# HISTORY

OF THE

# Indian Tribes of Hudson's River;

THEIR

ORIGIN, MANNERS AND CUSTOMS; TRIBAL
AND SUB-TRIBAL ORGANIZATIONS;
WARS, TREATIES, ETC., ETC.

BY

E. M. RUTTENBER

*Ira J. Friedman Division*
KENNIKAT PRESS
Port Washington, N.Y.

HISTORY OF THE INDIAN TRIBES OF HUDSON'S RIVER

First published in 1872
Reissued in 1971 by Ira J. Friedman Division, Kennikat Press
Library of Congress Catalog Card No: 78-154049
ISBN 0-8046-8095-7

Manufactured in the United States of America

EMPIRE STATE HISTORICAL PUBLICATIONS SERIES NO. 95

# PREFACE.

THE pioneer in new fields of historic inquiry encounters many obstacles from which those who follow the more beaten paths of investigation are exempt, and especially so if the inquiry involves conclusions differing materially from those which have been generally accepted. The experience of the author in prosecuting the investigations, the results of which have been embodied in the work which is now submitted to the public, have been no exception to this rule. Not only had the history of the Indians who occupied the valley of Hudson's river never been written, but the incidental references to them, in the histories of nations more prominent at a later period — treating them as mere fragmentary bands without organization or political position among the aboriginal nations — being regarded as erroneous, the inquiry involved the rejection, to a very great extent, of the conclusions of others, and the investigation and analyzation of original sources of information. To extract the truth and embody it in consistent narrative, has involved no little labor and research, and the careful weighing of words; and, although the results may not be stated in the clearest terms or the most flowing rhetoric, nor entirely without error, they are nevertheless believed to fully sustain the conclusion that the tribes in question have a history which entitles them to a high rank in the annals of aboriginal nations, and which assigns to them native abilities as distinguished, eloquence as pure, bravery and prowess as unquestionable, as was possessed by those who, preserved for a greater time in their national integrity by their remoteness from civilization, became of more esteem in their relations to the government but less noble in their purposes.

It has been the object of the author to trace the history of the Indians from the earliest period; to show their original position in the family of nations, and that which they subsequently maintained; the wrongs which they suffered, and the triumphs which they won; their greatness and their decay. In the narrative, liberal use has been made of current histories, so far as their statements were found to be in accordance with the facts. Acknowledgment, it is believed, has been fully made, and even to an extent which is not customary. Very full notes have been introduced for the purpose of explaining the text and enabling the reader to judge of the correctness of the conclusions drawn therefrom. As far as possible the narrative has been divested of the recitation of events which do not pertain to it, and though necessarily running beyond the limits of the territory regarded as the valley of the Hudson, has been as closely confined to it as possible, too closely perhaps, as it is believed that the eastern

Indians have the same claim to consideration as a confederacy as the western.

The work is submitted to the judgment of the public, with a desire that the author may be lost in the theme which he has presented, and the truth of history vindicated in behalf of a people that have left behind no monuments to their memory save those erected by their destroyers.

NEWBURGH, N. Y.

The Half Moon off Yonkers.

# Indian Tribes of Hudson's River.

## CHAPTER I.

HUDSON IN THE MAHICANITUK — HIS INTERCOURSE WITH THE INDIANS — THEIR TRADITIONS CONCERNING HIS VISIT.

SAILING under the auspices of the Dutch West India Company, HENRY HUDSON, an intrepid English navigator, moored his vessel, the Half Moon, on the morning of September 3d, 1609, in the waters of the river which now bears his name. Lingering off Sandy Hook a week, he passed through the Narrows, and anchored in what is now Newark bay. On the 12th, he resumed his voyage, and slowly drifting with the tide, anchored over night, on the 13th, just above Yonkers, the great river stretching on before him to the north and giving to his ardent mind the hope that he had at last discovered the gateway to the Eastern seas. On the 14th, he passed Tappan and Haverstraw bays; and sailed through the majestic pass guarded by the frowning Donderberg, and anchored at night near West Point, in the midst of the sublimest scenery of the mountains. On the morning of the 15th, he entered Newburgh bay, and reached Katskill; on the 16th, Athens; on the 17th, Castleton; on the 18th, Albany. Here he remained several days, sending an exploring boat as far as Waterford, and sadly learning that he had reached the head of navigation, and that the Eastern passage was yet an unsolved problem. His return voyage began on the 23d; on the 25th, he anchored in Newburgh bay; reached Stony point on the 1st of October; on the 4th, Sandy Hook, and sailed from thence

Newburgh Bay.

to Europe, bearing with him the information which he had collected, not the least of which in importance was that in relation to the native lords whom he had met on the banks of the river he had discovered, and who then broke the silvery surface of its waters with their light canoes and awoke the echoes of its mountain sides with their wild choruses, of whose power it was an emblem, on the waters of which, as they faded away in the north, was wafted their war shallops into tributaries that stretched on to the lakes and the great river of Canada, bearing with them the prestige of savage supremacy.

Hudson first met the Indians near the Narrows, where they came on board his vessel " clothed in mantles of feathers and robes of fur, the women, clothed in hemp, red copper tobacco pipes, and other things of copper they did wear about their necks;" of arms they brought none, their mission was peace; but he "durst not trust them." Suspicion breeds suspicion, and suspicion leads to violence. Sending an exploring boat up the river the next day, it was attacked, on its return to the ship, and one of the English sailors, John Coleman, was killed by an arrow shot in the throat.[1] He was buried upon the adjacent beach, the first European victim of an Indian weapon on the Mahicanituk. The offense which had been committed by himself and his companions is not stated, but may be inferred. They were far from the ship, the night came on and a thick cloud of rain and fog settled over them; seeing their condition, the Indians sprang to their boats to rescue them, fear seized them, the savage was more dreaded then the tempest, a falcon shot was hurled at the approaching canoes, the swift arrow replied, and "in the fight one man was slain and two more hurt." Day after day the Indians came on board, brought tobacco and Indian wheat, and oysters and beans, "making show of love," but he "durst not trust them." They brought their women and children with them, but he "durst not trust them." At Yonkers they came on board in large numbers; here he detained two of them, and dressed them in red coats, and though they jumped from the ports and swam away, their detention was not the less a violation of the laws of hospitality, so they regarded it, for when they had reached the shore they called to him "in scorn."

At Katskill he found a "very loving people and very old men." They brought on board "Indian corn, pumpkins, and tobacco," and used him well. At Castleton they were very sociable, and the "master's mate went on land[2] with an old savage, a governor of the country, who carried him to his house and made him good cheere." "I sailed to the shore," he says, "in one of their canoes, with an old man who was chief of a tribe consisting of forty men and seventeen women. These I saw there in a house well constructed of oak bark, and circular in shape, so that it had the appearance of being built with an

---

[1] Coleman's point is the monument to this occurrence.

[2] It has been assumed on the authority of a quotation alleged by De Laet to have been made from a journal kept by Hudson, that the place of this visit was in latitude 42° 18′, or in the vicinity of the present city of Hudson. (*N. Y. Hist. Soc. Coll.*, 1, 300). The journal kept by Juet was not only the official record of the voyage, but is very precise in its statements as to who visited the shore in this, and in other instances. He does not give the latitude, but from the ship's log it would seem that the place was "six leagues higher," up the river than that fixed by De Laet, and that it was at Schodac or Castleton.— *O'Callaghan*, 1, 37; *Brodhead*, 1, 31; *Collections of the New York Historical Society*, 2d Ser. 1, 326.

arched roof. It contained a large quantity of corn and beans of last year's growth, and there lay near the house, for the purpose of drying, enough to load three ships, besides what was growing in the fields. On our coming to the house two mats were spread out to sit upon, and some food was immediately served in well-made wooden bowls. Two men were also dispatched at once, with bows and arrows, in quest of game, who soon brought in a pair of pigeons which they had shot. They likewise killed a fat dog,[1] and skinned it in great haste, with shells which they had got out of the water. They supposed that I would remain with them for the night;" but when they saw that he desired to return to the ship and that he would not remain, they supposed he "was afraid of their bows and arrows, and taking their arms they broke them in pieces and threw them in the fire."

At Albany, Hudson repaid the old governor for his entertainment. The Indians flocked to visit his vessel, and he determined to try some of their chief men to see " whether they had any treachery in them." " So they took them down into the cabin, and gave them so much wine and *aqua vitæ* that they were all merry. In the end one of them was drunk, and they could not tell how to take it." At night they all departed, except the old man who had taken the *aqua vitæ;* " he slept all night quietly." On the following day they came again, and when they saw that their chief had recovered from his debauch they were glad. They returned to their castle and " brought tobacco and beads " and gave them to Hudson, " and made an oration, and showed him all the country round about." " Then they sent one of their company on land again, who presently returned and brought a great platter full of venison, dressed by themselves," and caused Hudson " to eat with them ; then they made him reverence, and departed, all save the old man " who had found the Indian's paradise with the white man's rum. But he took his departure the next day, and two days after returned, bringing " another old man with him " from the place where " the loving people " had first been met. He too brought belts of wampum beads and gave them to Hudson, " and shewed

Probably a black bear.

him all the country thereabout, as though it were at his command. So he made the two old men dine with him, and the old man's wife; for they brought two old women, and two young maidens of the age of sixteen or seventeen years with them, who behaved themselves very modestly." No doubt more wine was served at this dinner, but the *aqua vitæ* was evidently omitted, for the party took their departure at one o'clock.

On his return voyage " the loving people " met Hudson again, and " would have him go on land and eat with them ; " but the wind was fair, and he would not yield to their request. Very sorrowfully the old man, who had made the request in behalf of himself and his people, left the ship, although comforted with presents and with the assurance that his new friends would come again. Passing down through the Highlands, the Half Moon was becalmed off Stony point, and " the people of the mountains " came on board and wondered at the " ship and weapons." One canoe kept " hanging under the stern," and its occupant was soon detected in pilfering from the cabin windows. When detected, he had secured a " pillow and two shirts, and two bandeliers ; " but the " mate shot at him, and struck him on the breast, and killed him." The Indians were frightened and fled away, some in their canoes, others jumping into the water. A boat was lowered to recover the articles which they had taken, when one of them who was in the water seized hold of it " thinking to overthrow it," but " the cook seized a sword and cut off one of his hands and he was drowned." At the head of Manhattan island the vessel was again attacked. It was here that Hudson had attempted to kidnap two young men, who, on their escape, had called to him " in scorn " at their betrayal. One of these men, accompanied by his friends, now came out to the ship in their canoes. They were not suffered to enter the vessel, and falling behind it, discharged their arrows at it ; " in recompense whereof" six muskets replied " and killed two or three of them." The Indians retreated, and from a point of land renewed the attack ; but " a falcon shot " killed two of them, and " the rest fled into the woods;" " yet they manned off another canoe, with nine or ten men," through which a falcon shot was sent, killing one of its occupants. Then the sailors discharged their muskets, and "killed three or four more of them." "So they went their way," and the Half Moon was hurried down into the bay, "clear from all danger," carrying thence to Holland, in Hudson's simple narrative, an epitome of the subsequent history of the intercourse of the Indians with the Europeans; the clash of customs, the violence, the intoxicating cup.

To most of the Indians the advent of Hudson's ship was a strange spectacle. For over an hundred years the white-winged messengers of the old world had been wafted by them; in the further south, the white man was not a stranger, but not before had his sails been folded on the breast of their waters, nor the voice of trumpet and cannon reverberated through their solitudes. All this was new and strange; the Great Spirit had come to them; the signals of a mighty change passed before their vision. Their traditions repeat that almost with the appearance of Hudson in the lower bay, they began to collect on the shores and headlands, gazing in astonishment on the strange sight; that when they first saw the Half Moon they " did not know what to make of it, and could not comprehend whether it came down from heaven or from the devil." Some of them " even imagined it to be a fish, or some monster of the sea, and accordingly a strange report of it soon spread over the land." It was at length agreed among them "that, as this phenomenon moved towards the land, whether it was an animal or not, or any thing that had life in it," would soon be apparent. Runners from the shore went back and forth, and messengers were sent to the chiefs of the country to send in their warriors. As the ship approached they concluded it was "a large canoe or house, in which the great Manitto himself was, and that he was probably coming to visit them." Every thing was put in order to entertain him ; " the best of victuals was prepared, and plenty of meat for sacrifice procured, and idols or images examined and put in order, to appease him in case he was angry." Other runners soon arriving, declared it to be a " large house of various colors, full of people, yet of quite a different color from themselves, that they dressed in a different manner, and that one, in particular, appeared altogether red, which must be the Manitto himself." The crew of the Half Moon soon hailed them with a loud shout, which so frightened them that some were for running away, yet they feared to give offense and remained.

Meanwhile Hudson kept on his course, and the Indians continued to collect on the banks of the river, expressing their curiosity in the strongest manner. Establishing intercourse at last, they ventured on board the ship, where they were saluted "in a friendly manner, and they returned the salute after their manner." " They are lost in admiration both as to the color of the skin of these whites, as also of their manner of dress; yet most as to the habit of him who wore the red clothes, which shone with something they could not account for. He must be the Great Manitto, but why should he have a white skin?" Then they sat down to eat with their strange visitant, " a large and elegant *hockhack* was brought forward by one of the Manitto's servants, and something poured from it into a small cup or glass, and handed to the Manitto. He drank it, had the cup refilled, and had it handed to the chief next to him to drink. The chief receives the glass, but only smells at it, and passes it on to the next chief, who does the same. The glass thus passes through the circle without the contents being tasted by any one, and is on the point of being returned again to the red-clothed man, when one of their number, a spirited man and great warrior, jumps up, harangues the assembly on the impropriety of returning the glass with the contents in it; that the same was handed them by the Manitto in order that they should drink it, as he himself had done before them; that this would please him; but to return what he had given to them might provoke him, and be the cause of their being destroyed by him. And that since he believed it for the good of the nation that the contents offered them should be drank, and as no one else was willing to drink it, he would, let the consequence be what it might; that it was better for one man to die than for a whole nation to be destroyed. He then took the glass, and, bidding the assembly a farewell, drank it off. Every eye was fixed on their resolute companion, to see what an effect this would have upon him; and he soon beginning to stagger about, and at last dropping to the ground, they bemoan him. He falls into a sleep, and they view him as expiring. He awakes again, jumps up, and declares that he never before felt so happy as after he had drank of the cup. He wishes for more. His wish is granted; and the whole assembly soon join him, and become intoxicated. Then the man with the red clothes distributed presents to them of beads, axes, hoes, stockings, and other articles, and made them understand that he would return home and come again to see them, bring them more presents and stay with them awhile, but should want a little land to sow some seeds, in order to raise herbs to put in their broth."

But from their dream of trusting love they had a speedy awakening. Their traditions state that the promise made by Hudson to return again was fulfilled the following season, and that they "rejoiced much at seeing each other again; but the whites laughed at them, seeing that they knew not the use of the axes, hoes, etc., they had given them, they having had those hanging to their breasts as ornaments, and the stockings they had made use of as tobacco pouches. The whites now put handles or helves in the former, and cut trees down before their eyes, and dug the ground, and showed them the use of the stockings. Here a general laughter ensued among the Indians, that they had remained for so long a time ignorant of the use of so valuable implements, and had borne with the weight of such heavy metal hanging to their necks for such a length of time. They took every white man they saw for a Manitto, yet inferior and attendant to the supreme Manitto, to wit: to the one which wore the red and laced clothes.

"Familiarity daily increasing between them and the whites, the latter now proposed to stay with them, asking them only for so much land as the hide of a bullock would cover or encompass, which hide was brought forward and spread on the ground before them. That they readily granted this request; whereupon the whites took a knife, and beginning at one place on this hide, cut it up into a rope not thicker than the finger of a little child, so that by the time this hide was cut up, there was a great heap; that this rope was drawn out to a great distance, and then brought round again, so that the ends might meet; that they carefully avoided its breaking, and that upon the whole it encompassed a large piece of land; that they were surprised at the superior wit of the whites, but did not wish to contend with them about a little land, as they had enough; that they and the whites lived for a long time contentedly together, although the whites asked from time to time, more land of them and proceeding higher up the Mahicanituk,[1] they believed they would soon want all the country."

[1] The Iroquois, it is said, called the river the Cohatatea, while the Mahicans and the Lenapes called it the Mahicanituk or " the continually flowing waters." The Dutch gave it the name of Mauritius river, as early as 1611, in honor of their stadtholder, Prince Maurice, of Nassau. Hudson called it the River of the mountains, a name which the French adopted in Rio de Montagne. The English first gave it the name of Hudson's river by which, and North river, the latter to distinguish it from the Connecticut or East river, and from the Delaware or South river, it has since been known.

Henry Hudson.

## CHAPTER II.

### Origin, Manners and Customs, etc.

THE origin of the North American Indians, is a subject which has engrossed the attention of learned men for over two hundred years, and yet the question, "By whom was America peopled?" remains without satisfactory answer. In 1637, Thomas Morton wrote a book to prove that the Indians were of Latin origin. John Joselyn held, in 1638, that they were of Tartar descent. Cotton Mather inclined to the opinion that they were Scythians. James Adair seems to have been fully convinced that they were descendants of the Israelites, the lost tribes; and, after thirty years residence among them, published in 1775, an account of their manners and customs, from which he deduced his conclusions.[1] Dr. Mitchill, after considerable investigation, concluded "that the three races, Malays, Tartars and Scandinavians, contributed to made up the great American population, who were the authors of the various works and antiquities found on the continent." DeWitt Clinton held, that " the probability is, that America was peopled from various quarters of the old world, and that its predominant race is the Scythian or Tartarian." Calmet, a distinguished author, brings

---

[1] "Observations and arguments in proof of the American Indians being descended from the Jews: 1. Their division into tribes. 2. Their worship of Jehovah. 3. Their notion of a theocracy. 4. Their belief in the ministration of angels. 5. Their language and dialects. 6. Their manner of counting time. 7. Their prophets and high priests. 8. Their festivals, fasts and religious rites. 9. Their daily sacrifice. 10. Their ablutions and anointings. 11. Their laws of uncleanness. 12. Their abstinence from unclean things. 13. Their marriages, divorces, and punishments of adultery. 14. Their several punishments 15. Their cities of refuge. 16. Their purifications and ceremonies preparatory to war 17. Their ornaments. 18. Their manner of curing the sick. 19. Their burial of the dead. 20. Their mourning for the dead. 21. Their raising seed to a departed brother. 22. Their choice of names adapted to their circumstances and the times. 23. Their own traditions, the accounts of our English writers, and the testimony which the Spanish and other authors have given concerning the primitive inhabitants of Peru and Mexico."— *Adair.*

forward the writings of Hornius, son of Theodosius the Great, who affirms that "at or about the time of the commencement of the Christian era, voyages from Africa and Spain into the Atlantic ocean were both frequent and celebrated;" and holds that "there is strong probability that the Romans and Carthagenians, even 300 B. C., were well acquainted with the existence of this country," adding that there are "tokens of the presence of the Greeks, Romans, Persians, and Carthagenians, in many parts of the continent." The story of Madoc's voyage to America, in 1170, has been repeated by every writer upon the subject, and actual traces of Welsh colonization are affirmed to have been discovered in the language and customs of a tribe of Indians living on the Missouri. Then the fact is stated that "America was visited by some Norwegians," who made a settlement in Greenland, in the tenth century. Priest, in his *American Antiquities*, states that his observations had led him "to the conclusion that the two great continents, Asia and America, were peopled by similar races of men."

It is not necessary to add to this catalogue. Men equally learned with those whose opinions have been quoted, see no obstacle in the way of an opinion that America received her population as she did her peculiar trees, and plants, and animals, and birds. The geologist examines the relics of the west, and where imagination fashions artificial walls, he sees but crumbs of decaying sandstone, clinging like the remains of mortar to blocks of greenstone that rested on it; discovers in parallel intrenchments a trough that subsiding waters have ploughed through the centre of a ridge, and explains the tessellated pavement to be but a layer of pebbles aptly joined by water; and, examining the mounds, finds them composed of different strata of earth, arranged horizontally to the very edge, and ascribes their creation to the power that shaped the globe into vales and hillocks.[1] The mounds, it is true, may have been selected by the aborigines as the site of their dwellings, fortifications, or burial places; but the mouldering bones, from hillocks which are crowned by trees that have defied the storms of many centuries, the graves of earth from which they are dug, and the

[1] *Hitchcock.*

feeble fortifications that are sometimes found in their vicinity, afford no special evidence of connection with other continents.[1] "Among the more ancient works" of the west, says another writer,[2] "there is not a single edifice, nor any ruins which prove the existence, in former ages, of a building composed of imperishable materials. No fragment of a column, nor a brick, nor a single hewn stone large enough to have been incorporated into a wall, has been discovered. The only relics which remain to inflame the curiosity, are composed of earth."

To add force to this sweeping blow at the beautiful theories that have been woven, the learned Agassis disputes the idea of the unity of the races through Adam; while other writers pretty clearly demonstrate that the theory of the lost tribes of Israel has no foundation in fact. Dr. Lawrence, in his *Lectures on Physiology, Zoology, and the Natural History of Man*, sums up the whole argument by saying that, "in comparing the barbarian nations of America with those of the eastern continent, we perceive no points of resemblance between them, in their moral institutions or in their habits, that are not apparently founded in the necessities of human life."

This is apparently the reasonable conclusion of the whole matter, for to pass intelligent judgment, the aborigines of America must be taken as they were found, and not as they may have appeared after years of association with Europeans, an association necessarily producing a mingling of ancient customs with those learned from missionaries, or copied under the impulse of imitation. These early lessons were taught by men of all nations, the Dutch, the French, the Spanish, and the English, and, before their advent, by the Norwegians. It would be strange indeed, under all the circumstances, if the aborigines did not have grafted upon them some resembling features of all nations. Sir William Johnson, than whom no man had better opportunity to form a correct judgment, after considering the whole matter, concluded that all theories were defective for this reason; saying, that the Indians residing next to the English settlements had lost a great part of their traditions, and had so

---

[1] Warren in *Delafield's Antiquities*.    [2] *Drake's Picture of Cincinnati*.

blended their customs with those of the Europeans as to render it "difficult if not impossible to trace their origin or discover their explication," while those further removed had nevertheless been visited by traders, and especially by French Jesuits, who had "introduced some of their own inventions which the present generation confound with their ancient customs."[1] Until many of the nations of the old world can satisfactorily explain the origin of their own race, it is hardly worth while to endeavor to make our aborigines any further kindred with them than that the same Almighty Power called them into being and endowed them with common instincts.

Verazzano,[2] who sailed along the coast of North America in 1524, speaks of the natives whom he met in the harbor of New York, as "not differing much," from those with whom he had intercourse at other points, "being dressed out with the feathers of birds of various colors." His description being the earliest is of the most merit, for at that time they were untainted by association with Europeans. In person, he says, they were of good proportions, of middle stature, broad across the breast, strong in the arms, and well-formed. Among those who came on board his vessel were "two kings more beautiful in form and stature than can possibly be described; one was about forty years old, the other about twenty-four." "They were dressed," he continues, "in the following manner: The oldest had a deer's skin around his body, artificially wrought in damask figures, his head was without covering, his hair was tied back in various knots; around his neck he wore a large chain ornamented with many stones of different colors. The young man was similar in his general appearance." In size, he says: "they exceed us," their complexion tawny, inclining to white, their faces sharp, their hair long and black, their eyes black and sharp, their expression mild and pleasant," "greatly resembling the antique." The women, he says, were "of the same form and beauty, very graceful, of fine countenances and pleasing appearance in manners and modesty." They wore no clothing "except a deer skin ornamented like those of the men." Some

---

[1] *Documentary History of New York*, IV, 431.

[2] *Collections of the New York Historical Society*, 2d Series, I, 45.

had "very rich lynx skins upon their arms, and various ornaments upon their heads, composed of braids of hair," which hung down upon their breasts on each side. The older and the married people, both men and women, " wore many ornaments in their ears, hanging down in the oriental manner." In disposition they were generous, "giving away" whatever they had; of their wives they were careful, always leaving them in their boats when they came on ship-board, and their general deportment was such that with them, he says, " we formed a great friendship."[1]

Hudson's experience with them, in 1609, was somewhat different, but his references to their personal appearance are similar. "This day," he says, "many of the people came aboard, some in mantles of feathers, and some in skins of divers sorts of good furs. Some women also came to us with hemp. They had red copper tobacco pipes, and other things of copper they did wear about their necks."

The Dutch historians, Wassenaar, Van der Donck, and others, agree that the natives were generally well-limbed, slender around the waist, and broad-shouldered; that they had black hair and eyes, and snow white teeth, resembling the Brazilians in color, or more especially "those people who sometimes ramble through Netherland and are called Gipsies;" were very nimble and swift of pace, and well adapted to travel on foot and to carry heavy burthens. "Generally," says one writer, "the men have no beards, some even pluck it out. They use very few words, which they previously well consider. Naturally they are quite modest and without guile, but in their way haughty enough, ready and quick witted to comprehend or learn, be it good or bad. As soldiers, they are far from being honorable, but perfidious and accomplish all their designs by treachery; they also use many stratagems to deceive their enemies, and execute by night almost all their plans that are in any way hazardous. The thirst for revenge seems innate in them; they are very pertinacious in self-defense, when they cannot escape; which, under other circumstances, they like to do; and they make little of death, when it is inevitable, and despise

---

[1] *Collections of the New York Historical Society*, 2d Series, I, 46.

all tortures that can be inflicted on them at the stake, exhibiting no faint-heartedness, but generally singing until they are dead.

Their clothing is described as having been most sumptuous. The women ornamented themselves more than the men. "All wear around the waist a girdle made of the fin of the whale or of sewant." The men originally wore a breech-cloth, made of skins, but after the Dutch came those who could obtain it wore " between their legs a lap of duffels cloth half an ell broad and nine quarters long," which they girded around their waists, and drew up in a fold "with a flap of each end hanging down in front and rear." In addition to this they had mantles of feathers, and at a later period decked themselves with " plaid duffels cloth " in the form of a sash, which was worn over the right shoulder, drawn in a knot around the body, with the ends extending down below the knees. When the young men wished to look especially attractive, they wore " a band about their heads, manufactured and braided, of scarlet deer hair, interwoven with soft shining red hair." " With this head-dress," says Van der Donck, " they appear like the delineations and paintings of the Catholic saints," and, he adds, " when a young Indian is dressed in this manner he would not say *plum* for a bushel of plums. But this decoration is seldom worn unless they have a young woman in view."

The dress of an Indian belle was more attractive than any which civilized life has produced. Says the writer last quoted, " The women wear a cloth around their bodies, fastened by a girdle which extends below their knees, and is as much as an under coat ; but next to the body, under this coat, they wear a dressed deer skin coat, girt around the waist. The lower body of this skirt they ornament with great art, and nestle the same with strips which are tastefully decorated with wampum. The wampum with which one of these skirts is ornamented is frequently worth from one to three hundred guilders. They bind their hair behind in a club of about a hand long, in the form of a beaver's tail, over which they draw a square cap, which is frequently ornamented with wampum. When they desire to be fine they draw a headband around the forehead, which is also ornamented with wampum, etc. This band confines the hair smooth, and is fastened behind, over the club, in a beau's knot. Their head dress forms a handsome and lively appearance. Around their necks they wear various ornaments, which are also decorated with wampum. Those they esteem as highly as our ladies do their pearl necklaces. They also wear hand bands or bracelets, curiously wrought, and interwoven with wampum. Their breasts appear about half covered with an elegantly wrought dress. They wear beautiful girdles, ornamented with their favorite wampum, and costly ornaments in their ears. Here and there they lay upon their faces black spots of paint. Elk hide moccasins they wore before the Dutch came, and they too were most richly ornamented." Shoes and stockings they obtained from the Dutch, and also bonnets.

Plurality of wives was, to some extent, in vogue among them. " The natives," says Van der Donck, " generally marry but one wife and no more, unless it be a chief who is great and powerful; such frequently have two, three or four wives, of the neatest and handsomest of women, and who live together without variance." Minors did not marry except with the advice of their parents or friends. Widowers and widows followed their own inclinations. Their marriage ceremonies were very simple. Young women were not debarred signifying their desire to enter matrimonial life. When one of them wished to be married she covered her face with a veil and sat covered as an indication of her desire. If she attracted a suitor, negotiations were opened with parents or friends, presents given and the bride taken.

Chastity was an established principle with married females. To be unchaste during wedlock was held to be very disgraceful. " Many of the women would prefer death, rather than submit to be dishonored." No Indian would keep his wife, however much he loved her, when he knew she was unchaste. Divorce frequently came from disagreements, and was a simple form. The wife was handed her share of the goods and put out of doors by the husband, and was then free to marry another. In cases of separation the children followed the mother, and were frequently the cause of the parents coming together again. The man who abandoned his wife without cause left her all her property, and in like manner the wife the husband's. Foul and impertinent language was despised by them. All romping, caressing and wanton behavior they spoke of with contempt, as indirect alurements to unchastity, and reproved such conduct in the Netherlanders. The Dutch made wives of many of them and retained them, refusing to leave them for females of their own country.

Most of the diseases incident to females of the present day were unknown to them. Before confinement it was their custom to retire to a secluded place near a brook, or stream of water, and prepare a shelter for themselves with mats and covering and food, and await delivery "without the company or aid of any person." After their children were born, and especially if they were males, they immersed them some time in the water, no matter what the temperature, and then swathed them in warm clothing and gave them great attention. Several days after delivery they returned to their homes, but until the child was weaned, had no commerce with their husbands, holding it to be disgraceful and injurious to their offspring.

In sickness they were very faithful to each other, and when death occurred the next of kin closed the eyes of the deceased. The men made no noise over the dead, but the women made frantic demonstrations of grief, striking their breasts, tearing their faces, and calling the name of the deceased day and night. Their loudest lamentations were on the death of their sons and husbands. On such occasions they cut off their hair and burned it on the grave in the presence of all their relatives, painted their faces pitch black, and in a deer's skin jerkin mourned the dead a full year. In burying their dead the body was placed in a sitting posture, and beside it were placed a pot, kettle, platter, spoon, money and provisions for use in the other world. Wood was then placed around the body, and the whole covered with earth and stones, outside of which palisades were erected, fastened in such a manner that the tomb resembled a little house.[1] To these tombs great respect was paid, and to violate them was deemed an unpardonable provocation.

[1] *Documentary History of New York*, IV, 127.

Their fare or food was poor and gross, "for," says one Dutch writer, "they drink water, having no other beverage." They eat the flesh of all sorts of game, "even badgers, dogs, eagles, and similar trash which Christians in no way regard." All sorts of fish were eaten, as well as "snakes, frogs and such like." Their mode of cooking without removing the entrails was not palatable to the Dutch. In addition to their meats they made bread of Indian meal and baked it in hot ashes, and make a "pap or porridge, called by some sapsis, by others dundare (literally boiled bread), in which they mixed beans of different color which they raised." The maize from which their bread and sapsis were made was raised by themselves, and was broken up or ground in rude mortars. They observed no set time for meals. Whenever hunger demanded, the repast was prepared. Beavers' tails, the brains of fish, and their sapsis,[1] ornamented with beans, were their state dishes and highest luxuries. They knew how to preserve meat and fish by smoking, and when on a journey or while hunting, carried with them corn roasted whole. At their meals they sat on the ground.

Their occupations were hunting, fishing and war. When not on the war path they repaired to the rivers and caught fish or to the forests and hunted deer, fawns, hares and foxes, "and all such," says the narrator who adds, "the country is full of game; hogs, bears, leopards, yea, lions, as appears by the skins which were brought on board." The beaver was most highly prized by them, not only for its food and fur, but for the medicinal uses of the oil obtained. The women made clothing of skins, prepared food, cultivated the fields of corn, beans and squashes, made mats, etc., but the men never labored until they became too old for the field, when they remained with the women and made mats, wooden bowls and spoons, traps, nets, arrows, canoes, etc.

Their houses were for the most part built after one plan, differing only in lengths. They were formed by long, slender hickory saplings set in the ground, in a straight line of two rows, as far asunder as they intended the width to be and con-

---

[1] "The crushed corn is daily boiled to a pap which is called *suppaen*."

tinued the rows as far as they intended the length to be. The poles were then bent towards each other in the form of an arch and secured together, giving the appearance of a garden arbor. Split poles were then lathed up the sides and roof, and over this was bark, lapped on the ends and edges, which was kept in its place by withes to the lathings. A hole was left in the roof for smoke to escape, and a single door of entrance was provided. Rarely exceeding twenty feet in width, these houses were sometimes a hundred and eighty yards long. "In those places," says Van der Donck, "they crowd a surprising number of persons, and it is surprising to see them out in open day." From sixteen to eighteen families occupied one house, according to its size. A single fire in the centre served them all, although each family occupied at night its particular division and mats.

Their castles were strong, firm works, and were usually situated on the side of a steep, high hill, near a stream of water with a level plain on the crown of the hill. This plain was enclosed with a strong stockade, which was constructed by laying on the ground large logs of wood for a foundation, on both sides of which oak palisades were set in the ground, the upper ends of which crossed each other and were joined together: against the rude assaults of rude enemies, these castles were a safe retreat. Inside of their walls they not unfrequently had twenty or thirty houses, so that a clan or tribe could be provided for in winter. Besides their strongholds, they had villages and towns which were enclosed or stockaded. The latter usually had woodland on one side and corn land on the other. Near the water sides and at fishing places they not unfrequently had huts for temporary occupancy; but in the winter they were found in their castles which were rarely, if ever, left altogether.

Their weapons of war were the spear, the bow and arrows, the war club and the stone hatchet, and in combat they protected themselves with a square shield made of tough leather. A snake's skin tied around the head, from the centre of which projected the tail of a bear or a wolf, and a face not recognizable from the variety of colors in which it was painted, was their uniform. Their domestic implements were of very rude construction. Fire answered them many purposes and gained for them the name of Fireworkers. By it they not only cleared lands, but shaped their log canoes and made their wooden bowls. Some of their arrows were of elegant construction and tipped with copper, and when shot with power would pass through the body of a deer as certainly as the bullet from the rifle. The more common arrows were tipped with flint, as well as their spears, and required no little patience and skill in their construction. When they came to obtain guns from the Dutch they were remarkably expert with them.

Their money consisted of white and black zewant (wampum),[1] which was " nothing more nor less than the inside little pillars of the conch shells " which the sea cast up twice a year. These pillars they polished smooth, drilled a hole through the centre, reduced them to a certain size, and strung them on threads. Gold, silver or copper coins they had none. Their standards of value were the hand or fathom of wampum, and the *denotas* or bags which they made themselves for measuring and preserving corn. Such was their currency and such their only commercial transactions. To obtain wampum they made war and took captives for whom they demanded ransom, or made the weaker tribes tributaries to the stronger.

[1] There were two kinds of wampum in early use by the Indians, as a standard of value, the *purple* or black and the *white*. The purple was made from the interior portions of the *venus mercenaria*, or common conch. The white was wrought out of the pillar of the periwinkle. Each kind was converted into a kind of bead, by being rounded and perforated, so as to admit of being strung on a fibre of deer's sinew. This was replaced after the discovery, by linen thread. The article was highly prized as an ornament, and as such constituted an object of traffic between the sea coast and the interior tribes. It was worn around the neck ; also as an edging for certain pieces of their garments ; and when these strings were united, they formed the broad wampum belts by which solemn public transactions were commemorated. As a substitute for gold and silver coin, its price was fixed by law. Three *purple* beads of wampum, or six of *white*, were equal to a stuyver among the Dutch, or a penny among the English. Some variations, however, existed in its value, according to time and place. A single string of wampum of one fathom, ruled at five shillings in New England, and is known in New Netherland to have reached as high as four guilders, or one dollar and sixty-six cents. The old wampum was made by hand and was an exceedingly rude article. After the discovery, the Dutch introduced the lathe in its manufacture, polished and perforated it with exactness, and soon had the monopoly of the trade. The principal place of its manufacture was at Hackensak, in New Jersey. The principal deposit of sea-shells was Long Island, where the extensive shell banks left by the Indians, in which it is difficult to find a whole shell, show the immense quantities that were manufactured.

They were not skilled in the practice of medicines, notwithstanding the general belief on that subject. They knew how to cure wounds and hurts, and treated simple diseases successfully. Their general health was due more to their habits than to a knowledge of remedies. Their principal medical treatment was the sweating bath. These were literally earthen ovens, into which the patient crept, and around which heated stones were placed to raise the temperature. When the patient had remained under perspiration for a certain time he was taken out and immersed suddenly in cold water, a process which served to cure or certainly cause death. The oil which they obtained from beavers was used in many forms and for many purposes; among others for dizziness, for trembling, for the rheumatism, for lameness, for apoplexy, for toothache, for earache, for weak eyes, for gout, and for almost all ills. The Dutch took to this remedy and attached to it great value.

As the term is generally understood, they had no religion, but in its place a rude system in which they looked

"Through nature up to nature's God."

Good and evil spirits they recognized, and to them appealed in sacrifice and fires. Their minister or priest was called *kitzinaeka*. It was his duty to visit the sick and exorcise the evil spirits; or, failing, to see the usual rites for the dead performed. He had no home of his own, but lodged were it pleased him, or where he last officiated; was not permitted to eat any food prepared by a married woman, but that only which was cooked by a maiden or an old woman, and altogether lived "like a Capuchin." [1] To the sun, moon and stars they paid particular attention. The first moon following that at the end of February they greatly honored. They watched its coming and greeted its advent with a festival, at which they collected from all quarters and reveled "in their way with wild game or fish," and drank clear river water to their fill. This was their new year; this moon the harbinger of spring. The harvest moon, or the new moon in August, they also honored with a feast, in

---

[1] Wassenaar, *Documentary History of New York*, III, 28.

acknowledgment of the product of their fields and their success in the chase.

They fully recognized the existence of God, who dwelt beyond the stars, and in a life immortal expected to renew the associations of this life.[1] But to them God had less to do with the world than did the devil, who was the principal subject of their fears, and the source of their earthly hopes. No expeditions of hunting, fishing or war were undertaken unless the devil was first consulted, and to him they offered the first fruits of the chase, or of victory. "On such occasions," says one of the early writers, "conjurors act a wonderful part. These tumble, with strange contortions, head over heels, beat themselves, leap, with a hideous noise, through and around a large fire.[2] Finally they set up a tremendous caterwauling, when the devil, as they say, appears in the shape of a ravenous or harmless animal; the first betokens something bad, the other good; both give information respecting coming events, but obscurely, which they attribute to their own ignorance, not understanding the devil's right meaning when matters turn out differently." For the spiritual they cared nothing; but directed

Devil Worship.

---

[1] The belief of *Maikans* regarding the separation of the soul, is, that it goes up westward on leaving the body. There it is met with great rejoicing by the others who died previously; there they wear black otter or bear skins, which among them are signs of gladness. They have no desire to be with them.—*Wassenaar.*

[2] This dance of the Indians was called *kinte-kaying*. It was observed on the

their study principally to the physical, " closely observing the seasons." Their women were the most experienced star-gazers, scarce one of whom could not name them all, give the time of their rising and setting, their position, etc., in language of their own. *Taurus* they described as the horned head of a big wild animal inhabiting the distant country, but not theirs; that when it rose in a certain part of the heavens, then it was the season for planting. The firmament was to them an open book wherein they read the laws for their physical well-being, the dial plate by which they marked their years.

They were not without government and laws, although both partook of the nomadic state. They had chief and subordinate rulers, and general as well as local councils. Their sachem was their local ruler and representative. Their general councils were composed of the sachems of different families or clans. But these councils assembled only in case of war, or other matters requiring concerted action. In all other respects the tribes or clans acted independently, and declared war and made peace without reference to their neighbors, unless the contest was such that assistance was desirable, in which case invitations to alliance were sent out by messengers. All obligations acquired their force from the acceptance of presents. In making agreements or sending messages they took as many little sticks as there were conditions or parties in their proposals.[1] If the contracting parties agreed on all, each party, at the conclusion, laid his presents at the feet of the other. If the presents be mutually accepted, the negotiation is firmly concluded, but if not, no further proceedings were had unless the applicant changed the conditions and the presents. On occasions of importance, a general assembly was held at the house of the chief

eve of engaging in expeditions of war or hunting. When taken prisoners and about to suffer torture, they asked permission to dance the *kinte-kaye*. The first dance witnessed by the Europeans was by the savages assembled on the point of land just above Newburgh, which still bears the name of *Dans kammer*, or dance chamber.

[1] " As to the information which you observe I formerly transmitted to the governor of New York, concerning the belt and fifteen bloody sticks sent by the Missiosagaes, the like is very common, and the Indians use sticks as well to express the alliance of castles as the number of individuals in a party. These sticks are generally about six inches in length and very slender, and painted red if the subject is war, but without any peculiarity as to shape.—*Documentary History of New York*, IV, 437.

sachem in order that a full explanation might be made. At these assemblies the will of the sachem was supreme, for although permitting full debate, mutiny was punished by death.

Lands held by them were obtained by conceded original occupation or by conquest. If conquered, original right ceased and vested in the conquerors; if reconquered, the title returned to its original owners. This rule they applied also to the sale of lands to the Dutch. As often as they sold to the latter and subsequently drove off the settlers, so often was repurchase necessary, and, if it was not made, cause of grievance and future war remained. Some respect was paid to the rights of property, and whenever it was stolen, it was ordered returned.[1] Although the reputation attaches that they were a "thieving set," yet the fact is that in almost every stated case the Dutch were the aggressors, the Indians only making reprisals for that of which they had been despoiled.

Rank was known among them; nobles, who seldom married below their rank, as well as a commonalty.[2] These conditions were hereditary, for although one of the commonalty might rise to prominence, the sachemship descended as long as any one was found fit to rule, and regents frequently governed in the name of a minor. The oldest or first of a household or family represented it "with or unto the chief of the nation." Military distinction was conferred by merit without regard to families or birth. The lowest might become a chief, but the rank died with its possessor, unless his posterity followed in his footsteps, in which case his titles were transmitted. Those of hereditary rank, however, were not esteemed, unless they were distinguished for activity, bravery and understanding, and such they honored greatly.

Their armies, or warriors, were composed of all their young men, among whom were even boys of fifteen, and were not without some of the forms of organization and discipline known to civilized nations. Each clan or canton had its war chiefs,

---

[1] "Notwithstanding misdemeanors are not punished, wicked acts are of rare occurrence. Stolen property, whenever discovered, is ordered by the chief to be restored. If any one commit that offense (stealing) too often, he is stripped bare of his goods." — *Documentary History*, IV, 129; *Wassenaar*, *Ib.*, III, 44.

[2] "Though this people do not make such a distinction between man and man as

or captains, as the Europeans called them,[1] who stood in rank according to the services by which they had distinguished themselves, the one highest in the qualifications of prudence, cunning, resolution, bravery, and good fortune, had powers equivalent to a commanding general. In times of war, the tribes were under rigid martial law; nothing was done without the consent of the war captains; no warrior could leave the troop without forfeiting his honor and the highly esteemed advantages of promotion.

To begin a war was called "taking up the hatchet," and could not be done without what were regarded as the most just and important reasons. The death of a warrior at the hands of a neighboring tribe, was not always a cause for war. The murderer could be surrendered or the offense atoned by presents; but when a warrior was killed and scalped, or when, as with the *Mohawks*, the hatchet was left sticking in the head of the victim, it was regarded as a declaration of war. In such cases the war captains summoned their followers and addressed them: "The bones of your murdered countrymen lie uncovered; they demand revenge at our hands, and it is our duty to obey them; their spirits loudly call upon us, and we must satisfy them; still greater spirits watching over our honor, inspire us with a resolution to go in pursuit of the murderers of our brethren. Let us go and devour them! Do not sit inactive! Follow the impulse of your hereditary valor! Anoint your hair! Paint your faces! Fill your quivers! Make the woods echo with your voices! Comfort the spirits of the deceased, and revenge their blood!" The work of preparation for the field was speedily performed; the weapons of war were collected, a pouch of parched corn and maple sugar prepared, and the body painted black. Then came the war dance and

---

other nations, yet they have high and low families; inferior and superior chiefs, whose authority remains hereditary in the houses. The military officers are disposed of only according to the valorous prowess of each person."— *Documentary History of New York*, IV, 128.

[1] A captain among the Indians, is what we should call a commander or general. He has several subordinate officers, in proportion to the number of troops under his command. The rank of captain is neither elective nor hereditary. The first occasion to this appointment is generally a dream, early in life, which a young man or his friends interpret as a destiny for the office of captain. He therefore endeavors to attain the necessary qualifications for this dignity, and to prove his prowess by feats of valor.— *Loskiel*.

war song;[1] and the paths of the forest received the avenging horde, to return to peace only when compelled by necessity or the intervention of mediators.

The ceremonies of war and peace were somewhat different when the alliance of one tribe with another was called. In such cases an embassy was dispatched bearing a piece of tobacco, a belt of wampum, and a hatchet with a red handle. The tobacco invited a friendly smoke and consideration, the belt described by certain figures the tribe against whom alliance was desired, and the hatchet determined the purpose. The principal captain of the embassy made a speech, on delivering these credentials of his authority. If the belt was accepted, nothing more was said, that act being considered a solemn promise to lend every assistance; but if neither the hatchet was lifted up nor the belt accepted, it was understood that the tribe would remain neutral. The consideration of the matter was usually circumspect and slow, and the decision regarded with no little reverence.

The lives of prisoners taken in war were rarely spared, except those of women and children, who were treated leniently and adopted by their conquerors to recruit their numbers. Male prisoners were subjected to great torture, usually by fire, and a savage cunning indeed was practiced in prolonging the sufferings of the victims. The next of kin was an avenger and might inflict death on a murderer, provided he was enabled to do so within twenty-four hours. After the lapse of that time the avenger himself was liable to death if death came by

---

[1] Heckewelder gives the following as the war song of the Lenape warriors:
"O poor me!
Who am going out to fight the enemy,
And know not whether I shall return again,
To enjoy the embraces of my children
And my wife.
O poor creature!
Whose life is not in his own hands,
Who has no power over his own body,
But tries to do his duty
For the welfare of his nation.
O thou Great Spirit above!
Take pity on my children
And on my wife!
Prevent their mourning on my account!
Grant that I may be successful in this attempt,
That I may slay my enemy,
And bring home the trophies of war
To my dear family and friends,
That we may rejoice together.
O take pity on me!
Give me strength and courage to meet my enemy.
Suffer me to return again to my children,
To my wife!
And to my relations!
Take pity on me and preserve my life,
And I will make thee a sacrifice."

his hand. A murderer was seldom killed after the first twenty-four hours were passed, but he was obliged to remain concealed; meantime his friends endeavored to reconcile the parties, and offered a blood atonement of wampum. If peace was agreed upon it was usually accompanied by the condition that the nearest relatives of the murderer, whether men, women or children, on meeting the relatives of the murdered person, must give way to them. But an offense unatoned was unforgiven, and, though years might elapse, vengeance was certain if opportunity offered.

Great faults were charged against the Indians, and great faults they doubtless possessed when judged from the standpoint of a different civilization. Were the line strictly drawn, however, it might be shown that, as a whole, they compared favorably with nations upon whom light had fallen for sixteen hundred years. This at least appears to their credit, that among them there were none who were cross-eyed, blind, crippled, lame, hunch-backed or limping; all were well-fashioned, strong in constitution of body, well-proportioned and without blemish. Until touched and warped by wrong treatment, wherever they were met, whether on the Potomac, the Delaware, the Hudson, or the Connecticut, they were liberal and generous in their intercourse with the whites. More sinned against than sinning, they left behind them evidences of great wrongs suffered, their enemies being the witnesses.

## CHAPTER III.

### NATIONAL AND TRIBAL ORGANIZATIONS, TOTEMIC CLASSIFICATIONS, POLITICAL RELATIONS, ETC.

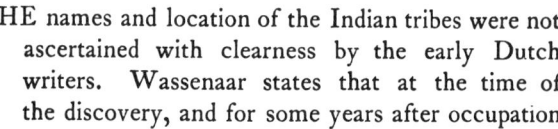HE names and location of the Indian tribes were not ascertained with clearness by the early Dutch writers. Wassenaar states that at the time of the discovery, and for some years after occupation by the Dutch, the *Maikans* or *Mahicans*, held twenty-five [1] miles on both sides of the river in the vicinity of Fort Orange ; that the *Maquas*, or *Mohawks*, resided in the interior ; that Fort Orange was erected on the lands of the *Mahicans*, whose castle was on the opposite (east) side of the river. De Laet writes in 1625, that the *Maquas* held the west shore, and Wassenaar concludes with a similar statement ; but if it is considered that the history of the latter was written at different periods extending from 1621 to 1632, his account will be found entirely consistent with itself as well as with De Laet's. South of Fort Orange the classifications of these writers is almost wholly by chieftaincies or cantons. Van der Donck, writing twenty years later, does not appear to have obtained more definite knowledge than his predecessors.

From information subsequently obtained, however, and especially that furnished by treaties and other documentary papers, it would appear that at the time of the discovery the *Mahicans* held possession, under sub-tribal organizations, of the east bank of the river from an undefined point north of Albany to the sea, including Long Island ; that their dominion extended east to the Connecticut, where they joined kindred tribes ; that on the west bank of the Hudson they ran down as far as Catskill, and west to Schenectady ; that they were met on the west by the territory of the *Mohawks*, and on the south by chieftaincies

---

[1] Seventy-five English miles.

acknowledging the supremacy of the *Minsis*, a totemic tribe of the *Lenni Lenapes*, and that the territory of the latter extended thence to the sea, and west to and beyond the Delaware river. Pending the early operations of the Dutch traders, this original classification was somewhat changed. The *Mahicans* sold a considerable portion of their lands on the west side of the river to Van Rensselaer, retaining only a castle at Cohoes falls and one at Katskill, and admitted the *Mohawks* to territorial sovereignty north of the Mohawk river. Although the latter were not in possession by castles and villages, it may be admitted that, practically, as early as 1630, three great divisions or nations were represented on the Hudson: The IROQUOIS,[1] the MAHICANS, and the LENNI LENAPES, or Delawares as they were more modernly known. The first of these nations, the IROQUOIS, was represented by a tribe called by themselves *Kayingehaga*; by their enemies, the Mahicans, the *Maquas*; by the Dutch, *Makwaes*; by the English, *Mohawks*, and by the French *Agniers*. The IROQUOIS CONFEDERACY [2] was, at this time, composed of five tribes under the modern names of *Mohawks*, *Oneidas*, *Onondagas*, *Cayugas*, and *Senecas* and bore the title of *Aquinoshioni* or *Konoshioni*, that is, Cabin-makers, or People of the Long House, as applied to their territorial possessions and national organization. That "long house" subsequently reached from the banks of the Hudson to the shores of Lake Erie, and from the Katskill range to the St. Lawrence — the Eastern door guarded by the *Mohawks* and the western by the *Senecas*.

The traditions held by the *Iroquois* respecting their origin and confederate organization,[3] are that, like the Athenian, they sprung from the earth itself. In remote ages they had been confined under a mountain near the falls of the Osh-wah-kee,

---

[1] The appellation, *Iroquois*, was first applied to them by the French, because they usually began and finished their discourses or *palaver* with the word *hiro*, which means either "I say," or "I have said," combined as an affix with the word *koné*, an exclamation expressing joy or sorrow according as it was pronounced long or short."—*Garneau's History of Canada*.

[2] *Colden's History of the Six Nations; Schoolcraft's Notes on the Iroquois; Dunlap's Hist. New York; Yates & Moulton's History New York; O'Callaghan's New Netherland; Brodhead's New York*, etc.

[3] The Iroquois tribes are classed by Gallatin in three divisions: eastern, western, and southern. The eastern consisted of the confederation known as the Five Nations, the western of the Wy-

or Oswego river, whence they were released by *Tharonhyjagon*, the Holder of the Heavens. Bidding them go forth to the east, he guided them to the valley of the Mohawk, and following its stream they reached the Hudson, which some of them descended to the sea. Retracing their steps towards the west, they originated, in their order and position, the *Mohawks*, *Oneidas*, *Onondagas*, *Cayugas*, *Senecas*, and *Tuscaroras*, six nations; but the *Tuscaroras* wandered away to the south and settled on the Cautano, or Neuse river, in North Carolina, reducing the number to five nations.

Each of the tribes thus originated was independent of the others, and warred with each other, as well as with the surrounding tribes. *Tharonhyjagon* still remained with the tribes; gave them seeds of various kinds, with the proper knowledge for planting them; taught them how to kill and roast game; made the forests free to all the tribes to hunt, and removed obstructions from the streams. After this he laid aside his divine character and resolved to live with the *Onondagas*, that he might exemplify the maxims he had taught. For this purpose he selected a handsome spot of ground on the southern banks of the lake called *Teonto*, being the sheet of water now known as Cross lake.[1] Here he built a cabin, and took a wife of the *Onondagas*, by whom he had an only daughter, whom he tenderly loved, and most kindly and carefully treated and instructed. The excellence of his character, and his great sagacity and good counsels, led the people to view him with veneration, and they gave him the name of *Hi-a-wat-ha*, signifying a very wise man. From all quarters people came to him for advice, and in this manner all power came naturally into his hands, and he was regarded as the first chief in all the land. Under his teachings the *Onondagas* became the first among all the original clans. They were the wisest counselors, the best orators, the most expert hunters, and the bravest warriors.

andots, or Hurons, and the Attiouandarons, or neutral nation, north, and the Erigas and Andastes, or Guandastogues (Guyandots), south of Lake Erie; the southern, of the Tuscaroras, the Tutelos, and the Nottowas, of North Carolina.

The Tuscaroras and Tutelos removed to the north, the former in 1714 and the latter in 1758, and were incorporated in the Five Nations, the former becoming the sixth member of the confederacy.

[1] *Schoolcraft's Notes on the Iroquois*, 273.

Hence the *Onondagas* were early noted among all the tribes for their preeminence.

While *Hiawatha* was thus living in quiet among the " people of the hills," the tribes were attacked by a furious and powerful enemy from the north of the great lakes. This enemy advanced into the country and laid waste the villages, and slaughtered men, women and children, until the people had no heart to oppose the invaders. In this emergency they fled to *Hiawatha* for advice, who counseled them to call together all the tribes from the east, and the west, " for," said he, " our safety is not alone in the club and dart, but in wise counsels." He appointed a place on the banks of the Onondaga lake for the meeting, and thither the chiefs, warriors, and head men forthwith assembled in large numbers, bringing with them their women and children.

The council had been waiting for three days, but as yet *Hiawatha* was absent. Messengers were dispatched to hasten his attendance, but they found him gloomy and depressed. He told them that evil lay in his path, and felt that he should be called to make some great sacrifice; nevertheless he would attend the council. The talismanic white canoe, in which he always made his voyages, and which the people had learned to reverence, was got out and *Hiawatha* and his daughter took their seats. Gliding silently down the deep waters of the Seneca, the canoe reached the outlet and entered on the placid Onondaga. As the canoe of the venerated chief appeared, he was welcomed with loud shouts; but while he was measuring his steps towards the council ground, a long and low sound was heard, and instantly all eyes were turned upward, where a compact mass of cloudy darkness appeared, which gathered size and velocity as it approached, and appeared to be directed inevitably to fall in the midst of the assembly. Every one fled but *Hiawatha* and his daughter, who calmly awaited the issue. The force of the descending body was like that of a sudden storm; and hardly had *Hiawatha* paused, when an immense bird, with long distended wings, came down, with a swoop, and crushed the daughter to the earth. The very semblance of a human being was destroyed in the remains of the girl, and the head and neck of the bird were buried in the ground from the force of the fall.

*Hiawatha* was inconsolable for several days; but at length took his place in the council and the deliberations opened. The subject of the invasion was discussed by several of the ablest counselors, and various plans proposed to foil the enemy. *Hiawatha* listened to the debate, and at its conclusion bade the warriors depart until the next day when he would unfold his plan, which he felt confident would ensure safety.

The council again met; and with even more than ordinary attention the people listened to the words of their great chief. *Hiawatha* counseled them, that "to oppose these hordes of northern tribes singly and alone, would prove certain destruction;" that to oppose them successfully, the tribes must unite in " one common band of brothers," must have one voice, one fire, one pipe, and one war club. In the confederacy which he proposed should be formed, the several tribes were assigned the position they were to thereafter occupy; and, in conclusion, he urged them to weigh well his words; that if they should unite in the bond he had proposed, the Great Spirit would smile upon them, and they would be free, prosperous and happy; but if they rejected it, they would be "enslaved, ruined, perhaps annihilated forever."

The tribes received the address in solemn silence; and the council closed to deliberate on the plan recommended. Assembling the next day, the union of the tribes into one confederacy was discussed and unanimously adopted. Pending this result, *Hiawatha*, warned by the death of his daughter that his mission was accomplished, prepared to make his final departure from earth. Before the council dispersed, he recounted the services he had rendered to his people, and urged them to preserve the union they had formed. "If you preserve this," said he, "and admit no foreign element of power, by the admission of other nations, you will always be free, numerous and happy. If other tribes and nations are admitted to your councils, they will sow the seeds of jealousy and discord, and you will become few, feeble and enslaved. Remember these words, they are the last you will hear from the lips of *Hiawatha*. The Great

Master of breath calls me to go. I have patiently waited his summons. I am ready to go. Farewell." As his voice ceased, sweet sounds, from the air, burst on the ears of the multitude ; and while all attention was engrossed in the celestial melody, *Hiawatha* was seen, seated in his white canoe, in the mid-air, rising with every choral chant that burst out, till the clouds shut out the sight and the melody ceased. Every warrior now plucked a feather from the great bird as a memorial, and took their departure.[1]

The precise date of the formation of the confederacy cannot, of course, be ascertained. Pyrlaus, a missionary among the *Mohawks*, states as the result of his investigations, that the alliance took place " one age, or the length of a man's life, before the white people came into the country." Another writer fixes the date at 1414 ; while a third confirms the statement of Pyrlaus.[2] Whatever may have been its date, it was a practical and effective alliance by which the democratic principle, which was the basis of the government of the cantons, was extended to the expression of the national will. The general head had few powers, but the determination of the tribes, in regard to matters in which they had a common interest, when announced from the general council at Onondaga, carried with it the united voice of an empire. The active government was confined to the tribes or cantons, which were independent states. Each had its own chiefs, civil and military, and its own council, and was represented in general councils by sachems exercising the power of delegates. These delegates, however, spoke the popular will of the tribes they represented, and to determine their action they were not permitted to approve any measure which the tribe had not endorsed by an unanimous vote. Indeed, the unanimous principle was the ruling one of the confederacy. Tribes might declare war and conclude peace, and exercise all powers of sovereignty on their own account,

---

[1] *Schoolcraft's Notes*, 278, etc.

[2] *Schoolcraft's Notes*, 118, 120, etc. " The time when the confederacy was formed is not known, but it was presumed to be of a recent date, and the Oneidas and Cayugas are said to have been compelled to join it. Those two tribes were the younger, and the three others the older members of the confederacy." — *Gallatin.* " The Oneidas and Cayugas are their children." — *Zinzendorf.*

but national or confederated action required the concurrence of all the tribes, and hence, when a decision was made, it was clothed with all the power of the most full popular will.[1] There was no female suffrage among them, and yet females had the power, by adoption, to rescue prisoners from death, and to command a cessation of war. When so determined by the matrons, the braves returned from the conflict without compromiting the character of the tribe for bravery. But this feature in their customs was common to all the Indian nations. It remains to be shown that they had any forms of government peculiar to themselves. Their power was in their confederation, and in this they apparently differed from other nations only in the number of tribes and in the perpetuity of the organization, other nations securing the same results, in case of war, by temporary alliances.

A view of their national council is furnished by Loskiel, who says that in 1745, Spangenberg, one of the Moravian bishops, spent several weeks at Onondaga, and frequently attended its sessions. "The council-house was built of bark. On each side six seats were placed, each containing six persons. No one was admitted besides the members of the council, except a few, who were particularly honored. If one arose to speak, all the rest sat in profound silence, smoking their pipes. The speaker uttered his words in a singing tone, always rising a few notes at the close of each sentence. Whatever was pleasing to the council was confirmed by all with the word *nee*, or *yes*. And at the end of each speech, the whole company joined in applauding the speaker by calling *hoho*. At noon, two men entered, bearing a large kettle filled with meat upon a pole across their shoulders, which was first presented to the guests. A large wooden ladle as broad and deep as a common bowl, hung with a hook to the side of the kettle, with which every one might at once help himself to as much as he could eat.

---

[1] The difference between confederated and tribal action has many illustrations in the history of the times in which they took a conspicuous part. It became very difficult indeed to secure unity of action in favor of the English at different times, and in 1755 it was entirely defeated. In 1763, Johnson did not class the Senecas among the "friendly tribes," and in 1775 the English were compelled to resort to tribal alliances, in view of the determination of the council in favor of neutrality.

The whole was conducted in a very decent and quiet manner. Indeed, now and then one or the other would lie flat upon his back and rest himself, and sometimes they would stop, joke and laugh heartily."

The second of the national divisions was the MAHICANS, called by the Dutch, *Maikans*, and, by the French missionaries, " the nine nations of *Manhingans*,[1] gathered between Manhattan and the environs of Quebec." The several nations composing the confederacy have never been designated, although certain general divisions appear under the titles of the *Mahicans*, the *Soquatucks*, the *Horicons*, the *Pennacooks*, the *Nipmucks*, the *Abenaquis*, the *Nawaas*, the *Sequins*, and the *Wappingers*, which, in confederated action, may be classed under the generic name of *Abenaqui*, or *Wapanachki*, that is, Men of the East. The representative nation of the confederacy on the Hudson, the *Mahican*, appears to have taken original position there, and to have sent out subduing colonies to the south and east, originating other national combinations. To the noble stream upon which they were found by the Dutch they gave their name, the Mahicanituck; and kindled their ancient council-fire at Schodac, opposite the site of the present city of Albany. To trace their movements prior to the discovery, tradition and theory must be blended. It may be presumed that in the course of the ages they seized the head waters of the Connecticut, the Housatonic, and the Hudson, and from their inland position rolled a savage horde upon the sea-coast, giving birth to the Pequots and the Narragansetts,[2] and from thence overrunning the tribes on the southern part of the peninsula of New York and the adjacent islands, and reuniting with the parent stock as one independent tribe in the position in which they were found

---

[1] *Muhhekaneew* is the orthography of the original name as given by Dr. Edwards, for many years among them. The Dutch called them Mahikanders; the French knew them as the Mourigans and Manhingans; the English as the Mohiccons, Mohegans, Muhheeckanew, etc.

[2] Hubbard, referring to the Pequots, says that it was " commonly reported, about the time when New England was planted by the English," that they, " being a more fierce, cruel, and warlike people than the rest of the Indians, came down out of the inland parts of the continent, and by force seized upon the goodliest places near the sea, and became a terror to all their neighbors."—*Indian Wars*, 14. The relationship between the Mahicans and Pequots is so conclusively shown that one must have apparently originated the other.

by the Dutch under the names of *Wappingers, Montauks* and *Mahicans*.

The tradition which the *Mahicans* give of their origin states: " The country formerly owned by the Muhheakunnuk nation, was situated partly in Massachusetts, and partly in the states of Vermont and New York. The inhabitants dwelt chiefly in little towns and villages. Their chief seat was on Hudson's river, now it is called Albany, which was called Pempotowwuthut-Muhhecanneuw, or the fire-place of the Muhheakunnuk nation, where their allies used to come on any business whether relative to the covenants of their friendship or other matters. The etymology of the word Muhheakunnuk, according to original signification, is great waters or sea, which are constantly in motion, either ebbing or flowing. Our forefathers asserted that they were emigrants from west-by-north of another country; that they passed over great waters, where this and the other country are nearly connected, called Ukhkokpeck; it signifies snake water or water where snakes are abundant; and that they lived by side of a great water or sea, from whence they derive the name of Muhheakunnuk nation. Muhheakunneuw signifies a man of Muhheakunnuk tribe. Muhheakunneyuk is a plural number. As they were coming from the west they found many great waters, but none of them flowing and ebbing like Muhheakunnuk until they came to Hudson's river; then they said one to another, this is like Muhheakunnuk our nativity. And when 'they found grain was very plenty in that country, they agreed to kindle a fire there and hang a kettle, whereof they and their children after them might dip out their daily refreshment. That before they began to decay, our forefathers informed us that the Muhheakunnuk nation could then raise about one thousand warriors who could turn out at any emergency."[1]

The government of the *Mahicans* was a democracy. They had a chief sachem, chosen by the nation, upon whom they looked as conductor and promoter of the general welfare. This office was hereditary by the lineage of the wife of the sachem; that is, the selection of a successor, on the death of a

[1] *Massachusetts Historical Society Collections*, IX, 101. In some of its parts this tradition bears the impress of the theories entertained by the early missionaries.

sachem, was confined to the female branch of the family. The sachem was assisted by counselors, and also by one hero, one owl, and one runner; the rest of the nation were called young men or warriors. The sachem, or more properly king, remained at all times with his tribe and consulted their welfare; he had charge of the *mnoti*, or bag of peace, which contained the belts and strings used to establish peace and friendship with different nations, and concluded all treaties on behalf of his people. The counselors were elected, and were called chiefs. Their business was to consult with their sachem in promoting the peace and happiness of their people. The title of hero was gotten only by courage and prudence in war. When a war-alliance was asked, or cause for war existed with another tribe, the sachem and the counselors consulted, and if they concluded to take up the hatchet, the matter was put in the hands of the heroes for execution. When peace was proposed, the heroes put the negotiations in the hands of the sachem and counselors. The office of owl was also one of merit. He must have a strong memory, and must be a good speaker. His business was to sit beside his sachem, and proclaim his orders to the people with a loud voice; and also to get up every morning as soon as day-light and arouse the people, and order them to their daily duties. The business of runner was to carry messages, and to convene councils.[1]

Precisely what relation the *Mahicans* of the Hudson sustained to the *Mohegans* under Uncas, is not known. Uncas, it will be remembered, was a Pequot chief, and as such occupied a district of country between the Thames and the Connecticut, called Mohegoneak.[2] After an unsuccessful conflict with the tribe to which he belonged, he fled, with some fifty of his

---

[1] *Stockbridge, Past and Present*.

[2] The Pequot and *Mohegan* country lay to the south and east of the *Nehanticks* (in Lyme), from Connecticut river to the eastern boundary line of the colony, and north-east or north of its northern boundary line. This tract was thirty miles square, and Included the counties of New London, Windham, and the principal parts of the county of Tolland. The Pequot country proper was principally within the three towns of New London, Groton and Stonington. All the tract above this, as far north and east as has been described, was the Mohegan country; and most, if not all, the towns held their deeds from Uncas or his successors. Dr. Trumbull, in his *History of Connecticut*, expresses the opinion, that the Pequots and Mohegans were one tribe and took their names "from the place of their situation."—*Massachusetts Historical Society Collections*, IX, 79.

followers, to Hartford, where he formed an alliance with the English in 1638. In the subsequent wars between the English and the Pequots, he remained faithful to the former, and, when the Pequots were blotted out as a nation,[1] received a portion of its survivors as his reward. He subsequently became one of the most powerful chiefs of the country, and the petted favorite of the English of Connecticut. Originally of the same stock;[2] controlled by the same traditionary hostility to the Mohawks; influenced by the conflict for jurisdiction between the Dutch and the English to the Connecticut, it is not at all improbable that he was frequently found sustaining his brethren on the Hudson, and that they in turn recruited his numbers to some extent.[3] The organization under Uncas, however, was clearly distinct from that of the Hudson confederacy.[4] The latter were powerful in themselves, and in their recognized confederated allies, and successfully disputed the prowess of their Mohawk rivals.

The third of the great divisions or confederations represented on the Hudson was the LENNI LENAPES, a name which they applied to themselves, and which has had various interpretations, among others, that of original people, and unmixed people.[5] They were also called by the generic name of *Wapanachki*,

[1] By the terms of peace which closed the Pequot war, that nation were not to live in their ancient country, nor be called by their ancient name, but to become Narragansetts and Mohegans. The name of their ancient river was changed to Thames, and their territory was to be considered the property of the English.—*Rhode Island Historical Society Collections*, III, 177.

[2] "And the identity of name between the *Mahicans* of the Hudson and the *Mohegans* of East Connecticut, induces the belief that all those tribes belonged to the same stock."—*Gallatin*, II, 34. "The *Pequots* and *Mohegans* were apparently originally of the same race with the *Mohicans*, *Mohegans*, or *Mohicanders*, who lived on the banks of the Hudson."—*De Forest's History of the Indians of Connecticut*.

[3] "Some *Mahicanders* are at Hartford in consultation with others the rivers and Northern Indians."—*Col. Nichols, June 25, 1666; Colonial History*, III, 117.

[4] This fact cannot be too distinctly recognized. The *Mohegans* were an exclusively Eastern Connecticut tribe and in alliance with the government of that province; the *Mahicans* of New York differed from them in their dialect, in the territory which they occupied, and in their alliances; having in the latter respect a nominal representation with the authorities of New York and a positive one with Massachusetts. The *Mohegans* of Connecticut were one of the very few tribes whose organization and subsequent history is a matter of record; the *Mahicans* of the Hudson ante-date all human knowledge.

[5] "The term *Lenape*," says Schoolcraft, "appears to carry the same meaning as *inaba*, a male, and the word was probably used nationally, and with emphasis in the sense of men." "I have called them simply *Lenape*, as they do themselves in most instances."—*Heckewelder*.

or Men of the East.[1] Their territory extended from the Katskill mountains south to the Potomac, occupying the region watered by the Hudson, the Delaware,[2] the Susquehanna and the Potomac. The site of their ancient council-fire was at what is now Philadelphia, on the bank of the *Lenapewihituk*, or Delaware river; *Lenape*, the term given to themselves, and *ituk* a geographical equivalent for the English word domain or territory.[3]

According to tradition[4] handed down from their ancestors, the *Lenni Lenapes* resided for many centuries in a very distant country, in the western part of the American continent. Having resolved to move eastward, they set out in a body in search of a new home; and after a long journey and many nights encampment, (i. e., halts of one year at a place), they reached the *Namaesi Sipee* (Mississippi), where they fell in with another nation, the *Mengwe*, or Iroquois, who had also emigrated from a distant country for the same purpose. The region east of the Mississippi was occupied by the *Allegewi* (Alleghany), a powerful and partially civilized people, having numerous large towns defended by regular fortifications and entrenchments.[5]

[1] "These people are known and called by all the western, northern and some of the southern nations by the name of Wappanachki, which the Europeans have corrupted into Apenaki, Openagi, Abenaquis, and Abenakis. All these names, however differently written, and improperly understood by authors, point to one and the same people, the Lenape, who are by this compound word called People at the rising of the Sun, or as we would say Eastlanders; and are acknowledged by near forty tribes, whom we call nations. All these nations, derived from the same stock, recognize each other as Wappanachki, which among them is a generic name."—*Heckewelder*.

[2] Their territorial possessions on the Hudson are clearly defined. Onderis Hocque, one of their chiefs, declared to the Esopus clans, at the treaty of 1660: " Ye must not renew this quarrel. This is not your land; it is our land. Therefore repeat not this, but throw down the hatchet. Tread it so deeply in the earth that it shall never be taken up again."

In the controversy in reference to the Hardenbergh tract, in 1769, one Dr. Shuckburgh stated that he was present at a conference in 1734, in which the chiefs of Schoharie, Seth and Hance, " told the Esopus or Delawares that if they ever attempted to sell lands west of the Katskill hills, they would kill them." An Oneida Indian, whose father was chief sachem of Oneida, " and their oracle in all matters of antiquity," heard his " father often say that the lands on the east of the Delaware was the property of the River Indians or Delawares."—*Johnson Manuscripts*, XVII, 159.

[3] The capital of the nation was subsequently removed to Shamokin, and from thence to Wyoming.

[4] No value whatever attaches to these traditions. That which is here recited gives to them a western origin, in face of their eastern name.

[5] "It is generally believed that the *Allegewi*, or *Alleghans*, were of Welsh origin. This belief rests on the supposed voyage of Madoc to this continent in the twelfth century. The Welsh tradition is,

In this country the *Lenape*, on their arrival, asked to settle. This request was denied by the *Allegewi*, but permission was granted to pass through the territory, and seek a settlement further eastward. No sooner had they commenced to cross the Mississippi, however, than the *Allegewi*, perceiving the vast numbers of the *Lenape*, furiously attacked them. The result of this treachery was a long and bloody war between the *Lenape* and their allies the *Mengwe*, on the one side, and the *Allegewi* on the other. The latter, after protracted contest, finding themselves unable to make head against the formidable alliance, and that their very existence, as a distinct tribe, was threatened, abandoned their ancient seats and fled down the Mississippi, from whence they never again returned. Of course, their lands were divided by the conquerors.

For a long period — some say for several centuries — the *Mengwe* and *Lenape* dwelt in peace together, and both nations rapidly increased in numbers. At length some of the more enterprising of the *Lenape* huntsmen and warriors crossed the mountains, pursued their travels near to the great salt-water lake (Atlantic), and discovered the great river (Delaware). Going on still further eastward through the *Sheyickbi* country, they came to another great stream (the Hudson). On their return home they gave so flattering an account of the excellence and richness of the regions thus discovered, as to induce the general belief that this was the land which the Great Spirit designed for

that Madoc's company landed on some part of New England or Virginia, and in process of time spread over a great part of America. The investigations showing the existence of *white people* in the valley of the Mississippi, and that they were of Welsh origin, are very interesting. This people spoke the Welsh language to a considerable extent, and claimed Welsh origin. For more than a century and a half, the existence of this people in the interior of our country, has been traced."— *Yates and Moulton.* "They occupied a large portion of the western area of the State of New York, comprising the valley of the Alleghany river to its utmost source, and extending eastwardly an undefined distance. Our authorities do not leave us in doubt, that this ancient people, who occupy the foreground of our remote aboriginal history, were a valiant, noble and populous race, who were advanced in arts and the policy of government and raised fortifications for their defense, which are extended over the entire Mississippi valley, as high as latitude 43°, and the lake country, reaching from Lake St. Clair to the south shore of Lake Ontario, and the country of the Onondagas and Oneidas."— *Schoolcraft.* Priest traces the *Allegewi* from the lake country to the "vale of Mexico, where they finally and permanently rested," and where they assumed the name of *Aztecas*, or people of the lakes. The course of migration is marked by the mounds where they "rested," or dwelt temporarily on their journey.— *American Antiquities.*

their permanent abode. Though emigrating at first in small numbers, the great body of the nation at last settled on the four great rivers, Delaware, Hudson, Susquehanna and Potomac, and kindled their council-fire in the centre of their possessions. Here they became so numerous that their descendants were compelled to separate from them in branches, so that nearly forty tribes honored them with the title of *grandfather*,[1] a title which some of them continue to apply to the present day.[2]

In the government of the *Lenapes* the perfect liberty of the people was the fundamental law, and absolute unanimity the only recognized expression of the popular will. A more perfect system of checks and balances the wisdom of civilized nations has not devised. They were divided in three tribes, the *Unami*, the *Unalachto*, and the *Minsi*, or the Turtle, the Turkey, and the Wolf. Each tribe had its chief and each chief his counselors, the latter composed either of experienced warriors or aged and respectable fathers of families. In times of peace nothing could be done without the consent of the council unanimously expressed. The chiefs were required to keep good order, and to decide in all quarrels and disputes ; but they had no power to command, compel, or punish ; their only mode of government was persuasion and exhortation, and in departing from that mode they were deposed by the simple form of forsaking them. The constant restraint which they were under made them, in general, the most courteous, affable and hospitable of men. Their legislative hall was usually in a building provided for that purpose ; the counselors were called together by a servant ; in the centre of the room a large fire was kindled, and tobacco, pipes, and provisions provided, and the matter under consideration disposed of after alternate smoking, eating and deliberation, but with the utmost gravity.

In national matters the chief of the *Unami* was first in rank and constituted the head or king. For this reason, while he must be a member of that tribe, the selection of his successor, in case of his death, was made by the ruling chiefs of the other

---

[1] The tribes acknowledging this relation addressed the *Lenni Lenapes* with the title of *Mochomes*, that is to say, their *grandfather*, and were received with the appellation of *Noochwissah* or *my grandchildren.*—*Yates and Moulton.*

[2] Schoolcraft admits that there is some reason to acquiesce, " to a certain extent,"

tribes. He was required to maintain the peace and covenants with other nations, and to that end to carry on a kind of correspondence with them that he might always be acquainted with their disposition towards his people. He also sent out embassies, with the advice and consent of the other chiefs. He was liable to removal in case of neglect of duty, or for suffering any of his people to commit offenses which might involve the nation in war. If, after being admonished of his duty he was still neglectful of it, he was forsaken and his power was at an end. National councils were a duplication of tribal councils, except that they were composed of representatives selected by the chiefs and counselors of the tribes and their assemblage held at the capital. In times of war the powers of the civil government were suspended. A chief could not declare war without the consent of his captains, nor could he accept a war-belt except to transmit it to them, and finally, the captains could not declare war unless by unanimous assent. When war was formally declared, the care of the people passed into the hands of the captains. When terms of peace were proposed, civil government was resumed; the chief again took his place; the captains placed the proposals in his hands, and he had power to accept or reject them. If he accepted the proposals, he took the hatchet from the hands of the chief captain, and desired him to sit down. This constituted a truce, and was followed by the appointment of embassadors to conclude a treaty. All the proceedings were accompanied by the gravest demeanor, and the most impressive dignity. "No stranger could visit their councils without a sensation of respect."

Law and justice, as civilized nations understand those terms, were to them unknown, yet both they had in a degree suited to their necessities. Assaults, murders, and other acts regarded as criminal offenses by all nations, were so regarded by them, but the execution of punishment was vested in the injured family, who were constituted judges as well as executioners,

in both the claim to antiquity and their ancient position, in the great Algonquin family of the *Lenapes*. He says: "It is believed that there are no members of this generic family of tribes, certainly none of the existing tribes in the north and west, who are known to us personally, who do not acknowledge the ancient *Lenapes* under the title of grandfather."

and who could grant pardons or accept atonements. The rights of property they understood and respected; and half their wars were retaliatory for the taking of their territory without making just and proper compensation. There was not a man among them that did not know the bounds of his own land as accurately as though defined by a surveyor's chain. Their customs were their unwritten laws, more effective than those which fill the tomes of civilized governments, because taught to the people from infancy and woven into every condition and necessity of their being. Their chiefs were poor and without revenue, yet the treasury of the nation was never exhausted. A more perfect democracy will never exist among the nations of the earth, and in this respect it was distinguished from the government of the Iroquois, the latter more nearly resembling a republic from the greater number of tribes represented in national councils, but in other respects scarcely presenting a single contrasting feature.

The names given to the *Lenape* tribes were from their totems. Each Indian nation was not only divided into tribes and chieftaincies or family clans, but had peculiar totemic classifications. Totems were rude but distinct devices or family symbols, denoting original consanguinity, and were universally respected. They were painted upon the person of the Indian, and again on the gable end of his cabin, "some in black, others in red." The wandering savage appealed to his totem, and was entitled to the hospitality of the wigwam which bore the corresponding emblem. They had other and various uses, but the most important was the representation which they made of the tribe or family to which they belonged or were made the emblems. The *Iroquois* had nine, forming two divisions, one of four tribes and the other of five. Of the first division the emblems were the Tortoise, the Wolf, the Bear, and the Beaver. The second division, and subordinate to the first, were the Deer, the Potatoe, the Great Plover, the Little Plover, and the Eagle. The *Mohawks* were represented by the totem of the Bear.[1] The *Lenni Lenapes* had three totemic tribes: the Turtle, or

---

[1] The Mohawk sachems who presented their condolence at Albany, in 1690, on the taking of Schenectady, said: "We are all of the race of the bear, and the bear you know never yields while one drop of blood is left. We must all be bears."—*Schoolcraft*.

*Unami*;[1] the Turkey, or *Unalachto*, and the Wolf, or *Minsi*. The totems of the *Mahicans* were the Bear,[2] the Wolf, and the Turtle. The Turkey and Turtle tribes occupied the seacoast and the south-western shore of the Hudson, while the Wolf or *Minsi*, being much the most warlike of the three, served as a sort of shield to their more peaceful brethren, and watched the movements of the *Mengwe* or Iroquois. Their territory extended from the Katskill mountains to the head waters of the Delaware and Susquehanna rivers, and was bounded on the east by the Hudson; their council-fire was lighted at Minisink.[3] The Turkey tribe joined the *Minsi* on the south somewhere about Stony point. On the west bank of the river, therefore, there were but two totemic *Lenape* tribes. Above the *Minsi* came the *Mahican* totem of the Wolf, and on the east bank the Bear of that nation. Below the *Mahicans* from Roeloff Jansen's kill to the sea, the Wolf again appeared as the totem of the *Wappingers;* while the *Montauks* bore the emblem of the Turtle.[4] The prevailing totem of all the Hudson river cantons was the Wolf, borne alike by *Minsis*, *Wappingers* and *Mahicans*,[5] leading the French to call them all *Loups* or wolves, and affording Mr. Schoolcraft the basis for his

---

[1] "The Turtle tribe, among the *Lenapes*, claims a superiority and ascendancy over the others because of their *relation* to the great tortoise, a fabled monster, the *Atlas* of their mythology, who bears, according to their traditions, this great island, as they term the world, on his back; and also superior because he is amphibious."—*Yates and Moulton's History*. Politically the Turtle and Turkey tribes were associated in the same government, while the Minsis had a distinct organization.

[2] "The Bear tribe was considered the leading totem and entitled to the office of chief sachem."—*Mahican Tradition*. They appear to have been in occupation in the vicinity of Albany.

[3] The location was about ten miles south of Maghackemek, in the present state of New Jersey. "The third tribe, the Wolf, commonly called the *Minsi*, which we have corrupted into *Monseys*, had chosen to live back of the two other tribes, and formed a kind of bulwark for their protection, watching the motions of the *Mengwe*, and being at hand to afford their aid in case of rupture with them. The *Minsi* were considered the most warlike and active branch of the Lenape. They extended their settlements from the Minisink, a place named after them, where they had their council seat and fire, quite up to the Hudson; and to the west, or southwest, far beyond the Susquehanna; their northern boundaries were supposed originally to be the heads of the great rivers Susquehanna and Delaware, and their southern boundaries that ridge of hills known in New Jersey by the name of Muskanecum, and in Pennsylvania, by those of Lehigh, Coghnewago, etc."—*Heckewelder*.

[4] The classification is not positive. There were other than the Turtle totem on the island.

[5] "*Mohegan* is a word, the meaning of which is not explained by the early writers; but if we may trust the deductions of philology, it needs create little uncer-

argument that the name of the Mahican confederacy was from its prevailing totemic emblem.

For dividing the territory of the *Mahicans* at Roeloff Jansen's kill, and again at Long Island, there is other than totemic authority. In regard to the former, the affidavit of King Nimham is on record, under date of October 13, 1730, in which it is stated that the deponent was "a River Indian of the tribe of the *Wappinoes*, which tribe was the ancient inhabitants of the eastern shore of Hudson's river, from the city of New York to about the middle of Beekman's patent," in the northern part of the present county of Dutchess ; " that another tribe of River Indians called the Mayhiccondas were the ancient inhabitants of the remaining eastern shore of said river ; that these two tribes constituted one nation." The testimony in regard to the *Montauks* is not so clear and positive, but is sufficiently so to indicate their status at the time of the discovery, whatever may have been their subsequent political relations. On the earliest maps the island is assigned to the *Mahicans*. DeRasieres, writing in 1626, states that its occupation was then by the " old Manhattans," and intimates that they were conquered " by the Wappenos." While all the eastern Indians were called Wappenos,[1] or Wapenacki, the reference, in this instance, is clearly specific, not general, and evidently refers to the Wappinoo or Wappinger branch of the Mahicans, who, whatever may have

---

tainly. In the *Mohegan*, as spoken at the present time by their lineal descendants, the Stockbridges of Wisconsin. *Maihtshow* is the name of the common wolf. It is called, in the cognate dialects of the Algonquin, *Myegan* by the Kenistenos, and *Myeengun* by the Chippewas, etc. In the old Algonquin, as given by La Hontan, it is *Mahingan*, and we perceive that this was the term adopted by the early French writers for the Mohegans. The term itself, it is to be understood, by which the tribe is known to us, is not the true Indian, but has been shorn of a part of its true sound by the early French, Dutch and English writers. The modern tribe of the Mohegans, to whom allusion has been made, called themselves *Muhhekaniew*. * * *Mohegan* was a phrase to denote an enchanted wolf, or a wolf of supernatural power. This was the badge of arms of the tribe, rather than the name of the tribe itself."—*Schoolcraft*. Compare with the statement of Capt. Hendrick, quoted *ante*, p. 42.

[1] Their various tongues may be classed into four distinct languages, namely, Manhattan, Minqua, Savanoo and Wappanoos. With the Manhattans we include those who live in the neighboring places along the North river, on Long Island, and at the Neversink ; with the Minquas, we include the Senecas, the Maquas, and other inland tribes. The Savanoos are the southern nations and the Wappanoos the eastern. Van der Donck, *N. Y. Hist. Soc. Coll.*, 2d Series, I, 206; Wassenaar, *Doc. Hist.*, III, 46.

been their origin, seized the southern part of the peninsula and adjacent islands, and established themselves in the Highlands. Long anterior to Nimham's affidavit, however, the *Montauks* were severed from the *Mahicans*, and became tributaries to the Dutch and to the English.

The original supremacy of the IROQUOIS CONFEDERACY is assumed by almost every writer of Indian history. "From their ancient fortresses," says one of their ardent but not altogether truthful admirers, "war parties continually went forth; their war-cry sounded from the lakes to the far west, and rolled along the banks of the Mississippi and over the far-off fields of the south. They defeated the *Hurons* under the very walls of Quebec, put out the council-fires of the *Gahkwas* and the *Eries*,[1] eradicated the *Susquehannocks*[2] and placed the *Lenapes*, under tribute. The terror of their name went wherever their war canoes paddled, and nations trembled when they heard the name of Konoshioni." Another asserts that "long before European discovery, the question of savage supremacy had been settled on the waters of the Cahohatatea;" that the "invincible arms" of the *Iroquois* "humbled every native foe." In view of the undeniable fact that there is not a single well-attested case of subjugation by the *Iroquois* until nearly half a century after "European discovery," these fulsome panegyrics may very properly be subjected to analysis.

While conceding to the *Iroquois*, and to their immediate representative on the Hudson, the *Mohawks*, much of the credit which has been claimed for them, justice to other nations will compel the acknowledgment that the former were aided in their conquests and preserved in their integrity to a very great extent by their early alliances with the Europeans, and especially by their constitution, by the English of New York, as an armed police over the unarmed tribes; and further, that there is scarce a recorded conquest by them that is not tinged by the unmis-

---

[1] The *Eries* were seated on the southern shores of the lake which still bears their name. We only know that they were an *Iroquois* tribe, and that they were destroyed in 1655.— *Gallatin*. The *Gahkwas*, or *Kahkwahs*, were also an *Iroquois* tribe, and are supposed by some to have been the same with the *Eries*; by others that they were subsequently known as the *Hurons*.— *Schoolcraft*.

[2] The Susquehannocks were seated on the Susquehanna river and Chesapeake bay. They were defeated, in conflict with the English, at their fort near Co-

takeable fact that the subjugated tribe was contending against civilized as well as savage foes. In their early wars the Dutch took no part, except to exchange for their furs the munitions of war which they wanted, and to cultivate with them, for the purposes of trade, peace and friendship. To both, this friendly intercourse was desirable, and to both a necessity. When the English came in possession of the province, the wars in which the Indians had taken part and were then engaged, the alliances which they had formed with the French, and the positions which they respectively occupied, made an alliance with the *Iroquois* but the perfection of a condition of things which had had the growth of over half a century, and which were destined to still further development.

This fact appears more clearly in connection with contemporaneous events. The settlement of Canada was commenced in 1604, under a patent granted by Henry IV to Pierre du Gast. In 1609, the year in which Hudson ascended the Mahicanituck, Champlain discovered the lake which now bears his name. At this time the *Mohawks* were at war with the northern tribes, and by the mere force of the circumstances under which he was placed, he formed an alliance with the latter, even agreeing to assist them against their enemies. The first result of this alliance was at a meeting of war parties of the *Mohawks* and *Hurons* on Lake Champlain at which the former were defeated, mainly perhaps by the power of the French arquebuses.[1] From that period the tide of *Algonquin* success rolled

lumbia, with the loss of several hundred warriors, and in this weakened state were conquered by the Oneidas and incorporated with that tribe. When they had forgotten their language they were sent back to the Susquehanna and became known as the Conestogas.— *Gallatin*.

[1] This battle was fought on the morning of the 30th July, 1609. Champlain with four of his men, and accompanied by some 200 *Hurons*, were engaged in exploring Lake Champlain, when a party of hostile *Mohawks* appeared. As the Indian practice was against fighting on the water, both parties hurried to the shore, where they pitched for battle. The Mohawks hastily entrenched themselves with trees "at the point of a cape which runs out into the lake from the west side." By agreement, hostilities were suspended until the next morning, when the *Hurons* led the attack. Running to within two hundred feet in front of their enemy, they stopped and divided into bands on the right and left, leaving Champlain and his men in the centre. The sudden appearance of the Frenchmen, and the peculiarity of their arms, produced extreme astonishment in the *Mohawk* ranks; but what was their dismay when the first report of the arquebuses fell upon their ears, and they beheld two of their chiefs fall dead and a third dangerously wounded. The contest was of short duration. The *Mohawks* broke and fled. Many were killed, and some taken prisoners. Not

along the northern frontiers of the *Iroquois*, and carried terror into the ranks of the *Onondagas*.[1] Obtaining arms and powder from the Dutch, the confederacy recovered its position, and in turn harassed the French and their Indians in wars which were yet open when the jurisdiction of the Dutch was exchanged for that of the English.

That the Dutch were neutrals is evident from their treaties with the Indians. Their first settlement was among the *Mahicans* at what is now Albany, and their intercourse was mainly, if not entirely, with that nation until 1623, when it is stated, the *Mahicans*, *Mohawks*, *Oneidas*, *Onondagas*, *Cayugas*, and *Senecas*, as well as the " far off *Ottawa* Indians," came " and made covenants of friendship," with them, bringing to commander Joris " great presents of beaver and other peltry, and desired that they might come and have constant free trade with them, which was concluded upon."[2] It is not to be presumed that the nations named were present at one time, for they were not at peace with each other; there is no mention made by the Dutch historians of any acknowledgment of subjugation by any of the tribes, so minutely described in one of the early histories of New York,[3] and accepted apparently without examination by subsequent writers. The deducible fact is that none of the tribes were granted special privileges, and that there was not the slightest distinction made between them in the terms of the compact.

During the difficulties with the Indians in the vicinity of Fort Amsterdam in 1645, it is said that Director Kieft visited Fort Orange and made a treaty with the *Mohawks* and *Mahicans* by which their friendship was secured. Although O'Callaghan[4] magnifies the consequence of the *Mohawks* in this transaction, and assumes that their " name alone, inspired terror among all the tribes west of the Connecticut ; over whom they claimed to be sovereign, and from whom they exacted tribute,"

---

one of the *Hurons* was killed ; and they celebrated their victory on the field of battle in dancing and singing.— *Yates and Moulton.*

[1] The incursions of the French exploring parties may have been the very " northern hordes," to resist whom the confederation was formed in the manner so graphically described in the story of Hiawatha.

[2] *Wassenaar*, VII, 11 ; *Doc. Hist.*, III, 35, 51.

[3] *Yates and Moulton's Hist. New York*, 346, 347.

[4] *Hist. New Netherland*, I, 355.

his statements are defeated by the association of the *Mahicans* in the treaty, by the facts which he subsequently quotes, and by the whole tenor of contemporaneous history. In 1659, the *Mohawks* visited Fort Orange for the first time to ask special favors, and the first visit to them, in an official capacity, was made by the Dutch soon after. There is nothing in the proceedings of either conference which establishes any other fact than that the *Mohawks* desired an accommodation which the Dutch were willing to grant only to an extent that should prevent the alliance of the former with the tribes then threatening hostilities. In 1660, they were included in the peace at Esopus, but neither in its negotiation nor its terms was there distinction made between the parties to that treaty. Three years later Stuyvesant distinctly refused to employ them. The advantage to the *Iroquois* from their treaty of free trade was great, but it was made so only by the bar which their proximity to Fort Orange interposed to the supplying of other nations with whom they were at war.

The treaty between Nicolls, on the part of the English, and the *Iroquois*, was one of necessity. With the *Mahicans* the English were already in treaty ; with the *Iroquois* alone they had none. Nothing was changed by it, but the change which subsequently came was due to other causes, and those causes precisely what they were a hundred years later. It required more than half a century to develop the result of the opposing French and English Indian alliances, even admitting that the result was practically determined on this continent. The war between the French Indians and the *Iroquois* at the north was one of alternate successes and reverses, with positive advantages undetermined ; but at the south, where the French alliance was without power, the *Lenapes, Minsis, Susquehannas, Andastes*,[1] and other tribes became tributary to their ancient enemies. With the progress of the French in the west, and the gathering

---

[1] Note 3, *ante* p. 35. Raffeix, the French missionary, writes, in 1672 : "God preserve the *Andastes*, who have only three hundred warriors, and bless their arms to humiliate the Iroquois and preserve to us peace and our missions."— *Brodhead*, II, 193. The wars of the five nations against their own kindred, as in the case of the *Andastes, Eries, etc.,* are one of the unexplained passages in their history.

thither of tribes retreating before the civilization which was rolling upon them, the condition of even the subjugated tribes improved, while the integrity of the *Iroquois* was compromised. What the French lacked in position they made up in zeal, and pushed their priests and their fire-arms together. Their success was far greater than the English could wish. The *Mohawks* were shorn of an entire canton of converts; the flower of the *Mahicans* became the trophies of the priests; the *Senecas*, who could call out more warriors than their four associate tribes combined, were detached almost entirely, two small villages only retaining their allegiance to the English. A hundred years of war and diplomacy gave the French a very strong position, and correspondingly elevated the tribes with which they were in alliance. The English were compelled to dictate the removal of the *petticoat* from the *Lenapes*, while the *Mohawks* were reduced to numbers comparatively insignificant, notwithstanding the efforts made to recruit them. How the contest would have ended had the French remained in possession of Canada and the west, cannot be assumed; but the presumption is not unreasonable, that, while the English may not have been swept out of possession, the prowess of the *Algonquins* would have been chanted where now the notes of applause embalm the memory of the *Iroquois*.

The inquiry has its specific form in the alleged subjugation of the *Mahicans* and in the period assigned to the subjugation of the *Lenapes* as having been anterior to the advent of the Europeans. The *Mahicans* were the most formidable competitors of the *Iroquois*. Equal in courage, equal in numbers, equal in the advantages of obtaining fire-arms from the Dutch and in their subsequent alliance with the English, they marched unsubdued by the boasted conquerors of America. When the Dutch first met them they were in conflict with the *Mohawks*, and that conflict was maintained for nearly three-quarters of a century, and until the English, who were in alliance with both, were able to effect a permanent settlement. Gallatin, writing upon this subject, says: "Judge Smith, in his *History of New York*, published in 1756, says, that 'When the Dutch began the settlement of this country, all the Indians on Long

Island and the northern shore of the sound, on the banks of Connecticut, Hudson's, Delaware, and Susquehanna rivers, were in subjection to the Five Nations, and, within the memory of persons now living, acknowledged it by the payment of an annual tribute: " He gives no authority for the early date he assigns to that event. The subsequent protracted wars of the Dutch with the Manhattan and the Long Island Indians, and the continued warfare of the Mohawks against the Connecticut Indians, are inconsistent with that account, which is clearly incorrect with respect to the Mohikander River Indians, or Mahicans. These are mentioned by De Laet as the mortal enemies of the Maquas. It was undoubtedly the interest of the Dutch to promote any arrangement, which, by compelling the Mahicans to remain at peace, would secure their own trade. If they succeeded at any time, the peace was but temporary. We learn from the Relations of the French missionaries, that war existed in 1656, between the Manhingans and the Mohawks, and that these experienced a severe check in 1663, in an attack upon a Manhingan fortified village, and Colden admits that the contest was not at an end until 1673. 'The trade of New York,' he says, 'was hindered by the war which the Five Nations had at that time with the River Indians;' and he adds that the governor of New York 'obtained a peace between the Five Nations and the Mahikanders or River Indians.'[1] It is also certain that those Mohikander or River Indians were not reduced to the same state in which the Delawares were placed. It is proved by the concurring accounts of the French and English writers, that, subsequently to the peace of 1673, they were repeatedly, indeed uniformly, employed as auxiliaries in the wars of the Five Nations and the British against the French."[2]

This conclusion is not only abundantly sustained by the records referred to, but by an analysis of the testimony which has been relied upon as indicating an opposite result. The latter is confined, first, to traditional reverses sustained by the *Mahicans* on Wanton island, near Katskill, and at Red Hook, in Dutchess county, the bones of the slain at the latter place

---

[1] *Colden's Six Nations*, chap. ii, 35.   [2] *Gallatin's Indian Tribes*, II, 43, 44.

being, it is said, in monumental record when the Dutch first settled there; and second, to the statements by Michaelius and Wassenaar. The traditional evidence is entirely worthless as to the results involved, and at best can only be accepted as proof of sanguinary conflicts; while the statements by Michaelius and Wassenaar, based as they were on information received from others, are almost wholly at variance with positive records. The former writer states that in the war of 1626, the *Mohawks* were successful and that the *Mahicans* fled and left their lands unoccupied;[1] the latter affirms that "war broke out" again in 1628, "between the *Maikens*, near Fort Orange, and the *Makwaes*," and that the former were beaten and driven off.[2] Admitting that both writers refer to the same occurrence, and that there is no conflict in date, the retirement spoken of could only have included a single canton or chieftaincy. That the *Mahicans*, as a nation, did not leave their lands unoccupied nor surrender their possession, appears from the title deeds which they gave to Van Rensselaer in 1630, the validity of which was never questioned; from the treaty made with them by Kieft, and from their participation in the wars with the Dutch at Fort Amsterdam. To these facts it may be added that deeds from King Aepjin show that his council-fire was kept burning at Schodac[3] as late as 1664; that one of the castles of the nation, that at Cohoes, was in occupation by them as late as 1660, and that the records of the commissioners of Indian affairs show an organization, distinct from that which was recognized by Massachusetts but clearly subordinate to it, for over half a century after the English succeeded the Dutch in the government.

It only remains to harmonize these facts with the statements referred to. That, as already intimated, a canton or chieftaincy

---

[1] "The business of furs is dull on account of a new war of the *Maechibaeys* (Mohawks) against the *Maikans* at the upper end of this river. There have occurred cruel murders on both sides. The *Maikans* have fled and their lands are unoccupied, and they are very fertile and pleasant."—Michaelius, *Colonial History*, II, 769.

[2] "In the beginning of this year (1628) war broke out between the *Maikans*, near Fort Orange, and the *Mohawks*, but these beat and captured the *Maikans* and drove off the remainder, who have retired towards the north by the Fresh river, so called, where they begin to cultivate the soil; and thus the war terminated."—Wassenaar, *Documentary History*, III, 48.

[3] It is not certain that Schodac was the original capital of the nation. The probabilities are that it was, and that it was subsequently removed to Westenhuck, in the valley of the Housatonic.

of the nation retired from the west bank of the river at or about the time spoken of by Michaelius and Wassenaar, is not only probable, but its movements can apparently be traced and the territory which it "left unoccupied" very nearly defined. The explanation is found in the title deeds which were subsequently given by the tribes who were parties to the conflict. Their examination shows that the *Mohawks* only claimed the right of conquest over lands north of the Mohawk river and in part particularly embraced in the Kayaderossera patent. South of the Mohawk river they never either claimed or sold lands on the Hudson, and even north of that point their claim, although traditionally conceded, was subsequently disputed.[1] Whatever may have been the extent of the territory which they claimed, however, it is apparent that it was limited and that it did not include or extend to the east side of the river, nor involve the subjugation of the nation. The retiring canton was an advanced post on the frontiers, pushed forward, it may be reasonably supposed, by superior prowess, and maintained until peculiarly exposed. The point to which it removed is not positively stated;[2] but the evidence is sufficient to indicate pretty certainly that it was known as the *Soquatucks* or *Socoquis*,[3] in the alliances of 1664, and in the subsequent history of the nation.

If there is no evidence of prior subjugation, there is certainly none establishing that condition after the advent of the English. The nation was almost continually in conflict with the *Mohawks*, and in its last war with them maintained itself with success. A more extended reference to this war and its results may be proper. The eastern Indians were involved in the contest as well

---

[1] It is asserted that the *Mahicans* admitted the conquest of the lands west of the Hudson embraced in the Saratoga (Schuylerville) tract; yet from the Johnson Manuscripts it appears that they claimed them in 1767, to "the prejudice," as Johnson says, "of *Mohawk* rights."— *Johnson Manuscripts*, IV, 170, 173.

[2] Wassenaar says, "towards the north near the Fresh river."

[3] *Brodhead's Hist.*, I, 732; *Col. Hist.*, IX, 66. Probably called *Soquatucks* from Soquans, or Suckquans, their chief sachem. Their classification as Saco Indians (*note* *Col. Hist.*, IX, 475), does not correspond with their assignment "towards Lake Champlain," (*Ib.*, 795), or with the very plain statement by Talon: "Two Indian tribes, one called the *Loups* (Mahicans) and the other the *Socoquis*, inhabit the country adjoining the English, and live, in one respect, under their laws, in the same manner as the *Algonquins* and *Hurons* do under those of his majesty. I perceive in these two tribes, by nature arrant and declared enemies of the Iroquois, a great inclination to reside among the French." After King Philip's

as the *Mahicans*.[1] In 1662, Director Stuyvesant succeeded in establishing peace between the contestants, but when the *Mohawks* carried presents to the English fort at Penobscot to confirm the same, they were attacked and slain.[2] The connection of the Hudson river chieftaincies with the war which followed cannot be distinctly traced, but there is some data upon the subject. In *Kregier's Journal of the Second Esopus War*, it is said that residents at Bethlehem, in the present county of Albany, were warned, in the fall of 1663, by a friendly Indian, to remove to a place of security; that "five Indian nations had assembled together, namely the *Mahikanders*, the *Katskills*, the *Wappingers*, those of Esopus, besides another tribe of Indians that dwell half-way between Fort Orange and Hartford;" that their "place of meeting was on the east side of Fort Orange river, about three (nine) miles inland from Claverack,"[3] and that they were "about five hundred strong." Again: "Hans the Norman[4] arrived at the redoubt with his yacht from Fort Orange; reports that full seven thousand Indians had assembled at Claverack, on the east side, about three (nine) miles inland, but he knows not with what intent."[5] The intent soon became apparent. Under date of June 21, 1664, Brodhead writes: "War now broke out again. The *Mahicans* attacked the *Mohawks*, destroyed cattle at Greenbush, burned the house of Abraham Staats at Claverack, and ravaged the whole country on the east side of the North river." The operations of the Jesuit missionaries were seriously hindered; prisoners taken on either side were burned or eaten; the *Mohawks* were weakened and their pride humbled. Such were the results of the war at the close of 1668.[6]

In the spring of 1669, a *Mohawk* embassy visited Quebec, and asked that their nation might be "protected from the *Mahi*-

---

war, a portion of them appear to have returned to the Hudson, where they were incorporated with the *Mahicans* at Schaticook. The greater portion, however, ultimately found their way to Canada, where, with fragments of other tribes, they were known as the St. Francis Indians.—*Doc. Hist.*, I, 27; *Col. Hist.*, III, 482, 562; IV, 684, 715.

[1] On the other hand, war was raging furiously between the *Mohawks* and the Mohegans, who had been joined by the *Abenaqui* nations.—*Shea's Charlevoix*, III, 45; *Drake's Book of the Indians*.

[2] *Brodhead's New York*, I, 732.

[3] The village of Claverack was five miles from the Hudson. It was known by the Indian name of *Potkoke*.

[4] Norman's kill, in Albany, takes its name from this person.

[5] *Documentary History*, IV, 83, 85.

[6] *Brodhead*, II, 99, 146.

*cans* by the king of France, to whom their country now belonged by the force of arms." In this they were successful so far at least as to secure the cooperation of the Jesuit missionaries in resisting an attack by the *Mahicans* on the palisaded village of Caghnawaga. This attack was made on the eighteenth of August, 1669. The *Mahicans* retired after two hours fighting; and the *Mohawks*, descending the river in canoes, hid themselves below them in an ambuscade which commanded the road to Schenectady, at a place called Kinaquariones, where a conflict ensued in which, although at first successful, the *Mohawks* were put to flight.[1] The *Mohawks* then induced the *Oneidas*, *Onondagas* and *Cayugas* to make common cause with them; and four hundred confederate warriors went to surprise a *Mahican* fort " situated near Manhattan." But this enterprise failed, and the *Iroquois* returned home with two wounded.[2] In April, 1670, Governor Lovelace visited Albany, charged, among other things, with the duty of making peace between the *Mohawks* and *Mahicans*; but it was not until August of the succeeding year that the negotiations were consummated.[3] What the terms of peace were is not stated, and can only be inferred from the subsequent treatment of the tribes who were parties to it, who are described as being " linked together in interest," and who were uniformly treated as equals even in the selection of representative chiefs to visit England. At no stage of their history are they represented as the dependents of the Five Nations. This will more fully appear from their connection with the wars with the Dutch,

---

[1] Drake states that the *Mahicans* and their allies marched into the Mohawk country, led by the principal sachem of Massachusetts (*Pennacooks?*) named Josiah, alias *Chekatabut*, a wise man, and stout man of middle stature. After a " journey of two hundred miles," they arrived at the *Mohawk* fort, " when, upon besieging it some time, and having some of their men killed and sundry others sick, they gave up the siege and retreated. The *Mohawks* pursued them, got in their front, and from an ambush, attacked them and a great fight ensued. The *Mohawks* were finally put to flight by the extraordinary bravery and prowess of *Chekatabut* and his captains; but victory was purchased by the death of their chosen leader. This was a severe stroke, and although the war continued, it was not with that spirit in which it had been commenced."

[2] *Brodhead's New York*, II, 161.

[3] *Assize Record*, II, 732; *Brodhead's New York*, II, 181. Colden says that peace was not established until 1673. The following entry is made in *Assize Record*, IV, 116: " March 7, 1671. Mendowasse, sagamore from Hackinsack, Anmanhose from Haverstroo, Meggenmaiker, sagamore of Tappan, in behalf of themselves and Neversincks, having understood that peace had been made between the Maquas and Mahikanders, asked permission to visit, etc."

their treaties with the English and their official relations with the governments of New York and Massachusetts.

That the *Mahicans* experienced great changes is unquestioned. To a considerable extent their position involved this. Though spared on the north and east, they were exposed to the incoming civilization on the west and south. The *Wappingers* suffered terribly in their wars with the Dutch: from the rapacity of the traders at Fort Orange they recoiled. If their national councilfire was originally at Schodac, it was subsequently removed to the valley of the Housatonic,[1] where, under the name of W-nahk-ta-kook, it was known to the authorities of Massachusetts and to the English missionaries; under that of Westenhuck, to the Moravians, and under that of Stockbridge, preserved the line of kings and linked the past with the present history of the nation.[2] To the English of New York, however, this council-fire was little known. Cut off by the boundary line of Massachusetts it was officially recognized by that province, while the authorities of New York maintained their official relations with an organization which is represented as existing "above and below Albany," and known as the *Mahicander* or River Indians. This organization was strengthened by the results of King Philip's war. In that war the *Pennacooks*[3] had taken part, and at the close of the campaign of 1675, found winter quarters among their kindred "near Albany." After the disastrous conflict of August 12th, of the succeeding year, in which Philip was killed, they again retreated "towards Albany," some two hundred and fifty in number, but were pursued and attacked by the English, near the Housatonic river, and a number of them killed. The main body of them, however, made good their retreat to the Hudson, where a portion of

---

[1] The Housatonic was originally known as the Westenhook river, south of Westenhuck.— (*Sauthier's Map*). It was the boundary line of the neutrality which was established by the *Iroquois* and the *Mahicans* with the French Indians in the war of 1704. "The inhabitants of this Province who lived on the west side of that river followed all their occupations in husbandry as in times of peace, while at the same time the inhabitants of New England were in their sight exposed to the merciless cruelty of the French and their Indians."—*Colonial History*, VI, 371.

[2] *Stockbridge, Past and Present*, 39; *History of Missions of United Brethren*, II, 56, 115, 130; *Memorials Moravian Church*, I, etc.

[3] The *Pennacooks*, Schoolcraft says, "occupied the Coos country, extending from Haverhill to the sources of the Connecticut." The French classed them among the *Mahican* tribes, and such they

them remained near the Dutch village of Claverack, and the remainder, some two hundred in number, passed over to Potick, an old *Mahican* village at Katskill.[1] The French immediately made overtures to them, through their associates who had found refuge in Canada, and Connecticut invited them to homes within her borders. Governor Andros, with equal promptness and from a similar motive,[2] invited them to settle at Schaticook, in the present county of Rensselaer, near the confluence of the Hoosic with the Hudson, in company with the *Mahicans* who were established there. This offer was accepted and a flourishing colony soon came into existence, which was patronizingly called by the *Mohawks*, our children.

The historical narrative need not be further anticipated. In passing, however, it may be remarked that it cannot be admitted that while "the *Pequots* and *Mohegans* claimed some authority over the Indians of the Connecticut, those extending westwardly to the Hudson appear to have been divided into small and independent tribes, united, since they were known to the Europeans, by no common government," as stated by Gallatin. That conclusion was based upon information less perfect than that which has since been obtained, and not only so but is in conflict with the previous findings of that author. There was nothing in their action inconsistent with the clearly understood powers of chieftaincies; but much that implies obligation to national authority. The entire peninsula south of the Highlands was under the sovereignty of the *Wappingers*, as a tribal division of the *Mahicans*, and the offenses of the Dutch were resented by the nation and the tribe. As early as 1622, the imprisonment of the chief of the *Sequins* aroused the *Mahicans* to that extent that the offending agent of the Dutch was compelled to leave the country; in the war of 1643, the Dutch were surprised to find their boats attacked above the Highlands, by Indians with whom they were ignorant of ever having had any

appear to have been from the statements of Gov. Moore and others pending the efforts to secure their removal to the Hudson river after their disastrous defeat in the war under King Philip. At the time of the discovery they were a powerful tribe.—*Schoolcraft's Ind. Nat.*, v, 222, *etc.*

[1] *Hubbard's Indian Wars*, 94, 98, 188; *Colonial History*, iv, 902, *etc.*; *Brodhead's New York*, ii, 294.

[2] The Indians began to have a value in the hands of the French as well as the English. To both parties they were the most effective soldiers that could be pro-

difficulty, and subsequently the Indian fortresses of the Highlands became the receptable of Dutch prisoners. The Dutch knew very little of tribal organizations or tribal laws. To each village they gave the dignity of a tribe, and undertook to hold with them separate covenants. The *Mahicans* made a very wide distinction between the Dutch at Fort Orange and those at Fort Amsterdam, and it was not until Kieft made his treaty with them in 1645, that he had peace. With the subsequent crumbling up of the clans more exposed to European influences, and the debris which remained after the retirement of their more active members, the result was the same in all parts of the country, whether *Mahicans*, *Lenapes*, or *Mohawks*.

In considering the political relations of the LENAPES they should be regarded as the most formidable of the Indian confederacies at the time of the discovery of America, and as having maintained for many years the position which subsequently fell to the *Iroquois*, rather than as having been subjugated by the latter anterior to the advent of the Europeans. Their tradition that they were "the head of the *Algonquin*[1] nations,[2] and held the *Mengwe* in subjection," is not without confirmation. The precise time at which the latter condition was reversed, cannot be stated; but the causes leading thereto are now pretty correctly ascertained. Their long house was invaded alike by the Europeans and the *Iroquois*, with special advantages to the latter in position, and in the facility with which they could obtain arms.[3] The tradition which they gave of their subjuga-

cured. The great error of Massachusetts was the war which she made upon them, as she subsequently learned.

[1] "The primitive language which was the most widely diffused, and the most fertile in dialects, received from the French the name of *Algonquin*. It was the mother tongue of those who greeted the colonists of Raleigh at Roanoke, of those who welcomed the Pilgrims at Plymouth. It was heard from the Bay of Gaspe to the valley of the Des Moines, from Cape Fear, and, it may be, from the Savannah, to the land of the Esquimaux; from the Cumberland river of Kentucky to the southern bank of the Mississippi."—*Bancroft*, III, 237.

[2] "The Delawares were the head of all nations. All nations except the Mingoes and their accomplices, were united with them and had free access to them; or in their own words, according to their figurative manner of expressing themselves, the united nations had *one house, one fire, and one canoe*."—*Heckewelder*.

[3] "Clean across this extent of country (namely from Albany to the Potomac), our grandfather had a long house, with a door at each end, which doors were always open to all the nations united with them. To this house the nations from ever so far off used to resort, and smoke the pipe of peace with their grandfather. The white people coming from over the great

tion is that the *Iroquois*, finding the contest in which they were engaged, too great for them, as they had to cope on the one hand with the French, and on the other with native prowess, resorted to a master stroke of intrigue. They sent an embassy to the *Lenapes* with a message in substance as follows : That it was not well for the Indians to be fighting among themselves at a time when the whites, in even larger numbers, were pressing into their country ; that the original possessors of the soil must be preserved from total extirpation ; that the only way to effect this was a voluntary assuming, on the part of some magnanimous nation, of the position of the women or umpire ; that a weak people in such a position would have no influence, but a power like the *Lenapes*, celebrated for its bravery and above all suspicion of pusillanimity, might properly take the step ; that, therefore, the *Aquinoshioni* besought them to lay aside their arms, devote themselves to pacific employments, and act as mediators among the tribes, thus putting a stop forever to the fratricidal wars of the Indians.

To this proposition the *Lenapes* listened cheerfully, and trustfully consented ; for they believed it to be dictated by exalted patriotism, and to constitute the language of genuine sincerity. They were, moreover, themselves very anxious to preserve the Indian race. At a great feast, prepared for the representatives of the two nations, and amid many ceremonies, they were accordingly made women, and a broad belt of peace entrusted to their keeping. The Dutch, so the tradition continues, were present on this occasion, and had instigated the plot. That it was designed to break the strength of the *Lenapes* soon became evident. They woke up from their magnanimous dream, to find themselves in the power of the *Iroquois*. From that time they were the cousins of the *Iroquois*, and these were their uncle.[1]

While this tradition bears the impress of theory upon a subject in regard to which little was known, and while it is much

---

water, unfortunately landed at each end of this long house of our grandfathers, and it was not long before they began to pull the same down at both ends. Our grandfather still kept repairing the same, though obliged to make it from time to time shorter; until at length the white people, who had by this time grown very powerful, assisted the common enemy, the *Maquas*, in erecting a strong house on the ruins of our grandfathers."—*Relation by an aged Mahican, given by Heckewelder*

[1] *Life and Times of David Zeisberger*, 45, 46.

less clear than that already quoted, as from a *Mahican*, it is not wholly unsupported. The *Lenapes* did, to a very considerable extent, act in the capacity of mediators, and the Dutch traders did no doubt have part in terminating the hostilities between them and the *Iroquois*. It is a singular fact, too, that of all the nations subjugated by the *Iroquois*, the *Lenapes* alone bore the name of women. While the council-fires of other nations were " put out," and their survivors merged in the confederacy, that of the *Lenapes* was kept burning, and their civil government remained undisturbed. The proposition, however, is that both of the results stated were in accordance with the terms of the peace which the English government negotiated, and not of prior *Iroquois* diplomacy.

The historic causes leading to the subjugation of the *Lenapes* is to be found in the circumstances and position of the nation, as compared with the *Iroquois*; the one with territory invaded by Europeans at different points, the other assailed only on one border by the French, against whom they were sustained by " free trade " with the Dutch and by subsequent more positive alliance with the English. To the establishment of the lordship and manor of Rensselaerswyck, and its village of Beaverwyck, the *Iroquois* were primarily indebted for their subsequent position in the family of Indian nations. That manor was organized under an independent charter with powers not delegated to the West India Company at Fort Amsterdam, especially in the matter of the sale of fire-arms to the Indians. At its trading-houses arms could be had for furs; there the doors were open to the *Mohawks* and the *Mahicans*, who guarded well the special advantages which they enjoyed. These advantages were great; the former were enabled by them to push their conquests, the latter to maintain independence. This is clearly deducible from the records which were made by the Dutch, in connection with the wars at Fort Amsterdam in 1643,[1] in which it is said that the traders from Rensselaerswyck, " perceiving that the *Mohawks* were craving for guns, which some of them had already received, paying for each as many as twenty beavers, and for a pound of powder as many as ten or twelve guilders, came down to Fort

[1] *Journal of New Netherland*, Doc. Hist., IV, 1, etc.

Amsterdam, in greater numbers than usual, where guns were plenty, purchasing them at a fair price, realizing in this way considerable profit. This extraordinary gain was not long kept secret. The traders coming from Holland soon got scent of it, and from time to time, brought over great quantities, so that the *Mohawks*, in a short time, were seen with fire locks and powder and lead in proportion." The record continues : " Four hundred armed men knew how to make use of their advantage, especially against their enemies, dwelling along the river of Canada, against whom they have now achieved many profitable forays where before they had but little advantage. This caused them also to be respected by the surrounding Indians even as far as the sea-coast, who must generally pay them tribute ; whereas, on the contrary, they were formerly obliged to contribute to these. On this account the Indians, in the vicinity of Fort Amsterdam, and as the record elsewhere shows, especially the *Minsis* of New Jersey and the Delaware, " endeavored no less to procure guns, and through the familiarity which existed between them and the people " at New Amsterdam, " began to solicit the latter for guns and powder, but as such was forbidden on pain of death, and could not remain long concealed in consequence of the general conversation, they could not be obtained. This greatly augmented the hatred which stimulated them to conspire against us, beginning first with insults which they everywhere indiscreetly uttered, railing at us as *materiotty*, that is to say cowards."

In regard to the time at which the subjugation of the *Lenapes* took place or was acknowledged, there is wide divergence in statement. Smith's assertion that it was prior to European occupation, is generally denied ; while Brodhead's assumption that it was in 1617, is without foundation in contemporaneous or subsequent facts. Nor could subjugation have been as early as 1643 or 1645, when Kieft made his treaty with the *Mohawks* and *Mahicans*, for the Swedes were then supplying the *Minsis* with arms. In 1660, the latter, through their chief, could declaim to their dependents at Esopus, in the presence of the *Mohawk* embassador, " this is not your land ; it is our land, therefore repeat not this," [1] and no *Mohawk* chief ever made utterance with more authority. A terrific contest was then raging between the *Senecas* and the *Minsis*, and the former came to Fort Orange and demanded, by virtue of the treaty of Esopus (1660), a higher price for their furs. "We require, said they, sixty handsful of powder for one beaver. We have a vast deal of trouble collecting beavers through the enemy's country. We ask to be furnished with powder and ball. If our enemies conquer us, where will ye then obtain beavers?" Director Stuyvesant, so the record says, replied by giving them a keg of powder, but entreated them to make peace with the *Minsis* so that the Dutch might "use the road to them in safety." Three years later the Dutch were in terrible alarm. A body of six hundred *Senecas* attacked the fort of the *Minsis* on the Delaware, and were put to flight and pursued northward for two days. Unable to cope with them single-handed, the *Senecas* solicited the aid of the *Mohawks*, and with them continued the struggle. The transition of the province from the Dutch to the English found the contest undecided, and not only so but the *Mohawks* expressly asking the English to make peace "for the Indian princes with the nations down the river," [2] as they had pleaded with the governor of Canada for protection against the *Mahicans*. In a letter from Governor Lovelace, February 24, 1665, it is said that negotiations for peace were then pending between the Esopus Indians, the South Indians, and the Novisans, on the one part, and the *Senecas* and *Mohawks* on the other, and that the magistrates of Ulster were directed to encourage the same; and under date of August 13, 1669, the same officer writes that "Perewyn lately made sachem of Hackinsack, Tappen, and Staten Island," had visited him "to renew and acknowledge the peace between them and the Christians; also, between them and the *Maquas* and *Sinnecas*, the which they say they are resolved to keep inviolable." He ordered that the matter be "put on record to be a testimony against those that shall make the first breach." [3] It was about this time that tradition gives the story of a great battle between

---

[1] *O'Callaghan's New Netherland*, II, 417.
[2] *Colonial History*, III, 67.
[3] *Assize Records*, II, 408.

the contestants in the Minnisink country, and the probabilities are that the peace spoken of was its result. But whatever the date, the *Minnisinks*, a north-western family of the *Minsis*, as well as the *Tappans*, were under the obligations of subjugation in 1680, for Paxinosa or Paxowan as he was sometimes called, sachem of the former, was required to furnish forty men to join the *Mohawks* in an expedition against the French.[1] In 1693-4, these tribes paid tribute to the *Senecas*.[2] The inference is that if the peace which was made with the *Minsis*[3] was not made until after the English came in possession of the province, that the subjugation of the *Lenapes* did not take place at an earlier period.

And this conclusion agrees with the almost infallible test of title to lands. The *Iroquois* never questioned the sales made by the *Lenapes* or *Minsis* east of the Delaware river, but only asserted the rights acquired by conquest in accepting, in 1743, the clearly false boundaries which the proprietaries of Pennsylvania had given to lands which had been purchased from the *Lenapes* in 1686. Whatever title the *Iroquois* had could not have been acquired when this sale was made. The findings of Gallatin in this particular are confirmed by all the title deeds in New York and New Jersey. In New Jersey the *Minsis* were paid for lands which they held *prior* to subjugation long after actual subjugation had taken place and possession ceased, for the simple reason that they were not conquered lands. In whatever aspect the question is considered, the same result is reached.

That the subjugation of the *Lenapes* was complete, there is no denial. The famous speech of Canassatiego, at Philadelphia, in 1742 : "We conquered you, we made women of you ; you know you are women ; we charge you to remove instantly ; we don't give you liberty to think about it," is' not more conclusive than the admission of Tedyuscung : "I was styled by my uncles, the Six Nations, a woman, in former years, and had no

---

[1] *Council Minutes*, Aug. 7.
[2] *Colonial History*, IV, 98.
[3] The terms Minquas, Minsis, Monseys, and Munsies are convertible. The Minquas who sold lands on the Delaware were the same persons who appeared at Esopus in 1660. The treaty which was concluded by the one was concluded by the other.

natchet in my hand but a pestle or a hominy pounder." But through the thick gloom which shrouds the history of their subjugation, through all the degradation and reproach which was heaped upon them as " a nation of women," there runs a thread of light revealing their former greatness, pleading the causes of their decay, promising that their dead shall live again. Not in the eternal darkness which shuts in the *Eries* is that light lost, but from its prison house breaks in brilliancy, redeeming the past, and wringing from their ancient subjugators, shivering under adverse fortune, the greeting — BROTHERS.

## CHAPTER IV.

### Analysis of Tribes and Chieftaincies.

WASSENAAR and De Laet supply the earliest account of the subtribal divisions, or chieftaincies of Indians occupying the valley of the Hudson. The former writes: " Below the *Maikans* are situate these tribes: *Mechkentowoon* and *Tappents*, on the west side; *Wickagjock* and *Wyeck*, on the east side. Two nations lie there lower down at Klinkersberg.[1] At the Fisher's Hook[2] are the *Pachany*, *Warenecker*, *Warrawannankoncks*. In one place, Esopus, are two or three tribes. The *Manhates* are situated at the mouth." The latter corrects the geography of his predecessor and gives the location of what he calls tribes[3] more accurately. Commencing at New York, he says: " On the east side, on the main land, dwell the *Manhattans*, a bad race of savages, who have always been very obstinate and unfriendly towards our people. On the west side are the *Sanhickans*, who are the deadly enemies of the *Manhattans*, and a much better people. They dwell along the bay, and in the interior. The course of the river is north-east and north-north-west according as the reaches extend. Within the first reach, on the west bank of the river, where the land is low, dwell the *Tappans*. The second reach of the river extends upwards to a narrow part named by our people Haverstroo; then comes the Seylmaker's-reach, as they call it, and next a crooked reach, in the form of a crescent, called Kock's-reach. Next is Hoge-reach; and then comes Vossen-reach, which extends to Klinkersberg. This is succeeded by Fisher's-reach, where on the east side of the river, dwell a nation of savages named *Pachami*. This reach extends to another narrow pass, where on the west, is a

---

[1] The first title given to Butter Hill.
[2] The bend in the river opposite Newburgh, forming a hook by the confluence of the Matteawan creek.
[3] A tribe was an union of families, but as here used designated families.

point of land that juts out [1] covered with sand, opposite a bend in the river, on which another nation of savages, the *Waoranecks*, have their abode at a place called Esopus. A little beyond on the west side, where there is a creek and the river becomes more shallow, the *Warranawankongs* dwell. Next comes another reach called Klaverack ; then comes Backerack, John Playsier's-rack, and Vaste-rack as far as Hinnenhock. Finally the Huntenrack succeeds as far as Kinderhook; further on are Sturgeon's-hook and Fisher's-hook, over against which, on the east side dwell the *Mahicans*."

Van der Donck, who wrote thirty years later, places the *Manhattans* on the island, and above them Indian villages which he names *Saeckkill, Wickquaskeck, Alipkonck, Sin-Sing, Kestaubuinck, Keskistkonck, Pasquuasheck,* and *Noch-Peem,* south of and in the highlands. On the south side of Wappinger's kill he locates three villages under the general name of *Waoranecks,* and above them and occupying both sides of the river south of the " Groote Esopus R.," he places the *Wappingers*. On the west side he locates the *Neve-Sincks* opposite Staten Island, then the *Raritans;* opposite Manhattan Island, *Haverstroo;* below Verdrietigehoeck, the *Tappans;* between Murderer's creek and the Dans-Kammer, the *Waranwankongs;* then the *Wappingers,* and west of the Esopus, the general title of " Minnessinck of te l'Landt von Bacham."

Were the question of location left to these writers and to the early maps, the inquiry might well be abandoned as hopeless. Fortunately, however, Indian treaties and title deeds supply information which, though still imperfect,[2] enables a division of territory and location of subtribes to be made with tolerable accuracy. From these sources the following classifications are mainly derived :

I. The chieftaincies of the MONTAUKS were:

1st. The *Carnarsees,* who claimed the lands now included in the county of Kings, and a part of the town of Jamaica.

---

[1] Dans-Kammer point.

[2] "There being no previous survey to the grants, their boundaries are expressed with much uncertainty, by the Indian names of brooks, rivulets, hills, ponds, falls of water, etc., which were and still are known to very few Christians. Sometimes the grant is of the land that belonged to such an Indian by name, or is bounded by such an Indian's land, but to

Their principal village was about the site of the village of Flatlands, where there is a place which still retains the name of Canarsee, and was, perhaps, the residence of the sachem. This chieftaincy was of considerable power in 1643, when it stood at the head of the Long Island tribes who were engaged in the war with the Dutch. Penhawitz was the first sachem known to the Dutch, by whom he was styled the Great Sachem of Canarsee. The names of the chiefs in 1670, as given in a deed for the site of the present city of Brooklyn, were Peter, Elmohar, Job, Makagiquas, and Shamese.

2d. The *Rockaways*, who were scattered over the southern part of the town of Hempstead, which, with a part of Jamaica and the whole of Newtown, constituted the bounds of their claim. Their main settlement was at Near Rockaway. The first sachem known to the Dutch was Chegonoe. Eskmoppas appears to have been sachem in 1670, and Parnau in 1685.

3d. The *Merricks, Merokes,* or *Merikokes,* as they have been denominated, who claimed all the territory south of the middle of the island, from Near Rockaway to the west line of Oyster bay. Their principal village was the site of the present village of *Merick*. Their sachem in 1647, was Wantagh.

4th. The *Marsapequas* or *Marsapeagues*, who had their settlement at a place called Fort Neck, and thence eastward to the bounds of Islip and north to the middle of the island. At Fort Neck the remains of two Indian forts were recently still visible. One was upon the most southerly point of land adjoining the salt meadow, nearly of quadrangular form and about thirty yards in extent on each side. The other was on the southernmost point of the salt meadow adjoining the bay, and consisted of palisades set in the meadow. The place is now covered with water. The chieftaincy was prominent in the war of 1643 and suffered severely. After this they appear to have been on friendly terms with the Dutch; and in the Esopus war of 1663, contributed forty-six men to Kregier's forces.[1]

prove that any particular spot belonged to any particular Indian, I believe is beyond human skill, so as to make it evident to any indifferent man."— *Colden, Documentary History*, I, 383, 384. Nevertheless many such localities have been and can be proved with positive accuracy. In hundreds of old surveys the hills, streams, etc., by which the tracts were bounded are as clear as the marks of modern surveyors.

[1] *O'Callaghan*, II, 482.

Tackapousha, sachem in 1656, was also chief sachem of the western chieftaincies on the island.

5th. The *Matinecocks*, who claimed jurisdiction of the lands east of Newtown as far as the west line of Smithtown, and probably to the west side of Nesaquake river. They were numerous and had large villages at Flushing, Glen Cove, Cold Spring, Huntington and Cow Harbor.[1] A portion of the chieftaincy took part in the war of 1643 under Gonwarrowe; but the sachem at that time remained friendly to the Dutch, and through his diplomacy succeeded in establishing peace. Whiteneymen (one-eyed) was sachem in 1643, and Assiapam in 1653.

6th. The *Nesaquakes* or *Missaquogues* possessed the country east of the river of that name to Stony brook and from the sound to the middle of the island. The principal settlement of the tribe was on the site of the present village of Nesaquake where the sachem probably resided. Coginiquant was sachem in 1656.

7th. The *Seatalcats* or *Setaukets*, whose territory extended from Stony brook to Wading river. Their village was upon Little Neck. They are said to have been a numerous family. Warrawakin sachem, 1655; Gil, in 1675.

8th. The *Corchaugs* owned the remainder of the territory from Wading river to Oyster ponds, and were spread upon the north shore of Peconic bay, and upon the necks adjoining the sound. From the many local advantages which their situation afforded, there is reason to suppose that they were, as regards numbers and military power, a respectable clan. Momometon sachem in 1648.

9th. The *Manhassets*, who occupied Shelter island, Hog island, and Ram island. Their principal settlement was on Shelter island; and the residence of their sachem on what is now known as Sachem's Neck. Tradition affirms that they could once bring into the field more than five hundred fighting men. From their exposed situation they were, like other clans on this part of the island, made tributary to the *Pequots*, *Narragansetts* and *Mahicans* alternately. Poygratasuck, a brother to

---

[1] *Thompson's Long Island.* Van Tienhoven represents them to consist of only thirty families in 1650.

Wyandance, was sachem in 1648, and is spoken of as possessed of capacity and courage. Yokee, or Youghco, sachem in 1651.

10th. The *Secatogues*, who joined the *Marsapequas* on the west and claimed the country as far east as Patchogue. The farm owned by the Willett family, at Islip, is supposed to have been the site of their village. The bounds of their tract were from Connectquut river on the east to the line of Oyster bay on the west, and from the South bay to the middle of the island. They were so much reduced by wars and disease that when settlements were made among them their lands were comparatively deserted. Winnequaheagh was sachem in 1683.

11th. The *Patchogues*, or *Onchechaugs*. Their jurisdiction extended from Patchogue east to West Hampton, and their villages at Patchogue, Fire Place, Mastic, Moriches and West Hampton. Tobaccus sachem in 1666.

12th. The *Shinecocks*, who claimed the territory from West Hampton to East Hampton, including Sag harbor, and the whole south shore of Peconic bay. Nowedonah was sachem in 1648, and Quaquasho, or The Hunter, in 1691.

13th. The *Montauks*.[1] This chieftaincy was acknowledged both by the Indians and the Europeans, as the ruling family of the island. They were indeed, the head of the tribe of *Montauks*, the other divisions named being simply clans or groups, as in the case of other tribes. DeRasieres and Van der Donck class them as " old Manhattans." They were considerable in numbers; distinguished for the hospitality which they extended to the Dutch traders and early settlers, and no less so for their subsequent hostility. Holding in their possession the treasure chest of all the Indian nations, they were especially exposed to invasion by the more powerful tribes bordering on the sound. At the time of the discovery they were a part of or under tribute to the *Mahicans*. Wyandance, their sachem, was also the grand sachem of Paumanacke, or Sewanhackey, as the island was called. Nearly all the deeds for lands were confirmed by him. His younger brothers, Nowedonah and Poygratasuck, were respectively sachems of the *Shinecocks* and the *Manhassets*. His residence was upon Montauk, and

---

[1] Metowacks, *Brodhead;* Matuwacks, *Yates* & *Moulton;* Montauks, *Thompson.*

the body of his followers lay in the immediate vicinity. During the wars of the *Mahicans*, the *Montauks* were subjugated by or compelled to pay tribute to the *Pequots*. After the destruction of the latter nation in 1637, the *Mahicans* again asserted their authority, but about that time the *Montauks* accepted the protection of the English and paid tribute to the governor of New Haven. In 1653, they were engaged in war with the *Narragansetts*, or rather the latter attacked them "as the friends and tributaries of the English."[1] A considerable number of the *Montauks* perished in this war.

On the division of the island in 1650, between the English and the Dutch, the English taking the eastern, and the Dutch the western part, the jurisdiction of Wyandance was nominally divided, Tackapousha being elected sachem of the chieftaincies in possession of the Dutch, viz: Marsapequas, Merikokes, Carnarsees, Secatogues, Rockaways, and Matinecocks. In the winter of 1658, the small pox destroyed more than half the clan, while Wyandance lost his life by poison secretly administered. The remainder, both to escape the fatal malady, and the danger of invasion in their weakened state, fled in a body to their white neighbors, who received and entertained them for a considerable period. Wycombone succeeded his father, Wyandance, and being a minor, divided the government with his mother, who was styled the Squa-sachem. Lion Gardiner and his son David acted as guardians to the young chief, by request of his father made just before his death. At Fort Pond, called by the Indians *Konk-hong-anok*, are the remains

---

[1] Thompson ascribes the cause of this war to the refusal of the Montauk monarch to join in the plan for exterminating the Europeans. Roger Williams writes to the governor of Massachusetts in 1654: "The cause of the war is the pride of the barbarians, Ascassascotick, the Long Island sachem, and Ninigret, of the Narragansetts. The former is proud and foolish; the latter proud and fierce."— *Thompson's Hist. Long Island; Drake's Book of the Indians.*

Lion Gardiner, in his *Notes on East Hampton*, relates, that the Block Island Indians, acting as the allies of the *Narragansetts* attacked the *Montauks*, during King Philip's war, (1675), and punished them severely. The engagement took place on Block Island, whither the *Montauks* went in their canoes, and upon landing, fell into an ambuscade. He says: "The Montauk Indians were nearly all killed; a few were protected by the English and brought away. The sachem was taken and carried to *Narragansett*, he was made to walk on a large flat rock that was heated by building fires on it, and walked several times over it singing his death song, but his feet being burned to the bones, he fell and they finished the tragical scene as is usual for savages."— *N. Y. Hist. Soc. Coll.*, 1849, 258.

of the burial ground of the chieftaincy, and here once stood the citadel of the monarch, Wyandance.[1]

II. The chieftaincies of the WAPPINGERS were :

1st. The *Reckgawawancs*.[2] This chieftaincy has been generally known by the generic name of *Manhattans*,[3] and is so designated by Brodhead and other historians. The site of their principal village is now occupied by that of Yonkers, and was called Nappeckamak. This village, says Bolton,[4] was situated at the mouth of the Neperah, or Saw Mill creek. On Berrien's Neck, on the north shore of the Spuyten Duyvel creek, was situated their castle or fort, called Nipinichsen. This fort was carefully protected by a strong stockade and commanded the romantic scenery of the Papirinimen, or Spuyten Duyvel, and the Mahicanituk, the junction of which two streams was called Shorackappock. It was at this castle that the fight occurred between Hudson and the Indians on his return voyage,[5] and

---

[1] *Thompson's History of Long Island.*

[2] Bolton gives them the name of *Nappeckamaks*, but that title does not appear in the records except as the name of their village at Yonkers.

[3] Custom would, perhaps, warrant the continuance of the name as designating a chieftaincy, but the evidence is conclusive that it was not used by the Indians in any such connection, but was a generic term designating not only the occupants of the island now called Manhattan, but of Long Island, and the mainland north of Manhattan Island. The term Manhattan indicates this, being apparently from Menohhunnet, which in *Eliot's Bible*, is given as the equivalent of islands, or as applied to the people, "the people of the islands."—(*Historical Magazine*, I, 89). The statements of the Dutch historians confirm this interpretation. Van der Donck and Wassenaar agree that there were four languages spoken by the natives, namely, the Manhattan, Minqua, Savanoo, and Wappinoo. "With the Manhattan," says Van der Donck, "we include those who live in the neighboring places along the North river on Long Island and at the Neversink." De Rasieres, writing in 1628, as a personal witness, says : "Up the river the east side is high, full of trees, and in some places there is a little good land, where formerly many people have dwelt, but who for the most part have died or have been driven away by the Wappenos." Again, referring to Long Island, he says : "It is inhabited by the old Manhattans (Manhatesen); they are about two hundred or three hundred strong, women and men, under different chiefs whom they call sackimes (sachems)." De Laet says : "On the east side on the main land, dwell the Manhattans." Block, whose vessel was burned in the lower bay in 1614, and who there built another, was fed and protected by the Manhattans, not on Manhattan Island, but, as appears by the statements of the Long Island Indians, this care and protection was in the territory and on the island of the latter. Under this explanation there is no contradiction in the statements of Hudson, De Laet and other writers, as compared with the *Albany Records*, that the name Manhattan, is "from or after the tribe of savages among whom the Dutch made their first settlement;" nor with that contained in a paper describing New Netherland (*Documentary History*, IV, 115): "So called from the people which inhabited the main land on the east side of the river."

[4] *History of Westchester County.*

[5] "Whereupon two canoes full of men, with their bowes and arrowes shot at us

it was also at this point that he first dropped anchor on his ascending voyage. They held occupation of Manhattan island and had there villages which were occupied while on hunting and fishing excursions. In Breeden Raedt their name is given as the *Reckewackes*, and in the treaty of 1643, it is said that Oritany, sachem of the Hackinsacks, " declared he was delegated by and for those of Tappaen, Reckgawawanc, Kicktawanc, and Sintsinck."

The tract occupied by the *Reckgawawancs* on the main land was called Kekesick, and is described as " lying over against the flats of the island of Manhates." It extended north including the site of the present village of Yonkers, and east to the Broncks river. Their chiefs were Rechgawac, after whom they appear to have been called, Fecquesmeck, and Peckauniens. Their first sachem known to the Dutch, was Tackarew, in 1639. In 1682, the names of Goharis, Teattanqueer and Wearaquaeghier appear as the grantors of lands to Frederick Phillipse. Tackarew's descendants are said to have been residents of Yonkers as late as 1701. The last point occupied by the chieftaincy was Wild Boar hill, to which place its members had gathered together as the Europeans encroached upon them. Traces of two burial grounds have been discovered on their lands.

2d. The *Weckquaesgeeks*.[1] As early as 1644, this chieftaincy is known to have had three entrenched castles,[2] one of which remained as late as 1663, and was then garrisoned by eighty warriors. Their principal village was on the site of Dobb's Ferry; it is said that its outlines can still be traced by numerous shell beds. It was called Weckquaskeck, and was located at the mouth of Wicker's creek, which was called by the Indians Wysquaqua. Their second village was called Alipconck. Its

---

after our sterne; in recompense whereof we discharged six muskets, and killed two or three of them. Then above an hundred of them came to a point of land to shoot at us. There I shot a falcon at them, and killed two of them; whereupon the rest fled into the woods. Yet they manned off another canoe with nine or ten men, which came to meet us. So I shot a falcon, and shot it through, and killed one of them. Then our men with their muskets, killed three or four more of them. So they went their way."—*Hudson's Journal*.

[1] This name appears to be local, although there is some reason for regarding it as generic.

[2] "Journal of New Netherland," *Documentary History*, IV, 15.

site is now occupied by the village of Tarrytown. Their territory appears to have extended from Norwalk on the Sound, to the Hudson, and to have embraced considerable portions of the towns of Mount Pleasant, Greenburgh, White Plains, and Rye; it was very largely included in the Manor of Phillipsborough. Their sachem, in 1649, was Ponupahowhelbshelen; in 1660, Ackhough; in 1663, Souwenaro; in 1680, Weskora, or Weskomen, and Goharius his brother; in 1681, Wessickenaiuw and Conarhanded his brother. Their chiefs are largely represented in the list of grantors of lands.

3d. The *Sint-Sinks*. This chieftaincy does not appear to have been very numerous. Their name is perpetuated in the present village of Sing-Sing, which was called Ossing-Sing, where they had a village. Another village was located between the Sing-Sing creek and the Kitchawonck, or Croton river, and was called Kestaubuinck. Their lands are described in a deed to Frederick Phillipse, August 24, 1685, and were included in his manor. The grantors were Weskenane, Crawman, Wappus, Mamaunare and Weremenhore, who may or may not have been chiefs.

4th. The *Kitchawongs*, or *Kicktawancs*. The territory of this chieftaincy appears to have extended from Croton river north to Anthony's Nose. Their principal village, Kitchawonck, was at the mouth of the river which bears their name. They also had a village at Peekskill, which they called Sackhoes. Their castle or fort, which stood at the mouth of the Croton, is represented as one of the most formidable and ancient of the Indian fortresses south of the Highlands. Its precise location was at the entrance or neck of Teller's point (called Senasqua), and west of the cemetery of the Van Cortlandt family. Their burial ground was a short distance east of the castle; a romantic and beautiful locality. The traditionary sachem of the chieftaincy was Croton. Metzewakes appears as sachem in 1641; Weskheun in 1685, and, in 1699, Sakama Wicker. There was apparently a division of the chieftaincy at one time, Kitchawong appearing as sachem of the village and castle on the Croton, and Sachus of the village of Sackhoes or Peekskill. Sirham was sachem of the latter in 1684. Their lands were principally included in the manor of Cortlandt, from which was subsequently erected the towns of Cortlandt, Yorktown, Somers, North Salem and Lewisborough.

5th. The *Tankitekes*.[1] The lands occupied by this chieftaincy are now embraced in the towns of Darien, Stamford, and New Canaan, in Connecticut, and Poundridge, Bedford, and Greenbush, in Westchester county. They were purchased by Nathaniel Turner, in behalf of the people of New Haven, in 1641, and are described in the deed as the tracts called Toquams and Shipham. Ponus was sachem of the former and Wasenssne of the latter. Ponus reserved a portion of Toquams for the use of himself and his associates, but with this exception their entire possessions appear to have passed under a deed without metes or bounds. The chieftaincy occupies a prominent place in Dutch history through the action of Pacham, "a crafty man," who not only performed discreditable service for Director Kieft, but was also very largely instrumental in bringing on the war of 1645.

6th. The *Nochpeems*. This chieftaincy occupied the highlands north of Anthony's Nose.[2] Van der Donck assigns to them three villages: Keskistkonck, Pasquasheck and Nochpeem on the Hudson. Their principal village, however, appears to have been called Canopus from the name of their sachem. It was situated in what is now known as Canopus hollow, one of the most fertile sections of Putnam county. The residence of Canopus is said to have been on a hill in the south-east part of

---

[1] Brodhead locates this chieftaincy at Haverstraw, but his authorities are not at all clear. For example, it is said that an offending member of the Hackinsacks, had gone "two days' journey off among the Tankitekes; "Pacham, the subtle chief of the Tankitekes near Haverstraw." Haverstraw was not two days' journey from Hackinsack, certainly. His location is also defeated in the person and history of Pacham, whose name he previously gives to a chieftaincy in the highlands. O'Callaghan locates them on the east side of Tappan bay, and Bolton in the eastern part of Westchester from the deeds which they gave to their lands. The latter is clearly correct.

[2] Wassenaar locates here the Pachany; and Brodhead, on authorities which appear to him sufficient, follows him under the name of Pachimis. In Breeden Raedt they are called Hogelanders, while in the treaty of 1644 (*O'Callaghan*, 1, 302), they are called Nochpeems, a title which corresponds with the name of one of their villages on Van der Donck's map. It is not impossible that the Tankitekes extended into the highlands on the east, and that their chief Pacham held sway there, and hence the name; but the treaty record of 1644 appears to be a sufficient answer to this theory. It is certainly safe to designate them by a title by which they were officially known.

the town of Putnam Valley, and was included in the deeds for the manor of Cortlandt. The remainder of their lands passed into the hands of Adolph Phillipse, under a title which was the subject of controversy for years, and in reference to which a delegation of chiefs visited England accompanied by king Nimham. Those who have regarded these chieftaincies as " independent tribes, united, since they were known to the Europeans, by no common government," may examine this controversy with profit. The grantors of the deed were Angnehanage, Rauntaye, Wassawawigh, Meanakahorint, Meahem, Wrawermneuw, and Awangrawryk, and was for a tract from Anthony's Nose to the Matteawan creek, and from the Hudson three miles into the country. The latter line Phillipse stretched to twenty miles.[1]

7th. The *Siwanoys*; also known as " one of the seven tribes of the sea-coast." This chieftaincy was one of the largest of the *Wappinger* subdivisions. They occupied the northern shore of the sound, " from Norwalk twenty-four miles to the neighborhood of Hell-gate." How far they claimed inland is uncertain, but their deeds covered the manor lands of Morrisania, Scarsdall and Pelham, from which were erected the towns of Pelham, New Rochelle, East and West Chester, North and New Castle, Mamaroneck, Scarsdall, and parts of White Plains and West Farms; other portions are included in the towns of Rye and Harrison, as well as in Stamford. There is also some reason for supposing that the tract known as Toquams and assigned to the *Tankitekes*, was a part of their dominions. A very large village of the chieftaincy was situated on Rye Pond in the town of Rye. In the southern angle of that town, on a beautiful hill now known as Mount Misery,[2] stood one of their castles. Another village was situated on Davenport's Neck. Near the entrance to Pelham's Neck was one of their burial grounds. Two large mounds are pointed out as the sepulchres of the sachems Ann-Hoock and Nimham. In the town of West

---

[1] *Land Papers,* XVIII, 127, etc.

[2] This hill is said to have acquired its present name from the fact that a large body of Indians were there surprised and cut to pieces by the Huguenots of New Rochelle, in retaliation for a descent upon their place. If such a battle took place it has no official record. The story is mythical.

Chester they had a castle upon what is still known as Castle Hill neck, and a village about Bear swamp, of which they remained in possession as late as 1689. Their ruling sachem, in 1640, was Ponus, whose jurisdiction was over tracts called Rippowams and Toquams, and the place of whose residence was called Poningoe. He left issue three sons, Omenoke, Taphance and Onox; the latter had a son called Powhag. In 1661, Shanasockerell, or Shanorocke, was sachem in the same district, and, in 1680, Katonah and his son Paping appear as such. Of another district Maramaking, commonly known as Lame Will, was sachem in 1681. His successor was Patthunck, who was succeeded by his son, Waptoe Patthunck. The names of several of their chiefs occur in Dutch history as well as in the early deeds. Among them are Ann-Hoock, alias Wampage, already noticed, who was probably the murderer of Ann Hutchinson,[1] and Mayane, spoken of in 1644 as "a fierce Indian, who, alone, dared to attack, with bow and arrows, three Christians armed with guns, one of whom he shot dead; and, whilst engaged with the other, was killed by the third," and his head conveyed to Fort Amsterdam. The occurrence served to convince the Dutch that in offending against the chiefs in their immediate vicinity, they were also offending those of whose existence they had no previous knowledge.[2] Shanasockwell is represented as "an independent chieftain of the *Siwanoys*," of the island called Manussing.

8th. The *Sequins*. This was a large chieftaincy; its principal seat was on the west bank of the Connecticut river and its jurisdiction over all the south-western Connecticut clans, including those designated by Van der Donck as the *Quirepeys*, the *Wecks*, the *Makimanes*, and the *Conittekooks*, and classified by De Forest[3] as the *Mahackenos*, *Unkowas*, *Paugussetts*, *Wepawaugs*, *Quinnipiacs*, *Monteweses*, *Sicaoggs*, *Tunxis*, etc. Their lands on the Connecticut were included in a purchase made by the West India Company, June 8, 1633, and on them was erected the Dutch trading post and fort known as "Good Hope."

---

[1] Nothing was more common among the Indians than to give to a warrior the name of his victim.

[2] *Documentary History*, IV, 14.

[3] *De Forest's History Indians of Connecticut.*

The tract is said to have been sixty miles in extent.[1] Subsequently (1643), Sequin, from whom the chieftaincy took its name, covered his deed to the Dutch by one to the English, in which he included "the whole country to the Mohawks country."[2] By the fortunes of war, the Pequots compelled the *Sequins*, the *Siwanoys*, and a portion of the *Montauks*, to pay them tribute,[3] but this condition was only temporary. In the subsequent war between the English and their allies and the Pequots, the national existence of the latter was destroyed. There are many reasons for presuming that the *Sequins* were an enlarged family of *Wappingers*, perhaps the original head of the tribe from whence its conquests were pushed over the southern part of the peninsula.[4]

9th. The *Wappingers.* North of the Highlands was the chieftaincy historically known as the *Wappingers*,[5] and acknowledged as the head of the chieftaincies of the tribal organization of that name occupying the territory from Roeloff Jansen's kill

---

[1] The deed recites the agreement between Van Curler, on the part of the company, "and the sachem named Wapyquart or Tatteopan, chief of Sickenames river, and owner of the Fresh river of New Netherland, called in their tongue Connetticuck," for the purchase and sale of the lands named, "on condition that all tribes might freely, and without fear or danger," resort thither for purposes of trade.—*O'Callaghan*, I, 150. The *Sickenames*, from whom the title was obtained, are described as "living between the Brownists (the Puritans) and the Hollanders," and that "all the tribes on the northern coast were tributary to them." Sequin denied the validity of their deed and sold to the English. The Dutch quarreled with the *Sickenames* (Pequots), and the latter invited the English to settle at New Haven; subsequently quarreled with them also, and were destroyed.—*O'Callaghan*, I, 157; *De Forest's Indians of Connecticut.*

[2] *Farmington Town Records, De Forest.*

[3] The tradition is recited by O'Callaghan that the *Sequins* had original jurisdiction, but lost it after three pitched battles with the *Pequots*. There is a strange mixing up of tribes in the story, and especially in that of the original sale, in which the transaction is made to appear "with the knowledge of Magaritiune," the Wappinoo chief of Sloop's bay.—*O'Callaghan*, I, 149, 150, 157. "After the overthrow of Sequin, the *Pequots* advanced along the coast and obliged several tribes to pay tribute, and sailed across the sound and extorted tribute from the eastern inhabitants of Sewan-Hackey.—*De Forest's History Indians of Connecticut,* 61.

[4] *Ante*, p. 41.

[5] *Ante*, p. 41. The chieftaincy must have borne some other name, but what is not known. Among the Moravians they were known as the *Wequehachkes*, or the people of the hill country. Governor Lovelace, in a letter to Governor Winthrop of Massachusetts, Dec. 29, 1869 (*New York Assize Record*), writes: "I believe I can resolve your doubt concerning what is meant by the Highland Indians amongst us. The *Wappingers* and *Wickeskeck*, etc., have always been reckoned so." It is entirely possible that the tribal name was *Wequehachke*, or *Wickeskeck*, or *Weckquaesgeek*, and that *Wappingers* is local. In all their official relations, however, and in the recognition of Nimham, they were known as the *Wappingers.*

on the north to Manhattan island on the south. What their family clans were on the north is not known, nor where their capital. On Van der Donck's map three of their villages or castles are located on the south side of the Mawenawasigh, or Great Wappinger's kill, which now bears their name. North of that stream they appear to have been known as the Indians of the Long Reach, and on the south as the Highland Indians. Among their chiefs Goethals and Tseessaghgaw are named, while of their sachems the names of Megriesken and Nimham[1] alone survive. Of their possessions on the Hudson there is but one perfect transfer title on record, that being for the lands which were included in the Rombout patent, in which "Sackeraghkigh, for himself and in the name of Megriesken, sachem of the Wappinger Indians," and other Indians therein named as grantors, conveyed the tract beginning on the south side of the Matteawan creek and running along the Hudson north to a point five hundred rods beyond "the Great Wapping's kill, called by the Indians Mawenawasigh," thence east, keeping five hundred rods north of said creek, "four hours' going into the woods," thence south to the south side of Matteawan creek, and thence west "four hours' going" to the place of beginning — a district now embraced in the towns of Fishkill, East Fishkill, etc., in Dutchess county.

Although it is so stated on Van der Donck's map of New Netherland, and assumed by Gallatin as a fact, there is no evidence that the *Wappingers* extended west of the Hudson, but, on the contrary, the conclusion is certain that they did not. The record of the Esopus wars and the sales of lands show what and who the latter were. The error of Van der Donck's informants was in confusing totemic emblems, and similarity of dialect, with tribal jurisdiction. The totem of the *Wappingers* as well as that of the Esopus clans, was the Wolf, as already stated, while below the Highlands came the Turkey of the

[1] "Daniel Nimham, a native Indian and acknowledged sachem or king of a certain tribe of Indians known and called by the name of *Wappingers*, represents that the tribe formerly were numerous, at present consists of about two hundred and twenty-seven persons; that they have always had a sachem or king whom they have acknowledged to be the head of the tribe, and that, by a regular line of succession the government of the tribe descended to the said present sachem."— *New York Land Papers*, xviii, 127.

*Lenapes*, constituting a clear distinction from their neighbors on the opposite shore. Gallatin strengthens the error by introducing the fact that the *Wappingers* were a party to the treaty of Easton, but was evidently without knowledge that they were recent emigrants from New York.[1]

III. The MAHICANS.

The territory of the *Mahicans* joined the *Wappingers* and *Sequins* on the south, and stretched thence north, embracing the head waters of the Hudson, the Housatonic and the Connecticut, and the water-shed of lakes George and Champlain. The chieftaincies of the tribe have a very imperfect preservation, but its general divisions are indicated by the terms: 1. The *Mahicans*, as applied to that portion occupying the valley of the Hudson and the Housatonic; 2. The *Soquatucks*, as applied to those east of the Green Mountains; 3. The *Pennacooks*, as applied to those occupying the territory "from Haverhill to the sources of the Connecticut;" 4. The *Horikans*, who occupied the Lake George district, and 5. The *Nawaas* immediately north of the *Sequins* on the Connecticut. The first of these general divisions was again divided into at least five parts, as known to the authorities of New York, viz: 1. The *Mahicans*, occupying the country in the vicinity of Albany; 2. The *Wiekagjocks*, described by Wassenaar as " next below the *Maikens*;" 3. The *Mechkentowoons* lying above Katskill and on Beeren or Mahican Island; 4. The *Wawyachtonocks*,[2] who apparently resided in the western parts of Dutchess and Columbia counties, and 5. The *Westenhucks*, who held the capital of the confederacy. At the time of the discovery those embraced in the first subdivision had a castle on what is now known as Haver island, called by them Cohoes, on the west side of the river, just below Cohoes falls, under the name of Monemius' castle, and another on the east bank and south of the first, called Unuwat's castle.[3] At

---

[1] *Johnson Manuscript*, IV, 54.

[2] The name is local, and is applied, in a petition by William Caldwell and others in 1702, to a "tract of unappropriated lands in ye hands of ye Indians, lying in Dutchess county to ye westward of Westenholks creek, and to ye eastward of Poghkeepsie, called by ye Indians by ye name of Wayaughtanock." In the proceedings of a convention held at Albany in 1689, the name is applied to the Indians who are called the Wawyachteioks or Wawijachtenocks.

[3] Map of Rensselaerswyck, *O'Callaghan's New Netherland*; *Wassenaar, Documentary History*, III, 43.

or near Schodac was Aepjin's castle.[1] Nine miles east of Claverack was one of the castles of the *Wiekagjocks*, and on Van der Donck's map two of their villages, without name, are located inland north of Roeloff Jansen's kill. Potik and Beeren island[2] were for many years in the possession of the *Wechkentowoons*. The villages of the *Wawyachtonocks* are without designation, but it is probable that Shekomeko,[3] about two miles south of the village of Pine Plains, in Dutchess county, was classed as one of them, as well as that of Wechquadnach or Wukhquautenauk, described as "twenty-eight miles below Stockbridge." Kaunaumeek, where the missionary, Brainerd, labored, and which he describes as "near twenty miles from Stockbridge, and near about twenty miles distant from Albany eastward;"[4] Potatik, located by the Moravians on the Housatonic "seventy miles inland," and Westenhuck or Wnahktakook, the capital of the confederacy, were villages of the *Westenhucks*, subsequently known as the Stockbridges.[5] That their villages and chieftaincies were even more numerous than those of the *Montauks* and *Wappingers* there is every reason to suppose, but causes the very opposite of those which led to the preservation of the location of the latter, permitted the former to go down with so many unrecorded facts relating to the tribe, as well as to their neighbors, the *Mohawks*, whose four castles only appear on record instead of seven as affirmed by the Jesuit missionaries.[6]

But these subdivisions are of no practical importance. In tribal action they were as unknown as the merest hamlet in

---

[1] *Brodhead*, I, 77; *Albany County Records; Stockbridge Tradition*.

[2] Literally Bear's island, so called no doubt from the totem of its occupants.

[3] "Shacomico, a place in the remotest part of that county (Dutchess) inhabited chiefly by Indians, where also live three Moravian priests with their families in a blockhouse, and sixteen Indian wigwams round about it."—*Documentary History*, III, 1014.

[4] "The place as to its situation, was sufficiently unpleasant, being encompassed with mountains and woods."—*Brainerd's Diary*. The Indians removed from this village to Stockbridge, in 1744. The site of the hut which Brainerd occupied is marked by a pine tree growing up from the centre of what was once his only room, and the bridge near by is called Brainerd's Bridge.—*Stockbridge, Past and Present*, 69.

[5] Westenhuck and Stockbridge were two distinct places. The former was among the hills south of Stockbridge.—*Sauthier's Map*. After the establishment of the reservation and mission at Stockbridge the Indian village was mainly, if not entirely, deserted. Many of the tribe removed to Pennsylvania, and others united with the mission.

[6] Local research would, it is believed, develop forty villages in the territory of the Mahicans.

the voice of a civilized state; in other respects, as free as the most perfect democracy. Had the lands upon which they were located been sold in small tracts and opened to settlement at an early period, they would not have escaped observation and record; but the wilderness was a sealed book for many years, and there are those who still write that it was without Indian habitations. Such, too, was the dream in regard to the lands of the *Iroquois*, until Sullivan's blazing torch lighted the hills and valleys with the crackling flames of forty burning villages.

On the 8th of April, 1680, the *Mahicans* sold their land, on the west side of the Hudson, to Van Rensselaer, or at least so much thereof as was "called Sanckhagag," a tract described as extending from Beeren island up to Smack's island, and in breadth two days' journey." The grantors were Paep-Sikenekomtas, Manconttanshal and Sickoussen. On the 27th of July, following, the same gentleman bought from Cattomack, Nawanemit, Abantzene, Sagisquwa and Kanamoack, the lands lying south and north of Fort Orange, and extending to within a short distance of Monemius' castle, and from Nawanemit, one of the last named chiefs, his grounds, "called Samesseeck," stretching on the east side of the river, from opposite Castle island to a point facing Fort Orange, and thence from Poetanoek, the mill creek, north to Negagonse. Seven years later he purchased an intervening district "called Papsickenekas," lying on the east bank of the river, extending from opposite Castle island south to a point opposite Smack's island, including the adjacent islands, and all the lands back into the interior, belonging to the Indian grantors, and, with his previous purchases, became the proprietor of a tract of country twenty-four miles long, and forty-eight miles broad, containing, by estimation, over seven hundred thousand acres, now comprising the counties of Albany, Rensselaer, and part of Columbia.[1]

Deeds of a later period for lands in the same vicinity are recorded in Albany county records. One is given "in the presence of Aepjen and Nietamozit, being among the chiefs of the

---

[1] *O'Callaghan's New Netherland*, I, 122, 123, 124; *Map of Manor of Rensselaerswyck, Documentary History*, III, 916; *Map of Rensselaerswyck, O'Callaghan's New Netherland*, I, 204.

Mohikanders;" another defines the tract conveyed, as "the fast bank where the house of Machacnotas stood," and another conveys an island called "Schotack or Aepjen's island." Two immense tracts were sold to Robert Livingston, July 12th, 1683, and August 10th, 1685, and subsequently included in a patent to him for the manor of Livingston. The grantors were the following "Mahican Indian owners:" Ottonowaw, a cripple Indian; Tataemshaet, Oothoot, Maneetpoo, and two Indian women named Tamaranchquae and Wawanitsaw, and others in the deed named.[1] The lands between Livingston and Van Rensselaer were taken up in small parcels, some of them without purchase. Sales east of the Taghkanick mountains, in the state of Connecticut, are recorded, and among others that of a tract to Johannes Diksman and Lawrence Knickerbacker, now in the town of Salisbury, the grantors being Konaguin, Sakowanahook and others "all of the nation of Mohokandas." Almost touching the shore of the southern extremity of Lake Champlain, "Mahican Abraham" asserted his proprietorship, indicating tribal possession seventy miles north of Albany. In view of these records there is no difficulty in determining the value of the assertion that the *Mahicans* were driven back to the Housatonic "by their implacable enemies, the *Mohawks*." The more important proposition is, how came the former west of the Hudson, if the prowess of their rivals was so supreme?

Reference has already been made to the capital or council-fire of the nation as having been at Westenhuck. That the original capital was at Schodac is affirmed by the Dutch records and by the traditions of the tribe, and accords with the interpretation of the name itself. Like other tribes, they recoiled before the incoming civilization, and sometime between 1664 and 1734, removed their national seat to Westenhuck where it was known to the authorities of Massachusetts,[2] as well as to the Moravian missionaries. "In February, 1744," says Loskiel,[3] "some Indian deputies arrived at Shekomeko from Westenhuck, to inquire whether the believing Indians would live in friendship

---

[1] *Documentary History*, III, 612, 617.  [3] *History of the Moravian Missions.*
[2] *Stockbridge Past and Present.*

with the new chief." In 1751, he writes at Gnadenhutten, in Pennsylvania: "Two deputies were likewise sent to the great council of the Mahikan nation at Westenhuck, with which they appeared much pleased, and as a proof of their satisfaction made Abraham, an assistant at Gnadenhutten, a captain."[1] Again: "The unbelieving Indians at Westenhuck, made several attempts to draw the Christian Indians in Shekomeko into their party." "Brother David Bruce," it is added, "paid visits to Westenhuck, by invitation of the head chief of the Mahican nation," of whom it is said: "the above mentioned chief of Westenhuck, who had long been acquainted with the brethren, departed this life." This chief was Konapot, whose name has been preserved in the records of the Stockbridge mission, and who is described by Hopkins as "the principal man among the Muhhekaneok of Massachusetts." By the records of Massachusetts, it appears that, in 1736, the Westenhuck sachem visited Boston, accompanied by the chiefs from Hudson's river, as one people, while the former, when known as the Stockbridges, came to Albany in 1756, and were received as the actual representatives of the *Mahicans*, instead of those known as such to the authorities of New York. The fact that Westenhuck was the point selected for missionary labor, by the Society for the Propagation of the Gospel in Foreign Parts, is additional proof of its importance. Though the extremities of the nation withered under the adverse influences by which they were surrounded, the heart remained in vigor long after that of its rivals had been consumed.

IV. The chieftaincies of the UNAMIS were:

1st. The *Navisinks* or *Neversincks*. This chieftaincy inhabited the Highlands south of Sandy Hook. It was with them that Hudson had intercourse after entering the bay of New York. He describes them as civil in their deportment, and disposed to exchange such products of the country as they had for knives, beads and articles of clothing. It was at their hands, also, that John Coleman, one of Hudson's crew, lost his life

---

[1] Abraham, whose Indian name was Schabash, was one of the chiefs of Shekomeko. He was converted by the Moravians and removed with them to Pennsylvania, from whence he returned as stated. He subsequently became the head of the Mahicans of Pennsylvania. — *Mem. Morav. Chnrch.*

on the 6th of September, 1609. Passachquon was sachem in 1663.

2d. The *Raritans*, who occupied the valley and river which still bears their name. They were first called *Sanhikans*, or Fire-workers. They were divided, it is said, in two sachemdoms and about twenty chieftaincies. From their title deeds it would appear that the two sachems were Appamanskoch and Mattano or Mattenon.[1] Their territory on the Hudson included the valley of the Raritan, and from thence to the sea.[2] The Dutch had some difficulties with them in 1641, but soon after that year they removed to the Kittateny mountains, and were subsequently known in Dutch history only through the deeds which they gave to their lands. They were not a warlike race, but peaceable in disposition, as became the traditional totem which they bore. Their treatment under the English of New Jersey, was liberal and just. No bloodshed or violence was permitted, nor occupation of their lands without purchase. Their possessions finally dwindled down to about three thousand acres in the township of Eversham, Burlington county, on which a church was erected. This land they obtained permission to sell, in 1802, when the remnant of the clan removed to Oneida lake, N. Y., and from thence, in 1824, to a tract on Lake Michigan, where they united with the Brothertons.

3d. The *Hackinsacks*. The territory occupied by this chieftaincy was called Ack-kin-kas-hacky, and embraced the valley of the Hackinsack and Passaic rivers. Their number, in 1643, is stated at a thousand souls, of whom about three hundred were warriors. Their council-fire was kindled at Gamoenapa, the aboriginal for Communipau. They took prominent part in

---

[1] Deed for Raritan meadows, 1651; Deed to Denton and others, 1664.

[2] " The district inhabited by a nation called Raritangs, is situated on a fresh water river, that flows through the centre of the low lands which the Indians cultivate. This vacant territory lies between two high mountains, far distant the one from the other. This district was abandoned by the natives for two reasons; the first and principal is, that finding themselves unable to resist the Southern Indians, they migrated further inland; the second, because this country was flooded every spring." — *Documentary History*, IV, 29. Some of our historians, with characteristic zeal for the Mohawks, ascribe the removal of the Raritans to the incursions of the former. It is not possible to determine who the " Southern Indians" named in the text were, but it is not an improbable supposition that they were Shawanoes.

events of 1643-44, but subsequently appear only as mediators in the person of their sachem Oritany,[1] who enjoyed to a rare old age the confidence of his people and of the surrounding chieftaincies, as well as that of the Europeans. He is spoken of in 1687, as very aged, and as delegating his authority in a measure to Perro. The lands of the chieftaincy embraced Jersey City, Hoboken, a part of Staten island,[2] Wehawken, Newark, Passaic, etc.

4th. The *Aquackanonks*. Their sachem, in 1676, was Captahem or Captamin. Their territory, or at least a portion of it, was called Haquequenunck or Acquackanonk, and included the site of the present city of Paterson.[3] They are also described as occupying a considerable portion of the centre of New Jersey.

5th. The *Tappans*. The relations existing between this chieftaincy and the *Hackinsacks* were very intimate, so much so as to lead some to suppose that they were a part of Oritany's sachemdom. Their separate authority and jurisdiction, however, is clearly established. Their territory extended from the vicinity of Hackinsack river to the Highlands.[4] De Vries purchased lands from them in 1640, which he describes as " a beautiful valley under the mountains, of about five hundred acres, within an hour's walk of Gamoenapa," the principal village of the *Hackinsacks*. On some of the early maps their village is located some miles back from the river, but in the attempt, on the part of the Dutch governor, to collect tribute from them, in 1640, it appears that access could be had to them by sending up a sloop, indicating that in the summer at least they had a representative position on the Hudson. In the treaty of 1745, Sessekemick represented them and appears to have acted under the counsel of Oritany. In the sale of Staten island, Taghkospemo appeared as their sachem, and there is

---

[1] " I, Oratum, am sagamore, and sole proprietor of Hackingsack, lying and being on the main land over against the Isle of Manhattans."—*Deed to Edward Gove, Oct. 5, 1664.*

[2] Staten island, by the Indians called Eghquaous, appears to have been owned in partnership by the *Raritans*, the *Hackinsacks* and the *Tappans*.—*Deed to Van der Cappellen*, 1659.

[3] Deed to Hans Diderick and others, March 25, 1676. Oritany, who was then living, had no part in this deed.

[4] " Within the first reach, on the western bank of the river, where the land is low, there dwells a nation of savages, named *Tappans*."—*De Laet, New York Hist. Soc. Coll.*, 2d series, I, 298.

evidence that his sachemship had much earlier date. Their name survives in Tappan bay, which probably bounded their possessions on the Hudson.

6th. The *Haverstraws*. North of the *Tappans* and inhabiting a territory, the westward boundaries of which are not clearly defined, were the *Haverstraws*, so called by the Dutch,[1] but whose aboriginal name appears to have been lost.[2] They took some part in the early wars, but would seem to have been absorbed by the *Tappans* after the supremacy of the English. Stony point was the northern limit of their territory, as indicated by the deed to Governor Dongan subsequently embraced in the Evans patent. In a deed to Balthazar De Hart, July 31, 1666, confirmed to him by letters patent from Cateret, and Council of New Jersey, April 10, 1671, and subsequently by patent from the Governor of New York, the tract conveyed is described as "all the land lying on the west side of Hudson's river, called Haverstraw, on the north side of the hills called Verdrietinge hook, on the south side of the highlands, on the east of the mountains, so that the same is bounded by Hudson's river and round about by the high mountains."[3] This description embraces precisely the western boundary of Haverstraw bay. The deed was executed by Sackewaghgyn, Roansameck, Kewegham, and Kackeros. By deed to Stephen Van Cortlandt in 1683, it would appear that they had either moved further north or had more northern territory, the tract conveyed being described as lying opposite Anthony's nose, from the "south side of a creek called Senkapogh, west to the head thereof, then northerly along the high hills as the river runneth to another creek called Assinapink, thence along the same to Hudson's river." The deed was executed by " Sackagkemeck, sachem of Haverstraw, Werekepes, and Kaghtsikoos." Don-

---

[1] Named by our people Haverstroo."— De Laet.

[2] O'Callaghan gives the name of "Sessegehout, chief of *Reweghnome*, of Haverstroo," but it is not clear that that was the name of the chieftaincy, although the presumption is strongly in its favor.— *O'Callaghan's New Netherland*, II, 509, note.

[3] This purchase covered what were subsequently called "the Christian Patented lands of Haverstraw," and by that title formed the boundary in part of several patents. The original grant from Cateret was predicated on the supposition that the tract was within the limits of New Jersey.

gan's purchase in 1685 covered this tract, and had as one of its grantors Werekepes, who was also a grantor to Van Cortlandt. From Verdrietig hook to Stony point may be assumed as the territory of the *Haverstraws*.

V. The chieftaincies of the MINSIS were:

1st. The *Waoranecks*. This chieftaincy has been variously located. Van der Donck places them in the Highlands on the east side of the river and south of Matteawan creek, and De Laet on the west side as occupants of the Esopus country.[1] Wassenaar agrees with De Laet in locating them in the Fisher's hook.[2] The territory which was inhabited by them on the Hudson may be regarded as described with sufficient accuracy in what is known as Governor Dongan's two purchases (1684–'85), the first of which extended from the Paltz tract to the Danskammer, and the second from Dans-kammer to Stony point. In the first, the limits of the Esopus Indians, or *Warranawonkongs*, are defined as terminating at the Dans-kammer, and in the second the jurisdiction of what are therein called "the Murderer's kill Indians," is admitted as from the Dans-kammer to Stony point. Their western boundary cannot be so satisfactorily defined. From the fact that the same names, in part, appear as grantors of the Dongan tract, of the Cheesecock tract, and of a tract to Sir John Ashhurst,[3] the latter covering sixteen miles square, commencing at a point eight miles from the Hudson on the south side of "the Murderer's kill," it may be inferred that that boundary terminated with the natural watershed of the Hudson. Were not De Laet's location sufficiently clear, there are other reasons for assuming that the "Murderer's

---

[1] "This reach (the Fisher's) extends to another narrow pass, where, on the west side of the river, there is a point of land that juts out covered with sand, opposite a bend in the river, on which another nation of savages, the *Waoranecks*, have their abode."— *DeLaet*.

[2] At Fisher's hook are *Pachany, Warenocker, Warrawannankonckx.— Documentary History*, III, 28.

[3] The duplication of signatures indicates what may be called overlapping boundaries. The grantors, who were principal owners, are generally so stated, and the subsequent signatures classed as "inferior owners." Thus in the Haverstraw purchase, Sackagkemeck appears as sachem or principal, and Werepekes as an "inferior owner." In the Dongan purchase, Werepekes signed as sachem, and Sackagkemeck as an inferior. In the Cheesecock and Ashhurst deeds Moringamaghan, or Moringamack, is the principal, while in the Dongan deed he appears in a subordinate position. These overlapping boundaries entered very largely into consideration in fixing the limits of the Dongan purchase.

kill Indians" of 1685, were the *Waoranecks* of 1625. The name by which they were last designated was that of the creek now called " Murderer's ; " their first name disappears from the early records almost simultaneously with the appearance of the latter,[1] and with the general classification of " Esopus Indians," while the territory assigned to them had no other known occupants, rich though it was in all the elements of favorite hunting grounds. The *Waoranecks* participated in the Esopus wars, if not in the wars at Fort Amsterdam, and at the Dans-kammer celebrated those frightful orgies called kinte-kaying, regarded by the Dutch as devil worship. Their relations with the Esopus Indians[2] were such that there can be no hazard in classing them as one of the " five tribes," so called, of the Esopus country. Their sachem in 1685, was Werekepes, or Werepekes, and Moringamaghan[3] and Awessewa principal chiefs.

Maringoman's Castle.

2d. The *Warranawonkongs*.[4] This was the most numerous of the Esopus chieftaincies. Their territory extended from the

[1] This creek is first called Murderer's on Van der Donck's map, 1656, and was so called doubtless from events occurring during the first Esopus war.

[2] Esopus is supposed to be derived from *Seepus*, a river. Reichel says : " A Sopus Indian, or *a lowlander*."

[3] Maringoman's " castle" and Maringoman's " wigwam" are spoken of in different deeds. The first was on the north end of the Schunamunck mountain on the south side of Murderer's creek, in the present town of Bloominggrove, and is particularly described as being " opposite the house where John McLean now (1756), dwells, near the said kill." He subsequently removed to what is called a " wigwam," which stood " on the north bank of Murderer's creek, where Col. Matthews lives." The location is in Hamptonburgh, on the point of land formed by the junction of the Otter kill and the Grey Court creek, by which Murderer's creek is formed, and which takes its name at that point, as though some dark memory was associated with the name of its owner.

[4] " A little beyond, on the west side,

Dans-kammer to the Katskill mountains, or more properly perhaps to the Saugerties, and embraced the waters of the Shawaugunk, the Wallkill and the Esopus rivers. Their principal castle was in the Shawangunk country, although a very considerable one was on the Esopus river, known as Wiltmeet. The "oldest and best of their chiefs," Preummaker, was killed in the war of 1663, as was also Papequanaehen. In their treaty with Stuyvesant, in 1664, they were represented by Sewackenamo, sachem, and Onackatin and Powsawagh, chiefs. In the subsequent treaty of 1669, the five sachemdoms of the Esopus country were represented in the persons of Onackatin, Napashequiqua, Sewackenamo, Shewotin, and Calcop. In the Dongan purchase of 1684, Pemerawaghin appears as chief sachem.

3d. The *Mamekotings*. The district inhabited by the *Mamekotings* was west of the Shawangunk mountains and is still known as the Mamakating valley. Their history is so intimately blended with that of the Esopus Indians that identification is impossible further than by title. They were evidently one of the " five tribes," and may be designated as the third.

4th. The *Wawarsinks*. The fourth of the Esopus chieftaincies, the *Wawarsinks*, inhabited the district of country which still bears their name. Separate from the Esopus Indians they have no history.

5th. The *Katskills*. The fifth and last of the Esopus chieftaincies [1] inhabited the territory north of Saugerties, forming the eastern water-shed of the Katskill mountains,[2] including the Sager's creek, the Kader's creek, and the Kats kill, from which latter they took their name.[3] They were the "loving people" described by Hudson; a neutral and not very courageous peo-

---

where there is a creek, and the river becomes more shallow, the *Warranawonkongs* reside."— *De Laet.*

" These following Esopus Indians."— *Deed to Wm. Loveridge.*

[2] In giving the boundaries of the Coeyman's purchase, O'Callaghan states that the line followed Coxackie creek to its head; then ran west until it struck the head of the waters falling into the Hudson, all the land on which belonged to the Katskill Indians; the waters flowing west to the Schoharie creek being the property of the *Mohawks.*— *History of New Netherland,* 1, 435.

[3] Brodhead locates here some families of *Nanticokes,* and it is possible that when that nation " disappeared without glory," some of its members were induced thither either as recruits of the *Minsis* or the *Mohawks,* but their more considerable emigration was to Pennsylvania.

ple, as may be inferred from Kregier's account of them.[1] Their chief, in 1663, was known as Long Jacob. Mahak Niminaw sachem in 1682.[2] Above the *Katskills* came the *Mechkentowoons* of the *Mahicans*, but with boundary undefined.

6th. The *Minnisinks*. West of the Esopus country, and inhabiting the Delaware and its tributaries were the *Minsis* proper of whom a clan more generally known as the *Minnisinks* held the south-western parts of the present counties of Orange and Ulster, and north-western New Jersey. Van der Donck describes their district as "Minnesinck of 'tLandt van Bacham," and gives them three villages: Schepinaikonck, Meochkonck, and Macharienkonck, the latter in the bend of the Delaware opposite Port Jervis, and preserved perhaps in the name Mahackemeck.[3] On Sauthier's map, Minnisink, the capital of the clan, is located some ten miles south of Mahackemeck, in New Jersey. Very little is known of the history of the clan as distinguished from the tribe of which they were part, although the authorities of New York had communication with them, and the missionary, Brainerd, visited them. Tradition gives to them the honor of holding the capital of the tribe in years anterior to the advent of the Europeans. Defrauded and maltreated, they subsequently exacted a terrible compensation for their wrongs.

VI. The IROQUOIS.

1st. The *Mohawks*. The territory occupied by the *Mohawks* has already been sufficiently described, as well as that of their associate tribes of the Iroquois confederacy. The *Mohawks* had no villages immediately upon the Hudson, although they

---

[1] "Examined the Squaw prisoner and inquired if she were not acquainted with some Esopus Indians who abode about here? She answered that some Katskill Indians lay on the other side near the Sager's kill, but they would not fight against the Dutch."— *Documentary History*, IV, 48.

[2] "Mahak Niminaw shall have, as being sachem of Katskill, two fathoms of duffels and an anker of rum when he comes home."— *Deed to Wm. Loveridge.*

[3] On the east bank of the Neversink river, three miles above Point Jervis, on the farm now or late of Mr. Levi Van Etten, exists an Indian burial ground, the graves covering an area of six acres. Skeletons have been unearthed, and found invariably in a sitting posture, surrounded by tomahawks, arrow-heads, etc. In one grave was found a sheet iron tobacco box containing a hankerchief covered with devices, employed doubtless to preserve the record of its owner's services. Not far from the grounds is the Willehoosa, a cavern in the rocks on the side of the Shawangunk mountain. It contains three apartments, each about the size of an ordinary room. Indian implements of various kinds have been found there.

claimed title to the lands north of the Mohawk river. Their principal villages or castles, in 1677, were on the north side of the Mohawk, in the present counties of Montgomery and Herkimer, and were: 1. Cahaniaga, or Gandaougue, by the Dutch called Kaghnewage, and more modernly known as Caghnawaga; 2. Gandagaro, or Kanagaro; 3. Canajorha, or Canajoharie, and 4. Tionondogue or Tionnontoguen. The first contained twenty-four houses; the second, sixteen; the third, sixteen, and the fourth thirty.[1] Tionondogue was the capital of the tribe. It was destroyed by the French in 1667, and rebuilt about one mile further west. It was again destroyed by the French in 1693, but does not appear to have been rebuilt, as soon after that time Canajoharie is spoken of as the "upper Mohawk castle."[2] It was at the latter that Hendrick and his brother Abraham resided, as well as Joseph Brant. The house occupied by the former, and also by the latter, was situated near what is now known as "Indian castle church," in Danube, Herkimer county. Caghnawaga was the scene of early conflict between the *Mohawks* and the *Mahicans;* it was destroyed by the French in 1693, and subsequently by the Americans. It was long known as the "lower Mohawk castle," and occupied the site of the present village of Fonda, Montgomery county. Gandagaro passed out of existence with the second French invasion, or at least is lost to the records after 1693. In 1690, a new castle was erected at the mouth of Schoharie creek and called Tiononderoge, after the name of the ancient capital of the tribe, but was more generally known as "the castle of the praying Maquas." It was situated on the site of what was subsequently known as Fort Hunter. Its occupants were called the Schoharie Indians. It was among them that several families of Esopus Indians were settlers in 1756. After the revolution the *Mohawks* had neither castles nor villages in their ancient territory.

2d. The *Oneidas*, etc. The *Oneidas* had, in 1677, one town, "the old Oneida castle," as it was called, containing one

---

[1] *Colonial History*, III, 250; *Brodhead's New York*, II, 129. Pierron, the Jesuit missionary, it is said, visited every week seven Mohawk villages, but they are not located.
[2] *Colonial History*, VI, 850.

hundred houses; the *Onondagas*, a palisaded town of one hundred and forty houses, and a village of twenty-four houses;[1] the *Cayugas* three towns, and the *Senecas* four.[2]

The capital of the confederacy was the village of Onondaga, on the lake of that name, the principal settlement of the *Onondagas*. Bishop Cammerhof, who visited it in 1751, says, "Onondaga, the chief town of the six nations, situated in a very pleasant and fruitful country, and consisting of five small towns and villages, through which the river Zinochsaa runs." In the Relations of the Jesuit missionaries it is said: "The word *Onnota*, which signifies in the *Iroquois* tongue, a mountain, has given the name to the village called Onnontaé, or as others call it, Onnontagué, because it is on a mountain; and the people who inhabit it consequently style themselves Onnontaé-ronnons, or Onnontagué-ronnons."

[1] The great villages of the Onnontagues consists of one hundred cabins.— *Colonial History*, IX, 375.

[2] *Colonial History*, III, 250. This was the number then known. It is subsequently stated that forty towns existed in the three western cantons.— *Journal of Sullivan's Expedition*.

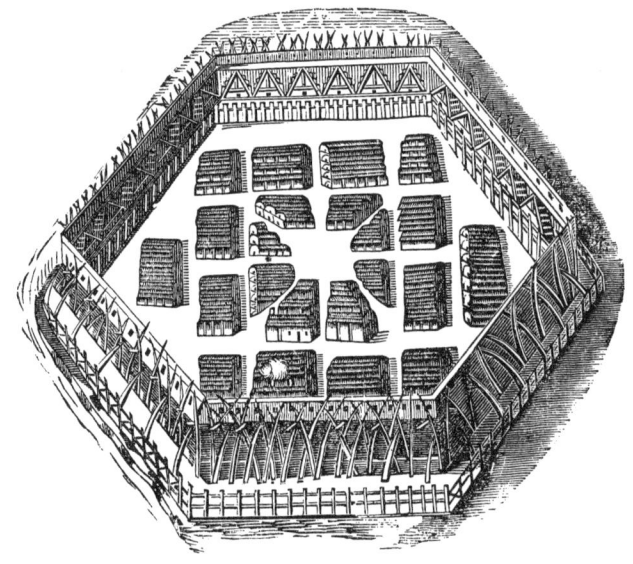

Indian Fort.
ONONDAGA, THE CAPITAL OF THE FIVE NATIONS — 1609.

## CHAPTER V.

### The Indians under the Dutch — The Manhattan Wars — From the Discovery to the Peace of 1645.

FROM the first hour of Hudson's appearance in the waters of the Mahicanituk, to the last of the domination of Holland, there was an antagonism between the Dutch and the Indians with whom they came in contact in the vicinity of Manhattan island, and a conflict which was apparently irrepressible. While in the territory of the *Mahicans* proper Hudson met "loving men," in that of the *Wappingers* and the *Minsis*, he dyed the waters of the river which he had discovered with the blood of those who were encouraged by his overtures to a violation of laws to which they were strangers, and his exit was amid the terrifying war-cries of a people enraged by the slaughter of kindred, and clouds darkened by their quivering arrows.[1]

Subsequent events in no degree mitigated the hostility which was then awakened. When the traders followed Hudson they paused not until they had reached the jurisdiction of those with whom his intercourse had been friendly. There they maintained kindly relations with the Indians, and around their trading posts, Fort Nassau, and subsequently Fort Orange,[2] hed neutral ground between the contending *Mahicans* and *Mohawks*.[3] But this alliance of friendship did. not relieve the Dutch from apprehended attacks on the part of those whom Hudson had

---

[1] *Hudson's Journal; ante*, p. 11.

[2] The first, or Fort Nassau, was erected on what was called Castle island, now known as Boyd's island, a short distance below the Albany ferry. It was a building twenty-six feet wide and thirty-six feet long, enclosed by a stockade fifty-eight feet square, and the whole surrounded by a moat eighteen feet wide. Its armament consisted of two large guns and eleven swivels, and the garrison of ten or twelve men. The location proved unfortunate, in consequence of the exposure to the spring freshets, and in 1618 it was removed to the banks of the Tawalsontha creek, now called the Norman's kill, from whence it was soon after removed further north and located in the vicinity of what is now South Broadway, Albany, and called Fort Orange, by which name, and that of Beaverwyck, the small settlement which gathered around it, was known until 1664.

[3] *Ante*, p. 54.

offended, and it was deemed prudent to erect a fort on what was then known as Prince's island, and to garrison it with sixteen men for the defense of the river below."[1]

Contemporaneous circumstances contributed to keep alive this feeling. One Jacob Eelkins,[2] who had been in superintendence of the trade at Fort Nassau, in the summer of 1622 ascended the Connecticut to traffic, and while there treacherously imprisoned the chief of the *Sequins* on board his yacht, and would not release him until a ransom of one hundred and forty fathoms of wampum had been exacted. The offense was resented by all the tribes, and by none more so than by the *Mahicans*. To appease them, Eelkins was discharged, and apparently in further overture to them, Krieckbeck, the Dutch commander at Fort Orange, in 1626, joined them, with six men, on a hostile expedition against the *Mohawks*.[3]

Other causes of grievance were not wanting. The sale of fire-arms to the *Mahicans* and *Mohawks* at Fort Orange and the refusal to sell to the chieftaincies in the vicinity of Fort Amsterdam [4] was a constant irritation, to allay which the Dutch traders treated the Indians at the latter place with great familiarity, invited them to their houses, admitted them to their tables, and gave them wine, until they came to regard such civilities as their due and to resent their absence. Then the cattle of the Dutch roamed at large, "without a herdsman," and "frequently came into the corn of the Indians, which was unfenced on all sides, committing great damage there. This led to complaints on their part and finally to revenge on the

---

[1] *Wassenaar, Documentary History*, III, 35. The location of this fort has never been positively ascertained.

[2] *Wassenaar, Documentary History*, III, 45; Brodhead, I, 146, 168.

[3] *Brodhead*, I, 168. The expedition was not successful. Krieckbeck and three of his men were killed, and the *Mahicans* put to flight. The *Mohawks* did not resent the alliance further than to roast and eat one of the Dutch soldiers, a man named Tyman Bouwensen; but Minuit deemed it prudent, during the continuance of hostilities, to remove the Dutch families to Fort Amsterdam, and to direct the garrison at Fort Orange to observe strict neutrality in the future.

[4] Precisely to what extent the Indians in the vicinity of Fort Amsterdam were supplied with arms in 1643, does not appear. It is said by the Eight Men, in October of that year: "These Indians are, on the contrary, strong and mighty; have, one with the other, made alliances with seven different tribes, well supplied with guns, powder and ball." (*Colonial History*, I, 190); yet there is not a single case of the use of fire arms by the Indians recorded. Even in their most desperate defenses bows and arrows are alone spoken of as their weapons.

cattle, without sparing even the horses." In 1626, a *Weckquaesgeek* Indian, accompanied by his nephew, who was a "small boy," and another savage, while on their way to the fort to trade, were met and robbed by men in the employ of Minuit, the Dutch director, and in the melee the *Weckquaesgeek* was killed. The act was unknown to the Dutch at the time, but the boy treasured a revenge which he forgot not to exact in manhood.

As the Dutch settlers took up lands on Long Island and the New Jersey shore, they made frequent complaints that their cattle were stolen by the Indians. Regarding the latter as the aggressors in all cases, Director Kieft, who had in the meantime succeeded Minuit, determined, in 1639, to demand from them tribute, not only as compensation, but to aid in establishing his government over them, and for that purpose sent an armed sloop to the *Tappans* to exact contributions of corn and wampum. The Indians expressed their astonishment at this proceeding, and denounced " the sakema of the fort" for daring to attempt such exactions. Sneers and reproaches followed. "The sakema," they said, "must be a mean fellow; he had not invited them to come and live here, that he should now take away their corn." A formal conference was held with the Indians, but the latter refused to yield the contributions asked.

An open rupture soon followed. Some pigs were stolen from De Vries's plantation on Staten island, as it subsequently appeared "by the servants of the company, then (1640) going to the South river to trade, and who landed on the island to take in wood and water;" but, as Kieft professed to believe, by the Indians. He accused the *Raritans* of the offense, and, on the sixteenth of July, commissioned Secretary Van Tienhoven to proceed, with one hundred men, to their territory and demand satisfaction. The *Raritans* denied the commission of the offense, and satisfied the secretary; but the troops under him were bent on mischief, and scarcely had he left them when they made an attack, killed several of the Indians, took one of their chiefs

---

[1] *De Vries, New York Historial Society Collections,* 2d series, I, 263; *Breeden Raedt, Documentary History,* IV, 101, 102.

captive, and mangled the body of another. The *Raritans* retaliated by attacking De Vries's plantation, killed four of his planters and burned his dwelling and tobacco house. Kieft followed with a proclamation announcing the policy of extermination, and offering a bounty of ten fathoms of wampum for the head of every *Raritan* which should be brought to him. Holding their own grievances in abeyance, some of the Long Island warriors took up the hatchet against the *Raritans*, and brought in at least one head for the director's gratification, but the great body of the Indians refused the tempting offer.

Meanwhile the *Weckquaesgeek* boy had grown to manhood, and determined to exact his long meditated atonement for the death of his uncle. Taking with him some beaver skins to barter, he stopped at the house of one Claes Smit, "a harmless Dutchman," and while he was stooping over a chest in which he kept his goods, the savage seized an axe and killed him by a blow on the neck; then quickly plundering his abode, escaped to the woods. Kieft demanded satisfaction, but the *Weckquaesgeeks* refused to deliver up the murderer. He then summoned all the heads of families of Manhattan to a meeting and laid the matter before them, especially asking if it was not just that the murder should be avenged, and if in case the *Weckquaesgeeks* would not surrender the murderer, it would not be "just to destroy the whole village" to which he belonged; and if so, in what manner, when, and by whom such chastisement should be inflicted. The meeting referred the proposition to "twelve select men," who, with greater discernment of the consequences of an open rupture with the Indians than the director, reported that while the murder should be avenged they thought "God and the opportunity should be taken into consideration," and that in the meantime the director should make suitable arrangements for sustaining an attempt at inflicting punishment. In case hostilities should be inaugurated, they thought the director should "lead the van," while the community should "follow his steps and obey his commands." They advised, however, as an offset to this quiet bit of sarcasm, that before anything else was done the director should send up a shallop to the *Weckquaesgeeks* to demand of them "once, twice, yea for a third time," the surrender of the murderer in a "friendly manner."

Offended and bent on war, Kieft "would not listen." Remaining inactive until November, he consulted each of the "twelve" separately on the question of immediate hostilities ; but the latter remained firmly opposed. In the winter he repeated this consultation, and urged that the Indians were absent from their village on hunting expeditions, and that arrangements should be made at once to destroy them. The "twelve" consented, unwillingly, and on assurances that an attack should only be made after repeated solicitations had failed to secure the surrender of the murderer. Kieft did not long delay an attempt to execute his atrocious design. In March (1642), he dispatched a company of eighty men, under command of Ensign Hendrick Van Dyck, with instructions to fall upon the *Weckaquaesgeeks*, " who lay in their village suspecting nothing," and punish them with fire and sword. Fortunately the guide missed his way, and the expedition was compelled to return to Fort Amsterdam "in all the mortification of failure." The result, however, was that the Indians, on discovering the trail of Kieft's men, and detecting his intention, became alarmed and asked that peace might be maintained. Kieft consented on condition that the murderer of Smit was delivered up, and on this basis a treaty, as it was called, was concluded with them. But it was not fulfilled by either of the contracting parties ; the arrest of an Indian, whose action had been in strict accordance with the laws and customs of his tribe, was a process of very difficult accomplishment.

Soon after this occurrence the Dutch were terribly frightened. Miantonomo, the " principal sachem " of the *Narragansetts*, having a controversy pending with Uncas, visited the Manhattans with an hundred men, and passed through all the *Mahican* villages to secure their alliance for the destruction of his rival. The Dutch, however, gave to him a different mission. From a whispered suspicion it grew to public clamor, that the embassy had no less an object than to secure the union of all the Indians in a " general war against both the English and the Dutch." The story spread to New England, where its falsity was demonstrated;[1] but in the meanwhile the inhabitants at New Amsterdam saw the hand of hostile Indians in every thing; believed that they had attempted to destroy the settlement by setting fire to its powder-magazine, and the director by poisoning him " or enchanting him by their deviltry."[2]

The storm passed over only to be succeeded by another. The *Hackinsacks* and *Tappans* had hitherto escaped special irritating collisions with the Dutch. True, the *Tappans* had resisted the attempt to place them under tribute, but this attempt appears to have been abandoned. De Vries[3] had settled among the latter, after the disaster which befel him on Staten island, and by kindly treatment had won their confidence. Circumstances, however, forced them to take up the hatchet. Contrary to the advice of the director, and in opposition to the wishes of a majority of the *Hackinsacks*, one Myndert Van der Horst[4] purchased a tract near Communipaw and made settlement thereon. While visiting this settlement a *Hackinsack* warrior became intoxicated, and was robbed of his beaver-skin coat. When the stupor passed off and he became conscious of the imposition which had been practiced upon him, he vowed he would go home for his bow and arrows and shoot the "roguish Swannekin" (as the Dutch were called), who had taken his things, and faithfully did he keep his vow. Watching his opportunity, he shot one of the colonists, Garret Jansen Van Voorst, as he was thatching the roof of one of Van der Horst's houses. The chiefs of his tribe, anxious to keep unbroken friendly relations with the Dutch, hastened to De Vries to secure his counsel and intercession. They dared not go to Fort Amsterdam for fear Kieft would keep them prisoners, but they were willing to make the " blood atonement of money " customary among the tribes, and offered two hundred fathoms of wampum to the family of

[1] *Hubbard's Indian Wars*, 44.
[2] The superstitious fears of the Dutch and the English were alike strongly worked upon by the skill of the Indians in jugglery.
[3] De Vries purchased from the Tappans a tract of about five hundred acres in April, 1640; made settlement thereon the subsequent year, and gave to it the name of Vriesendael.
[4] Myndert Myndertsen Van der Horst purchased and located on a tract "within an hour's walk of Vriesendael." His plantation extended from Archer Cul bay north towards Tappan, and included the valley of the Hackinsack river. The head quarters of the settlement were about five or six hundred paces from the principal village of the Hackinsacks.

the murdered man as the price of peace. Persuaded by De Vries, who became answerable for their safe return, the chiefs visited the fort with him, and there repeated their offer. Kieft refused to accept the wampum, and demanded the murderer. The chiefs could not comply; the murderer had sought refuge among the *Tankitekes*, and besides he was the son of a chief and could not be surrendered. They then renewed their expiatory offer, but it was again refused, and they returned to their homes hopeless of effecting reconciliation.

These collisions and causes of grievance culminated in the winter of 1643, when Director Kieft threw off all disguise and disgraced even savage modes of warfare by a blackening hypocrisy and a massacre more terrible than any of which their annals bear record. In February of that year a party of eighty *Mahicans*, "each with a musket on his shoulder," made a descent on some of the old Manhattan chieftaincies, for the purpose of collecting tribute which had been withheld.[1] Surprised, and wholly unable from inferiority in arms to cope with their adversaries, the assailed Indians fled to Fort Amsterdam for protection, leaving seventeen of their number dead and a considerable portion of their women and children prisoners in the hands of their enemies. The Dutch kindly cared for the fugitives and supported them for fourteen days; but, again alarmed for their safety, they scattered themselves among the *Hackinsacks* and *Tappans*, while others fled to Vriesendael to beg assistance and protection. De Vries promised to do all in his power for them, and accordingly went, in a canoe, through the floating ice, to Fort Amsterdam, to ask Kieft to assist him with some soldiers. The director, however, claimed that he had none to spare; and the next day the Indians left Vriesendael, some going to

[1] Brodhead and others assert that this foray was by Mohawks. The documentary proof, however, is that it was made by the Mahicans. "The *Mahican* Indians, who, surprising, slew full seventy of them"— *Colonial History*, 1, 151. "The *Mahicanders* dwelling below Fort Orange, who slew," etc.— *Ibid.*, 184. "The Indians, the *Mayekanders*, who came from Fort Orange "— *De Vries*. The conclusion that it was by the Mohawks is apparently based on the hypothesis that the *Mahicans* would not attack those regarded as their own people, and that the *Mohawks* alone were armed. The fact distinctly appears, however, that not only were the *Mahicans* armed, but that the " old Manhattans " had neglected to pay them the tribute due from conquered tribes. That no other chieftaincies than those of the Weckquaesgeek district were visited, is additional proof that it was by the *Mahicans*.

Pavonia[1] among the *Hackinsacks*, who were "full a thousand strong," and others to Rechtauck (now Corlear's hook) where they occupied some cabins which had been erected by the *Reckawancks*.

Made acquainted with these facts, the people of New Amsterdam were divided in opinion as to the proper policy to be pursued. The majority, under the lead of De Vries, counseled patience, humanity and kindness, such as had been extended to the fugitives when they first fled thither for protection. Another party, headed by Van Tienhoven, provincial secretary, masking their action under professions of indignation at the shedding of innocent Christian blood, clamored for the extermination of the Indians. A petition was circulated by the latter, and obtained some signatures, reminding the director that God had now supplied the "opportunity" which the "twelve" had suggested should be awaited, and asking permission to "attack and destroy the enemy which had been delivered into" their hands, and "that one party, composed of freemen, and another of soldiers, be dispatched to different places against them."[2] The petition was resisted by De Vries and others, who warned the director against so gross a breach of Indian and civilized laws of hospitality; but Keift, who had long before taken his position on the subject, readily' complied with the request of the petitioners, and issued an order that the Indians should be attacked by two divisions, one at Pavonia and the other at Corlear's hook, the former to be by the soldiers under the command of Sergeant Rodolf, and the latter by the burghers headed by Maryn Andriaensen.[3]

---

[1] Michael Pauw purchased from the Indians the tract now included in Hoboken and Jersey City, and established there a colony to which he gave the name of Pavonia.—*Brodhead*, 1, 203.

[2] *Colonial History*, III, 146; *O'Callaghan*, I, 266; *Brodhead*, I, 349. The Narrative is principally by De Vries.

"[3] We, therefore, hereby authorize Maryn Adriansen, at his request, with his associates, to attack a party of savages skulking behind Corlear's hook, or plantation, and act with them in every such manner as they shall deem proper and the time and opportunity shall permit. Sergeant Rodolf is commanded and authorized to take under his command a troop of soldiers and lead them to Pavonia, and drive away and destroy the savages being behind Jan Evertsen's, but to spare, as much as possible, their wives and children, and to take the savages prisoners.* * The exploit to be executed at night, with the greatest caution and prudence. Our God may bless the expedition. Done Feb. 24th, 1643."—*O'Callaghan*, I, 267, 268.

The plan was executed on the night of the 25th of February. The Indians had gathered behind Pauw's settlement at Pavonia, unsuspicious of attack from those to whose shelter they had fled, and were sleeping in conscious security when the work of death commenced. Loud shrieks first announced to DeVries, who was watching at Fort Amsterdam, that the slaughter had begun, but these shrieks were succeeded by the stolid indifference with which the red man always met his fate, and nothing was heard but the report of fire-arms. Neither age nor sex were spared. Warrior and squaw, sachem and chief, mother and babe, were alike massacred. DeVries describes the terrible tragedy in pointed language. Children were taken from the arms of their mothers and butchered in the presence of their parents, and their mangled limbs thrown into the fire or the water. " Other sucklings had been fastened to little boards, and in this position they were cut to pieces. Some were thrown in the river, and when the parents rushed in to save them, the soldiers prevented their landing and let parents and children drown." The next morning some of the Indians, who had escaped the midnight slaughter, came to the fort begging for shelter, but instead of receiving it, were killed in cold blood or thrown into the river.[1] Continues DeVries, " some came running to us from the country, having their hands cut off; some lost both arms and legs; some were supporting their entrails with their hands, while others were mangled in other horrid ways, too horrid to be conceived. And these miserable wretches, as well as many of the Dutch, were all the time under the impression that the attack had proceeded from their Indian enemies "— were unwilling to believe that men professing the Christian name could be guilty of so gross a violation of Christian principles.

With an aching heart, DeVries returned to his home, and had scarcely arrived when some of the fugitives gathered around him. " The Fort Orange Indians have fallen upon us," said they, " and we have come to hide ourselves in your fort." " It is no time to hide yourselves in the fort; no Indians have done

[1] " I am told for a fact that a certain skipper, Isaac Abrahamsen, having saved a boy, and hidden him under the sails, in order to give him to one Cornelius Melyn, towards morning the poor child, overcome with cold and hunger, made some noise, and was heard by the soldiers, eighteen Dutch tigers dragged (him) from

this deed; it is the work of the Swannekens," answered De Vries, and he led the fugitives to the gate, "where stood no sentinel," and bade them seek shelter in the forest depths. Meanwhile the victorious expeditions returned to Fort Amsterdam and reported, as the result of their work, that eighty Indians had been slaughtered at Pavonia and thirty at Corlear's hook, while with them were thirty prisoners. Kieft received his freebooters and soldiers with thanks, rewards and congratulations; while Van Tienhoven's mother, forgetful of the finer feelings which do honor to her sex, amused herself, it is stated, by kicking about the heads of the dead men which had been brought in as trophies of the midnight slaughter.[1]

The first notes of triumph had barely faded from the air, however, ere the hand of revenge was made red with the blood of the Dutch. Kieft, in the exultation of the moment, sent out foraging expeditions to collect corn. One of these expeditions seized two wagon loads from the Long Island Indians, who lost three of their number in endeavoring to save their property. In retaliation, the *Montauk* and the *Hackinsack* and *Tappan* chieftaincies made common cause with the *Weckquaesgeeks*,[2] who had suffered in the February attack, and who had learned fully that the Dutch, and not the *Mahicans*, had been the principals in the massacre of their kindred, and the tomahawk, the scalping knife and the firebrand executed the work of vengeance. "From swamps and thickets the mysterious enemy made his sudden onset. The farmer was murdered in the open field; women and children, granted their lives, were swept off into long captivity; houses and bouweries, hay-stacks and grain, cattle and crops, were all destroyed."[3] Even Vriesendael did

under the sails, in spite of the endeavors of the skipper, cut (him) in two and threw (him) overboard."—*Breeden Raedt*.

[1] *O'Callaghan*, 1, 269. "It is a scandal for our nation," says the author of *Breeden Raedt*, "and if silence would have remedied it, I should never have mentioned it."

[2] The narrative speaks of the *Weckquaesgeeks*, the *Sint-Sings*, and the *Kicktawancs* in different places.

[3] *Brodhead*, 1, 354. "Almost all the bouweries were also destroyed, so that only three remained on the Manhattes, and two on Staten island, and the greater part of the cattle were destroyed. Whatever remained of these had to be kept in a very small enclosure, except in Rensselaer's colonie, lying on the North river, in the neighborhood of Fort Orange, which experienced no trouble and enjoyed peace, because they continued to sell firearms and powder to the Indians even during the war against our people."—*Report, etc., Colonial History*, 1, 151.

not escape the general calamity. The outhouses, and crops and cattle were destroyed. DeVries and his colonists, however, escaped into the manor house or fort, which had been constructed with loop-holes for musketry, and were standing on their defense, when an Indian whom DeVries had sheltered on the morning of the massacre came up to the besiegers, related the occurrence and told them DeVries was "a good chief." The Indians at once raised the siege, and expressed their regret that they had destroyed the cattle; they would let the little brewery of their Dutch friends stand, although they longed for the copper kettle to make barbs for their arrows.[1]

The Dutch were thrown into great consternation and fled to Fort Amsterdam for protection, with bitter upbraidings on their lips against the director. He met them defiantly at first, and professed to have been controlled by the wishes of Andriaensen; but the latter denied the assertion, and carried his determination to escape the popular condemnation into an attempt upon the life of the director.[2] But the accumulating evidences of desolation brought ruler and people to repentance. For that mercy which he had refused to extend to the helpless Indians, Kieft besought the people to ask of the Most High, and to that end appointed a day of fasting and prayer, in his proclamation confessing that the calamities which had overtaken them was doubtless owing to the sins which he and his people had committed. While the latter humbled themselves before God, they had little charity in their hearts for the direct author of their calamities, and asked one another, "Did ever the duke of Alba do more evil in the Netherlands?"

Matters assumed a more favorable aspect in the spring. The Long Island Indians, although previously rejecting the overtures made by the director for peace, and denouncing him as a "corn thief," became more tractable when the planting season came on, and sent from the wigwams of Penhawitz, "their great chief," three delegates to Fort Amsterdam, desiring that negotiations might be opened. De Vries and Alferton were at once

---

[1] *De Vries*, 269; *New York Historical Society Collections*, 2d series, I, 269; *Brodhead*, I, 255.

[2] "What devilish lies art thou reporting of me? but by the promptness of the bystanders the shot was prevented, and he was arrested."— *Colonial History*, I, 184.

appointed to accompany them, and setting out on the 4th of March, came to Rechquaakie or Rockaway, where they found Penhawitz, surrounded by nearly three hundred warriors and a village of thirty wigwams. The next day they were conducted into the woods about four hundred yards off, where they found sixteen chiefs of the *Montauks*, with whom the conference was conducted in the Indian form.[1] De Vries invited the chiefs to accompany him to Fort Amsterdam, under the assurance of presents and peace. The latter embraced the offer, and, to the number of eighteen, embarked in a large canoe and reached the fort in the evening. After some days spent in negotiation a treaty was concluded on the 25th, and the chiefs dismissed with presents and solicited to bring to the fort the chiefs of the river families " who had lost so many " of their number. The Long Island sachem accordingly went to Hackinsack and Tappan, but weeks elapsed before negotiations were concluded. Oritany, sachem of the *Hackinsacks*, after consultation with his allies, finally appeared at Fort Amsterdam, clothed with authority to conclude a peace both for his own and the neighboring chieftaincies. The opportunity was embraced by the director and the following treaty agreed to:

" This day, the twenty-second of April, 1643, between William Kieft, director general and the council of New Netherland, on the one side, and Oratatum, sachem of the savages residing at Ack-kinkashacky, who declared that he was delegated by and for those of *Tappaen, Reckawawanc, Kitchawanc,* and *Sint-Sinck,* on the other side, is a peace concluded in the following manner, to wit:

[1] " We were awakened and led by one of the Indians in the woods upwards of 400 paces from the house, where we found sixteen chiefs from Long Island, who placed themselves in a circle around us. One of them had a bundle of small sticks. He was the best speaker, and commenced his speech. He related that when we first arrived on their shores, we were sometimes in want of food; they gave us their beans and corn, and let us eat oysters and fish; and now for recompense we murdered their people. He here laid down one little stick; this was one point of accusation. The men whom in your first trips you left here to barter your goods till your return, these men have been treated by us as we would have done by our eye-balls. We gave them our daughters for wives, by whom they had children. There are now several Indians, who came from the blood of the Swannekins and that of Indians; and these their own blood were now murdered in such villainous manner. He laid down another stick."—*De Vries, New York Historical Society Collections*, 2d series, 1, 271.

"All injustices committed by the said natives against the Netherlanders, or by the Netherlanders against said natives, shall be forgiven and forgotten forever, reciprocally promising, one the other, to cause no trouble, the one to the other; but whenever the savages understand that any nation not mentioned in this treaty, may be plotting mischief against the Christians, then they will give to them a timely warning, and not admit such a nation within their own limits."[1]

This peace was one of necessity on the part of the Indians. The *Hackinsack* sachem received his presents, but complained of their insufficiency, saying that his young men would only regard them as a trifling atonement; and such they not only were, but they were received as the sachem had indicated. At midsummer the sachem visited Vriesendael and stated that the young men of his people were urging war; that some had lost fathers and mothers in the February massacre, and all were mourning over the memory of friends; that the presents which had been given to them were not worth the touch, and that they could be no longer pacified. At the request of De Vries, the sachem accompanied him to Fort Amsterdam, where, on repeating his complaint, Kieft replied that he should cause his young Indians who wanted war, to be shot. Kieft then offered him two hundred fathoms of wampum, but the sachem spurned the bribe, and, after promising to do his best to pacify his people, went his way.

With the renewal of difficulties in New England, in September (1643), war again broke out at New Amsterdam. "Pachem, a crafty man, ran through all the villages, urging the Indians to a general massacre." The first aggressive act was by the *Wappingers*,[2] who seized a boat coming from Fort Orange, killed two men and took four hundred beaver skins. Others followed this example, " so that they seized two boats more," but were driven off, with the loss of six of their number, in

---

[1] *O'Callaghan* I, 277. *De Vries, Collections New York Historical Society*, 2d series, I, 270. It will be observed that neither the *Weckquaesgeeks* or *Manhattans* are mentioned in the treaty, a fact which indicates the local character of both titles.

[2] *Doc. Hist.*, IV, 12. The Dutch were surprised at the attack by the *Wappingers*, and protested that they had never had any trouble with them. In this they were mistaken, as the testimony shows that nearly all their troubles were with that tribe.

attacking the fourth boat. "Nine Christians, including two women," were killed in these captured boats, one woman and two children remaining prisoners. "The other Indians," continues the narrative, "so soon as their maize was ripe, followed this example, and through semblance of selling beavers, killed an old man and woman, leaving another man with five wounds, who, however, fled in a boat with a little child on his arm, who, in the first outbreak had lost father and mother, and now grandfather and grandmother, being thus twice rescued from the hands of the Indians, first when he was two years old." Nor was this all. Under the pretense of warning from approaching danger, the Indians visited dwellings and killed the inmates, and applied the brand to factories and outbuildings. The few families who had settled in the Esopus country abandoned their farms in alarm, and universal fear pervaded the province.

Kieft now called his people together again, and a committee of "eight men" was appointed to consult with him for the defense of the colony. Before any arrangement had been made, however, the *Weckquaesgeeks* attacked the plantation of Ann Hutchinson,[1] killed that extraordinary woman and her married daughter and son-in-law, and carried off captive her youngest daughter.[2]

Throgmorton's settlement [3] was next attacked and the buildings burned, the inhabitants escaping in their boats. Eighteen victims, however, were added to the revenges of the Indians. Pavonia was attacked and four bouweries burned under the very guns of "two ships of war and a privateer." From the

---

[1] The history of Ann Hutchinson is pretty generally known. With Roger Williams, she was banished from Massachusetts, as "unfit for the society" of her fellow-citizens. She followed Williams to Rhode Island, but fearing the power of Massachusetts would reach her there, removed, in 1642, to Manhattan and settled on a point now known as Pelham's neck.

[2] "The Indians set upon them and slew her and all her children, save one that escaped (her own husband having died before), a dreadful blow! Some write that the Indians did burn her to death with fire, her home and all the rest that belonged unto her, but I am not able to affirm by what kind of death they slew her."— *Wild's Rise, Reign and Ruin of the Antinomians.* "The daughter of Ann Hutchinson remained a prisoner four years, when she was delivered to the Dutch governor at Fort Amsterdam, who restored her to her friends. She had forgotten her native tongue, and was unwilling to be taken from the Indians."— *O'Callaghan.*

[3] Throgmorton was another refugee from Massachusetts. His settlement was a few miles west from that of Ann Hutchinson, and included the point now known as Throg's neck.

highlands of the Hudson to the highlands of the sea, the war-whoop was reechoed, and at a single blow "from the *Neversincks* to the valley of the *Tappans*, the whole of New Jersey was once more in the possession of its aboriginal lords."[1] Fort Amsterdam afforded the only place of shelter, and thither the colonists fled. "There women and children lay concealed in straw huts, while their husbands and fathers mounted guard on the ramparts above." The whole force of the Dutch was scarce two hundred and fifty men, while the Indians were represented by fifteen hundred of their most expert warriors, including the *Wappingers* of the Connecticut river, under the lead of Mayane, with whom the Dutch claimed they had never had any difficulty, but who then learned "for the first time that he and his Indians had done" them "much injury."[2] The position of the Dutch was perilous in the extreme. The Indians literally hung upon their necks with "fire and sword."[3] Had they known their own strength, the last refuge of the colonists would have fallen before them, but judging from their own modes of warfare, they feared to attack the fort and contented themselves with sweeping off the exposed plantations and with the terror which their presence inspired.[4]

Director Kieft now solicited aid from New England, offering "twenty-five thousand guilders" for one hundred and fifty men, and as a further consideration that New Netherland should be mortgaged to the English for the payment of the sum offered. Relief was also solicited from Holland; but these applications were attended with only partial success, and the Dutch were thrown on their own resources, aided by a few English volunteers under the command of Captain John Underhill.[5] Two

---

[1] The prowess of the *Iroquois* is affirmed in that they once placed Quebec in siege, yet Fort Amsterdam, more formidable than Quebec, was twice laid waste by the Indians in its vicinity.

[2] *Documentary History*, IV, 14.

[3] *Colonial History*, I, 182.

[4] "They rove in parties continually around day and night on the island of Manhattans, slaying our folks not a thousand paces from the fort, and 'tis now arrived at such a pass, that no one dare move a foot to fetch a stick of fire wood without a strong escort.— *Col. Hist.*, I, 206, 211.

[5] This Underhill was a terrible scourge to the Indians. Engaged in New England wars, he spared neither the aged nor the young. "He could justify putting the weak and defenceless to death, for says he, 'the Scripture declareth women and children must perish with their parents'— 'we had sufficient light from the word of God for our proceedings.'"— *Trumbull.*

companies were soon organized, one of sixty-five and one of seventy-five men, and the work of retaliation commenced. The second company was composed of forty burghers under Captain Pietersen, and thirty-five Englishmen under Lieutenant Baxter; Councillor La Montagne acting as general. This company passed over to Staten island; but found that the Indians, who had fallen back from the vicinity of the fort some time previously, had also abandoned their houses. Five or six hundred skepels of corn rewarded the invaders, but nothing was accomplished beyond its removal. Returning to the fort, the company was increased to one hundred and twenty men and sent to the Weckquaesgeek country. Landing at Greenwich in the evening, from three yachts, they marched the entire night, but found nothing. Retreating through Stamford, they were told by the English that there were Indians in that vicinity. Scouts were sent out who returned with the location of an Indian village. Twenty-five men were at once dispatched thither, and succeeded in killing a number and in capturing an old man, two women and some children. One of the captives offered to lead the expedition to the castles of the *Weckquaesgeeks*. Sixty-five men were sent with him and three castles found, but they had no tenants. Two of them were burned, and, after marching some thirty miles, the expedition returned, " having killed only one or two Indians, taken some women and children prisoners, and burnt some corn."

Meanwhile Underhill,[1] with a company of Dutch and English, had passed over to Long Island to attack the *Canarsees* under Penhawitz. After landing, the force was divided; Underhill and fourteen Englishmen were to attack a small village at Hempstead, and Captain Pieter Cock, and General La Montagne, with eighty men, were to reduce the more considerable village of Mespath. Both were successful; one hundred and twenty Indians were reported as having been killed, with a loss to the attacking forces of one man killed and three wounded.[2] Seven prisoners were turned over to Underhill by the English minister, Fordam, at Hempstead. They had been arrested for stealing pigs and had been confined in Fordam's cellar. Under-

---

[1] He held the rank of sergeant-major.  [2] *Documentary History*, IV, 16.

hill killed three of the seven in the cellar; two were towed in the water until they were drowned, and two were taken to Fort Amsterdam, where, after a short time, they were turned over to the soldiers "to do as they pleased with," and by whom they were dispatched in the most brutal manner.[1]

The third and last expedition was now organized. Underhill having visited Stamford and learned that a large number of Indians had assembled in one of their villages in that vicinity, a force of one hundred and thirty men was dispatched under his command to destroy them. Passing up the sound in three yachts, he landed at Greenwich, where he was compelled to remain over night, in consequence of a severe snow storm. Piloted by an Indian, he marched in the morning to the northwest "up over stony hills over which some must creep," and arrived in the evening about three miles from the village. Halting until ten o'clock, the march was resumed, and the village reached about midnight. Says the narrator: "The order was given as to the mode to be observed in attacking the Indians; they then marched forward towards the houses, being three rows set up street fashion, each eighty paces long, in a low recess of the mountain, affording complete shelter from the north-west wind. The moon was then at the full, and threw a strong light against the mountain so that many winter days were not brighter than it then was. On arriving there the Indians were wide awake, and on their guard; so that ours determined to charge and surround the houses sword in hand. They demeaned themselves as soldiers and deployed in small bands,

[1] "The first of these savages having received a frightful wound, desired them to permit him to dance what is called the kinte-kaye, a religious use observed among them before death; he received, however, so many wounds, that he dropped down dead. The soldiers then cut strips from the other's body, beginning at the calves, up the back, over the shoulders and down to the knees. While this was going forward Director Kieft and his councillor, Jan De la Montagne, a Frenchman, stood laughing heartily at the fun, and rubbing his right arm, so much delight he took in such scenes. He then ordered him to be taken out of the fort, and the soldiers bringing him to the beaver's path (he dancing the kinte-kaye all the time), threw him down, cut off his partes genitales, thrust them into his mouth while still alive, and at last, placing him on a millstone, cut off his head. * * There stood at the same time some twenty-four or twenty-five female savages, who had been taken prisoners, and when they saw this bloody spectacle, they held up their arms, struck their mouths, and in their language exclaimed: 'For shame! For shame! such unheard of cruelty was never known among us.'"— *Documentary History*, IV, 105.

so that we got in a short time twelve dead and one wounded. They were so hard pressed that it was impossible for one to escape. In a brief space of time there were counted one hundred and eighty dead outside the houses. Presently none durst come forth, keeping within the houses, discharging arrows through the holes. The general (Montagne) remarked that nothing else was to be done, and resolved, with Sergeant Major Underhill, to set the huts on fire, whereupon the Indians tried every means to escape, not succeeding in which they returned back to the flames, preferring to perish by the fire than to die by

Massacre of the Weckquaesgeeks.

our hands. What was most wonderful is, that among this vast collection of men, women and children, not one was heard to cry or to scream. According to the report of the Indians themselves the number then destroyed exceeded five hundred; some say full seven hundred, among whom there were also twenty-five *Wappingers*, our God having collected together there the greater part of our enemies to celebrate one of their festivals,[1] from which escaped no more than eight men in all, of whom even those were severely wounded." The work of sword and

[1] The Indians had doubtless assembled for their annual festival of the first moon following that at the end of February.— *Ante*, p. 27.

of fire having been completed in a manner so satisfactory to the humane and Christian Underhill and the equally pious Montagne, the expedition returned to Stamford bearing with them fifteen wounded. Two days after, the force reached Fort Amsterdam, where joy bells rang their welcome.[1]

The Indians now solicited peace, and a treaty was brought about through the intervention of Underhill. Mamaranack, chief of the *Sint-Sings*, Mongockonone of the *Weckquaesgeeks*, Pappenoharrow from the *Nochpeems*, and the *Wappingers* from Stamford, presented themselves at Fort Amsterdam, in the early part of April, 1644, and having pledged themselves that they would not henceforth commit any injury whatever on the inhabitants of New Netherland, their cattle and houses, nor show themselves, except in a canoe, before Fort Amsterdam, should the Dutch be at war with any other chieftaincies; and having further promised to deliver up Pacham, the chief of the *Tankitekes*, peace was concluded, the Dutch promising, on their part, not to molest the Indians in any way.

The Long Island chieftaincies were not included in this arrangement, and the Dutch determined to employ some of the friendly Indians there against those who were hostile. Whiteneymen, sachem of the *Matinecocks*, with forty-seven of his warriors, was secured and dispatched with a commission to do all in his power "to beat and destroy the hostile tribes." The sachem's diplomacy, however, was better than his commission, and he returned to Fort Amsterdam in a few days empowered by the Long Island chiefs to negotiate a treaty of peace, which was at once concluded and pledges exchanged of eternal amity. Gonwarrowe, a chief of the *Matinecocks*, who was present, became surety for the *Hackinsacks* and *Tappans*, for whom he solicited peace,[2] which was granted, on the condition that neither canton should harm the Dutch, and that they should not afford shelter to hostile Indians.

Director Kieft then visited Fort Orange and solicited the negotiation and mediation of the *Mohawks* and *Mahicans* to secure

---

[1] "A thanksgiving was proclaimed on their arrival."— *New York Documentary History*, IV, 17.

[2] A semblance of peace was attempted to be patched up last spring, by a foreigner with one or two tribes of savages to the north.— *Col. Hist.* I, 210; *O'Callaghan's New Netherland*, I, 302.

peace with the remaining insurgents, and on their advice the latter agreed to conclude a treaty of which the record is in these words:

"Aug. 30, 1645. This day, being the 30th August, appeared at Fort Amsterdam before the director and council in the presence of the whole commonalty, the sachems in their own behalf, and for sachems in their own neighborhood, viz: Oratany, chief of *Ackkinkeshacky*, Sesekennick and Willem, chiefs of *Tappaans* and *Reckgawawank*, Pokam and Pennekeck, who were here yesterday, and did give their power of attorney to the former, and took upon them the responsibility for those of *Ouany* and its vicinity, viz: those of *Majauwetumemin*, those of *Marechhourick*, *Nyeck* and their neighbors, and Aepjen, who personally appeared, speaking in behalf of the *Wappinex*, *Wiquaeshex*, *Sint-Sings* and *Kitchtawanghs*.

"1. They conclude with us a solid and durable peace, which they promise to keep sincerely, as we oblige ourselves to do in the same manner.

"2. And if (which God in his mercy avert), there should arise any difficulty between us and them, war shall not be renewed, but they shall complain to our governor, and we to their sachems; and if any person should be murdered or killed, justice shall be directly administered on the murderer, and henceforth we shall live together in amity and peace.

"3. They may not come on the island Manhattan with their arms in the neighborhood of Christian dwellings; neither will we approach their villages with our guns, except we are conducted thither by a savage to give them warning.

"4. And whereas there is yet among them an English girl,[1] whom they promise to conduct to the English at Stamfort, which they yet engage to do; and if she is not conducted there, she shall be guided here in safety, while we promise to pay them the ransom which has been promised by the English.

"All which we promise to keep religiously throughout all New Netherlands. Done in Fort Amsterdam, in the open air, by the director and council in New Netherlands, and the whole commonalty, called together for this purpose; in the presence

---

[1] Supposed to have been the daughter of Ann Hutchinson.

of the *Maquas* embassadors, who were solicited to assist in this negotiation, as arbitrators, and Cornelius Anthonisson, their interpreter and arbitrator with them in this solemn affair. Done as above."

The original was signed with the mark of Sisindogo, the mark of Claes Norman, the mark of Oratany, the mark of Auronge, the mark of Sesechemis, the mark of Willem of Tappan, the mark of Aepjen, sachem of the *Mahicans*, and William Kieft, La Montagne, and other Dutch officials and witnesses.[1]

Thus terminated a war which had been waged for over five years. Both parties had suffered severely. Sixteen hundred Indians, it is said, perished, while the Dutch pointed to " piles of ashes from the burnt houses, barns, barracks and other buildings, and the bones of the cattle," and exclaimed: " Our fields lie fallow and waste; our dwellings and other buildings are burnt; not a handful can be planted or sown this fall on all the abandoned places. All this through a foolish hankering after war; for it is known to all right thinking men here, that these Indians have lived as lambs among us until a few years ago, injuring no one, and affording every assistance to our nation."[2]

[1] *Collections of the New York Historical Society*, 2d series, I, 275. *Col. Hist.* I, 210.

[2] *Colonial History*, I, 210.

The mark  of Aepjen

sachem of the Mahicans.

## CHAPTER VI.

### THE ESOPUS WARS.—FROM THE PEACE OF 1645 TO THE PEACE OF 1664.

SCARCELY had the peace of 1645 been concluded before the Dutch resumed their former intercourse with the Indians, as well as their former modes of promoting trade. The town of New Amsterdam was largely given up to the sale of brandy, tobacco and beer, and Indians were daily seen "running about drunk," through the streets. Every advantage was taken by the Dutch. The Indians were employed as servants, and defrauded of their wages; they were induced to drink, and while intoxicated were robbed of their furs or of the goods which they had purchased; they had standing complaint in regard to the sale of arms at Beaverwyck, and found cause of grievance in the value which the Dutch attached to the lands which they had sold, which led them to believe that they had not been paid a sufficient price for them. The *Minsis* were especially aggrieved, and when the Swedes made their appearance on the South river and offered them arms and ammunition in exchange for their furs, their contempt for the Dutch was openly expressed.

The Dutch, on the other hand, protested their innocence of the causes of complaint charged against them, and made up quite a formidable bill of grievances in their own justification. The Indians "without any cause," so far as they knew, had " not only slain and killed many animals, such as cows, horses and hogs," to the immigrants belonging, but had " cruelly murdered ten persons," one in the second year after the peace had been concluded, one in the year 1651, four in the year 1652, three in the year 1653, and one in the year 1654. The murderers had been demanded under the treaty of 1645, but the Indians had refused to give them up, and the government, "for the sake of peace and out of consideration for the good and advantage of the country and its people," had not attempted to enforce redress.[1] Granting that the offenses recited had been committed, they only prove that they were in retaliation for outrages inflicted on the Indians, for the testimony in all similar cases is that the latter were not wanton murderers.[2] The wrongs which they suffered found no fitting record at the hands of the Dutch, but their acts of retaliation were detailed with horror, and were exceeded, when opportunity offered, in the cold-blooded vengeance which was inflicted upon them.

Hostilities were not long delayed. A squaw, detected in stealing peaches from the garden of Hendrick Van Dyck, at New Amsterdam, had been killed by him, and her family determined to avenge her death. Availing themselves of the organization of a war party of *Wappingers*, then about to make descent upon some neighboring tribe, they prevailed upon them to stop at New Amsterdam, and aid them in enforcing the "blood atonement," which their laws demanded. On the morning of the fifteenth of September, 1655, "sixty-four canoes full of Indians," were beached on the shore, and, "before scarcely any one had yet risen," their occupants, "five hundred men, all armed,"[3] scattered themselves throughout the town, and, "under the pretense of looking for northern Indians," entered dwellings by force and "searched the premises" with more than the zeal of modern officers in quest of fugitives. They offered no personal violence, however, and their sachems readily attended a conference, called by the authorities, and promised to take their departure in the evening. But they failed to do so. The object for which they came was not accomplished. In the evening they were joined "by two hun-

---

[1] Petition of October, 1655, *Dutch Manuscripts*, vol. IV, office of secretary of state, Albany, as translated by Dr. O'Callaghan in *Indian War of* 1655.

[2] The Indians promptly confessed their wrong in the first of the cases recited, and sent a deputation to the director to solicit forgiveness and renew their covenant of peace. They wished to live in friendship, but were sorely provoked by their Dutch neighbors. The director promised that he would surely punish offenders against them if the Indians would complain directly to him. He accepted their gifts and made them presents in return, and they departed "very much satisfied."

[3] Brodhead says the Indians were supposed to number nineteen hundred men, of whom from five to eight hundred were armed. The text of the Dutch manuscript, however, is "five hundred," and even that number was a large complement for sixty-four canoes. Councillor La Montagne, upon whose "opinion," Brodhead evidently bases his statement,

dred armed Indians," and with them renewed the search. About eight o'clock, they detected Van Dyck, and an arrow was almost instantly winged to his breast. One Leendertsen, in attempting to protect him, was "threatened with an axe."[1] The cry of murder was raised by the Dutch, and the burgher guard rushed from the fort, " without any orders, some through the gate, others over the walls, so that they came into conflict with the Indians." The latter were "lying about the shore," evidently preparing to take their departure as they had promised. In the attack upon them two of the guard were killed and three wounded, while of their own number three were left dead.[2] Meanwhile they had embarked in their canoes, and, " taking their course across the river, landed on the western side ; and commenced the work of retaliation for the attack which had been made upon them and for the loss which they had suffered. A house at Hoboken was soon in flames, and those at Pavonia speedily followed. Every family, with the exception of one, was destroyed ; every man killed, " together with all his cattle," and a large number of women and children taken into captivity. Staten island was next visited, and its ninety colonists and flourishing bouweries shared the fate of those at Pavonia. For three days the carnage continued, and at its close " full fifty" of the Dutch had been " murdered and put to death ; over one hundred, mostly women and children," were in captivity ; " twenty bouweries and a number of plantations" had been burned with " full twelve to fifteen hundred skepels of grain," and five or six hundred head of cattle either killed or driven off. In addition to those killed and captured, three hundred colonists were ruined in estate, and the aggregated damages were computed at two hundred thousand guilders or eighty thousand dollars.

At the time of this occurrence, Director Stuyvesant, who had succeeded Kieft, was absent with his soldiers on an expedition to South river, and a messenger was immediately sent for his return. Meanwhile, as the tidings of the disaster spread, the

disagrees with all of his contemporaries, and was apparently determined to give good reason for the great fright which he suffered.

[1] Neither Van Dyck nor Leendertsen appear to have been killed.
[2] Opinion of Fiscal Van Tienhoven, O'Callaghan's *Indian War of* 1655, 40.

inhabitants fled in terror to the fort as to a city of refuge. The English villages on Long Island sent word that the Indians had threatened to kill the Dutch who resided there, and that the English themselves would share the same fate if they offered any assistance to the Manhattans, even to the extent of sending them food. Lady Moody's house at Gravesend was again attacked. The settlers at Esopus abandoned their farms, lest they should be cut off. Even New Amsterdam was not secure; bands of Indians wandered over the island, destroying all who came in their way. Ten Frenchmen were enrolled to guard the house and family of the absent director, while the Dutch themselves kept within the fort.

In the midst of the terror which prevailed, Stuyvesant and his soldiers returned, and the confidence of the colonists was soon restored. Soldiers were sent to the out settlements, an embargo was laid on vessels about to sail, and passengers able to bear arms were ordered not to depart " until it should please God to change the aspect of affairs." A plank curtain was thrown up, to prevent the Indians scaling the city walls, and no persons, on any account, were to go into the country without permission, nor unless in numbers sufficient to ensure their safety.

The fury of the Indians, however, had spent its force and they retreated, after dividing their prisoners, a portion of whom were taken to the highlands, and the remainder retained with the *Hackinsacks*. The latter, finding them an incumbrance, sent Captain Pos, who had been taken at Staten island, with proposals for their ransom. Not returning as soon as was expected, the Indians sent another messenger with word that all the prisoners should be brought to Paulus hook in two days. Pos returned, and in a few days brought from the chief of the *Hackinsacks* fourteen prisoners, " men, women and children," as a token of his good will, " in return for which he requested some powder and ball. Stuyvesant sent him a Wappinger and an Esopus Indian in exchange, and also some ammunition, of which he promised a further supply when other prisoners should be brought in. Pos, accompanied by two influential citizens, conveyed this message, and soon returned with twenty-eight of the captives and another message that from twenty to twenty-four others would be restored on the receipt of a proper quantity of friezes, guns, wampum and ammunition, but they would not exchange the prisoners for Indians, ransom was the order of their laws. Stuyvesant then asked the ransom price " for all the prisoners *en masse*, or for each individually," and received the answer, " seventy-eight pounds of powder and forty staves of lead, for twenty-eight persons." This offer was accepted, and thirty-five pounds of powder and ten staves of lead additional sent, but no more prisoners were returned, the highland chieftaincies having determined to retain them as hostages. No measures were taken to punish the Indians. The Dutch were clearly at fault, in the opinion of Stuyvesant,[1] and he turned a deaf ear to those who clamored for war, and who in return charged him with winking " at this infraction of the peace." The settlers gradually returned to their avocations, but under restraints which were more conducive to personal safety, and comparative quiet prevailed.

The Long Island tribes under Tackapousha, who had been assigned to the jurisdiction of the Dutch under the treaty with the English at Hartford in 1650, came forward and repudiated all connection with the outbreak which had occurred. Not only were they innocent of participation in it, but since they had withheld tribute from the *Wappingers*, they had been repeatedly attacked by them. Said their speaker : " Our chief has been twelve years at war with those who have injured you, and though you may consider him no bigger than your fist, he would yet prove himself strong enough. He has hitherto sat, his head drooping on his breast, yet he still hoped he should be able to show what he could achieve." Henceforth the western *Montauk* chieftaincies were the friends of the Dutch, and soon after renewed with them their treaty of alliance.[2]

---

[1] "We concur in the general opinion that the Indians had, on their first arrival, no other intention than to wage war against the savages on the east end of Long Island. We have come to this conclusion from various reasons too long to be detailed here; and that a culpable want of vigilance, and a too hasty rashness on the part of a few hot-headed spirits, had diverted the Indians [from their purpose] and been the cause of the dreadful consequences and enormous losses." — *O'Callaghan's Indian War of 1655.*

[2] The following is the treaty referred to :

"Articles of agreement betwixt the governor of New Netherland, and Tackapausha, March ye 12, 1656:

" 1. That all injuries formerly passed in the time of the governor's predecessors,

But there was no general peace. The conflict was remembered, and the Indians, as well as the Dutch, stood on guard. The scene of combat, however, was changed. The settlers at Esopus,[1] who had returned after the panic of 1655, continued for some time unmolested ; but, as in other places, they soon devoted the largest portion of their time and means to the purposes of trade. The examples of the traders at New Amsterdam were readily copied. Familiarity, brandy and other liquors, were called to their aid, and with results similar to those which had already disgraced the Dutch character. The Indians suffered wrongfully, and in retaliation (1657) " one of the settlers was killed, the house and out buildings of another were burned, and the settlers were forced, by threats of arson and murder, to plow up the patches of land where the savages planted their maize."[2] The white population consisted, at that time, of between sixty and seventy persons, who were in no condition for defense. They wrote at once to Stuyvesant, imploring him to send " forty or fifty soldiers to save the Esopus." The

shall be forgiven and forgotten, since ye sd year 1645.

" 2. That Tackapausha being chosen ye chief sachem by all the Indian sachems from Mersapege, Maskahnong, Secatong, Meracock, Rockaway and Canorise, with ye rest, both sachems and natives, doth take ye governor of ye New Netherland to be his and his people's protector, and in consideration of that to put under ye sd protection, on thiere lands and territoryes upon Long Island, so far as ye Dutch line doth runn, according to the agreement made att Hartforde.

" 3. The governor doth promise to make noe peace with the Indians that did the spoile at ye Manhattans the 15th September last, likewise to include the sachem in it.

" 4. That Tackapausha shall make no peace wh ye sd Indians, without ye consent and knowledge of the governor, and sd sachem doth promise for himself and his people to give no dwelling place, entertainment nor lodging to any of ye governor's, or thiere owne enemies.

" 5. The governor doth promise, between this date and six months, to build a house or forte upon such place as they shall show upon the north side, and the house or forte to be furnished with Indian trade and commodities.

" 6. The inhabitants of Hempsteede according to their patent, shall enjoy their purchase without molestation from ye sachem or his people, either of person or estate ; and the sachem will live in peace with all ye English and Dutch within this jurisdiction. And the governor doth promise for himself and all his people to live in peace with the sd sachem and all his people.

" 7. That in case an Indian doe wrong to a Christian in his person or estate, and complaint be made to the sachem, hee shall make full satisfaction ; likewise if a Dutchman or Englishman shall wrong an Indian the governor shall make satisfaction according to Equity."

[1] The precise time at which settlement was made at Atkarkarton, now Kingston, is not known, although it is assumed that a fort or trading post was erected there as early as 1614. The reference in the text is to the first known European settlers who removed thither, in company with Capt. Thomas Chambers, from Panhoosic, now Troy, in 1652.

[2] *Documentary History*, IV.

governor responded by immediately visiting the scene of disturbance with a company of soldiers, where he arrived on the 30th of May. The following day, being Ascension Thursday, the settlers assembled at the house of Jacob Jansen Stol for religious service. The governor met them there and explained to them the difficulties under which they were placed, by their isolated positions, and recommended that they should unite at once in a village, which could be easily defended from the attacks of the Indians. To this they objected on the ground of want of time to give care to their crops and to remove their dwellings and erect palisades; and asked that the soldiers be permitted to remain until after harvest. This request Stuyvesant refused; but promised that if they would agree to palisade at once the ground to be selected for a village, he would remain with them until the work was completed.

While these proceedings were being held, some twelve or fifteen Indians, accompanied by two of their chiefs, arrived at the house of Stol, where the director was staying, with word that other sachems were deterred from coming to the conference which he had invited through fear of the soldiers. Stuyvesant gave his assurance that no harm should befall them, when about fifty additional Indians, with a few women and children, made their appearance, and seated themselves beneath an aged tree which stood without the fence, "about a stone's throw from the house." Accompanied only by an interpreter and two of his followers, Stuyvesant went out and seated himself in the midst of the Indians, when one of the chiefs arose, " and made a long harangue," detailing the events of the war waged in Kieft's time (1645), and how many of their tribe the Dutch had then slain, adding, however, that they had obliterated all these things from their hearts and forgotten them.[1]

Stuyvesant replied to this address, that those things had occurred before his time, and that the recollection of them had been "all thrown away" by the subsequent peace. He asked them, however, if any injury had been done them, in person or property, since he had come into the country. The Indians remained silent. Stuyvesant then proceeded to enumerate the

[1] *O'Callaghan's New Netherland*, II, 358.

various offenses which the Indians had committed on the Dutch. "Your overbearing insolence at Esopus," said he, "is known. I come to investigate this matter, and not to make war, provided the murderer be surrendered and all damage repaid. The Dutch never solicited your sachems for leave to come here. Your sachems have requested us, over and over again, to make a settlement among you. We have not had a foot of your land without paying you for it, nor do we desire to have any more without making full compensation therefor. Why then have you committed this murder? Why have you burned our houses, killed our cattle, and continue to threaten our people?"

To this harangue the sachems made no reply, but "looked on the ground." At length one of them arose and responded: "You Swannekins have sold our children the *boisson.*" It is you who have given them brandy and made them *cachens*, intoxicated and mad, and caused them to commit all this mischief. The sachems cannot then control the young Indians nor prevent them fighting. This murder has not been committed by any of our tribe, but by a *Minnisink*, who now skulks among the *Haverstraws*. It was he who fired the two houses and then fled. For ourselves we can truly say, we did not commit the act. We know no malice, neither are we inclined to fight, but we cannot control our young men."

Stuyvesant immediately arose, and hurled defiance at the young braves. "If any of your young people desire to fight, let them now step forth. I will place man against man. Nay, I will place twenty against thirty or forty of your hot heads. Now, then, is your time. But it is not manly to threaten farmers, and women and children who are not warriors. If this be not stopped, I shall be compelled to retaliate on old and young, on women and children. This I can now do by killing you all, taking your wives and little ones captive and destroying your maize lands; but I will not do it. I expect you will repair all damages, seize the murderer if he come among you, and do no further mischief." "The Dutch," he continued, "are now going to live together in one spot. It is desirable that you should sell us the whole of the Esopus land, as you have often proposed, and remove farther into the interior; for it is not good for you to reside so near the Swannekins, whose cattle might eat your maize and thus cause fresh disturbances."

The sachems promised to take the matter into consideration, and departed with their followers. While they were absent the settlers agreed that it would be for the best to adopt the counsel of the director, and left the selection of the site of the village to him. He " accordingly chose a spot at the bend of the kill, where a water front might be had on three sides ; and a part of the plain, about two hundred and ten yards in circumference, was staked out."[1] The erection of a stockade was immediately commenced, the Dutch, in this particular, adopting the mode of the Indians and drawing from them lessons in defensive warfare.

On the 1st of June, the sachems returned and solicited peace, expressing sorrow for what had passed. They felt deeply the shame that Stuyvesant had challenged their young men, and they had not dared to accept the wager, and hoped the fact would not be spread abroad. Presents were distributed to them in exchange for the wampum with which they had accompanied their proposals for peace ; but they were told a second time that they must surrender the murderer, and make good the damages they had committed. To these requirements they demurred ; and it was finally agreed that they should make compensation for damages, and sell the land for the projected village. They then retired, but returned again on the 4th with a final reply, which was that they would give the director the land he asked, " to grease his feet with, as he had taken so long a journey to visit them." They then renewed the assurance that they had thrown away all malice, and that hereafter none among them would injure a Dutchman. The director responded with like assurances ; and the Indians departed. The work at the village now went forward rapidly. After three weeks' labor, the lines of palisades were completed ; all the buildings removed ; a guard-house, sixteen feet by twenty-three, built in the north-east corner ; a bridge thrown over the kill, and barracks erected for

---

[1] *Brodhead*, 1, 649; *O'Callaghan*, II, 361. The village located by Stuyvesant was about three miles north-west from the centre of the present village of Kingston, at a bend in the Esopus creek near the residence now, or late, of Benjamin Smith. The Indians were probably residents of the castle of Wiltmeet.

the soldiers, of whom Stuyvesant detailed twenty-four to guard the infant settlement, and then returned to Fort Amsterdam.

Stuyvesant visited Esopus again in the fall of 1658, in order to obtain from the Indians a transfer of the remainder of their lands. Calling the chiefs together, he thus addressed them: " A year and a half ago you killed two horses belonging to Madame de Hulter, and attacked Jacob Adriaensen in his own house with an axe, knocked out his eye, mortally wounded his infant child, and not satisfied with this, burnt his house last spring. You, moreover, robbed him of his property, and killed a Dutchman in one of his sloops. You compelled our farmers to plow your land; threatened, at the same time, to fire their houses, and repeatedly extorted money from the settlers, who have already paid you for their farms. You have added threats and insults, and finally forced the colonists, at much expense, to break up their establishments and concentrate their dwellings. Various other injuries you have committed since that time, notwithstanding your promises. For all this we demand compensation; to enforce which, efficient measures will be taken, unless the terms we now propose be acceded to."

The demand was a bold attempt at extortion; the terms of peace not less so. The Indians were required to make a free surrender of all the Esopus lands so far as they had been explored by the Dutch, as indemnity for the expenses which the settlers had incurred in removing their dwellings and fortifying their village; the relinquishment of all claims held by the Indians against the settlers for labor or furs, and the payment to the latter of several hundred fathoms of wampum for damages. The Indians regarded the terms as hard, and stated that they had already been deprived of many of their maize fields without compensation. Such a demand was unexpected, and as many of their sachems were absent, they asked time for consultation. Stuyvesant generously agreed to allow them one night to consider what course they would pursue.

The next day (Oct. 16), the council again assembled, and the sachems expressed a willingness to make reasonable compensation for injuries. They would relinquish part of their claims against the settlers, and give some lands to those who had been injured; but they were poor and had no wampum. Then throwing down a beaver skin, the principal sachem reminded the director that he could well afford to be generous from the prospect of largely increased trade with the *Senecas*. Offering a wampum belt, he concluded: " A horse belonging to Jacob Jansen Stol broke into our corn-fields and destroyed two of our plantations. One of our boys shot it, for which we gave Stol seventy guilders in wampum. But this belt we now present, so that the soldiers may let us go in peace, and not beat us when we visit this place."

Stuyvesant's proposition in relation to land was left untouched by the sachem, and the director asked: " What do you intend to propose about the land?" The sachem replied, that " it belonged to the chiefs who were not here to-day, and we cannot, therefore, come to any conclusion on it." He promised, however, that they would return the next day and give their answer. The morrow came, but the chiefs did not return. Stuyvesant dispatched messengers to their wigwams to inquire their intentions, who returned with the answer that " the chiefs had made fools of them." Stuyvesant had overreached himself by his extravagant demand, and, chagrined and disappointed, departed for Fort Amsterdam, leaving Ensign Dirck Smith with fifty soldiers under instructions to guard the village properly, and not allow any Indians within the palisades; to act purely on the defensive, and to detail, from day to day, a proper guard to protect the husbandmen. A *ronduit*, or small fort, was also projected at the mouth of the Walkill, and the work of its construction commenced. Several chiefs came in, shortly after Stuyvesant's departure, and made a present to Stol as further indemnity for the injuries he had sustained. The offering was accompanied by a renewal of their request for the removal of the soldiers, and an exchange of presents. The former was declined, and in response to the latter the settlers had " nothing to grease the Indian's breasts. So the meeting was a dry one."

Notwithstanding the threatening aspect of Indian affairs, the settlement continued prosperous, and its occupants, increased in numbers and enjoying the protection of an armed force, became more and more disregardful of the rights of the red men.

During the summer of 1659, mutual distrust and suspicion prevailed. The settlers were disturbed by reports that the Indians intended a general massacre when the work of harvest should begin ; while the Indians regarded the presence of the soldiers as a menace, doubted the director's desire for peace, and feared that it was his intention to attack and destroy them, as he had not yet sent the presents he had promised them. A conference was held with the chiefs Aug. 17, but they denied that they had any hostile intentions. " We patiently submit," said they, " to the blows which have been inflicted on us ; yet the Dutch still plunder our corn." Laying down seventeen small sticks, the sachem added : " so many times have the Swannekins struck and assaulted us in divers places. We are willing to live in peace, but we expect your chief sachem will make us some presents. Otherwise he cannot be sincere." The conference was broken up without removing the feeling which existed between the parties ; and fresh rumors disturbed the settlers that the Indians were preparing bows and arrows and concentrating their strength for an attack. Familiar as the Dutch were with the customs of the Indians and the periods of their annual return from their hunting expeditions, and their almost constant preparation of the implements of the chase, they nevertheless now saw in them nothing but impending destruction.

Nor were the general relations existing between the Indians and the Dutch more favorable. Two soldiers, who had deserted from Fort Orange, were murdered by the *Mahicans*, and some of the *Raritans* had destroyed a family of four persons, at Mespath kil, in order to obtain possession of a small roll of wampum which, in an unguarded moment, had been exhibited to them, and excited their cupidity. The *Mohawks*, suffering under the blows of the French, had complaint against the Dutch, and sent a delegation to Fort Orange, where, on the sixth of September, 1659, the second official conference was held with them. The *Mohawk* speaker charged that the Dutch called his people brothers, and asserted that they were bound to them by a chain, but that this continued only so long as they had beavers, after which they were no longer thought of. They had favors to ask, however, and were not disposed to quarrel.

They were engaged in war with the French, and, finding themselves crippled by the liquor which the Dutch sold to their warriors, asked that the sale be stopped, the liquor kegs plugged up and the dealers punished. The gunsmiths refused to repair their arms when they had no wampum ; this was not generous, nor was it generous to deny to them powder and lead. The French treated their Indians more liberally, and their example should be considered. Their principal request, however, was for thirty men with horses, to cut and draw timber for the forts which they were building.

The commandant at Fort Orange could give no reply, but would submit the requests which had been made to the director, whose arrival was daily expected. But Stuyvesant did not arrive, and, after waiting several days, the authorities at Fort Orange, now thoroughly alarmed, resolved to send embassadors to the *Mohawks* to reply to their requests. At Caughnawaga, on the twenty-fourth, was held the first formal council with the *Iroquois* in their own country. The professions of friendship on the part of the Dutch were warm, and no doubt sincere, in view of their relations with other tribes. They would remain the brothers of the *Mohawks* for all time, and would neither fight against them nor leave them in distress when they could help them ; but they could not force their smiths to repair their " brothers' fire arms without pay, for they must earn food for their wives and little ones." The sale of brandy could not be stopped so long as the Indians would buy it. The director was angry that such sale was made, and had forbidden it ; let the chiefs also forbid their people. " Will ye," they asked, " that we take from your people their brandy and their kegs ? Say so before all those here present." Aid to build the *Mohawk* forts could not be given ; the Dutch were all sick, and the hills were so steep their horses could not draw the timber. But to aid them in their work they gave them fifteen new axes ; and to assist them in their wars, seventy pounds of powder and a hundred weight of lead were added to their stores.[1]

---

[1] It was at this conference that the Dutch speaker asserted that it was " now sixteen years " since an alliance had been formed with the *Mohawks*. Reference has already been made to this treaty. It will also be observed that the *Minsis* were not subjugated at that time. but were in condition to ask the alliance of the *Mohawks*.

The embassadors made no efforts to control the *Mohawks* in their wars, nor cared with whom they fought so long as the Dutch escaped; while the *Mohawks* cared as little for their white neighbors, their sole object being to obtain the munitions of war to continue their conflict with the French and their Indians. The request of the embassadors for the release of the French prisoners, the *Mohawks* would not grant; but they would refer the matter to their castles. They had little faith in the French, however, for they made treaties and did not observe them; and when hunting parties of the *Mohawks* were abroad, they were attacked by the French Indians, among whom a number of Frenchmen were always skulking to knock them on the head. In their request that the *Mohawks* would not aid the Esopus clans in an attack upon the Dutch, the embassadors were more successful, the chiefs promising that they would refuse their belts and have nothing to do with them.[1]

In the meantime hostilities had broken out in the Esopus country. Chambers[2] had employed a number of Indians to husk corn, and, on the night of the termination of their labor, they had asked for and obtained some brandy. A carouse followed, in the course of which another bottle of brandy was procured. When the debauch was at its height, one of them discharged his gun, loaded only with powder, which had the effect to alarm the village. One of them, more wise than his associates, deplored the act of his companion, and proposed that they should

---

[1] *O'Callaghan*, II, 389, etc.
[2] Thomas Chambers was of English birth. He settled at Panhoosic, now Troy, in the jurisdiction of Rensselaerswyck, in 1651, and from thence removed to the Esopus country in 1652, where he took part in the early Indian wars, became a captain in the Dutch service, and was elected delegate to the provincial assembly in 1664. His residence was near the confluence of the Walkill with the Hudson, and was built for the double purpose of a house and a fort, being square and loop-holed for musketry. By commercial and other speculations, he acquired a considerable tract of land, which was erected, by Gov. Lovelace, in 1672, into the manor of Foxhall, with power to hold certain courts and to appoint a steward to try causes arising between the vassals. Not satisfied with these honors, he determined to perpetuate his name in another form, and accordingly passed his estate to his heirs by the most intricate entail. The manor and title was to be held only by heirs bearing the name of Chambers. To this end, his first wife having died without issue, he married a widow Van Gaasbeck and adopted her children. He died in 1698, and was buried in his vault on the site of the residence now or late of Jansen Hasbrouck, at Rondout. His remains, with those of the Van Gaasbeck family, were removed in 1854. The name of the manor and its owner only live in history.

at once leave the place, urging that "he felt a sensation in his body that they would all be killed." His companions, however, laughed at his alarm. They had never harmed the Dutch — "Why should they kill us?" But the speaker still cherished his fears, and replied: "My heart feels heavy within me;" and again he entreated his companions to depart, but they refused, and, in conscious security, lay down upon their blankets to sleep.

Meanwhile Ensign Smith had yielded to the request of the villagers by dispatching Sergeant Stol to reconnoitre and report the cause of the disturbance. Stol, on his return, stated the facts, when Smith gave orders that the Indians should not be molested. Notwithstanding this order, Stol went among the villagers and invited them to unite in a sortie against the Indian encampment. Enlisting some ten or eleven persons [1] in the enterprise, he left the village and stealthily approached the sleeping Indians, who were aroused from their slumbers by a volley fired among them. Jumping up to escape, one was knocked on the head with an axe, a second was taken prisoner, a third fled, and a fourth, too deeply intoxicated to awake, "was hewn on the head with a cutlass," which roused him to consciousness and he made off. Stol and his valorous associates then returned to the village and recounted their deeds of noble daring, justifying their proceedings by the assertion that the Indians first attacked them, an assertion subsequently proved to be without foundation.

Ensign Smith, finding his orders disobeyed, and hostilities actually commenced by a people whose movements he could not control, determined to leave the settlers to their fate by returning with his command to Fort Amsterdam. Learning his intention, the settlers frustrated his design by chartering, on their own account, all the sailing vessels that lay at the shore in which he and his men intended to embark. The only alternative that remained to him was to send an express to the director, detailing the state of affairs and requesting his presence. With this purpose in view he sent an armed party, eighteen or nine-

---

[1] His associates were Jacob Jansen Van Stoutenberg, Thomas Higgins, Gysbert Phillipsen Van Velthuysen, Evert Pels, Jan Arentsen, Barent Harmaensen, Martin Hoffman, Gilles de Wecker, Abel Dircksen, and James the mason.— *O'Calla-*

*ghan*, II, 396.

[2] A full investigation into this affair by the proper authorities attached the blame entirely upon the men engaged in the foray.

teen in number, to the shore to forward dispatches. In the meantime, the Indians had gathered in considerable numbers, determined to avenge the attack which had been made upon their kindred. Observing the party which had been sent out by Smith, an ambuscade was formed, into which, on their return, the company fell and were immediately surrounded by the Indians, to whom thirteen of the party, including the officer in command and six soldiers, surrendered without any resistance, and were borne off into captivity.

Open war was now declared. The Indians, justly incensed against their Dutch neighbors, burned all the houses, barns, and harvests within their reach, and killed all the horses and cattle that fell in their way. Four or five hundred Indians invested the village, and, after vainly attempting to set it on fire, avenged themselves by burning at the stake eight or ten of the prisoners in their hands, among whom was Stoutenberg who had taken part in the attack on the sleeping Indians. It was a horrid ceremony. The victims were fastened naked to stakes, placed at some distance from each other encircling a large fire; their heads ornamented; their bodies painted. The dance of death was then held, and the work of torture commenced. The nails of the victims were pulled out, their fingers bitten off or crushed between stones, their skin scorched with fire-brands or torches, pieces of flesh cut from their bodies, and every kind of slow torture that savage ingenuity could suggest, inflicted; and, as one by one they were released by death, their bodies were cast into the blazing fire and consumed. Terror folded her wings in the hearts of the people who beheld the spectacle which they could not prevent; fathers gathered upon the ramparts, and mothers pressed their children to their arms, not knowing how soon the frail palisades might yield, and themselves be exposed to the pitiless mercy of the frenzied children of the forest.

For three weeks the village was held in siege, the little stockade fort on the brow of the hill resisting the skill of Indian warfare. Relief at length came. The express to Stuyvesant reached Fort Amsterdam on the 23d of September; but everything there was in the greatest consternation. The settlements on Long island were being ravaged, and another general Indian war was feared. Considerable time was lost in enlisting a company to proceed to the assistance of the Esopus settlers, and it was not until the 10th of October, that Stuyvesant set sail. He arrived at Esopus on the 11th, with a force of nearly two hundred men. Indian runners had preceded him and apprised their friends of his approach, and, a few hours previous to his arrival, the siege was raised and the beleaguering forces melted into the forests. Thither they could not be pursued, heavy rains having swollen the streams and made the trails impassible, and, having no employment for his force, Stuyvesant directed their return to Fort Amsterdam.

The authorities at Fort Orange now interested themselves in the matter, and obtained the cooperation of some *Mohawk* and *Mahican* chiefs, who visited the settlement, and succeeded in securing an armistice and the surrender of two prisoners held by the Indians. On the 28th of November, Stuyvesant came up, with the hope of making a permanent treaty, but the sachems refused to meet him. A conference was finally held on the 18th of December, and the Indians persuaded to bring in some supplies in exchange for powder; but they refused to make peace, denounced the truce which had been made as without binding authority, and retained their young prisoners, having killed all the others.

In the spring of 1660, peace having been concluded with the *Wappingers*, Stuyvesant determined upon active hostilities against the Esopus cantons; but the latter, shorn to a large extent of their allies, were not disposed to continue the contest, and accordingly secured the intercession of Goethals, the chief sachem of the *Wappingers*, that they might be included in the treaty which had been made with that tribe. Stuyvesant doubted their sincerity, and Goethals replied: " The Indians say the same of the Dutch." He assured Stuyvesant that Kaelcop, Pemmyraweck, and other Esopus sachems were anxious for peace, and that it was only the *kalebackers*[1] who were not inclined to treat, but that the chiefs would make them

---

[1] Indians who possessed guns were called *kalebackers*, and were generally the most idle and vicious of the Indian people.— *De Laet*.

come in. "What security can there be for peace, if the *kalebackers* desire war?" asked the director, but Goethals. could not reply. Stuyvesant then told him that the Esopus chiefs must visit him at Fort Amsterdam, if they desired peace. " They are too much frightened and dare not come," was the reply. Believing this to be true, Stuyvesant consented to visit Esopus and. hold a conference with the Indians.

While these negotiations were in progress, Ensign Smith was engaged in active service against the offending Indians. On the 17th of March he advanced, with forty men, nine miles into the interior, and attacked the Indian fort Wiltmeet, which was defended by some sixty Indians who fled at the first fire, leaving four of their number dead and twelve others prisoners. A large quantity of maize, peas, and bearskins, fell into the hands of the Dutch, and the fort was destroyed.

Stuyvesant arrived at Esopus on the 18th, but soon saw that all hope of negotiating a peace was at an end. He therefore sent the prisoners and plunder to Fort Amsterdam, and directed a vigorous prosecution of the war by a formal declaration (March 25th) against the Esopus Indians " and all their adherents." Smith now followed up the advantage he had gained by posting (April 4th) forty-three men in ambuscade, " over the creek among the rocks," but the Indians discovered the snare, and a general fight ensued in which three Indians were killed, two severely wounded, and one taken prisoner. This disaster produced a material change in the deportment of the Indians, who now most earnestly entreated for peace, and again obtained the intercession of neighboring chiefs in their behalf. On the 24th of May, three *Mahican* chiefs visited Fort Amsterdam, and declared that the Esopus Indians were willing to leave that country and transfer their land to the Dutch, in indemnity for the murder of the settlers, on condition that their friends in captivity should be surrendered and peace concluded. Security was demanded that the *kalebackers* also united in the request. Laying down four belts of wampum, " these," said Aepjin, the *Mahican* chief sachem, " are a guaranty that the *kalebackers* desire peace, and that we are authorized to treat in their behalf." Stuyvesant accepted the belts, but told the chiefs that peace would be concluded only when the Esopus chiefs would present themselves at Fort Amsterdam for that purpose. The director was then requested to liberate the captive Indians; but he declined, and in reply to the question: " What are your intentions as regards these men?" answered, " What have been done with the Christian prisoners?" Aepjin then requested that if the war was continued it might be confined to the Esopus country, and the director assured him that so long as his people observed peace, the Dutch would treat them as friends. The conference was concluded by the presentation of a blanket, a piece of frieze, an axe, a knife, a pair of stockings, and two small kettles, to each of the chiefs, who departed content. The next day, Stuyvesant issued an order banishing the Esopus prisoners to Curaçoa " to be employed there, or at Buenaire, with the negroes in the company's service." Two or three of the prisoners only were retained at Fort Amsterdam, to be punished " as it should be thought proper."

Meanwhile Ensign Smith pushed hostilities with vigor. On the 30th of May, guided by one of his prisoners, a force under his command discovered, " at the second fall of Kit Davit's kil," [1] about twelve miles west from the Hudson, a few Indians planting corn on the opposite bank. The stream being swollen, it was found impossible to cross, so he returned to the village, where he learned that the Indians had concentrated their force at an almost inaccessible spot about twenty-seven miles " up the river, beyond the above-mentioned fall, where it was pretty easy to ford " the kil. Thither Smith directed his force, but the Indians received notice of his approach by the barking of their dogs, and fled, leaving behind them Preummaker, " the oldest and best of their chiefs." [2] The aged sachem met his foes with the haughty demand, " What do ye here, ye dogs ? " aiming an arrow at them as he spoke. He was easily disarmed, and a consultation held as to how he should be disposed of. " As it

---

[1] Sager's kil, now called the Esopus creek. "The second fall" was the small stream entering the Esopus creek from the west, south of the old village. "Kit Davit's farm was about nine miles from Hudson's river."—*O'Callaghan*, II, 44.

[2] *O'Callaghan*, II, 411. "Preummaker's land," lying upon Esopus kil, within the limits of Hurley, was laid out for Venike Rosen, April 15, 1685.— *Land Papers*, II, 169.

was considerable distance to carry him," writes the ensign, " we struck him down with his own axe."

While Smith was thus carrying war into the heart of the Indian country, several of the sachems were seeking the mediation of the neighboring chiefs to secure a permanent peace. Sewackenamo called his warriors together to know their wishes. " We will fight no more," was the brief reply. The chief next assembled the squaws, and inquired " what seemed to them best ? " These answered, " That we plant our fields in peace and live in quiet." He then assembled the young men, who urged him to make peace with the Dutch, and declared that " they would not kill either hog or fowl any more." The sachem then proceeded to Gamoenapa to secure the assistance of the sachems of the *Hackinsacks* and *Tappans* in procuring a cessation of hostilities. While there a runner brought to him the intelligence of the death of Preummaker, which so unmanned him that " he knew not what to do." Leaving his *Hackinsack* friends to negotiate for him, he returned to his people with a heavy heart.

Oritany, of the *Hackinsacks*, bore the peace belts which were committed to him to Fort Amsterdam, and presented them to the director on the 2d of June. Stuyvesant assured him that the Dutch were disposed for friendship. " It is very strange, then," said the old sachem, whose notions of warfare differed somewhat from his hearers, " that your people were so recently engaged against the Indians, and have slain their aged chief." Stuyvesant replied, that it was customary among white men to exert all their strength until they had conquered a peace. Oritany then requested a suspension of hostilities while negotiations for peace were in progress. To this Stuyvesant consented with the proviso that the sachem should go at once to Esopus, accompanied by a Dutch interpreter, and learn for himself the wishes of the Indians. Oritany accepted the proposition, and took his leave saying, " Now I shall see for myself if the Esopus people contemplate any good." His mission was entirely successful, and he returned to Fort Amsterdam with a request to the director to visit Esopus and arrange a treaty.

On the 7th of July, Stuyvesant arrived at Esopus, accompanied by Captain Martin Kregier and Burgomaster Van Cortland, and sent messengers to acquaint the sachems of his arrival. Three days elapsed and no response came from the Indians. Summoning the chiefs of the *Mohawks*, *Mahicans*, *Wappingers*, *Minsis* and *Hackinsacks*, who had been invited to assist in the negotiations,[1] he addressed them as follows:

"Brothers: Ye all know well that we have not caused this war. After the Esopus savages burned three of our houses and murdered one of our men, a year ago, we forgave them and renewed the chain of friendship with them, promising the one to the other, that we should not thenceforth again wage war though a man was killed, but that the murderer should be surrendered and punished. Notwithstanding all this, the Esopus savages took some of our people prisoners, now ten moons since,[2] burnt several houses; besieged and stormed Esopus, though they pretended, during the siege, to be inclined to peace. They then consented to receive a ransom for the prisoners, but when the ransom was brought out to the gate, they carried it away by force, retained our prisoners, and murdered eight or nine of them afterwards in an infamous manner. Brothers: this it was that compelled us to take the hatchet.

"Brothers: On the earnest entreaties of Indian friends, who solicited peace on behalf of the Esopus savages, and on the intercession of the *Maquas*, the *Mahicans*, those of the Highlands, the *Minsis*, the *Katskills*, and other tribes, we concluded a truce with our enemies, who seemed much rejoiced, and solicited us to come in person and conclude a treaty. We came with our friends, yet those of Esopus hang back. They come not to us, nor speak one word of peace. Ye see clearly that it is not our fault. Brothers: The Esopus savages play the fool with you, as well as with us.

"Brothers: Our station will not permit us to remain here in uncertainty, any longer. Even ye are tired with waiting,

---

[1] The chiefs present on this occasion were: *Mohawks*, Adogbegnewalquo, Requesecade, Ogknekelt; *Mahicans*, Aepjin, Aupamut; *Katskill*, Kefe-weig, Machacknemenu; *Minsis*, Onderis Hocque, Kaskongeritschage; *Wappingers*, Isseschahya, Wisachganio; *Hackinsacks*, Oritany, Carstangh; *Staten island*, Warehan.—*O'Callaghan*, II, 419.

[2] Stuyvesant carefully avoided allusion to the immediate cause of the war, which had already been fixed against the Dutch.

and are as willing to depart as we. We request you to remember these our words. Communicate them to all the other sachems our brothers, and to all the Indians our friends, and tell them, as we have done before, that they must not meddle with the Esopus savages, nor suffer them to live among them. And now tell the Esopus savages we will yet wait till evening.

"Brothers: When yonder sun goes down, we depart if they be not here."

The sachems received this address with alarm, and immediately sent out messengers to the Esopus chiefs, urging them to attend the council. Towards evening Kaelcop, Sewackenamo, Nasbabowan, and Pemmyraweck appeared before the gate of the village. Immediately on their arrival, a grand council of all the inhabitants of Esopus, both Christians and Indians, was held. The Esopus sachems and the sachems of the tribes in attendance, and the villagers, being seated " under the blue sky of heaven," Stuyvesant signified that he was ready to hear the Esopus chiefs. Whereupon Onderis Hocque, of the *Minsis*, arose and thus addressed the assembly:

"The Indians of Esopus complained to us that they were involved in a heavy war with the Dutch. We answered them, 'Why did ye begin it? It is all your own fault, we cannot, therefore, help you in your necessity; but we shall intercede in your behalf, and do all in our power to obtain for you peace.' We have now brought a present, in return for that with which they solicited our assistance for a peace, which we now request in their behalf. If they cannot obtain it now, those of Esopus must return home weeping."

Stuyvesant replied: " Out of respect for the intercession of all our friends here present, we consent to a peace, if the *Mohawks* and *Minsis*, and all the other chiefs will be security that it shall be faithfully observed."

The *Mohawk* chief, Adogbegnewalquo, then addressed the Esopus chiefs: " The whole country is now convened in behalf of you, who began this quarrel, to procure you peace.[1] If

---

[1] At a later period the Mohawks considered the causes of the Esopus war, and reported that "all their zaakemaakers (sachems) lay the cause of the war on us," the Dutch, and this was also the verdict of the Katskill Indians.— *O'Callaghan*, II, 396.

this be once concluded, break it not again. If ye do break it and treat us with contempt, we shall never again intercede for you."

The *Minsi* sachem, Onderis Hocque, then addressed the Esopus sachems : " Ye must not renew this quarrel; neither kill horse nor cow, nor steal any property. Whatever ye want, ye must purchase or earn. Live with the Dutch as brothers. Ye cause us and the *Mohawks* great losses. This is not your land. It is our land. Therefore repeat not this,[1] but throw down the hatchet. Tread it so deep into the earth that it shall never be taken up again." He then presented them with a white belt, and, turning to the Dutch, he warned them not to renew this trouble, nor to beat the Esopus Indians in the face and then laugh at them. Then taking an axe from the Esopus sachem, he cast it on the ground, and trampled it in the earth saying, " Now they will never commence this quarrel anew."

Sewackenamo, the Esopus sachem, then arose and addressed the assembly : " The hatchet have we permitted to be taken from our hands ; and to be trodden in the ground. We will never take it up again."

At the conclusion of these ceremonies, Stuyvesant submitted the following as the conditions of the treaty :

" 1. All hostilities shall cease on both sides, and all injuries shall be mutually forgiven and forgotten.

" 2. The Esopus Indians, in compensation of damages, promise to transfer to the director-general all the lands of Esopus, and to directly depart thence without being permitted to return thither to plant

" 3. Further, the director-general promises to pay for the ransom of the captive Christians eight hundred schepels of maize, the half next harvest when the maize is ripe, the other half, or its value, in the harvest of the following year.

" 4. The Esopus Indians promise that they will keep this peace inviolate, and will not kill any more of our horses, cattle or hogs. Should such occurrence happen, then the chiefs oblige themselves to pay for it, or by refusal, that one of them shall remain arrested until the killed animal shall be paid for or made

[1] *Ante*, p. 67.

good; while the director-general, on his side, promises that the Dutch shall not do them any harm.

" 5. If the Dutch kill an Indian, or an Indian kill a Dutchman, war shall not be commenced on that account. Complaint thereof shall first be made, and he who committed the murder, shall be delivered to be punished as he deserves.

" 6. The Esopus Indians shall not approach the Dutch plantations, houses, or dwellings, armed; but may go and trade, unarmed as before.

" 7. Whereas the last war owes its origin to drinking, no Indians shall be permitted to drink brandy or any spirituous liquors, in or near any Dutch plantations, houses, or concentrations, but shall do it in their country or deep in the woods, at a great distance.

" 8. In this peace shall be included, not only the aforesaid tribes, but all others who are in friendship with the director-general, and among others, by the chiefs of Long island, Tapansaugh, with all their Indians; and if any act of hostility be committed against them, then the director-general engages himself to assist them.[1]

" 9. The aforesaid chiefs (the *Mohawks*, *Minsis* and others already named) as mediators and advocates of the Esopus nation, remain securities, and engage themselves that it shall be kept inviolate; and if any infraction be committed by the Esopus Indians, they engage themselves to assist the Dutch to subdue them.

" Thus done and concluded, near the concentration of Esopus, under the blue sky of heaven, in the presence of the Hon. Martin Kregier, burgomaster of the city of Amsterdam in New Netherland; Oloff Stevensen van Cortland, old burgomaster; Arent van Curler, commissary of the colonie of Rensselaerswyck, and all the inhabitants of Esopus, both Christians and Indians, on the 15th of July, 1660."

The day was far spent before the negotiations opened, and the shades of twilight had deepened into the night ere the ceremonies were concluded. The proposals submitted by Stuyvesant were accepted, the sachem, Sewackenamo, declaring, in

[1] *Ante*, p. 68.

the customary language of his people, that their friendship with the Dutch should last as long as the sun and moon gave light; as long as the stars should shine in the firmament, and the rivers flow with water. But before this conclusion, he had asked the director for the return of his kindred. Stuyvesant, who had already disposed of the prisoners in his hands, replied that they must be considered "as dead." The answer deeply grieved the sachem, the memory of their banished brethren was graven on the hearts of his people. But though sufferers by the war, their losses were not without some compensation. Among the prisoners held by them was the son of Evert Pels, one of the men who had led the midnight foray upon them. Just as he was being bound to the stake of torture, the incident which gave to American history the name of Pocahontas had its counterpart. The daughter of a chief stepped forward, in accordance with the customs of her people, and adopted the trembling captive as her own. In the depths of the forest he became her husband, and when the delivery of prisoners came, she was " unwilling to part with him or he with her." Adopted by the tribe, he returned with them to the wilderness, content to share their fortunes and their freedom.

Meanwhile affairs at Fort Orange wore a threatening aspect. In their greedy grasping for furs, a class of what were called runners had sprung up, who penetrated the woods to meet the Indians before they reached the town and secure their peltries. Their remuneration depended on the amount of property they secured for their principals, and to increase their gains they often had recourse to violence, wresting from the Indians their property against their will, after inflicting on them, in addition, personal injuries. The evil continued, despite the efforts of the authorities to correct it, until the *Mohawks* made complaint and threatened to break their treaty and leave altogether, adding, that unless the practice was discontinued, " perhaps matters might terminate as at Esopus." Stuyvesant, finding that no enforcement of law could be secured at the hands of the Beaverwyck traders, sent La Montagne thither with an armed force to patrol the woods and prosecute offenders. On the 22d of July, he went thither himself to meet a delegation of *Seneca* chiefs.

The proceedings of the conference [1] illustrate the nature of the alliance which at that time existed between the confederacy and the Dutch, as well as the relations of the former with the Esopus clans and the *Mahicans*. The *Seneca* speaker made a long harangue, in which he stated his complaint against the runners and the difficulty experienced by the Indians in negotiating the sale of their beavers without restraint, and demanded their ancient freedom of trade. They would no longer submit to being locked up by the Dutch, or kicked by those who wished to have their beavers, until "we know not where our eyes are." Several years ago, they had visited the Manhattans, and though they had offered presents, they received no answer; "no, not even one pipe of tobacco;" and they felt now as if they were about "to run against a stone." Still, they would make a few requests. They were involved in a heavy war with the French Indians and the *Minsis*, and could not obtain either powder or ball without beavers. "A brave warrior ought to have these for nothing."

"You are," continued the orator, "the chiefs of the whole country. We all look to you. We ask a piece of cloth for a beaver, and that it may be understood and henceforward be a rule, that we shall receive thirty yards of black and sixty yards of white zeawan for one beaver. Ye have been sleeping hitherto. With these three beavers we now open your eyes. We require sixty handsful of powder for one beaver. We have a vast deal of trouble collecting beavers through the enemy's country. We ask to be furnished with powder and ball. If our enemies conquer us, where will ye then obtain beavers?

"Ye have included us and the *Mohawks*, and the *Mahicans* in the peace of Esopus. Set now at liberty the Indians ye have taken prisoners there. We are sometimes obliged to pass by that path. It is good that brothers live together in peace. The French Indians meet the *Mahicans* near the Cohoes. This we regret. Brothers: We are united by a chain; ye too ought to mourn. This our speech is designed merely to rouse you from your slumbers. We shall return next spring to receive your conclusions. Warn the Dutch not to beat the Indians; otherwise they will say, 'We know nothing of this.'"

[1] *O'Callaghan*, II, 421, etc.

Stuyvesant replied, that when the chiefs were, "for the first time at the Manhattans, some two or three years ago," the tobacco was forgotten, but a roll would now be given to them to make them remember their agreement when they returned to their own country; that he had "made peace with the Indians at Esopus, at the solicitation of the *Mohawks*, the *Mahicans*, and other friends," so that they might use in safety the rivers and the roads; that as they had thanked him for making that peace, he solicited that they should "make peace with the *Minsis* and cultivate it," that the Dutch "might use the road to them in safety;" that he would now give them a whole keg full of powder, but that it "ought not to be used against the *Minsis*," but against the distant enemies from whom they captured the beaver; that he had forbidden the Dutch to maltreat any of the Indians, and that if the latter caught them doing so, they were at liberty "to beat them on the head until it could no longer be seen where their eyes stood." The price of cloth, however, he could not regulate, as it was brought from "beyond the great lake." With these assurances the chiefs departed to renew their conflict with their savage foes.

Three years of tranquillity succeeded the peace of 1660, during which the settlement at Esopus continued to increase in population. A new village was organized on the north-eastern portion of the "great plot," and the ronduit,[1] at the mouth of the Walkill completed. The Indians, however, were far from being satisfied with their Dutch neighbors. The new village was on land which they had not given to the Dutch; the new fort boded them no good, and the sting inflicted, by sending their brethren to exile and slavery, rankled in their breasts, and threats of vengeance were again heard. To quiet them Stuyvesant instructed the magistrates to announce that he would soon visit Esopus, give them presents and renew the peace; but this promise he failed to fulfill with that promptness that was necessary to satisfy the Indians of his sincerity. On the 5th of June, the promise was renewed, but the Indians still doubted, and replied that "if peace was to be renewed with them, the

---

[1] The location of this fort is supposed to have been at the place still bearing the aboriginal name of Ponckokie.

honorable herr director-general should, with some unarmed persons, sit with them in the open field, without the gate, as it was their custom to meet unarmed when renewing peace or conducting other negotiations.[1]

Without waiting for a reply to this condition, the Indians attacked the settlement, on the 7th of June, and, with tomahawk and fire-brand, executed the work of death. On the morning of that day, the settlers went forth to their fields as usual. About noon, bands of Indians entered the gates of both villages, and scattered themselves among the houses, ostensibly for the purposes of trade. Suddenly they attacked the inhabitants of the new village, and destroyed the buildings. "Some people on horseback" escaped and reached the old village, "crying out, ' The Indians have destroyed the new village!'" This was the signal to the Indians to attack the old village; the war whoop rang out, and the people were murdered "in their houses with axes and tomahawks, and by firing on them with guns and pistols." Women and children were seized and carried off prisoners; houses were plundered, and men, rushing to the defense of their families, were shot down by Indians concealed in their own dwellings. To aid in the work of destruction, the Indians set fire to the village on the windward side. The flames spread rapidly; but when at their height, the wind suddenly changed to the west and prevented further devastation. A rally of the inhabitants was now effected by the energy of Domine Bloom. The gun at the mill-gate was cleared and discharged with effect, and the settlers coming in from the fields, soon drove the Indians out. By evening all was still again, and the bereaved inhabitants kept mournful watch, during the night, along the bastions and curtains. Twenty-one lives were lost, nine persons were wounded, and forty-five carried off captives. The new village was "entirely destroyed, except a new uncovered barn, one rick, and a little stack of seed," and in the old village of Wiltwyck twelve houses were burned.[2] Writes Bloom,[3] of the scene after the Indians had retreated: "There lay the burnt and slaughtered bodies, together with those wounded by bullets and

[1] *Documentary History*, IV, 39.
[2] *Documentary History*, IV, 42, 44.
[3] *Documentary History*, III, 962.

axes. The last agonies and the moans and lamentations of many were dreadful to hear. I have been in their midst, and have gone into their houses and along the roads, to speak a word in season, and that not without danger of being shot by the Indians. The burnt bodies were most frightful to behold. A woman lay burnt, with her child at her side, as if she were just delivered, of which I was a living witness. Other women lay burnt also in their houses. The houses were converted into heaps of stones, so that I might say with Micah, 'We are made desolate ;' and with Jeremiah, ' A piteous wail may go forth in his distress.' The Indians have slain in all twenty-four souls in our place and taken forty-five prisoners."

The official record conveys in simple language a picture which leaves to the imagination but little office. Killed " in front of his house," " in his house," " on the farm," " burnt with her lost fruit," " burnt in her house," are but repeated in forms of detail until the blackened villages are again presented in the presence of the pitiless massacre, and the wails of the dying and the cries of the captives fade away in the wilderness. It was a terrible massacre ; but was it not terribly provoked ?

The fate of the redoubt was not known. On the morning of the 10th, ten soldiers were commanded to ride down and ascertain its condition. They returned with the statement that the Indians had not been seen there ; that fugitives from the new village had reached there, but the soldiers had not dared to venture to the assistance of the settlers. On the 16th, a troop of soldiers was sent to the redoubt to bring up ammunition and to convey letters to be dispatched to Fort Amsterdam for assistance. This company was attacked, on its return, at the first hill, and the skirmishing continued until after passing the second hill. One of the soldiers was killed and six were wounded ; the remainder reached Wiltwyck with their wagons and ammunition.

Immediately on the receipt of the dispatches which had been sent to him, Stuyvesant sent a commission to Fort Orange, to raise a loan, engage volunteers, and invite from the *Mahicans*, the *Mohawks* and the *Senecas*, the assistance which they had promised, under the treaty of 1660, in case of a revolt. The commissioner, however, found that the *Mahicans* and the *Mohawks* were at war, and that the *Senecas* had taken the field against the *Minsis*. From them no concerted action could be expected, while the people of Beaverwyck were in alarm lest the assistance which they had rendered to the *Senecas* should recoil upon their own heads. " The farmers fled to the patroon's new fort, Cralo, at Greenbush; the plank fence which inclosed Beaverwyck, and the three guns mounted on the church, were put in order; and Fort Orange, with its nine pieces of artillery, was prepared against an attack." [1]

Meanwhile a reenforcement of forty-two men, under command of Ensign Niessen, was sent from Fort Amsterdam to Wiltwyck, and measures taken to enlist a more considerable force. On the 26th, Burgomaster Martin Kregier, with additional men and a force of forty-six Long island Indians, was sent forward, and on the 4th of July, assembled at Wiltwyck in a general council of war. A few days after, five *Mohawk* and *Mahican* chiefs arrived from Fort Orange, on whose mediation a portion of the Dutch captives were restored; but to proposals for peace the Indians would not listen unless they were paid " for the land, named the Great Plot," and rewarded with presents at their Shawangunk castle within ten days. Scouting parties were then sent out by the Dutch, who succeeded in bringing in a few prisoners, from whom it was ascertained that the Indians had fallen back to their castle; that this castle was " defended by three rows of palisades, and the houses in the fort encircled by thick cleft palisades with port holes in them and covered with the bark of trees;" that in form it was quadrangular, but that the angles were " constructed between the first and second rows of palisades," the third row of palisades standing " full eight feet off from the others towards the interior;" and that the whole stood " on the brow of a hill " surrounded by tableland.[2]

An expedition for the reduction of this castle was at once organized, consisting of " ninety-one men of Kregier's company; thirty men of Lieutenant Stillwell's company; Lieutenant Couwenhoven with forty-one Long island Indians," acting under

[1] *Ante*, p. 60; Brodhead, I, 711.   [2] *Documentary History*, IV, 49. Appendix.

their treaty of 1656; six Manhattan Indians; thirty-five volunteers from the settlers, "and seven of the Honorable Company's negroes," with "two pieces of artillery and two wagons." The expedition started on the night of the 26th of July, under the guidance of Rachel la Montagne, who had been taken prisoner on the 7th and escaped; but she soon lost the trail, and the force was compelled to bivouac "until day-break," when the right road was found, and the march resumed. The progress was slow, however; "much stony land and hills" intervened; long swamps and frequent kils compelled halts and the construction of bridges, and mountain passes obliged the hauling of "wagons and cannon up and down with ropes." When about six miles from the castle, the expedition halted and one hundred and sixteen men were sent forward to surprise it. This force soon captured a squaw in a corn-field, who told them that the Indians had deserted the fort two days before. About six o'clock the entire expedition reached its destination, but found no foe to contest possession.

On the morning of the 28th, the captive squaw having informed them that the Indians had fallen back into the mountains with their prisoners, a company of one hundred and fifteen men started in search of them. The place where they were supposed to be was that from which Rachel Montagne had escaped, but when it was reached it was found that "they had left that place also." The Indian squaw could not tell them where her people had gone, but pointed out a mountain some miles distant where she thought they might be found, but the march thither was also fruitless. The squaw then pointed out another mountain, but as the Dutch had had quite enough of marching, and as it had become apparent that the Indians were fully advised of their movements, they returned to the castle. In the afternoon the corn-fields were cut down, and the maize and beans, which had been preserved in pits, were destroyed. Three days were spent in ravaging the country. "Nearly one hundred morgens (two hundred and fifteen acres) of maize" were cut down, and "above a hundred pits of corn and beans" burned. On the morning of the 31st, the castle and all the houses were set on fire, "and while they were in full blaze," the Dutch marched out in good order, and returned to Wiltwyck.

The settlers now engaged in harvesting their grain, and the soldiers guarded them while at work, which was prosecuted day and night. Rumors of another attack were rife. One Davids arrived from Manhattan, with a letter from Couwenhoven, who had been sent down to the Dans-kammer in a sloop to negotiate with the Indians, and who wrote that four hundred men were preparing to attack the fort; that the Indians "who lay there about on the river side made a great uproar every night, firing guns and *kinte-kaying*, so that the woods rang again." Davids himself had been on shore and slept one night with the Indians, who had four captives with them, one of whom, a female, informed him that the Indians were in force watching the reapers on the Great plot, and waiting opportunity to attack them.

Couwenhoven continued his negotiations, and on the 20th of August, brought up a woman and a boy whom he had redeemed. His sloop was furnished with supplies and returned to the Danskammer, and instructions issued to him to continue his efforts for the release of the captives; that failing in this, he should seize as many Indians as possible, "either on land, or by inducing them, with fair words," to trust themselves on his vessel. If he could do no better, if the Indians came thither with their captives, he was instructed to "endeavor to detain them on shore" "by means of intoxicating liquors," or by such other mode as he should deem expedient, until word could be conveyed to the fort, and arrangements made to surprise and seize them." The mission was not successful. The Indians took all the powder and brandy which were offered them, and called for more; but, beyond two children, no prisoners were released by them. To aid him, Couwenhoven employed a *Wappinger* sachem to visit them, "but when he had been two or three days with them in their new fort, two *Mohawks* and one *Minsi* came there with sewan and a long message, which rendered them so ill disposed towards him that they caused him to depart."

Kregier now determined to resume the offensive. On the 30th a council of war was called, at which it was "resolved and concluded to attack, with one hundred and twenty men, the Indians who reside in their new fort, about four hours farther than their first fort." The expedition started on the afternoon of September 3d, a young *Wappinger* prisoner acting as guide, under a promise of freedom, and Davids as interpreter. Considerable difficulty was experienced in the march, the streams being swollen and heavy rains prevailing. On the 5th, about noon, the first maize field was reached, and two squaws and a Dutch woman discovered gathering corn. Passing these without alarming them, the fort was discovered about two o'clock, " situate on a lofty plain." The force was divided for the purpose of surprise, but discovery was made by a squaw, " who sent forth a terrible scream, which was heard by the Indians," who rushed from the fort, on which they were at work, to their houses to secure their arms. From thence they sprang into their corn-fields which bordered the kil, and in almost a moment of time were on the opposite bank of the stream, where they courageously returned the Dutch fire. They soon retreated however, having lost their chief, Papequanaehen, and fourteen warriors, four women and three children killed ; and thirteen prisoners, " men and women, besides an old man," who, after accompanying his captors about half an hour, would go no further, and who was then taken aside and given " his last meal." Twenty Dutch prisoners were recovered, among whom was Mrs. DuBois and her children, around whose captivity tradition has thrown the story that at the time of the attack preparation was being made for her sacrifice at the stake, which was only delayed by the pleasure with which the Indians listened to the death-song which she chanted.[1] Unfortunately for the tradition, the Indians, at the time of the attack, were not constructing sacrificial fires or listening to death songs, but were completing their fort, which is described as " a perfect square with one row of palisades set all around, being about fifteen feet above and three feet below ground," with angles " of stout palisades, all of them almost as thick as a man's body, having two rows of port-holes, one above the other." Two of these angles were

---

[1] Record of the family of Louis Du Bois, 15 ; *Collections of the Ulster Historical Society*, vol. 1, part i, 44.

finished, and, when surprised, the Indians "were busy at the third angle." The Dutch found plunder in abundance, such as bear skins, deer skins, blankets, elk hides, etc., sufficient indeed to have well filled a sloop. Twenty-five guns were found, about twenty pounds of powder, thirty-one belts and strings of wampum, and indeed, all the movable wealth of the fugitives. Everything was destroyed except the ripening maize, and laden with spoil, and cheered by the gladness of the rescued captives, the expedition started for Wiltwyck. On the march one of the Indian children died, and its body was thrown into the creek; Indians were seen hovering around, but no attack was made, and on the 7th, about noon, the fort was reached.

The Indians, meanwhile, retreated to the Minnisink country. The loss which they had suffered was severe indeed, but it had fallen upon a single chieftaincy, of whom it is said " not more than twenty-seven or twenty-eight warriors, fifteen or sixteen women and a few children survived," and that these were " without houses or huts." [1] The confederated chieftaincies, however, " showed no signs of submission," and a new expedition was sent out against them. This expedition consisted of a force of one hundred and two soldiers, forty-six *Marsapequas* and six freemen. Leaving Wiltwyck on the 1st of October, it arrived at the castle destroyed on the 2d. The Indians had, meanwhile, returned to it and thrown the bodies of their dead comrades into five pits, from which " the wolves had rooted up and devoured some of them. Lower down on the kil four other pits were found containing bodies; and further on, three Indians with a squaw and child that lay unburied and almost wholly devoured by the ravens and the wolves." A terrible picture of desolation was spread out on either hand, where but a month before the Indian lords had exulted in their strength. The Dutch completed the work of destruction. The remains of the castle were pulled down, the wigwams burned, and all the

---

[1] O'Callaghan says the Indians were virtually destroyed, but the facts do not warrant the conclusion. In the attack of 1659, "the savages, estimated at four or five hundred warriors, harassed the Dutch day and night;" in that of 1663, "their numbers were estimated at about two hundred." Their losses subsequently could not have reduced them to the sixty stated. The Dutch had no confidence in such a state of facts, for they relaxed none of their vigilance.

maize which had been left was cut up and cast into the kil. Thence marching down the kil, " several large wigwams " were found, as well as " divers maize plantations," which were also destroyed. The expedition then returned to Wiltwyck.

Negotiations for the release of the captives still remaining in the hands of the Indians were again opened. On the 5th of November, one of the chiefs agreed to return them in ten days, for which purpose a truce was granted by Couwenhoven, whose sloop remained at the Dans-kammer. On the 7th, two children were brought in by a *Wappinger* chief, who accompanied them as a friend and who promised to bring in a captive woman whom he had purchased. This woman he brought in on the 13th, and received in exchange a *Wappinger*, called Splitnose, and one of the captive squaws and her child. On the 29th, the *Wappinger* again appeared and after satisfying himself that of the Indians in the hands of the Dutch none had died, said that six of the captives held by the Indians were then at the river side ; that the seventh had been sent for, and that all would be restored in three days ; but he was unable to redeem his promise. On the 2d of December he brought up two children, and stated that of the remaining five, three were in the hunting grounds and he could not find them, while the other two were detained by a sick squaw. He would, however, return them as soon he could obtain them, for which purpose he had already purchased Albert Heyman's oldest daughter. Whether the promise was fulfilled or not does not appear.

In this condition matters remained until the spring of 1664, when the Amsterdam chamber instructed Stuyvesant to continue the war until the Indians were exterminated. But Stuyvesant had on his hands a controversy with the English towns on Long island, in which was involved the jurisdiction of the West India Company, and was under the necessity of husbanding his strength for emergencies in which he might possibly be placed. Besides, wars were pending between the *Mohawks* and the *Mahicans* on the east, and the *Senecas* and the *Minsis* on the south, destroying trade and threatening to involve the Dutch settlements in the common destruction. Under the

[1] *Documentary History*, IV, 80, 81.

circumstances he deemed it prudent to entertain the solicitations of the neighboring chiefs for the establishment of peace with the Esopus cantons, especially as it was rumored that the English were encouraging the *Wappingers* and other tribes to unite in the general revolt.

Sending an invitation to the Esopus sachems and their friends to meet him in council at Fort Amsterdam, a large delegation assembled there, and the customary preliminaries being disposed of, Sewackenamo, sachem of the *Warranawonkongs*, arose, and calling several times in a loud voice on his God, BACHTAMO, prayed unto him to conclude something good with the Dutch, and that the treaty about to be formed, in the presence of the sachems assembled,[1] should be like the stick he grasped in his hand, firmly united, the one end to the other. Sigpekenano, a Long island chief, expressed his joy that peace was about to be concluded, and that the clan he represented was to share in its provisions. He hoped it would be a peace as firm and as compact as his arms, which he folded together; and then, presenting his right hand to the director, added: " What I say is from the fullness of my heart; such is my desire and that of all my people."

The next day (May 16) Stuyvesant submitted the treaty. By its terms all that had passed was to be forever forgotten and forgiven. The land already given to the Dutch as an indemnity, and now again " conquered by the sword," including the two Shawangunk castles, became the property of the Dutch; nor were the Indians to return thither to plant, nor to visit the village of Wiltwyck, nor any remote settlement, with or without arms. They were permitted, however, to plant near their new castle, and for the then present year only by their old castle, where they had already planted some seed. To prevent collisions in the future no Indian was to approach places where the Dutch farmers were pursuing agricultural labor, nor visit the village or the residences of the settlers. They might, however, trade at

---

[1] The chiefs in attendance were: *Esopus*, Sewackenamo, Onackatin, Powsawag; *Wappinger*, Tsees-sagh-gaw; *Kitchawan*, Megetsewacks; *Haverstraw*, Sessegehout; *Weckquaesgeeks* Sawanacoque; *Hackinsacks*, Oritany; *Staten Island*, Matheno; *Marsepeqau*, and *Reckheweck*, Slegpekenano, brother of Tackapousha, with twenty others of different chieftaincies acting in the capacity of embassadors.

the redoubt, in parties of three canoes at a time, by sending a flag of truce beforehand to give notice of their approach. For their accommodation on such occasions, a house was to be built beyond the creek, where they could leave their arms. Should a Dutchman kill an Indian, or an Indian a Dutchman, war was not to be declared; but a complaint was to be lodged against the murderer, who should be hanged in the presence of both the contracting parties. All damages by the killing of cattle, or injury of crops, were to be paid for, and the treaty annually ratified by the exchange of presents. For the faithful observance of the treaty the Hackinsack and Staten island sachems became sureties on the part of the Esopus sachems, and were bound to cooperate against either party who should violate its terms.

The signing of the treaty was announced by a salute from Fort Amsterdam, and caused universal satisfaction. In special commemoration of the event, Stuyvesant proclaimed a day of general thanksgiving, to be held throughout the province on the 31st of May. To still further strengthen the position of the Dutch, he sent a commission to the *Soquatucks*[1] to negotiate a peace between them and the *Mohawks*, for which purpose a conference was held at Narrington and a treaty concluded on the 24th. The day of thanksgiving was a day of peace throughout the settlements of New Netherland.

But the brooding clouds of war were not dispelled. While yet the Esopus conflict was pending, the *Mahicans* had been summoning their clans; the peace of Narrington was broken by the *Abenaquis*, who murdered the *Mohawk* embassadors, "instigated thereto, it is alleged, by the English;" the war was renewed; the *Mahicans* overran the country, killed a number of cattle at Greenbush, and "fired a house at Claverack, belonging to Abraham Staats, in which they burnt his wife and two children" (July 11). "Proceeding, next, in a body one hundred strong, against the *Mohawks*, they gave them battle, but the latter being more numerous, routed their assailants. The *Mohawks*, elated by success, pursued their foe, with whom

---

[1] The record says, "between the Maquaas and the Mahicans and Northern Indians."—*O'Callaghan*, II, 519, note.

they renewed the fight the next morning at break of day, but were repelled with great loss." Filled with alarm, the colonists at Fort Orange sent in hot haste to request the presence and advice of the director; but he had other duties to perform — the guns of the English fleet were echoing over the waters of the bay — a more formidable enemy was knocking at the doors of New Amsterdam.

Indian Inscription on
Rocks at Esopus.

## CHAPTER VII.

THE INDIANS UNDER THE ENGLISH.—TREATIES WITH THE FIVE NATIONS, THE MAHICANS AND THE ESOPUS INDIANS.— THE JESUITS AND THE WAR OF 1689.

THE English, under Richard Nicolls, took possession of Fort Amsterdam on Monday, September 6th, 1664, and immediately changed its name to Fort James. Nicolls was proclaimed deputy governor for the Duke of York, in compliment to whom he directed that the city of New Amsterdam should thenceforth be known as New York. Fort Orange surrendered on the 10th, and its name was changed to Fort Albany, after the second title of the Duke of York. Following this change came a conference with chiefs of the *Mohawks* and *Senecas*, representing the Five Nations, and the conclusion with them, and with the *Mahicans* of New York, of a treaty of peace and alliance, similar to that which had existed with the Dutch. By the terms of this treaty the independence and equality of the nations parties to it, was recognized, while the tribes not in alliance with them, but " under the protection " of, or in treaty with, the English were to be regarded as subjects of the crown, and to sustain, in that relation, the position of citizens for their protection and redress. These facts more clearly appear from its text, which is as follows :

" Articles made and agreed upon the 24th day of September, 1664, in Fort Albany, between Ohgehando, Shanarage, Soachoenighta, Sachamackas of ye *Maquaes;* Anaweed, Conkeeherat, Tewasserang, Aschanoondah, Sachamas of the *Synicks* on the one part, and Col. George Cartwright, in the behalf of Col. Nicolls, governor under his royal highnesse, the Duke of Yorke of all his territories in America, on the other part, as followeth, viz :

" 1. Imprimis. It is agreed that the Indian princes above named and their subjects, shall have all such wares and commodities from the English for the future, as heretofore they had from the Dutch.

" 2. That if any English, Dutch or Indian (under the protection of the English) do any wrong, injury or violence to any of ye said Princes or their subjects in any sort whatever, if they complain to the Governor at New Yorke, or to the officer in chief at Albany, if the person so offending can be discovered, that person shall receive condign punishment and all due satisfaction shall be given; and the like shall be done for all other English Plantations.

" 3. That if any Indian belonging to any of the Sachims aforesaid do any wrong, injury or damage to the English, Dutch or Indians under the protection of the English, if complaint be made to ye Sachims and the persons be discovered who did the injury, then the person so offending shall be punished and all just satisfaction shall be given to any of His Majesties subjects in any colony or other English plantation in America.

" 4. The Indians at Wamping and Espachomy and all below the Manhattans, as also all those that have submitted themselves under the protection of His Majesty, are included in these articles of agreement and Peace.

" In confirmation whereof the parties above mentioned have hereunto sett their hands the day and year above written. Signed, etc."

To the Five Nations proper some special concessions were made, which were included in the following supplemental articles, viz. :

" These articles following were likewise proposed by the same Indian Princes and consented to by Col. Cartwright in behalfe of Col. Nicolls, the 25th September, 1664.

" 1. That the English do not assist the three nations of the Ondiakes (Abenaquis), Pinnekooks, and Pacamtekookes, who murdered one of the Princes of the *Maquaes*, when he brought ransomes and presents to them upon a treaty of peace.[1]

" 2. That the English do make peace for the Indian Princes with the Nations down the River.[2]

" 3. That they may have free trade, as formerly.

---

[1] The Abenequis, or Eastern Indians.   [2] The Minquas, Esopus and Navison clans of Lenapes.

"4. That they may be lodged in houses, as formerly.

"5. That if they be beaten by the three nations above mentioned they may receive accommodation from ye English."[1]

This treaty, to be correctly interpreted, must be considered in connection with the former relations of the Indians to the governments of New Amsterdam and New England. The *Mahicans* proper were under treaty with both the English and the Dutch, but representative cantons immediately on the Hudson held a recognized intercourse with the latter. These were included in the treaty under the terms, "the Indians of Wamping and Espachomy, precisely as were those of Long island, who had recognized treaties, and who were specified " as below the Manhattans;" but the Massachusetts *Mahicans* required no such recognition, the change in the government not having affected the treaty which existed between them and the English. The fact that the treaty was made with representatives of the Five Nations has no significance other than that with them the English had no previous treaty. Whatever special terms there were in its provisions with them were included in the supplemental articles, and these related only to the questions of war and peace pending with tribes with whom the English were under treaty, and in reference to which negotiations were at once opened.[2] The new treaty made no other change in relation to the position of the representative tribes than was necessarily involved in the change of government. This clearly appears from the subsequent records of the commissioners of Indian affairs, in which the *Mahicans* uniformly appear as having not only formed a treaty with the Dutch in 1609, and to have renewed that treaty with the English, but as being " linked together in interest with the Five Nations," and consulted with and treated as allies of the government in the capacity of an independent nation.[3]

[1] *Colonial History*, III, 67.

[2] The war which was pending at the time this treaty was made was instigated by the English.— *O'Callaghan*, II, 519. The governor of New York and the governor of Massachusetts were the parties to the treaty between the *Mohawks* and the *Mahicans*. Governor Lovelace writes to Governor Winthrop, in 1669: "If all my letters arrived in your hands you will find them all of one tenor, viz: the earnest desire of the Maquas to conclude firm peace with the Mohicands."— *New York Assize Record*.

[3] *Colonial History*, IV, 744, 902, etc. In an address to the Massachusetts commis-

But English possession brought with it additional changes in the connection of the Indians with provincial authorities. To the boundary lines of territorial governments, which had already passed through and subdivided the *Mahicans* and the *Lenapes*, court districts and county lines were added. Indians of the same tribal families, who had hitherto been held responsible to and had their treaty relations with different governments and provinces, while consolidated in some respects, were further separated by special assignment to the charge of different court districts. Thus the *Wappingers* and those residing south of the highlands and Long island, had their treaty intercourse with the governor and authorities at New York; those north of the highlands on the east, and north of the highlands and south of the Katskills on the west, including principally the Esopus clans, were placed under the justices at Kingston, and the *Mahicans* on the east and those on Beeren island and north of the Katskills on the west, came directly under the authorities at Albany, at which place the general council-fire was lighted and intercourse held with the Five Nations and the *Mahicans*. While these divisions were the result in part of the established centres of population and treaty intercourse under the Dutch, they subsequently added materially to the disintegration of the river tribes, and gave to them much of that character of independent cantons which has been assumed as representing their political status. From this disintegration the Five Nations escaped, with results to their consolidated recognition which cannot be too highly estimated. That they would have been similar sufferers had they been similarly situated, the records of the negotiations with them after the war of the revolution, are a sufficient indication. Considered only as a whole and treated as a whole, they were a power; but treated with as independent tribes they were shorn of their strength. With them the history of the *Mahicans* and the *Lenapes* repeated itself with fearful emphasis.

The policy adopted by the English was liberal and reasonable, and contributed at least to the temporary improvement of the

---

sioners in 1744, the chiefs used the following language: "We are united with the Six Nations in one common covenant, and this is the belt which is the token of that covenant."

condition of the Indians. The frictions which had prevailed during the Dutch administration were very largely removed by a law declaring that "no purchase of lands from the Indians, after the first day of March, 1665," should be "esteemed a good title without leave first had and obtained from the governor and after leave so obtained;" that purchasers should bring before the governor "the sachem or right owner" of lands which were purchased "to acknowledge satisfaction and payment" for the same, when all the proceedings were to be entered on record and constitute a valid title. "All injuries done to the Indians of what nature soever," were made punishable on complaint and proof in any court, without cost to the complainant, "in as full and ample a manner as if the case had been between Christian and Christian." The contraband trade in fire-arms was broken up, and only those who were licensed were permitted "to sell guns, powder, bullets, lead, shot, or any vessel of burthen or row boat (canoes excepted)." The sale or gift to the Indians of "rum, strong waters, wine and brandy," without license, was forbidden under penalty of "forty shillings for each pint so sold or disposed of." To prevent difficulties arising from cattle straying upon the unfenced lands of the Indians, and to encourage the latter to fence their fields, the colonists were directed to assist them in "felling trees, riving and sharpening rails" and setting posts, allowing "one Englishman to three or more Indians." These reforms were eminently satisfactory to the Indians, although many abuses were subsequently perpetrated by those who were licensed under them. Not less so was the treaty stipulation that the privileges of trade were to be uniform, in all English plantations, to Indians in alliance with the government, and the fact that such alliance secured the friendship of the "great sachem." Tranquillity was soon established, and although the *Mohawks* and the *Mahicans* and *Abenaquis*, at the east, and the *Senecas* and *Minsis*, at the south, continued their struggle, the conflict was not around the centres of civilization. Gradually the *Minsis*, more immediately represented on the Hudson, yielded to the superior advantages possessed by their enemies, or to the inducements which the English offered; while those more remote made common cause with the French.

The annual renewal of the treaty with the Esopus Indians, required by its terms, was delayed until October, 1665, when, as their intercourse in the future was to be with the English, the treaty was rewritten in the English language, with such changes in its terms as the change in government required,[1] as appears from its text:

"An agreement made between Richard Nichols, Esq., Governor, under his Royall Highness the duke of York, and the Sachems and People called the Sopes Indians:

"That no act of hostility shall at any time bee committed on either part, or if any damage shall happen to be done by either party to the Corn, Cattle, Horses, Hoggs, Houses, or any other goods whatever of the other party, from the goods of the other party shall return be given upon demand for the same.

"2. That if any Christian shall wilfully kill an Indyan, or any Indyan a Christian, hee shall bee put to death. And the said Sachems do promise on their part, to bring any such Indyan to the officer in chiefe at the Sopes to receive his punishment there.

"3. That a convenient House shall bee built where the said Indyans may at any time lodge, without the Forts of the said Town, in which House the Indians are to leave their armes, and may come without molestation to sell or buy what they please from the Christians.

"4. That in case any Christian should kill an Indyan, or any Indyan a Christian, the peace shall not be broaken, or any Revenge taken before satisfaction is demanded by the one party and refused by the other, allowing a competent time for the apprehending of the offender, in which case the Indyans are to give Hostage, till the offender is brought to punishment, the said Hostage to be kindly treated and shall receive no other punishment but imprisonment.

---

[1] Compare with synopsis of treaty of 1664. The statement that Nicolls made the treaty the occasion for the purchase of additional lands, apparently indicated by the fifth section, appears to have been the expression in definite terms of the general language of the treaty of 1664, "the lands now conquered by the sword." The original manuscript of the treaty, and the wampum belt which the Indians gave in accepting it, are preserved in the office of the clerk of Ulster county. It was renewed at different periods until the Indians ceased to exist or had entirely removed to the west.

"5. That the said Sachems and their subjects now present do, and in the names of themselves, and their heirs forever, give, grant, alienate and confirm all their right and interest, claim or demand to a certain Parcell of Land, lying and being to the west and south west of a certain creek or River, called by the name of Kahanksen, and so up to the head thereof, where the old Fort was; And so with a direct line from thence through the woods and crosse the Meadows to the Great Hill, lying and being to the west or south west thereof, which Great Hill is to be the true west or south west Bounds of the said Lands. And the said creek called Kahanksen, the north or north east Bounds of the said Lands, herein mentioned, to be given, granted, and confirmed unto the said Richard Nicolls, governor under his Royal Highness, the Duke of York, or his assigns, by the said Sachems, and their subjects, forever, and to hold and enjoy the same as his free land, and Possession against any claim hereafter to bee madee by the said Sachems or their subjects, or any their heirs and successors.

"In token of the aforesaid Agreement, the aforesaid Sachems do deliver two small sticks, and in confirmation thereof, do deliver two more small sticks, to the said Richard Nicholls. And in the name of the Indyans their subjects, one of the subjects do deliver two other round small sticks, in token of their assent to the said agreement. And the said Richard Nicholls does deliver as a present to their Sachems three laced redd coates.

"6. The said Sachems doth engage to come once every year, and bring some of their young People, to Acknowledge every part of this agreement in the Sopes, to the end that it may be kept in perpetual memory.

"7. That all past Injuryes are buried and forgotten on both sides.

"8. That the young Sachem called Ningeerinoe hath Liberty for three years to plant upon a small neck of land, over against a small creek called Choughkanakanoe, unless the said young Sachem be warned off by order to remove, and give place to such Christians as shall have Order from the said Richard Nicolls, or his assignees, to plant there, at which time the said young Sachem is to receive a Blankett, by way of Curtesie, and to remove to the other side of the Creek, without delay, or claiming any future interest thereupon.

" 9. In consideration of the premises, the said Richard Nicolls doth farther give and pay to the said Sachems and their subjects, forty blanketts, twenty Pounds of Powder, twenty knives, six Kettles, Twelve Barrs of Lead, which payment we acknowledge to have received, in full satisfaction, for the premises, and do bind ourselves, our heirs and successors forever, to perform every part of this agreement, without any fraud or reservation of mind; and further, that we will maintain and justify the said Richard Nicolls, or his assigns, in the full and peaceable Possession of the said Tract of Land, Royaltyes and Privileges for ever, against any Nation of Indyans whatsoever, pretending right to the same.

" In testimony whereof we have sett our markes to two several writings, the one to remaine in the hands of the Sopes Sachems, the other upon record, this 7th day of October, 1665."

The parties to the treaty on behalf of the Indians were sachems Onackatin,[1] Naposhequiqua, Senakonama (Sewakanamo), and Shewotin. The signature of Nicolls and of the sachems was witnessed by " Jeremias Van Rensleiar, Philip Pieterson Schuyler, Robert Nedham, S. Salisbury and Edw. Sackville," and by the following " Esopus young men " : Pepankhais, Robin Cinnaman " a Pekoct sachem," Ermawamen, and Rywackus. One of the chieftaincies was apparently without a sachem ; the full number was completed in 1670, when, on the 11th of April, " a new made sachem of the Esopus Indians, named Calcop," appeared before the justices of Ulster and confirmed the agreement.

The *Minsis* proper maintained hostilities until 1675, when they yielded to what Dr Colden denominates " the full play of the warlike genius" of their enemies, but more properly, as already intimated, to the fearful disadvantages under which they were placed by the refusal of the English to supply them with firearms and powder, in accordance with the treaty with the *Senecas* and *Mohawks*, and were made tributary to the *Senecas*. In the east the contest still raged. Peace was made in 1675, but it

---

[1] Oghgotacton; his lands were near the present village of Walden. See appendix.

was one of accommodation on the part of the *Abenaquis* and their allies, many of whom sympathized with King Philip and eagerly shared his fate. Nor were they disheartened when, on the 12th of August, 1676, that great leader gave up his life. In that remarkable struggle for the restoration of the Indians to independence, one of the branches of the formidable alliance, the *Pennacooks*, was crushed and its fugitives, bleeding and torn, sought refuge in the friendly villages of their kindred on the Hudson. Reference has already been made to the immediate subsequent history and organization of these fugitives as the *Schaticooks*.[1] After their settlement, the authorities made no little effort to increase their number by inducing those who had found refuge elsewhere to remove to the lands assigned, and in this were partially successful. At the close of the French war of 1698, and subsequently, these efforts were renewed;[2] meanwhile a very considerable number of them had reached Canada, and were encouraged by the French to invite their brethren of New York, as well as their old *Mahican* allies, to unite with them. The result of these efforts was the organization of what was known as the St. Francis Indians.

Meanwhile an element other than that of war had been introduced to divide the Indian tribes. With the French, religious zeal and commercial ambition walked hand in hand, and the banner of the cross became the pioneer of that of France. No sooner had Champlain discovered the territory of the St.

---

[1] *Ante,* p. 62. The date of this organization, as well as the original classification of the elements of which the *Schaticooks* were composed, is distinctly stated by Earl Bellomont, the governor, in 1698 : " Our Skackoor or river Indians and which river Indians having been formerly driven out of those eastern parts by the people of New England."— *Colonial History,* IV, 380, 715. Colden fixes the date of their settlement as 1672, while one of their chiefs, speaking in 1700, states the occurrence as happening " six and twenty years ago," or in 1674.— *Colonial History,* IV, 744. As there was no war against the New England Indians by which an exodus of this kind would be made necessary prior to the downfall of Philip in 1676, and as the fugitives from that conflict are described by Hubbard as having fled towards Albany, the conclusion is that the *Schaticooks* were no other than the Indians described by him. There was another organization of Schaticooks, composed of New England and Hudson river Indians. They were located on Ten Mile river, so called, in the present county of Dutchess. This organization is particularly described by De Forest (*History Indians of Connecticut,* 407), as having been commenced by one Gideon Manwehu, a Pequot, sometime about 1735, and who succeeded in calling about him a hundred warriors.

[2] *Colonial History,* IV, 380, 715, 744, 902.

Lawrence than he was found declaring, that while the aggrandizement of France was earnestly to be desired, yet "the salvation of a soul was worth more than the conquest of an empire." At his instance, La Carnon, an ambitious Franciscan priest, entered the field as a missionary, and in 1616, penetrated the Mohawk country, passed to the north into the territory of the Wyandots and reached the river of Lake Huron. In 1633, the Society of Jesus succeeded the Franciscans with fifteen missionaries, the history of whose labors is connected with the origin of every established town in the annals of French America; "not a cape was turned, nor a river entered, but a Jesuit led the way."[1] The converts of these missionaries were at first from among the enemies of the Five Nations; the latter regarded them as foes, and in their incursions upon the *Hurons*, spared them not. The fate of the missionary village of St. Joseph and of Fathers Daniel, Lallemand and Brebeuf, and the captivity of Father Jogues, are but types of the toil and sacrifice which attended their labors, and of the heroism with which they met death. The fruit of their efforts was the possession by France not only of New France and Acadia, Hudson's bay and Newfoundland, but a claim to a moiety of Maine, of Vermont, and to more than a moiety of New York, to the whole valley of the Mississippi, and to Texas even, as far as the Rio Bravo del Norte, whither the flag of France followed their footsteps and reared colonies.

The Dutch gave very little attention to the movements of the missionaries, or to the extension of the dominion of France. Intent upon trade and having no ambition to extend their possessions beyond the three rivers which they claimed, the conversion of the Indians scarcely received from them a thought.[2] The missionaries improved their advantage, and in 1654, appeared in the territory of the *Onondagas*, where they found many *Huron* captives who had formerly received their instruction. Missions

---

[1] *Bancroft*, III, 122.

[2] Domine Megapolensis, who came over in 1643, under an agreement with Van Rensselaer, made some effort to learn the *Mohawk* language, with a view to preach to them in their castles, but without much success. A few Indians attended his preaching at Albany, but without understanding a word that he said. The claim that he was the predecessor of Eliot, has very little foundation, and none whatever in the aid which the government extended to him. *Brodhead*, I, 375, 376.

to the *Oneidas* and *Senecas* speedily followed; chapels sprang into existence, and long before the English obtained possession of New Amsterdam, the solemn services of the Roman church were chanted in the heart of their future province. The possession of these privileges, however, was not destined to be permanent. The *Oneidas* murdered three Frenchmen (1657), and the French retaliated by seizing *Iroquois*. Two years later the missionaries had abandoned the country, and the French and the Five Nations were again at war. Finding success hopeless without stronger military support, the aid of the king of France was invited, and scarcely had the English succeeded in planting the flag of St. George on the walls of Fort Orange, ere the colony of New France was protected by a royal regiment, and Courcelles, a veteran French soldier, established as its governor. The missionaries now renewed their work, and reestablished themselves in the territory of the *Senecas* and *Onondagas*, and converted one of the villages of the *Mohawks*.[1]

The progress of the French soon became more formidable. Serious inroads were made on the territory claimed by the English, and the *Iroquois* were gradually yielding to the efforts of the Jesuits. Except in the valor and good faith of the Indians more immediately under English influence, the province had no protection. The Jesuit fathers became spies, and, in 1682, were enabled to advise the governor of Canada, that circumstances had materially changed; that they were now accustomed to the woods, were acquainted with all the roads through them, and that the French could, from Fort Frontenac, fall on the *Senecas* in forty hours and crush them by an unexpected blow.[2] When Colonel Dongan came over, in 1683, as governor of New York, matters wore a threatening aspect indeed. He was under instructions to preserve friendly relations with the French, and besides this, was himself an earnest Catholic; but he was not blind to the danger which menaced the province, or slow to use his power to avert it. Wherever the French priests traveled they set up the arms of France in token of French

---

[1] Although the priests had no little difficulty with the *Mohawks*, they ultimately succeeded in converting the village or castle of Caghnawaga.

[2] *Documentary History New York*, 1, 97.

possession; Dongan gave to his *Iroquois* allies medals showing that they were British subjects, and caused the arms of the Duke of York to be erected in all their castles. The French invited their converts to Canada; Dongan solicited them to remain, and obtained a promise from those who had already gone to return. He would give them lands and priests and built them a church. In the fall of 1686, he sent fifty citizens of Albany and New York to winter with the *Senecas*, and used his influence with the *Mahicans* to join the *Iroquois* in an alliance for mutual defense.

Meanwhile the Duke of York (1685), under the title of James II, had succeeded the sensual Charles II, as king of England. The duke was an intense Catholic, and his elevation gave courage to the Jesuit fathers, who could now ask, with additional force, his aid in extending their work. Dongan appealed to him and endeavored to arouse him to the necessity of protecting the province and of maintaining the alliance with the *Iroquois*. "The Five Nations," said he, "are a bulwark between us and the French and all other Indians. This government has always been, and still is, at a great expense to keep them peaceable and annexed to this government, which is of that moment that upon any occasion I can have three or four thousand of their men upon call." The interests of trade also required this alliance, in his opinion, not less than the security of the English. To this end he asked for Catholic priests in the interests of the English, in order to oblige the French priests to retire to Canada and the "country be divested of the pretense for their presence." But James had already bound himself to Louis XIV in a treaty of neutrality; to that treaty his attention had been called by Louis, on complaint from La Barre, the governor of Canada, and if he had the disposition to aid Dongan, he was under obligations to avoid a rupture with France.

La Barre's administration was not a success. The *Senecas* attacked some French trading canoes, and after organizing a considerable force to proceed against them, he had fallen back without conflict, terrified at the rumor that Dongan had promised them the aid of "four hundred horse and four hundred foot" if they were attacked. The only fruit of his expedition was a treaty which he concluded with the *Onondagas*, *Oneidas* and *Cayugas*, the force of which may be inferred from the fact that only six hours were spent in its negotiation. His subordinates were disgusted at his proceedings, and refused to restrain their " sovereign contempt for the general's person." " His design," says Demeneles, " was to attack the *Senecas*, but instead of showing him any civility, they did not even condescend to come and meet him, and gave an insolent answer to those who proposed it to them. If people had anything to say to them, let them take the trouble to come and meet them." De Lamberville, the Jesuit missionary at Onondaga, alone sustained him. The difficulties of prosecuting war against the *Senecas* were not, in his opinion, properly estimated. The Indians would not be found in their villages or forts, but would prowl everywhere, " killing without if possible being killed." For the conflict they were ready; nay, had received " with joy " the intelligence that they were to be attacked, confident that in such an event they would be able to strip, roast and eat the French. The result of the affair was the removal of La Barre, the appointment of De Denonville as his successor, and the receipt by Dongan of instructions to observe strict neutrality.

The French were fully determined to attempt the destruction of the power of the *Iroquois*. Louis himself was convinced that such a step was necessary. De Denonville had examined the situation thoroughly, and had informed his royal master that the reputation of the French had been " absolutely destroyed " among the Indians, whether friends or enemies, by La Barre's conduct, and that unless this was arrested, nothing could avert a general rebellion, the ruin of trade and the extirpation of the French. War was necessary, too, " for the establishment of religion," which could not otherwise be successfully prosecuted. " Merit in the eyes of God," and the " possession of an empire of more than a thousand leagues in extent," from which " great commercial advantages" would eventually be derived, demanded the effort and the expense which it involved. The king responded with an addition to the French force; gave his entire approval to the war, and, in addition to the means to be employed, advised that prisoners be taken and sent to him for service as galley-slaves.

The work entrusted to Denonville was not long delayed. Treachery was resorted to, to secure prisoners. De Lamberville succeeded in decoying a considerable number of *Iroquois* chiefs into Fort Frontenac, on Lake Ontario, from whence they were removed in irons to Quebec and hurried to France;[1] Indian allies were called in, and arrangements for an aggressive movement consummated. He had no contemptible foe to encounter. " The *Iroquois* force," by his own authority, consisted of " two thousand brave, active men, more skillful in the use of the gun than the Europeans, and all well armed; besides twelve hundred *Mahicans* (Loups), another tribe in alliance with them as brave as they,"[2] to say nothing of the English whom he expected to assist them.

In July, 1687, he marched into the territory of the *Senecas*, and took formal possession " in the name of the king." On his way he was attacked by the *Senecas* with such vigor that he was obliged to bivouac on the field, and witness, without being able to prevent, the tortures which the *Senecas* inflicted on the prisoners who had fallen into their hands. In the morning the *Senecas* retreated, and on reaching their village it was found that they had destroyed it and abandoned their fort. The French cut up the growing corn without molestation, and successfully completed the construction of Fort Niagara. The campaign cost the lives of one hundred Frenchmen, ten French or Catholic Indians, and eighty *Senecas*. The latter appealed to Dongan, who supplied them with powder, lead and arms, and

---

[1] The number taken was twenty-seven, of whom " Taweeratt, the chief warrior of Cayouge," was one.— *Colonial History*, III, 560, 579. Father Millett was charged with being a party to their capture.—*Ib.* 621. The French account is that forty chiefs were taken prisoners, one of whom is called Orehaoué, " one of the most considerable chiefs of their nation."— *Colonial History*, IX, 464. " The general in chief of the entire Iroquois nation." — *Ibid.*, 465.

[2] The cooperation of the *Mahicans* with the *Iroquois* is frequently referred to in the French records, and in language indicative of their importance. The alliance referred to in the text, is spoken of as having existed for some time. In 1674, the *Mahicans* were at war with the *Ottawas*, and the *Senecas* became arbitrators to establish peace. In 1684, it is said " six or seven hundred *Mohegans* were preparing to go to the assistance of the *Iroquois*, as the *Ottawas* were aiding the French." The number of their warriors stated in the text is no doubt exaggerated, but there is no question that they could at any time bring more warriors to the field than the *Mohawks*.— *Colonial History*, IX, 259, 460, 466, etc.

called upon their allies to unite together to defend the territory which France had invaded. In addition to this a special meeting of the council was held at Fort James, and a bill passed for levying a tax of a " penny in the pound out of the estates of the freeholders," to aid in defraying expenses. Palisades were ordered for fortifying Albany and Schenectady, and the Five Nations were requested to send down " their wives, children and old men, lest the French fall upon them in winter; that they who come be settled, some at Katskill, and along the river," where they would be in security and in readiness to assist in the common defense should it be necessary. Every tenth man of the militia was ordered to Albany, and other measures taken for defensive war. " I will do what is possible for me to save the government from the French," said Dongan to De Denonville, " until I hear from the king, my master ;" and " advise Monsieur Denonville to send home all the Christians and Indian prisoners, the king of England's subjects, you unjustly do detain."

Meanwhile the *Senecas* remained on the war path. Dongan had offered his mediation for peace on condition that the captive chiefs should be restored, the fort in the *Seneca* country razed, and the spoils taken from that nation restored. To these propositions De Denonville would not listen. In July, 1688, the *Iroquois* advanced to dictate the terms. Haaskouaun, their chief, with five hundred warriors sat down before Quebec. Twelve hundred warriors remained within call. If in four days the French would concede to Dongan's terms, the place would be spared; 'if not, it would be overwhelmed. The French governor yielded, and on the sixth of September following abandoned Fort Niagara and the possession of the country south of the great lakes. The imprisoned chiefs, however, he did not restore.

In this situation matters remained until January, 1689, when James was driven from the throne of England by William, the Prince of Orange. France espoused the cause of the deposed king, and declared war against England, and on both continents the conflict was opened. Before the formal declaration came, however, the *Iroquois* had resumed hostilities. Visiting Albany in July, they acquainted the magistrates that the French had not returned their chiefs, and that they were resolved to be revenged.[1] From thence they proceeded to Canada, and on the twenty-fifth of August, fifteen hundred in number, they landed on the south side of the island of Montreal, burned the houses, sacked the plantations, and put to the sword all the men, women and children without the fortifications. " In less than an hour, two hundred people met death under forms too horrible for description. Approaching the town of Montreal, they made an equal number of prisoners, and after a severe skirmish became masters of the fort, and of the whole island, of which they remained in possession until the middle of October. In the moment of consternation, De Denonville ordered Fort Frontenac, on Lake Ontario, to be evacuated and razed. From Three Rivers to Mackinaw, there remained not one French town, and hardly even a post."[2]

Anticipating an aggressive movement on the part of the English and their allies, representation had already been made to Louis. Governor Andros, who had succeeded Dongan,[3] promptly declared his determination to regard his Indian allies as " subjects of the crown of England," and the French gave up all hope of detaching them even through the influence of their priests. To retain possession of the territory was their only expectation, coupled with a determination to inflict such injury as they could. Under these instructions Count de Frontenac was appointed governor-general, and with a considerable force landed at Quebec within forty days after the attack of the *Iroquois* on Montreal, and the first news he met, on entering the St. Lawrence, was an account of it. He determined to retaliate, not by marching against the *Iroquois*, but against their English allies who had furnished them with arms and were their supporters.[4] To carry out this determination an expedition was organized to be conducted in three divisions, the first to rendezous at Montreal and proceed towards Fort Orange ; the second, at the Three Rivers and make a descent on

---

[1] *Colonial History*, III, 599.
[2] *Bancroft*, III, 179. *Colonial History*, III, 621.
[3] New York was annexed to New England, under the government of Sir Edmund Andros, in 1688.
[4] Frontenac brought with him, as a peace offering to the *Iroquois*, the chiefs who had been treacherously betrayed and taken to France. They were subsequently restored to their people.

New England, and the third, to proceed by water for the reduction of Fort James. Count de Frontenac was to conduct the land expedition against Fort James, where he was to be met by the fleet under the command of Caffiniere, while the governor, De Callieres, was to conduct the expedition against Albany. The latter expedition left Montreal at the commencement of February, 1690. The point of attack was concealed from the Indian allies, by whom it was accompanied, until the place of destination was nearly reached, when a council was held and the destination announced. The Indians objected, and the conclusion was finally taken to attack Schenectady instead of Albany. Thither the invaders directed their steps, and on the morning of Sunday, February 10th, repeated the massacre by the *Senecas* and their allies at Montreal. The attacking force separated in two divisions, and entered the gates in two directions. At the point of junction, the shrill whoop of the savage burst upon the air, and the implements of death and the blazing torch completed the work of destruction. No house were spared in the town, except one belonging to Major Condre (Sanders), the commandant, who, with his men, surrendered to the French division on the promise of quarter, and that of a widow and her six children, in whose care the French commander, who had been wounded, was placed. The lives of between fifty and sixty persons, old men, women and children, who escaped the fury of the first attack, were spared. Upwards of eighty well built and well furnished houses were destroyed. Sixty men, women and children were killed, and twenty-seven carried away prisoners. A few succeeded in escaping and fled through the snow to Albany, a distance of twenty miles, and gave the alarm. Before the local forces could be rallied and the *Mohawks* and their allies called in, however, the French were far on the retreat. They were pursued by the *Mohawks*, who fell upon their rear and harassed them until they reached Montreal. The second expedition reached Salmon Falls, in New Hampshire, which place was burned; but the attack on New York was abandoned.

The people of New York were divided in sentiment in regard to the claims of William and James. Immediately following the announcement of the accession of William, Jacob Leisler, a captain of the militia, at the instigation of the friends of the Protestant king, took forcible possession of Fort James, in the name of William and Mary, while Nicholson, who had been appointed governor, fled to Europe. It was in the midst of these civil commotions that the atrocities at Schenectady terrified the people and calmed the domestic factions. New York, Massachusetts, and Connecticut united for the reduction of Montreal and Quebec. An expedition by land and water was agreed upon. Sir William Phipps was placed in command of the fleet, and the land forces assigned to the command of General Winthrop of Connecticut. The fleet arrived before Quebec about the middle of October, 1690, but the land forces only penetrated as far as Wood creek, in the present county of Washington, when sickness, want of provisions and dissensions among the officers, compelled a return. In the meantime, Quebec had been strengthened by the French, and bade defiance to the English fleet, which soon returned to Boston.

In 1691, Colonel Sloughter was appointed governor of the province, and, immediately on his arrival, Governor Leisler and his son-in-law Milborne, were arrested and executed for treason. This, with the renewing of the covenant chain with the *Iroquois*, was the only act of his administration, death having suddenly ended his career. His successor was Benjamin Fletcher, under whom, in the succeeding year, the English, with their Indian allies, carried on the war against the French, Capt. John Schuyler making a successful attack on the French settlements beyond Lake Champlain. In February, 1693, Frontenac invaded the *Mohawk* territory, surprised and burned their castles, killed many and took three hundred prisoners. The invasion cost the invaders thirty men, but the *Mohawks* were completely dispersed. The forces at Albany, accompanied by such *Mahicans* as could be rallied, hastened to their relief, pursued the retreating enemy and recovered most of the prisoners. Governor Fletcher reached Albany soon after, and so pleased were the stricken chiefs at the celerity of his movements that they gave to him the flattering title of Lord of the Great Swift

Arrow.[1] The tide of war then rolled along the frontiers of New England, and the settlements at Oyster river in New Hampshire, and Haverhill in Massachusetts, were destroyed, Hatfield and Deerfield, on the Connecticut, shared the same fate. In 1696, Frontenac invaded the territory of the *Onondagas*, but without much success,[2] while Indians in detached bands warred for the respective powers with which they were in alliance. In the year following the war terminated in September, by the peace of Ryswick, and the principal combatants withdrew. Collisions and acts of hostility continued between the *Iroquois* and the allies of the French, however, until two years later. Governor Bellomont was exceedingly anxious to so order the termination of these hostilities that the *Iroquois* should be placed in acknowledged supremacy over their foes, and the French governor was not less mindful of his own and the interests of his allies. The latter triumphed, and both parties laid down the hatchet at his feet on terms of equality. Through a feeling springing in part from this result, and in part from the antagonisms which had been engendered by the part which they had taken in the war, the assembly of New York, in 1700, made a law for hanging every Catholic priest that should come voluntarily into the province.

The part which the *Mahicans* and *Minsis* of the Hudson took in this war, is only incidentally stated. The alliance between the *Iroquois* and the former, was of no little magnitude in the opinion of the French, as has already been stated. That alliance appears to have been suggested by the *Mohawks*.[3] In reference to the more detached bands, the *Mohawk* speaker in the conference of 1683, advised: " The *Schahook* Indians, in our opinion, are well placed where they are — they are a good guard;

---

[1] These castles were three in number, and were destroyed on the 7th and 8th of February.— *Colonial History*, IV, 16, 20, 22. The *Mohawks* never forgot their punishment, but in after years repeated that they knew what it was " to be whipped and scourged by the French."

[2] *Bancroft*, III, 170.

[3] At a subsequent period the aid of the *Mahicans* was asked by the council at Onondaga. " Arnout Vielle, from Onondaga, Feb. 18, 1694-5, brought this message : The whole Five Nations send seven hands of wampum to inform the *Mahikanders*, or River Indians, that the Count Frontenac would fall upon the *Onondagas* in the spring. They desired the assistance of three hundred Christians, with as many River Indians and *Mahikanders* as can be got together."—*Colonial History*, IV, 123.

they are our children, and we shall take care that they do their duty. But you must take care of the Indians below the town so that they may be of more service to you. We advise you to bring all the river Indians to be under your subjection at Albany to be ready on all occasions." A portion of the *Minsis*, who had settled among the *Ottawas*,[1] had joined the French alliance. Governor Dongan asked the aid of the *Iroquois* to bring them home. " One of them," said he, " is worse than six of the others, therefore all means must be used to bring them home." The confederates accepted the mission, and induced a considerable number to return.[2] Governor Andros was not less positive in his personal overtures to them. When he visited the province in May, 1688, he invited their aid, and promised to give lands to those who might desire to locate their families.[3] At a meeting of the council, September 17th, 1689, it was ordered that Robert Sanders use his endeavors to procure the " Indians of the Long Reach, Wawyachtenok and Esopus to come up here (Albany) to lie out as scouts upon the borders of this county," and that the " Justices of the Peace of Ulster county assist him in persuading the Indians." On the 22d of February, 1690, it was ordered by the same body, " that the Indians living at Beere island and Katskill be persuaded to go and live at Katskill,[4] and be ready on all occasions to be employed as scouts or otherwise." In April following, the *Tappans*

---

[1] The *Ottawas* occupied the southwestern part of Canada at this time. They were almost constantly at war with the Five Nations, and also with the *Mahicans*. Their relations with the Esopus *Minsis* were intimate and friendly, and many of them came thither to trade with the English at Kingston. In 1691, a company of them, while visiting the Esopus country, fell victims to the small-pox.— *Colonial History*, III, 776, 778. In the *Land Papers*, official record is made that Punganis, whose land was near Walden, in Orange county, pledged the same to Robert Sanders as security for the payment of £70, that he had then (1689) been absent with the *Ottawas* for ten years, and that his brother " intending to go to the wars," wished Sanders to keep the land " till his brother pays him for it."—*Land Papers*, III, 22.

[2] *Colonial History*, III, 808.

[3] "Several Indians living on both sides Hudson's river came to His Excellency, some at Albany, and others at a town nigh the river called Kingstone; he commanded them to demean themselves quietly towards the Christians their neighbors, invited such as were gone elsewhere to return with their families, and that if they wanted land it should be laid out for them in convenient places."—*Colonial History*, III, 568.

[4] On a map accompanying *Proud's History of Pennsylvania*, *Katsban* is applied to a village immediately north of Saugerties creek, and *Katskill* to a village at the junction of the *Kader's* and the *Katskill* creek, west of the present village of Katskill. These two villages perhaps explain the text.

reported that they had sent twelve men to the *Senecas*, and should send more," and the *Kicktawancs* and other Westchester families stated that they had sent six of their number.[1] The *Schaticook* Indians were actively employed. In addition to their services as scouts, a large number of them joined in the pursuit of the French after the destruction of Schenectady, and also in the several expeditions against Canada. When the expedition under Winthrop returned, Captain John Schuyler voluntarily embarked, at Wood creek, with a company consisting of " twenty-nine English soldiers, one hundred and twenty Mohawk and Scahook Indians,[2] to go to Canada and fight the enemy." This force made the successful attack on the French beyond Lake Champlain, already noticed, and returned to Albany with nineteen prisoners and six scalps. The *Wappingers*, or " Indians of the Long Reach," as they were called, accepted the invitation to unite in the war, and with their head sachem and " all the males of the tribe able to bear arms," went to Albany,[3] and from thence to the field. A portion of them, however, appear as the allies of the French, and as such to have destroyed Hatfield and Deerfield, under the lead of Ashpelon, one of their chiefs.[4] While those who were allies of the English were absent, a large portion of their lands, embracing the present county of Putnam, were fraudulently entered by Adolph Phillipse, and after their return a fifty years' controversy was opened in regard thereto. The *Minnisinks* hesitated at first to embark in the war, and sent Paxinos, their chief, to New York to consult with Governor Dongan in regard to the

---

[1] April 5, 1690. The Indian Sachems of *Kightowan, Wossecamer, Wescawanus*, did promise to send six men to go against the French."— *Documentary History*, II, 237.

" April 19, 1690. The sachems of *Tappan*, called Mendoassyn, and a captain called Wigworakum, said that they had sent, fifteen days ago, twelve men to ye Maquase and Sinnekas, and when returne shall send more, being strong, in all sixty young men."— *Ibid*.

[2] " Mohawks, 92 ; River Indians, 66 ; the latter under Estewapo, Estowacamo, Wannesackes and Magataw."—*Colonial History*, III, 800, 802. The ranks of the Mohawks were frequently swelled in this manner.

[3] *Colonial History*, VII, 868.

[4] *Hubbard's History of New England*. An Indian called Quaetseitts, " who formerly lived on Hudson's river," is also mentioned as one of those who had " lately done mischief in Connecticut."— *Colonial History*, III, 562, 563. The governor of Canada, in 1698-'99, demanded of the Five Nations, among other conditions, the return of " a Mahikander Indian who is at Onondaga, a prisoner."— *Ib.*, IV, 498. These Indians had joined the French prior to or during the war.

matter.[1] They subsequently contributed their quota, however, and rendered important service.[2] The losses sustained by the *Iroquois* and their allies aggregated nearly one-half of the number engaged. The *Mohawks, Oneidas* and *Senecas* lost over one-half of their warriors, the latter being reduced from thirteen hundred to six hundred. The river Indians, however, were the greatest sufferers, having lost nearly two-thirds of the force which they contributed to the war.[3] Fifteen hundred Indians fell victims to the interests of the English, while the loss sustained by the allies of the French probably equalled that number. In addition to those lost in conflict, the *Iroquois* suffered the permanent detachment of the Praying Indians, who took up permanent residence " about four leagues above Montreal," and laid the foundation of that " formidable and fatal reduction " subsequently known as the *Caghnawaga* nation,[4] and more modernly as the *St. Regis* Indians. Assimilating with the French in faith, they soon did so in politics. They went off in small bodies, secretly, and after they had become located, drew to them considerable numbers of Schati-

---

[1] Paxinos has been classed as a Shawanoe chief, but such was not the case at this time, whatever he may have been subsequently.

[2] " Ordered, that a message be sent to Minnisinks to order them to send up their young men to Albany to join with the Five Nations against the French."— *Council Minutes*, May 6, 1688.

[3] This includes only those residing in the then county of Albany. The following return made to Gov. Fletcher in 1698, gives the strength and losses of the several tribes :

|  | Strength, In 1689. | In 1698. | Loss. |
|---|---|---|---|
| Mohawks, | 270 | 110 | 160 |
| Oneidas, | 180 | 70 | 110 |
| Onondagas, | 500 | 250 | 250 |
| Cayugas, | 320 | 200 | 120 |
| Senecas, | 1300 | 600 | 700 |
| River Indians, | 250 | 90 | 160 |
| Total, | 2820 | 1320 | 1500 |

*Colonial History*, iv, 337.

[4] " The French debauched many of our Five Nations to their Religion and Interest, actually drew several off to go and live in Canada, and laid the foundation of that formidable and fatal reduction which now forms the Cagnawaga na-

tion."— " Four hundred of our best Indians." — *Colonial History, of the State of New York*, iii, 836. " In the time of the last war the clandestine trade to Montreal began to be carried on by Indians from Albany to Montreal. This gave rise to the Konuaga or Praying Indians, who are entirely made up of deserters from the *Mohawks* and river Indians, and were either enticed by the French Priests or by our merchants in order to carry goods from Albany to Montreal, or run away from some mischief done here. These Indians now consist of about eighty fighting men and live about four leagues above Montreal. They neither plant nor hunt, but depend chiefly upon this private trade for their subsistence. These Indians in time of war gave the French intelligence of all designs here against them."—*Colden, Colonial History*, v, 732. " They became a thorn to the frontier towns and settlements of New England during the whole of the French war, and of the American Revolution."— *Schoolcraft*. They numbered, in 1745, two hundred and thirty fighting men.

*cooks* as well as of *Mohawks* and *Oneidas*.[1] The *Mohawks* felt the loss deeply, and exhausted every effort to reclaim the wanderers, but without avail.

Not only was foundation laid for the subsequent weakness of the *Iroquois* by the defection of the Praying Indians, but by the settlement among the *Lenapes* of the *Shawanoes* of Maryland and Virginia. At the outbreak of the war the *Shawanoes* were contesting the advance of the *Iroquois* in the south, and were also engaged in war with the *Cherokees*. In the latter they suffered severely, and but for the timely aid of the *Mahicans*, would have been destroyed. The *Lenapes* invited them to remove to their country ; the invitation being accepted, the *Minsis* brought the matter to the attention of the government of New York, in September, 1692, on an application to permit their settlement in the Minnisink country. The council gave its assent on condition that they should first make peace with the Five Nations.[2] This was soon effected, and the messengers departed, accompanied by Arnout Vielle, an interpreter, and three Christians, to visit the country of the *Shawanoes* and consummate the transfer.[3] On the 6th of February (1694), Major Peter Schuyler announced to the Five Nations, in conference at Albany, that " one of the Christians " had returned with the intelligence that seven nations or chieftaincies, " in all a thousand souls," were on their way.[4] Confirmation came also from

---

[1] The leader of the *Caghnawagas* was known to the French by the name of Kryn. A party led by him was prominent in the attack on Schenectady, and also on Salmon Falls. On their return from the latter expedition they were attacked by a party of *Algonquins* and *Abenaquis*, who, mistaking them for English *Mohawks*, killed two and wounded ten. " Among the slain was Kryn, the 'great *Mohawk* ;' whose death was the more deplored, because Frontenac and the Jesuits hoped that through his influence all the New York *Mohawks* would eventually be drawn to Canada."—*Brodhead*, II, 618 ; *Colonial History*, IX, 467.

[2] River Indians returned from a residence with the Shawanoes, brought with them some Shawanoes who intended to settle with the Minnisinks, asking permission to that end. Council directed that the Shawanoes, must first make peace with the Five Nations.— *Council Minutes*, Sept. 14, 1692

[3] " We are glad that the Shawanoes, who were our enemies, did make their application to you last fall for protection, and that you sent them hither to endeavor a peace with us ; also, that you have been pleased to send Christians along with them to their country to conduct them back again. We wish they were come to assist us against the common enemy."— *Answer of Five Nations*, July 4, 1693, *Colonial History*, IV, 43.

[4] " It seems the heavens are propitious unto us, for this day we have the forerunners of the Shawanoes Farr Indians come to town with one of our Christians that was sent thither, who gives us an

another quarter. Captain Arent Schuyler visited the *Minnisinks* in February, and there learned that the *Shawanoes* were expected early in the ensuing summer.[1] This expectation was realized, and the *Minsis* of the Hudson as well as those of the Delaware received to their embrace "the second son of their grandfather," after having given their pledge "to be faithful subjects of the king."[2]

At the time of the incorporation of the *Shawanoes* with the *Minsis*, the latter were at the lowest point in their history. Broken by their long wars with the *Senecas* and *Mohawks*, and scourged by the small pox,[3] they were but a remnant indeed of that proud people who had once successfully disputed the sovereignty of the continent. Their warriors hunted in fear; their chiefs trembled at the anger of the *Senecas*.[4] The *Shawanoes* were proud, warlike and cruel to an extent sufficient to draw

[1] "Enquiring after news, they told me that six days ago three Christians and two Shawans Indians, who went about fifteen months ago, with Arnout Vielle, into the Shawans country, were passed by the Mennisincks going for Albany to fetch powder for Arnout and his company: and further told them that said Arnout intended to be there with seven hundred of the said Shawans Indians, loaden with beaver and pelteries, at the time the Indian corn is about one foot high, which may be in the month of June."— *Colonial History*, IV, 98.

[2] *Council Minutes*, 1694.

[3] This malady was not confined to any district of country. Charlevoix says that in 1690 not less than fifteen hundred Indians perished in the Canada wilderness; and Ledwick writes in 1692, that of those residing in the vicinity of New Amsterdam: "The small pox took many of them away lately." Loskiel says that the Indians discovered a remedy in what he calls "fossil oil" (petroleum). He adds, "an old Indian in the small pox lay down in a morass to cool himself, and soon recovered. This led to the discovery of an oil spring in the morass, and since that time many others have been found, both in the country of the Delawares and the Iroquois." About the time spoken of by Loskiel, the epidemic was severe in the Esopus country. An entire company of *Ottawas* visiting there were among its victims. *Garneau's History of Canada*, I, 228; *New York Historical Collections*, 2d series, II, 249; *Loskiel's Moravian Miss.* 117.

account that they are coming with seven nations of Indians, with women and children, in all a thousand souls, and are upon their way hither with Arnout, the interpreter."— *Colonial History*, IV, 90. "In the intrim that they were treating with them (the Five Nations), Gerret Luykasse, with two of the Far Indians called Shawanoes arrives who brings news that Arnout, the interpreter, with a considerable number of those heathen, will be here next summer."— *Schuyler, Colonial History*, IV, 97.

[4] The Mennisinck sachems further said that one of their sachems and other Indians were gone to fetch beavor and pelteries which they had hunted, and having heard no news of them are afraid that the Sinneques have killed them for the lucar of the beavor, or because the Mennisincks have not been with the Sinneques as usual to pay their duty; and therefore desire that your excellency will be pleased to order that the Sinneques may he told not to molest or hurt the Mennisincks, they being willing to continue in amity with them — *Schuyler*, Feb. 1693, *Colonial History*, IV, 98.

from their enemies the name of Satans. On terms of peace with, but unsubdued by the *Iroquois*, their presence inspired the *Minsis*, and opened up to them a future in which their united war cry challenged the best efforts of their English and Indian foes. Half a century later they could say to their former rulers, the *Senecas*: " We have once been women and ashamed to look down at our petticoats, but as you have taken them off and encouraged us to begin a quarrel with the English, we are determined never to submit again to that ignominious state while there is one of us alive," [1] while a thousand warriors,

> "Quivered and plumed, and lithe and tall,
> And seamed with glorious scars,"

responded with rude but earnest approval.

[1] *Johnson Manuscripts*, IV, 131.

## CHAPTER VIII.

### THE MAHICANS IN COUNCIL — QUEEN ANNE'S WAR — MIGRATIONS — MISSIONARY LABORS — THE WAR OF 1746.

PEACE, such as had not fallen upon the wildernesses of the New World since the Europeans added their conflicting interests to the field of savage contests, prevailed at the opening of the eighteenth century. The contending tribes had buried the hatchet at Montreal, and *Senecas* and *Hurons*, *Onondagas* and *Ottawas*, *Mohawks* and *Ahenaquis*,[1] through their representatives smoked together the pipe of peace. Beside their ancient river the *Mahican* warriors hunted the deer, and their hand-maidens cultivated the fields, wove wampum in the woods, and chanted their maternal songs. Large numbers of them gathered around the "tree of welfare" which had been planted for them, and their dispersed New England relatives, at Schaticook, and in the councils with the tribes lifted up the voice of thanksgiving and proclaimed significant history. "We are glad to see you and your lady," said Soquans, the *Mahican* speaker, to Governor Bellomont at a conference at Albany, August 31st, 1700; "'Tis now about two years ago since we first saw you. The sun of peace shined then and so it does still. In the times of old there were not any Christians on this river, and the first Christians that came settled upon Rensselaer's land, whom we loved as soon as we saw them, and with whom we made a strict alliance and a covenant chain which has been kept inviolable ever since. This chain we are now come to renew. We are resolved to live and die here in this government, and do pray that our father will support and protect us." "I thank you for your kind expressions," replied Bellomont; "and you may be sure I will do every thing to maintain the covenant chain firm and steadfast. I should be

---

[1] Peace was established between the Abenaquis and the Five Nations, Oct. 7, 1700.—*Colonial History*, IV, 758.

very glad if you would invite your friends the *Pennacokes* and eastern Indians to come and settle with you. Since the Five Nations and you are linked together in interest, it would be an advantage to engage those other Indians in the same interest."[1] At a conference held July 18, 1701, Soquans again appeared with joyful heart. "We are now two hundred fighting men belonging to this county of Albany[2] from Katskill to Skachkook," said he, "and hope to increase in a year's time to three hundred. Our neighbors, the *Maquas*, have not been so fortunate, for their tree was burnt. We have been so happy and fortunate that our number is increased to that degree that we cannot all be shaded by one tree, and therefore desire that another tree, besides that at Skachkook, may be planted for us, for we are in hopes that our number will daily increase from other parts. It is now ninety years ago since the Christians first came here, when there was a covenant chain made between them and the *Mahikanders*, the first inhabitants of this river, and the chain has been kept inviolable ever since. We have been so happy as never to have had the least flaw or crack in the chain. There have been breaches round about us, and great differences, but that chain, wherein the *Maquas* and we are linked, has been kept inviolate, and we pray that our father will keep the same so forever." "We will plant you another tree," responded Lieutenant Governor Nanfan, "which shall be so large and flourishing that the branches will shade and cherish as many of your friends as will be persuaded to come and live with you. You know now by the experience of ninety years that we have the best laws and government in the world. You may depend upon it that I will do every thing to maintain the covenant chain firm and inviolate."[3]

Similar were the addresses delivered at a conference held by Governor Cornbury, on his first visit to Albany after his appointment: "You desired," said Soquans, "to know the number and strength of our people, which we now acquaint you with, viz: one hundred and ten Indians at Skachkook, and eighty-seven

---

[1] *Colonial History*, IV, 744.
[2] The county of Albany then embraced the entire country west of the Connecticut river, and north of Roelof's Jansen's kill on the east, and north of the Katskill mountains on the west.
[3] *Colonial History*, IX, 902, etc.

below the town (i. e., below Albany), in all one hundred and ninety-seven fighting men. You renewed the covenant chain two days ago (July 18, 1702), and we come now and ratify the same and make the chain stronger, which has been kept inviolable, between us and the Christians of this province, these ninety years. About twenty-six years ago, Sir Edmund Andros, then governor of this province, planted a tree of welfare at Skachkook, and invited us to come and live there, which we very luckily complied with, and we have had the good fortune ever since, that we have increased that tree, and the very leaves thereof have grown hard and strong; the tree is grown so thick of leaves and boughs that the sun can scarce shine through it, yea the fire itself cannot consume it; and we now desire, that our father may strengthen that tree and cause the leaves to grow so thick that no sun at all may shine through it."

The *Pennacooks* who had found refuge in Canada,[1] sent repeated invitations to their kindred at Schaticook to join them, promising them "houses, land and provisions," in the name of the French governor. These invitations were rejected, and Paasquin and Ackkonepak, two young *Pennacook* sachems, accompanied Soquans to Albany to acquaint the governor of their action. They were kindly received and their determination commended. "Tell your kindred," said Governor Cornbury, "to come and live with you. They shall not only have land assigned them gratis, but a fort shall be built of stockadoes to secure you and them from any sudden attempts of the enemy; your land is tough and hard, I will order next spring a plow to break up the ground for them to plant in, and they shall be protected and secured as well as any other Indians under the queen of England's protection. If they are inclined to be instructed in the Christian religion, the minister here shall teach them." And the Pennacooks accepted the mission, and went out after their brethren.

The relations existing between the government and the *Mahicans* under the treaty of 1664, had further illustration at this time. In August, 1702, Minichque, one of their sachems, while visiting Albany, was mortally wounded by a party of four

[1] *Ante*, p. 63.

negroes.  The authorities took immediate charge of him, nursed him tenderly, and arrested the offenders and brought them to trial.  Minichque and his brethren were satisfied, and the former, although lamenting that his death should have been caused by those who had " no courage nor heart," charged Soquans to make intercession for his murderers.  " Upon his death-bed," said Soquans, in performing this mission, " our great sachem desired that no revenge should be taken, saying that he forgave the offenders, and prayed that they might be reprieved."  " Since blood was shed, blood must be shed again," replied Cornbury, and on the 19th of August the principal offender was executed in atonement for the wrong which he had committed.

Through all these conferences[1] and proceedings, two principal facts are conspicuous : the equality of the *Mahicans* in all treaties with the authorities, from the earliest Dutch adventurers at Fort Orange to the more powerful occupation by the English, and the duality of the organization called the *Schaticooks*, in which the principals appear as *Mahicans* and the New England fugitives as *Pennacooks*.  Had equal fullness in record been made at earlier periods, the first point would not have so long been in obscurity.  That it finally appears is due to the wisdom of Governor Bellomont and to the selection of Colonel Peter Schuyler — than whom the *Mahicans* had no more sincere friend — as secretary to the commissioners of Indian affairs, under instructions, " upon any message from any or all of the Five Nations of Indians, or from the nation of Schakook or river Indians," to immediately call the commissioners together, and " to keep a record of all proceedings in reference thereto."  The faithfulness of this record preserves the truth of history, and places the *Mahicans* in the position which they justly occupied, but which had perhaps been clouded by the destructive wars through which they had passed, and the demoralization which had fallen upon them incident to their proximity to the marts of European

---

[1] Conferences with the Indians were not the most pleasant affairs. They were almost invariably held in the old Albany Court House.  Gov. Bellomont writes of one which he held with the Five Nations in October, 1700 : " My conference lasted seven days and was the greatest fatigue I ever endured in my whole life.  I was shut up in a close chamber with fifty sachems, who besides the stink of bear's grease, with which they plentifully daub'd themselves, were continually either smoking or drinking."— *Colonial History*, IV, 714.

traffic. Yet judged by this standard, their ancient rivals, the *Mohawks*, were not their peers. Zinzendorf writes of the latter that their passion for strong drink, by making them hopelessly indolent, had rendered them unworthy of their position as head of the Six Nations; that though chiefest in dignity, they were "despised because of their levity and paid off with the title," while the *Onondagas* were the actual " Judahs among their brethren." Years of intimate association with the Europeans had made the one " prophets without honor in their own country," while the absence of such association had magnified the dignity and prowess of the others.

The peace of 1698 was of short duration. James II, the dethroned king of England, died in exile in France in September, 1701, and Louis acknowledged the son of James as the successor to the throne. The death of King William followed in March, 1702, and Anne was declared his successor. The war which followed, and which was known in Europe as the war of the Spanish succession, was called in America, Queen Anne's war. It continued until the peace at Utrecht, April 11, 1713. New York scarce knew of its existence, although the province was put in condition for defense. The Indians, who had hitherto been the principal contestants and principal sufferers in these wars, were at peace. The Five Nations refused to break their treaties by attacking the *Abenaquis* who had espoused the cause of France, while the *Abenaquis* in turn refused to make war upon the Five Nations. But while New York escaped, New England was ravaged with ruthless hand. Casco, Wells, Deerfield, and Haverhill, were given to flame and sword; the aged and those of tender years shared the fate of the vigorous and manly; death hung on the frontiers; the prowling Indian seemed near every farm house. " There is," says Bancroft, " no tale to tell of battles like those of Blenheim, or Ramillies, but only one sad narrative of rural dangers and sorrows. The Indians stealthily approached towns in the heart of Massachusetts, as well as along the coast, and on the southern and western frontiers. Children, as they gamboled on the beach; reapers, as they gathered the harvest;

mowers, as they rested from using the scythe; mothers, as they busied themselves about the household, were victims to an enemy who disappeared the moment a blow was struck. Such were the sorrows of that generation."[1]

Special efforts were made, early in 1710, to induce the Five Nations and the *Mahicans* to violate their neutrality and embark in the conflict. The success of the French, in establishing themselves among the northern and western Indians, annoyed the English of New York, who saw in embroiling the peaceful tribes in war the only mode of arresting more formidable alliances. Nicholson, who had been appointed governor in 1688, and who had fled to England during the Leisler revolution, had met with some successes on the northern coast, and was anxious to have the Indians in the field as part of an expedition for the reduction of Quebec, which he had planned and in which he hoped to win unfading laurels. To promote the ends of both, and at the same time contribute to the relief of New England, he sailed for Europe, taking with him Colonel Peter Schuyler and representative chiefs of the *Mohawks* and *Mahicans*. On their arrival in England this delegation was received with marked distinction.[2] "Clothed like tragedy kings, by tailors of the theatre, taken in the coaches of state, they were waited upon by Sir Charles Cottrell, and, on the 19th of April, introduced to her majesty by the Duke of Shrewsbury. They were entertained by many noble persons, particularly the Duke of Ormond, who favored them with a review of the life-guards. Their portraits were taken and are now preserved in the British Museum, together with their names."[3] So much attention, so

[1] *Bancroft*, III, 216.
[2] *Bancroft*, III, 209.
[3] The best and most methodical account of the visit of these chiefs was published in the great annual history by Mr. Boyer, entitled "*The Annals of Queen Anne's Reign, for* 1710," from which the following is an extract: "On the 19th of April, *Te-Gee-Neen-Ho-Ga-Prow* and *Sa-Ga-Yeau-Qua-Prah-Ton* (King Hendrik, *Colonial History*, v, 358), of the Maquas; *Elow-Oh-Kaom* and *Oh-Yeath-Ton-No-Prow*, of the river sachems, and the *Ganajohhore* sachem, five kings or chiefs of the six nations, which lie between New England and New France or Canada, who lately came over with the West India fleet, and were clothed and entertained at the Queen's expense, had a public audience of Her Majesty at the palace of St James. They made a speech by their interpreter, which Major Pidgeon, who was one of the officers came with them, read in English to Her Majesty." Sir Richard Steele, in the *Tatler* of May 13, 1710, gives an account of the visit. Miner, in his *History of Wyoming*, endeavors to locate one of the visiting

great a display of the power and glory of England, had its effect ; the chiefs readily promised to return and rally their clans to the field; were hurried home with this promise fresh on their lips, and started on their mission of war.

Events moved slowly in the wilderness at that time, and a full year elapsed before the response came. On the 17th of August, 1711, the chiefs met Governor Hunter, with their warriors. The sachem of *Schaticook* brought thirty-eight men ; the *Mahicans,* fifty-eight under Wampasa, whom they had chosen as their captain ; the *Shawanoes,* twenty-six ; the *Mohawks* one hundred and forty, and the remaining tribes of the Five Nations, about five hundred. Each delegation was separately received, that of the Five Nations, on account of its numbers, being especially honored by a salute of five guns as they passed in review before Fort Albany. The conference opened on the 24th when, " each nation seated on the ground by themselves," Governor Hunter thanked them for their response to the queen's commands, and informed them that they would be expected to join General Nicholson in the expedition against Canada, which had been organized.[1] This expedition had already sailed from Boston, with seven veteran regiments, and was to be met by the colonial forces of New York, New Jersey and Connecticut, with their Indian allies, under the walls of Quebec.[2] Roasted oxen, barrels of beer, the firing of cannon, and some " private presents" to the proper chiefs, completed the work, and all professed their readiness to march at the queen's command.

The French were not idle spectators of these preparations, and in their efforts to defeat them brought out in strong colors the power and influence which they had established over their Indian allies through their priests. A great war festival was held at Montreal, and the war song chanted by seven or eight hundred warriors, many of whom were the flower of the *Iroquois* and *Mahican* nations, whom the priests had drawn thither.

---

chiefs among the Delawares, but is not sustained by the record. The Canajoharie chief, whose name is not given, died in England soon after his arrival. The first conference after their return was held at Albany, Aug. 10, 1711, of which the record says : " Some of ye sachems of ye Five Nations and river Indians, particularly those lately come from Great Britain, waited upon His Excellency, Gov. Hunter," &c. — *Colonial History,* v, 217.

[1] *Colonial History,* v, 267, etc.
[2] *Bancroft,* III, 221, etc.

From the far west the response was even more enthusiastic. Tribe after tribe, even the *Osages* and *Missouris*, sprang to the relief of the French. " Father," said they to Vaudreuil, " behold thy children compass thee round. We will, if need be, gladly die for our father — only take care of our wives and our children, and spread a little grass over our dead bodies to protect them against the flies."

Circumstances prevented actual collision. The fleet sailed from Boston, after many delays, only to be invested by heavy fogs, and to meet with the wreck of eight of the vessels of which it was composed and the loss of eight hundred and eighty-four men drowned.[1] The land forces were moved to the support of the fleet. "On the 29th of August," says Governor Hunter, " I left them all upon their march beyond Albany towards the lakes, completely armed, clothed, accoutred and victualled, to be followed next day by eight hundred Indians of the Five Nations and their allies from Albany." How far the march extended does not appear; it was arrested by the disaster to the fleet, and became a successful and unmolested retreat.

The *Tuscaroras*, of North Carolina, one of the southern tribes of *Iroquois*, did not escape from the war so fortunately. Resisting the encroachments of the proprietaries of Carolina, who had assigned their lands to the German Palatines, they were almost destroyed in their fort on the river Taw, on the 26th of March, 1713, having lost eight hundred in prisoners, who were sold as slaves to the allies of the English. The largest portion of the survivors of this disaster, "unwilling to submit and unable to contend," removed to the north, joined the confederated tribes of New York, and were accepted and established as the sixth nation, or " children," of the *Iroquois*.[2] They were located immediately west of, and in juxtaposition to,

---

[1] *Colonial History*, v, 277.

[2] At a conference at Albany, Sept. 25, 1714, the Five Nations, in their address to Governor Hunter, said : "We acquaint you that the Tuscarore Indians are come to shelter themselves among the Five Nations. They were of us and went from us long ago and are now returned, and promise to live peaceably among us, and since there is peace every where, we have received them. We desire you to look upon the Tuscarores that are come to live among us as our children who shall obey our commands and live peaceably and orderly."—*Colonial History*, v, 387.

the *Oneidas*,[1] and as they increased in strength became useful to their associates.[2]

Peace and intimate association with their European neighbors, which had proved so disastrous to the *Mahicans* in former times, did not improve their condition. They came regularly to the conferences, but in smaller numbers and in a condition betokening great indulgence in intoxicating liquors. At the conference of 1720, the commissioners specially commended their faithfulness to their covenant, as distinguished from the Five Nations, who had "suffered themselves to be deluded by the French and their emissaries," but did not hesitate to ascribe the poverty of which they complained to " drinking and laziness," and to advise them to " be sober and active in hunting and planting" in the future.[3] In 1722, Governor Burnet, in renewing the ancient covenant with them, remarked: " I need not tell you how destructive your intemperance has proved, and how much your people are diminished by your excessive drinking of rum, the women as well as the men being guilty of being often drunk. Let me advise you to be more sober in the future, and not to spend what you get by hunting in strong drink, and above all not squander your Indian corn for rum." But was it the fault of the Indians that the assertions of the governor were but too well founded? Said the *Mahicans* in their answer, through Ampamit [4] their speaker: " We are sensible that you are much in the right, that rum does a great deal of harm. We approve of all that you said on that point, but the matter is this, when our people come from hunting to the town or plantations and acquaint the traders and people that we want powder and shot and clothing, they first give us a large cup of rum, and after we get the taste of it we crave for more, so that in fine all the beaver and peltry we have hunted goes for drink, and we are left destitute either of clothing or ammunition. Therefore, we desire our father to order the tap or crane to be shut, and to prohibit the selling of rum, for as long as the Christians will sell rum

---

[1] " The *Oneidas*, the proprietors of that country, gave you a settlement then out of kindness."—*Johnson to Seth, chief of the Tuscaroras at Oghkwaga.*

[2] *Schoolcraft's Notes on the Iroquois*, 104, etc. *Gallatin*, 82, 83.

[3] *Colonial History*, v, 563.

[4] Said to have been chief of an island in the Hudson.

our people will drink it. We acknowledge that our father is very much in the right to tell us that we squander away our Indian corn, but one great cause of it is that many of our people are obliged to hire land of the Christians at a very dear rate, and to give half the corn for rent, and the other half they are tempted by rum to sell, and so the corn goes, and the poor women and children are left to shift as well as they can." And he might have added, that the land which they called their own was not unfrequently mortgaged to those who had furnished them corn, after defrauding them of that which they had produced, and the mortgages very promptly foreclosed.* Without this addition, however, Governor Burnet felt the force of the argument of this aboriginal prohibitionist, and took the point from his rebuke by remarking, in reply, that they " looked better" and were " better clothed " " than the other Indians, who do not live among the Christians," and that therefore they would do well " to stay among them." No promise did he give, however, that he appreciated and would enforce the divine command, " Lead us not into temptation," by preventing the sale of rum and the consequent plunder by which the Christian name was reproached. Commanding them to distribute their presents equally between those living above Albany and those living below Albany, he dismissed them.

The New England provinces maintained war with the eastern Indians for some years after peace had been established with France. The doctrine that the Indians had no rights which Christians were bound to respect, was firmly held by the successors of Underhill and Church, who hesitated not to provoke and continue hostilities when peace was within their reach. But the war grew tedious as well as disastrous, and the authorities there appealed to the *Iroquois* to take up the hatchet in their behalf.[1] The latter made loud protestations of what they would do, but contented themselves with hiding the hatchet in their bosoms and sending messengers to the *Abenaquis*. A year later (1724), the New England commissioners remonstrated with them,

---

[1] This overture was not to the Five Nations alone, but embraced the *Mahicans* and *Schaticooks*. Delegates from the tribes named were invited to Boston, and were there entertained with a feast and presents, as was customary in such negotiations. — *Niles' History, Massachusetts Historical Collections*, v, 347.

and charged that they had not only laid the hatchet by their side, but had accomplished nothing by negotiation. The reply was pointed : " The matter of peace rests with you," said their speaker ; " whenever you will give up the lands which you have wrongfully taken, and restore the hostages which you have retained without cause," peace can be secured. They had made full inquiry and were satisfied that the eastern Indians were not the aggressors, and they knew that should they attempt to force them to peace, a general war would ensue. " Though the hatchet lies by our side," continued their speaker, " yet the way is open between this place and Canada, and trade is free both going and coming, and so the way is open between this place and Albany and the Six Nations, and if a war should break out and we should use the hatchet that lays by our side, those paths which are now open would be stopped ; and if we should make war it would not end in a few days as yours doth, but it must last till one nation or the other is destroyed. We have been three times with the eastward Indians and could not prevail, and we know what whipping and scourging is from the governor of Canada. The eastern Indians seem to be inclined to peace, and inasmuch as we have tried three times and could not effect it, we would have you try them yourselves."[1] The *Iroquois* were in no humor to attack so formidable a foe as the *Abenaquis.* Their last conflict had been at least a drawn battle, and having formed a peace with them as well as with the governor of Canada, whose allies they were, they declined, as they did in 1704, to reopen a conflict which might involve their own existence. The name of *Mohawk!* if it once had terror[2] for the fugitive *Pequot,* upon whose head a price was set, had none for those who boasted that they received the first kiss of the morning sun— the tribute which they paid was not to the *Iroquois.*

The record of the years immediately subsequent is but a disconnected detail of migrations and reorganizations among the Indian tribes. In 1726, two of the sachems of the *Pennacooks,* at Schaticook, being dead, Governor Burnet appointed Wawiachech in their place. Instead of increasing in numbers as they had

[1] *Colonial History,* v, 723, 725.   [2] This is one of the fables of history, which is quoted by almost every writer.

anticipated, they steadily decreased by desertions to Canada. These desertions were explained, by those who remained, as being caused by debts which they had incurred and were unable to pay, or the payment of which they wished to escape.[1] While this explanation was not without some truth, the overtures made by the French, and the entreaties of their relatives, were probably the predominant impelling motives. Houses, lands, protection, and a more complete recognition by the government, were temptations that these wanderers, who, like Esau, had parted with their birthright for a mess of pottage, could not resist.

Nor were their *Mahican* neighbors fully satisfied with their condition. A considerable number of the better classes among them felt keenly the devouring curses to which they were exposed by their proximity to the established centre of trade, and fled from their devouring touch to the friendly embrace of their "grandfathers," the *Lenapes*, and settled beside the *Minsis* and *Shawanoes* in the valley of Wyoming at the forks of the Susquehanna.[2] Among the first of these emigrants was Keeperdo, or Mohekin Abraham, who, in 1730, left his lands at the mouth of Wood creek unoccupied. Whether he was the founder of the Pennsylvania organization or not does not appear; but the organization itself maintained a separate and recognized existence in all the changes of the *Lenapes* and their confederates. In those changes Keeperdo shared — accepted, with his associates, the reproach of "women," joined in the ceremonies of its removal, and, in 1771, was found in the Ohio country.[3]

---

[1] *Colonial History*, v, 798, 799.

[2] "We reached Skehandowa (April 23, 1737), where a number of Indians live,— Shawanos and Mahicanders."—*Memorials Moravian Church*, 1, 69.

[3] In the Manuscripts of Sir William Johnson, in the State Library (vol. 21, p. 40), is a letter endorsed: "Letter from Ohio concerning land —rec'd it Oct. 16th, 1771." This letter was from Mohekin Abraham, who writes: "I understand the Mohikans at Stockbridge are wanting to sell a certain tract of land lying above Albany, from the mouth of Wood creek upwards." This sale he requested to have stopped as he was the owner, that he was well known by many old people about Albany, and in conclusion says: "It may be reported that I am dead, as it is forty years since I left that country." Signed, "Mohekin Abraham, or Keeperdo." The tract was covered by a patent to Philip Skene, and embraced what was known as Skenesborough, now Whitehall, in the present county of Washington. Skene located thirty families on it in 1761. The Mahicans at Stockbridge claimed the ownership, but it does not appear that the tract was ever paid for. The letter of Keeperdo is important as defining more clearly the extent of the Mahican country.

As this band retreated towards the west, another appeared from the east in the territory of the *Mahicans*. Gideon[1] Mauwehu, a *Pequot* chief, originally of some prominence in that unfortunate nation, and whose natural abilities were of no ordinary stamp, with a few of his followers found a home in the present town of Dover, on Ten Mile river, in the county of Dutchess. Here he had lived but a short time, when, on one of his hunting excursions, he came to the summit of a mountain in the present county of Kent, Connecticut. Looking down from this eminence he saw the Housatonic winding through a narrow but fertile valley, shut in by wooded hills. Delighted with the scene, he returned to his wigwam, packed up his property, and journeyed with his family and followers to this new found land of quiet and plenty. From here he issued invitations to his old friends and to the *Mahicans* of the Hudson. Immigrants flocked in, and in ten years from the time of settlement, it was thought a hundred warriors had collected around him.[2] To his village he gave the name of Pishgachtigok, which had already been applied to that of the fugitive *Pennacooks* on the Hudson, and which there as well as on the Hudson,[3] was corrupted into Schaticook, by which it was known to the authorities of Connecticut, who subsequently established there a reservation on which the name of Mauwehu was represented for five generations.[4] What relation this organization sustained to the *Mahicans* does not appear, although the authority of the latter was no doubt recognized, so far as recognition was customary under tribal laws. With the authorities of New York, Mauwehu had no direct connection.

Almost simultaneously with the appearance of Mauwehu in the valley of the Housatonic, the axe of the pioneer was heard in its ancient forests. In 1722, Joseph Parsons and others purchased from the *Mahicans* there a tract of land embracing territory sufficient for two townships, and prepared to locate a

---

[1] A name given to him by the Moravian missionary, Mack, by whom he was baptized in 1743.—*Latrobe's Missions*, II, 43, 44, etc.

[2] *De Forest's History Indians of Connecticut*, 407, etc.

[3] The situations were similar and the name, Pisgachtigok, or the confluence of two streams, was applied to both.

[4] Eunice, the last of royal line, died on the reservation in 1860.

settlement. That which the people of New England then regarded as an absolute essential in such enterprises — a reservation for the use and support of a minister — was included in their charter. Subsequent investigation having proved that the location of a minister among them could be greatly promoted by availing themselves of the aid of the Society for the Propagation of the Gospel in Foreign Parts, and that the prospect of improving the condition of the *Mahicans* by direct association was better than through the intercourse had with them at the forts, where missionaries had been stationed, it was determined to make application to that society for a missionary. The application was granted, but on condition that the consent of the *Mahicans* should be first obtained. A committee accordingly visited them at Westenhuck in July, 1734. The relations existing between the *Mahicans* and the Massachusetts government being intimate and friendly — Konapot, the *Mahican* chief, having been commissioned captain, by Governor Belcher, and Umpachenee, his subordinate, made a lieutenant, in the colonial service — this consent was readily obtained. In September following, the Rev. John Sergeant was appointed to the mission and entered upon its duties in October. In 1735, the mission was definitely located on the W-nahk-ta-kook, or the Great Meadow, the great council chamber of the nation, where a township six miles square was laid out by the legislature as a reservation under the name of Stockbridge, by which name the *Mahicans* who were then located there, as well as those who subsequently removed thither, were known to the authorities of Massachusetts and New York.[1]

Following closely upon the establishment of the Stockbridge mission, the Moravians began their labors in the *Mahican* country. With a zeal remarkable for its voluntarily assumed sacrifices, and more pure than that which characterized the labors of other organizations, because without political interests to serve, they had pushed their way into the territory of the *Creeks* and

---

[1] *Stockbridge, Past and Present.* Twenty miles distant, at a village called *Kaunaumeek*, David Brainerd, a licentiate acting under similar authority, established a mission in 1743. He was aided in his labors, by a young Mahican, John Wauwaumpequnnaunt, and met with so much success that he was enabled to induce his people to remove to Stockbridge.

*Cherokees* of Georgia, in 1735. Driven thence by the political troubles with the Spaniards, they established a colony at Bethlehem, on the Delaware, and, in 1740, founded a mission in the present county of Dutchess. The pioneer in the latter field was Christian Henry Rauch, who arrived in New York, in July of that year, seeking missionary labor, and where he soon after met a company of *Mahicans* who were there to renew their covenant with the government. Ascertaining that he could converse with them in the Dutch language, he visited them repeatedly at their encampment, but found them almost invariably in a state of beastly intoxication on the liquor which the government had given them, ferocious in appearance and but little disposed to extend the encouragement which he sought. Finding them sober at last, he addressed two of their chiefs, Tschoop and Shabash, and obtained their consent to accompany them to their village as a teacher. Led by them he reached Shekomeko, in the district now known as Pine plains, on the 16th of August, and immediately commenced a work which was not without encouraging reward. Tschoop,[1] known as "the greatest drunkard among his followers," was converted; Schabash joined him soon after. At the end of two years thirty-one baptized Indians attended his ministrations, "all of the *Mahikander* tribe," and in 1743, the number had reached sixty-three.

Rauch's labors were not confined to Shekomeko alone. At Pisgachtigok, Mauwehu and his brother were among his converts, while at Wechquadnach,[2] or Pachquadnach, Totatik,[3] Westenhuck, and Wehtak,[4] he was not without sincere followers. At Shekomeko, Wechquadnach and Pisgachtigok, mission

---

[1] Schweinitz, in his *Life and Times of David Zeisberger*, says the name of this chief was Wasarnapah; his English name prior to his baptism, Job; and the name he received in baptism, John; that he never bore the name of Tschoop among his people, but that it originated among the Moravians in consequence of their German mode of pronouncing Job. Wasarnapah was the ruling chief at Shekomeko. He was a man of remarkable powers of mind, and in whose mien "was the majesty of a Luther." He died of small pox at Bethlehem, Aug. 27, 1746.

*Loskiel*, II, 93, 94. Schabash received in baptism the name of Abraham. He was subsequently elected chief or king of the Mahicans on the Delaware, and died at Wyoming in December, 1762.—*Memorials Moravian Church*, I, 147.

[2] Now North-east Centre, Connecticut. The name is preserved in Wachquadnach lake or Indian pond.

[3] On the east side of the Housatonic opposite the mouth of Poughtatuck creek.

[4] Or Wyatiack, near Salisbury, Litchfield Co., Conn.

houses were established, the success at the latter being greater than that at Shekomeko.  In this field Rauch, Gotleib, Buttner and Samuel Mack labored for twenty years, and until driven out by persecutions which their success provoked.  In the war of 1755, they were accused of being emissaries of the French ; subsequently they were arrested under the law of 1700, forbidding the presence of priests in the province without a license from the government ; the traders, whose traffic in rum was materially abridged by their teachings, lost no opportunity to misrepresent them and accuse them falsely ; finally, they were ejected from the lands at Shekomeko under a claim that they belonged to the white people and not to the Indians.  After a temporary rest at Wechquadnach and Pisgachtigok, they removed, with many of their followers, to Pennsylvania, where they formed a colony to which they gave the name of Freidenshutten, (tents of peace).  Their stay here was short.  Gnadenhutten (tents of grace) received them for a time, and from thence they shared the roving fortunes of the Moravians, followed in all their wanderings by their faithful *Mahican* converts.[1]

Meanwhile the commissioners of the society in Scotland for Propagating the Gospel had entered upon the work of diffusing Christian knowledge among the Indians, and had commissioned the Rev. David Brainerd to labor among the Delawares. Having transferred his mission among the *Mahicans* to the Rev. Mr. Sergeant, Brainerd visited the Delaware country in the spring of 1744.  At Minnisink he encountered the opposition of the Indians,[2] but established himself at the Forks of the Dela-

---

[1] *Heckewelder's Narrative; Life and Times of David Zeisberger ; Loskiel's History of the Mission of the United Brethren ; Memorials of the Moravian Church ; The Moravians in New York and Connecticut ; Documentary History of New York; Stone's Life of Brant*, etc.

[2] "I then set out on my journey toward Delaware ; and on May 10th, (1744), met with a number of Indians in a place called Minnissinks, about a hundred and forty miles from Kaunaumeek (the place where I spent the last year), and directly in my way to Delaware river.  With these Indians I spent some time, and first addressed their king in a friendly manner, and after some discourse, and attempts to contract a friendship with him, I told him I had a desire (for his benefit and happiness) to instruct them in *Christianity*.  At which he laughed and turned his back upon me and went away.  I then addressed another *principal* man in the same manner, who said he was willing to hear me.  After some time, I followed the *king* into his house, and renewed my discourse to him : but he declined talking, and left the affair to another, who appeared to be a rational man.  He began and talked very warmly near a quarter of an hour together ; he enquired why I desired the Indians to become

ware, at which place, and at Crossweeksung, "in New Jersey, towards the sea," he met with considerable success.[1] His brother, John Brainerd, about the same time, established a mission at Bethel, New Jersey, where he drew together a permanent congregation.

But the changes of this period were not confined to the *Mahicans* and *Lenapes*. It is said that in 1748, a band of fugitive *Nanticokes*, under their chief sachem, White, put themselves under the protection of the Six Nations at Conestoga on the Delaware.[2] If the Moravian missionaries were correctly informed, their presence was a source of weakness rather than of strength to their allies. Loskiel states that they "instructed the Delawares and Iroquois in preparing a peculiar kind of poison," which was capable of infecting whole townships and tribes with "disorders as pernicious as the plague," and that they "nearly destroyed their own nation by it." Their history, until their final disappearance in the west, was not particularly distinguished, perhaps for the reason stated by Loskiel.

A more important acquisition — at least temporarily — by the *Iroquois* at this time, was that of the *Mississagies* as the seventh nation of the confederacy. The *Mississagies* were a northern *Algonquin* nation whose place of residence was on the waters of

*Christians*, seeing the Christians were so much worse than the Indians. It was they first taught the Indians to be drunk, and *they* stole from one another, to that degree, that their rulers were obliged to hang them for it, and that was not sufficient to deter others from the like practice. But the Indians, he added, were none or them ever hanged for stealing, and yet they did not steal half so much; and he supposed that if the Indians should become Christians, they would then be as bad as those, and hereupon he said, they would live as their *fathers* lived, and go where their *fathers* were when they died. I then freely owned, lamented, and joined with him in condemning the ill conduct of some who are called Christians; told him these were not Christians at heart, that I hated such wicked practices, and did not desire the Indians to become such as these, and when he appeared calmer, I asked him if he was willing that I should come and see them again. He replied, he should be willing to see me again, as a *friend*, if I would not desire them to become *Christians*. I then bid them farewell, and prosecuted my journey towards Delaware."— *Brainerd's Mission*.

[1] He died in 1747, of consumption, a martyr to the work which he had undertaken.

[2] The Nanticokes, or tide water people, had their seats, when the Europeans first met them, on the eastern shore of Maryland. At the time of the removal referred to in the text they were not considerable in numbers. Gallatin says they were the allies of the Six Nations. Their lands in Maryland were sold, through the agency of Sir William Johnson, in 1760, and the money paid to the chiefs.— *Colonial History*, VIII, 117. They were repeatedly represented in the conferences with the Delawares and the Shawanoes.

a river which enters the north shores of Lake Huron, between Point Tessalon and La Cloche. In pushing the policy which the government of New York had established, of promoting trade by securing the alliance of Indian tribes with the Six Nations, the latter had been induced to open negotiations with many of their former enemies.[1] As one of the fruits of this policy, the *Necariages*, a remnant of the once powerful *Hurons*, or *Wyandots*, had been induced to visit Albany, in 1723, and to ask to be received as the seventh nation. The commissioners of Indian affairs accepted them as such,[2] but the confederates never acknowledged them. When the *Mississagies* tendered a similar alliance, however, they were received by the confederates, and at a conference, held at Albany on the 23d of August, 1746, were publicly acknowledged by them as the seventh nation.[3] The alliance did not long continue. When the war of 1755 broke out, it was found that the Six Nations were at war with their new allies.

A more permanent acquisition was that of the *Ochtayhquanawicroons*,[4] a *Tuscarora* clan,[5] who appeared on the Susquehanna river, in the present county of Broome, in 1722, and around whom subsequently gathered several *Mahican* families who had previously found homes with the *Mohawks*, but who had become "dissatisfied with the ruling politics[6] of that tribe;" *Skaniadaradigh-*

---

[1] In 1740, George Clark, then acting as governor, secured the assent of the Six Nations to the proposition to "take into the covenant chain all the nations of Indians lying to the westward and southward as far as the Mississippi," as the "most likely way to establish an universal peace among all the Indians and to make it lasting."

[2] *Colonial History*, v, 695. Schoolcraft classes the Necariages as the seventh nation, but admits that they were never so received. The fact appears to be that no nation was ever received into the confederate compact; even the Tuscaroras had no such relation. In all their national action but five tribes were represented.

[3] "We, the Six Nations, are now assembled together as one man, and we take in the Mississagies as the Seventh Nation; and what is now spoken by one mouth, are the joint and sincere thoughts of every heart."—*Colonial History*, vi, 321. The Mississagies numbered at that time eight hundred warriors. They were at treaty conference for the last time in 1755.—*Colonial History*, vii, 259.

[4] *Colonial History*, v, 675. They were subsequently called the Onoghquageys, Oghquagas, Aughquages, Ochquaquas, Onenhoghkwages, Auquaguas, Onehohquages, etc.—*Index Colonial History ; Proceedings of the Provincial Convention of New York*, ii, 340, 419, 423, etc.

[5] Dr. O'Callaghan says they were chiefly Mohawks (note, *Colonial History*, v, 675), but a different conclusion is clearly deducible from the conference minutes of Feb. 2, 1756, in which the name "Aughquages, as distinguishing the original organization, is immediately followed by that of Tuscaroras in brackets.—*Colonial History*, vii, 51. It is quite probable there were Mohawks residing among them.

[6] *Colonial History*, vii, 278. "A party

*roonas*, from Maryland,[1] a portion of the *Chugnuts*,[2] a Susquehanna family, and several clans of the *Minsis* or Esopus Indians living upon the east branch of the Delaware river;[3] They were not without favorable record in the wars of 1745 and 1755,[4] but derive their historic interest mainly from the distinguished services of their chief, Thomas King,[5] and from the fact that through them the history of the Esopus clans is linked with the war of the Revolution.[6]

At a later period, and apparently about 1746, the *Oneidas* sent off a colony from their principal castle, to a point about twelve miles from Oneida lake, where they established a settlement which they called Canowaroghere or Onawaraghharee,[7] and which was subsequently recognized as "the second Oneida castle." Several families of the Long island clans, dispossessed of their lands and surrounded by European settlers, were subsequently added to the colony,[8] giving to it influence in point of numbers.

Meanwhile the Esopus clans who had not followed the fortunes of their kindred, the *Minsis*, maintained their succession of sachems and held annual conferences with the justices at Kingston.[9] Thither came Ankerop, chief sachem, in 1722, and complained that a "white man had offered violence to an Indian

of Aughquages and Mahicanders under Thomas, an Aughquage chief.— *Ibid*, 187. The Mahicans here spoken of were entirely distinct from those who settled at an early period among the Lenapes, or those who were subsequently located at Otsiningo.— *Ibid.*, 104.

[1] *Colonial History*, VI, 983. Supposed to be a remnant of the Powhattan confederacy, who were removed under the treaty with Virginia in 1722, and called by Gallatin Sachdagughroonas. The date of their settlement at the north corresponds with that of the treaty with Virginia.— *Gallatin*, 58, 59.

[2] Their village was on the south bank of the Susquehanna, opposite Binghamton.

[3] "The Delaware Indians, who live on the east branch of the Delaware river, near the head of it, have given us the strongest assurances that they will live and die with us."— *Colonial History*, VII, 50.

[4] "I assure your excellency I never saw a people better inclined to assist us than they are."— *Colonial History*, VI, 361.

[5] This chief was actively employed as the principal deputy of the Five Nations in the treaties with the Lenapes and Shawanoes. He died at Charleston, South Carolina, after attending the congress of Indian nations at Scioto, in 1771. Johnson speaks of him as a man of "superior capacity and fidelity."— *Colonial History*, VIII, 290, 300, etc.

[6] *Proceedings of the Provincial Convention of New York*, I, 339, 808; ii, 340, 419, 423, etc.

[7] *Colonial History*, VII, 512, 611, etc.

[8] *Ib.*, VIII, 476.

[9] The records of these conferences are scattered, some being found at Kingston, others in the Clinton and Johnson papers in the State Library, and others in the office of the secretary of state.

whom he had met carrying rum," and the justices promised the punishment of the offender. The justices, on their part, charged that the Indians " had hired negroes to fight against the Christians," which the sachem denied. Not a conference passed without a claim for lands taken from the Indians without compensation, many of them entirely unfounded, according to the English interpretation of boundaries, but doubtless well founded in the absolute knowledge of the claimants, who, in their sales, had designated hills and not intervening valleys. The principal purpose of the conferences, however, appears to have been to dismiss the Indians with assurances of friendship, a few blankets and considerable rum. If they rapidly became a " contemptible people," it was in consequence of the influences by which they were surrounded. In their wanderings a few of them came under the teachings of the Moravians, and united with the *Mahican* converts in Pennsylvania, but to them as an organization no missionary work was undertaken. The people of Kingston cared little for their own improvement, much less for that of the Indians, and preferred rather to earn for themselves the sobriquet of "the Sodom of New York,"[1] than to perform those acts of charity and mercy which spring from a proper appreciation of the Christian character. Had they followed the exterminating policy of the Puritans it would have been more to their credit.

The *Wappingers*, too, maintained an organization on the Hudson amid all the changes which surrounded and attended them. Many of them had been drawn off to new homes; a few appeared among the Moravians and at Stockbridge, but the seat of the tribe remained in the highlands.[2] Nimham, who was made chief sachem in 1740, gave them prominence by service in the field and by his persistent efforts to recover lands of which they had been defrauded.

The result of these and other changes was, that at the close of the half century the *Lenapes* had an active, vigorous organization of five tribes; the *Iroquois*,[3] one of seven tribes, and the

---

[1] *Memorials of the Moravian Church*, I, 58.
[2] *Colonial History*, VII, 869.
[3] Including the original Lenape divisions with the addition of the *Shawanoes* and *Mahicans*. There were also several detached clans of minor importance associated with them.

*Mahicans*, although divided by provincial lines, one that could still call its followers from Quebec to Manhattan. Although the changes which had produced these new combinations were in a great degree the result alike of the selfish efforts of the European nations who were contesting the supremacy of the continent, and of the pressure of an incoming civilization, they were not less the work of aboriginal diplomats who had purposes of their own to serve. The lessons which Philip had taught his people and his allies were deeply impressed. Fugitives from the fields on which he had met disaster, bore them to congenial soil among the *Lenapes* and *Shawanoes*; to the north, among the *Abenaquis*, sharpening their desire for revenges which were unatoned; on the prairies of the west and amid the wildernesses of Canada, they were the theme of thought and preparation. The English saw the gathering storm and sought shelter behind their allies, the *Iroquois*; the French welded its gathering folds, and bade the avengers onward.

The war of 1744, while without positive results to the principal contestants, was the turning point in the supremacy of the *Iroquois*, as well as in the ardor of their attachment to the English. At the opening of the war a conference was held with them at Albany, in which Governor Clinton informed them of the condition of affairs, and asked their cooperation in promoting the mutual safety and defense of the English and themselves, " and the annoyance of the common enemy." The chiefs hesitated. " We cannot answer to every particular concerning the war," said they, " but do promise that we will keep all our people at home and there await orders. We are inclined to peace, till the enemy attack some of his majesty's subjects, and then we will join together to defend ourselves against them."[1]

The conference with them in October of the following year was not more successful. The chiefs thanked the governor for the information which he had given them concerning the war, but the hatchet which they accepted they would keep in their bosoms. " We are," said they, " in alliance with a great many nations, and if we should suddenly lift the hatchet without acquainting them, they would perhaps take offense at it.

[1] *Colonial History*, vi, 265.

We will, therefore, before we make use of the hatchet, send four of our people to Canada, to demand satisfaction for the wrongs they have done, and if they refuse, then we shall be ready."

In a word, they had determined to remain neutral, and to that end had had consultation with their allies as well as with the French. The general character of these consultations may be inferred from that which they held with the *Mahicans* at Stockbridge, in 1744, when, Mr. Sergeant states, the embassadors were met in the most cordial manner. "Uncle," said the *Mahican* chief, "I ask you a question. I hear you have agreed with the French *Mohawks* to sit still, in case of war between their friends and ours. You well know how that matter is. I desire you to tell me what we are to do in that affair. If you say we must sit still, we will sit still. If we are to see those Indians help their friends, we must help ours." "Cousin," replied the *Mohawk*, "the information you have received of our engaging with the French *Mohawks* to stand neuter in case of war between the French and English, is very true. Those Indians have promised us that they would not meddle with the war, but sit still in peace, and let the white people determine the dispute themselves. We have promised them the same, and desire you to join with us in the same peaceable disposition."

Neutrality was maintained until 1746, when the French and their Indians became the aggressors. Meanwhile the New England authorities had erected a chain of stockades and blockhouses along the frontier from Maine to the Connecticut river, and from thence across the Hoosic mountains to the territory of New York. Upon the Hoosic river, within the bounds of what is now the town of Adams, one of these blockhouses, known as Fort Massachusetts, was attacked in August, 1746, by a force under Vaudreuil, consisting of French troops and Indians numbering nine hundred and sixty-five men. The fort had but eleven effective defenders, who were compelled to surrender after a few hours' active resistance. The significance of this result was not in the loss of the fort, but in the fact that the enemy had crossed the Westenhuck and invaded neutral territory.

At the time of this occurrence a conference was being held at Albany, with the Six Nations, who as yet had given no evidence of intention to lift the hatchet. Governor Clinton had exhausted persuasive appeal; had told them that the king expected and ordered them to join with their whole force in the contest, thereby giving them "a glorious opportunity of establishing their fame and renown over all the Indian nations in America,' by the conquest of their "inveterate enemies, the French," who, however much they might "dissemble and profess friendship," would never forget the slaughter which the Five Nations had inflicted upon them in former years, and who, for the purpose of their destruction, were "caressing the nations" who had been their "most inhuman enemies," and who desired "nothing so much as to see the name of the Six Nations become decayed and forgot forever." The issue, as it was understood by the French and the Indians, was fairly stated, but it awoke no response.

When the news came that Hoosic had been attacked, the aspect of affairs was immediately changed. Three days after the governor's last appeal (August 23d), the chiefs replied: "Last year you gave us the hatchet to be made use of against your enemies. We accepted it and promised to make use of it if they should commit further hostilities, which they have now done by destroying Saraghtoga[1] and shedding a great deal of blood. Hitherto we have made no use of the hatchet, but as you now call upon us we are ready, and do declare, from the bottom of our hearts, that we will from this day make use of it against the French and their children." To this determination the *Mahicans* and the *Schaticooks* gave their assent.

But nothing more than a petty warfare followed. In New England the English suffered some disasters, but in New York they escaped, with the exception of an engagement near Schenectady, July 21st, 1748, the account of which is much confused, and the destruction, about the same time, of the residence of Mr. Keith, near Schaticook, and the slaughter of several of the members of his family, by a company of St. Francis In-

---

[1] A settlement on the Hudson in the vicinity of the present village of Schuylerville, from which the present name of Saratoga is derived.

dians.[1] On the part of the English, the *Mohawks* and *Mahicans* appear to have taken the field in some numbers, and to have lost warriors by death and captivity. At the Cedars they made a successful attack in the summer of 1747, but at the Cascades they were defeated with loss.

Pending formidable aggressive movements against the French, the war was closed by the treaty of peace at Aix la Chapelle. The news of the conclusion of this treaty reached Governor Clinton on the eve of the assemblage at Albany of a grand conference, with the Six Nations and their allies. Great effort had been made for the success of this conference, and in point of numbers these efforts were rewarded. If the Six Nations could do nothing else, they could always rally a host at a distribution of presents; the flow of rum was an attraction which they could not resist. Albany never saw such a gathering of painted warriors; a larger number never, perhaps, assembled in one place, or one in which there were more tribes represented. The enmities of years seemed to be forgotten; *Mahicans* and *Minsis* joined hands with the *Senecas*; the descendants of *Miantonimo* smoked the pipe with the *Mississagies*. Except in numbers, however, the conference was a failure. The " covenant chain " was brightened in ancient form, but instead of the command, " On to Canada ! " which Clinton had expected to issue, " Peace ! " was the injunction which fell upon the ears of the assembled chiefs.

The *Mohawks*, and *Mahicans*, the representative tribes addressed, were disappointed. While the other tribes in the English alliance had, with the exception of a few of their warriors, abstained from hostilities, they were seriously compromised. They had lost friends whose deaths were unavenged; the axe of the French was sticking in the heads of their people; in Canada prisons their brethren were rotting in irons; they had taken up the hatchet with reluctance, and would not lay it down until their friends were released and a definite proposal made guaranteeing their protection in the future. "We will still keep the hatchet in our hands," said the former; "we will still keep our hands on the cocks of our guns," said the latter. With them the question

[1] *Stone's Life and Times of Sir William Johnson*, 1, 350, 354.

of peace remained an open one until the exchange of prisoners was completed in June, 1750.[1] For two or three years later the *Mohawks* carried the hatchet in their hands, the English having neglected to call them together and remove it by a distribution of presents, a custom for which they had a most tenacious regard.

In the meantime, five tribes of the confederacy made peace with the French, asserting thereby not only their national independence but subscribing their totems to the declaration "that they had not ceded to any one, their lands;" that they "were not subjects of England."[2] To the French this was an important declaration. If the nations represented claimed independence, then could treaties be made with them and the foundation of territorial lines established; but if already under allegiance to Great Britain, the question of boundaries was still an open one. The *Mohawks* alone took their rank with the English; the practical division of the confederacy, upon a very vital point, was established, and a new element added to the controversy which had so long existed between the Indian nations and the English.

[1] *Colonial History*, x, 211.  [2] *Colonial History*, x, 187.

## CHAPTER IX.

THE WAR OF 1755 — REHABILITATION OF THE LENAPES AND SHAWANOES — THE CONSPIRACY OF PONTIAC.

THE treaty of Aix la Chapelle was a very imperfect paper. By its stipulations "all Nova Scotia, or Acadia, with its dependencies," was ceded to Great Britain; the "subjects of France, inhabitants of Canada," were not to "disturb or molest in any manner whatever," the Five Indian Nations which were "subject to Great Britain," nor the "other American allies" of that government; the boundaries between the English and French possessions, along the rivers St. Lawrence and Mississippi, and the limits even of Nova Scotia, one of the original causes of the war, were left entirely undetermined, and no provision was made for the removal of the forts which the French had erected at Crown point, or Lake Champlain, and at Niagara. The key to its interpretation, if such it had, was the status of the "Five Indian Nations" claimed as "subjects to Great Britain." If the nations referred to were not "subjects to Great Britain," then were the prohibitions of the treaty void, so far as they circumscribed the operations of the French or defined the boundaries of their possessions. Availing themselves of this interpretation, the French forstalled the English by securing from the *Onondagas*, *Senecas*, *Cayugas*, and *Oneidas*, the declaration already quoted that they were independent tribes, and resumed the prosecution of the policy, which they had inaugurated as early as 1731, of connecting the St. Lawrence with the gulf of Mexico by a chain of forts along that river to Detroit and down the Ohio to the Mississippi. While the English were disputing with them in regard to the Nova Scotia peninsula, La Galissoniére was sent out, in 1749, with three hundred men to trace and occupy the Ohio valley, and faithfully did he perform his work. At the mouth of every principal river plates of lead were deposited in the soil bearing the inscription, that, from the farthest ridge whence water trickled towards the Ohio, the country belonged to France, and the lilies of the Bourbons were nailed to forest trees in token of possession.[1]

The determination of the French reopened the original controversy. The establishment of the contemplated forts was fraught with danger to the English colonies. Not only would they cut off the western Indian trade, but would build up a power behind the English settlements which would be to them a perpetual menace, even if it did not involve their very existence as subjects of Great Britain. Self-interest as well as self-defense demanded that their construction should be anticipated if possible — if not, that their occupation by the French should be resisted. The colonies were themselves divided in regard to the jurisdiction to which they were respectively entitled by their charters; but, without waiting for the determination of the dispute, Virginia organized what was known as the Ohio company, for the ostensible purpose of securing the Ohio valley for the English world. Obtaining a patent in March, 1749, for five hundred thousand acres, this company sent out, in October, 1750, Christopher Gist to make treaties with the Indians and select locations for colonies, while Pennsylvania, for a similar purpose, dispatched George Croghan. At Logstown, these agents met and together prosecuted surveys, and consummated treaties, covering a broad expanse of territory, resting from their labors finally in the heart of the territory of the *Miamis*.

The *Senecas*, the *Lenapes*, and the *Shawanoes*, whose territory was thus invaded by the rival civilizations of Europe, at first received their visitors approvingly; but at length comprehending that they were to be the ultimate sufferers, remonstrated. "Where," said Tanadiarisson, the Half-King, as the ruling *Seneca* chief was called; "where lie the lands of the Indians? The French claim all on one side of the river, and the English all on the other;" and, repairing to the French commandant at Erie, he declared that it was the wish of his people that both parties should withdraw. Met with open refusal, he returned

[1] *Bancroft*, IV, 43 etc.; *Life and Times of Sir Wm. Johnson*, 1, 386, etc.

to his council, and added to the pending conflict a third party in interest — the aboriginal proprietors who were resolved to defeat the purposes of their European neighbors in such manner as opportunity should develop.

Strong in all the resources of civil and military centralization, the government of Canada moved with a resolution and celerity that for a time set at defiance the efforts of their slow-footed and divided adversaries. By the end of 1753, they had a connected line of forts, extending from Montreal to what is now called French creek, in Pennsylvania, but to which they gave the name of the Riviere aux Boeufs.[1] To this latter fort, Virginia sent, in December, Major George Washington, to demand the reason "for invading the British possessions in time of peace," and to warn the trespassers to retire. Civilly was he treated; the answer which he received was not unexpected. The French commandant knew no law but the orders of his general; to those orders he should "conform with exactness and resolution." The *casus belli* which Virginia sought was supplied.

Promptly voting £10,000, Virginia dispatched, in May, a force of one hundred and fifty men, under Washington, to the invaded territory, instructed "to make prisoners, kill or destroy all who interrupted the English settlements." Not a moment too soon did he reach the field. The French, sweeping down from Venango, had compelled the English to evacuate the trading post which they had established at the Fork,[2] and had occupied the place with fortifications. Warned by the Half-King, Washington hurried to the Great Meadows, where he held a conference with the friendly *Lenape* and *Seneca* chiefs. Before the rising sun of another day the French were attacked in ambush. An action of about a quarter of an hour ensued; ten of the French force were killed, including Jumonville, their commander, and twenty-one wounded.[3] Bearing tidings of the

---

[1] On account of the number of Buffalo found in its vicinity.— *Sparks's Washington*, II, 436.

[2] Now the city of Pittsburg, Pa. It was here that the Indian path separated, one leading to the Seneca country and the other to the west. Hence the name, the *Fork*.

[3] Washington was severely criticised for this attack, and was charged with the murder of Jumonville.— *Memoirs Hist. Soc. Penn.*, v, 45, etc.

disaster, a soldier reached the headquarters of the French commandant; a council of war was instantly assembled; its deliberations almost as instantly resulted in sending out an overwhelming force to meet and crush the advancing English. Washington fell back to the Great Meadows, where he threw up the breastworks of Fort Necessity and manned its feeble ramparts. But resistance was hopeless. Without supplies of ammunition or of food, capitulation was a necessity. Accepting permission to retire with his forces, Washington turned his face homeward. On the morning of the fourth of July, 1754, the French flag waved in triumph in the valley of the Ohio.

Not alone in the celerity of their movements had the French anticipated the English. With a zeal as remarkable as it was contagious among the Indians, they had pushed the alliances and strengthened the tribes immediately dependent upon them to an extent which had transferred to them the active power which had formerly been exercised by the Five Nations, when, armed by the English, they had first been commissioned a roving police over their contemporary tribes. In this respect the change had been wonderful indeed since the confederates rallied in the war of 1688. The liberality of the French had removed much of the ancient prejudice against them; the labors of the priests had won converts until in Canada the *Iroquois* were represented by as many organizations as they were in New York, who completely neutralized the action of the parent stocks; the *Mississagies*, the seventh tribe of the confederacy, had dropped from their ranks; the *Senecas* were estranged, and at Onondaga the council fire of the nation was constantly attended by the emissaries of France. As early as 1720, they began to appear in the character of mediators, rather than that of aggressive allies, and in 1745, they had with great difficulty indeed been brought out in even inconsiderable force in behalf of the English.

Perhaps this result was due in a great measure to the policy of the English in seeking through their alliances the promotion of trade; in neglecting to supply them with priests as self-sacrificing as were those sent out by France; in supplying the more immediate tribes with intoxicating liquors to their destruction, and in failing to cultivate the intimate relations with them which formed so conspicuous a feature of the policy of the French. Whatever the cause, the French experienced little difficulty in transferring to themselves the moral support of the *Senecas*, and in securing the active alliance of the *Lenapes* and *Shawanoes*, as well as of the more western tribes, and to direct their blows for the possession of the Ohio valley against the English as their worst enemies.

For their negative rather than their positive power, continued alliance with the confederates was desirable to the English. As enemies, they would be dangerous from their familiarity with the English settlements; as allies, they would still interpose a barrier to the incursions of their relatives in the Canada alliance. Their threats [1] intimidated Clinton; the rapidity with which events were culminating in hostilities, aroused the reluctant assembly; the funds necessary to provide presents for a renewal of the ancient alliance with them was voted, and Colonel Johnson dispatched to their castles to invite their attendance at a conference at Albany. The *Mohawks* responded sullenly : " Had any other person been sent, we would not move a foot ; " at Onondaga, the king declared he did not understand what the French and English intended to do in reference to the Ohio country, but for his people he could say, that they were already " so hemmed in by both, that hardly a hunting place was left, so that even if they should find a bear in a tree, there would immediately appear an owner of the land to challenge the property."

The conference at Albany was appointed for the fourteenth of June, 1754, and was to be held in conjunction with a convention of delegates from the several colonies, called to consider a plan for a general union for mutual protection. The attendance was not large; the colonies were not fully represented; the confederates were still halting between two opinions. The proceedings were opened with an address by acting governor De Lancey, in which the tribes were invited to " renew and strengthen their ancient covenant " with the English, and to call back the clans who had removed to the territory of the French. " The French," said he, " profess to be in perfect friendship with us

[1] *The Life and Times of Sir William Johnson*, 1, 422.

as well as with you. Notwithstanding this they are making continual encroachments upon us both. They have lately done so in the most insulting manner, both to the northward and westward. They are endeavoring to possess themselves of the whole country, although they have made express treaties with the English to the contrary. It appears to us that their measures must necessarily soon interrupt and destroy all trade and intercourse between the English and the several Indian nations on the continent, and will block up and obstruct the great roads, which have hitherto been kept open, between you and your allies and friends who live at a distance. We want, therefore, to know whether these things appear to you in the same light as they do to us, or whether the French, taking possession of the lands in your country, and building forts between the lake Erie and the Ohio, be done with your consent or approbation."

Hendrik accepted the belt, and replied that it should be taken to Onondaga for consultation. The confederates had been shamefully treated by their allies, while the French had used their utmost endeavors to bring them over in their favor. "This," said he, "is the ancient place of treaty, where the fire of friendship always used to burn; and 'tis now three years since we have been called to any public treaty here. 'Tis true there are commissioners here, but they have never invited us to smoke with them. But the Indians of Canada come frequently and smoke here, which is for the sake of their beaver. But we hate them. We have not yet confirmed the peace with them. 'Tis your fault, brethren, that we are not strengthened by conquest; for we would have gone and taken Crown point, but you hindered us. We had concluded to go and take it, but we were told that it was too late and that the ice would not bear us. Instead of this, you burnt your own fort at Saratoga, and run away from it, which was a shame and a scandal to you. Look about your country, and see, you have no fortifications about you; no, not even to this city. Look at the French; they are men; they are fortifying everywhere. But, we are ashamed to say it, you are all like women, bare and open without any fortifications." [1]

[1] *Colonial History*, VI, 870; *Life and Times of Sir Wm. Johnson*, I, 456, etc.

The *Mahicans* who acknowledged the jurisdiction of the authorities of New York, as well as those living under the government of Massachusetts, were present, and also the *Schaticooks*. The latter, replying to the governor, said : " Your honor may see that we are young and inexperienced, our ancient people being almost all dead, so that we have nobody to give us advice, but we will do as our fathers have done before us." The reception of the *Mahicans* from Stockbridge was delayed, the governor regarding them as belonging to Massachusetts. The records of the Indian commissioners were examined, and the fact made apparent that while under the territorial jurisdiction of Massachusetts, they were not the less the representatives of the *Mahican* nation ; that they had always been present at the treaties with the Five Nations, and had been included therein.[1] Their address was historical and forcible. Their fathers had first welcomed the Europeans and given them lands ; had formed with them a covenant chain which had never been broken. That chain they would now renew, rub bright and defend its links.[2]

The conference closed on the eighth of July. Every effort had been made to conciliate the chiefs, and presents and promises were lavished upon them. The heart of Hendrik grew happy. " We are highly pleased that all things have been so amicably settled," said he, "and hope that all that has passed between us may be strictly observed on both sides. If we do not hold fast by this chain of friendship, our enemies will laugh us to scorn." Thirty wagons conveyed to Schenectady the rum and other presents which he had received for his people ; in full faith that his lands would be protected, and a church built at Canajoharie, in which should be taught the principles of peace and good will, he departed.

While the conference with the Six Nations was as satisfactory as could have been expected, proceedings not directly connected therewith were had which ultimately destroyed not only the good which was anticipated, but plunged the confederates themselves into greater discord,[3] and aroused the *Lenapes* to war.

[1] *Colonial History*, vi, 865.
[2] *Colonial History*, vi, 881.
[3] *Colonial History*, vii, 956.

Sundry individuals of Connecticut had, after exploring the Susquehanna valley, determined to locate a settlement at Wyoming. The territory being regarded as the property of the Six Nations, although in the occupation of the *Lenapes* and their confederated clans, a deputation was sent to Albany to confer with them and effect its purchase. The governor of Pennsylvania promptly interposed objections to the procedure, and the delegates from that province were instructed to prevent its consummation if possible. The motive was entirely selfish. The proprietaries of Pennsylvania were also in attendance seeking the purchase of the same lands. The Connecticut agents succeeded, through the aid of Colonel Lydius. The tract purchased extended about seventy miles north and south, and from a parallel line ten miles east of the Susquehanna, westward two degrees of longitude, and included the whole valley of Wyoming and the country westward to the sources of the Alleghany. Failing to secure this tract for themselves, the proprietaries of Pennsylvania added to their purchase of 1737, "a tract of land between the Blue mountain and the forks of the Susquehanna river." These purchases were not made in open council with the representatives of the tribes, but from a few of the chiefs, several of whom were in a state of intoxication when they signed the deed of conveyance; but the purchasers, and especially the Connecticut company,[1] insisted upon their validity.[2]

The convention of deputies from the several colonies was continued in session until July 11th. A plan of union was agreed to and referred to the several colonial assemblies, and a declaration adopted recommending that the Indians in alliance with the English should be placed under a competent superintendency; that forts should be built for the security of each nation; that vessels of war should be placed on the lakes, and that any further advances of the French should be prevented. The latter only was approved; the union of the colonies failed. Regarding the transfer of powers to a confederate organization as too much of an encroachment upon the liberties of the people, the colonial assemblies refused their assent, while the parent

---

[1] Known as the Susquehanna company. It was organized in 1753.

[2] *Life and Times of Sir Wm. Johnson*, 1, 468, etc.

government rejected the plan on the ground that it favored the democratic at the expense of the aristocratic element.

The echo of Washington's guns on the Ohio meadows was speedily wafted to Canada, and scarcely had the last commissioner departed from Albany before the forests became alive with savage hordes let loose by the French upon the settlements. On the 28th of August, the St. Francis Indians fell upon Schaticook and Hoosic ; killed several persons, destroyed houses, barns and cattle, and swept off, either as prisoners or willing attendants, the remnant of *Pennacooks* residing there.[1] Bakerstown, in New Hampshire, was next visited, and there, as well at other points, men and women fell under the blows of their assailants, or were carried away captive.

Even more disastrous results were inaugurated in Pennsylvania and the Ohio country when the Albany purchases became known. The *Senecas* openly repudiated the contract. The lands which had been sold were theirs ; were occupied by their children and their allies, and they would not listen to its sale. Their principal chief, who had been one of the intoxicated grantors, was driven out from their cantons ;[2] the *Lenapes* and *Shawanoes* were urged to hostilities. The latter required but little encouragement. To them the famous " walking treaty," had been a sore grievance, a shameless fraud. That treaty was drawn by Penn in 1686, and conveyed an immense tract on the Delaware, the boundaries of which were described as beginning at a certain tree above the mouth of Neshamony creek ; thence by a course west-north-west to the Neshamony ; thence back into the woods " as far as a man could walk in a day and a

---

[1] On the 28th of August a party of French Indians, said to be of Bekancourt, a place between Quebeck and Montreal, made an incursion into this province and burnt the houses and barns full of grain at Hoosic, a place lying about eighteen or twenty miles east from that part of Hudson's river which is ten miles above Albany. They carried off with them the few remaining Indians at Schaticook, being between fifty and sixty in number, men, women and children. They had a little while before, when I was in Albany, assured me of their fidelity.— *Report of Gov. DeLancy, Colonial History*, vi, 909.

[2] Johnson says that this chief fled to the French for protection against his incensed people, but immediately adds : " A powerful party who followed his fortunes, took up arms shortly after, attacked a body of provincials at Lake George, whom he totally defeated, and killed forty-five. Since which he was concerned in the most important services against us, cut off some of our settlements, and occasioned the deaths of more than four hundred of our people."— *Colonial History*, vii, 956

half;" thence to the Delaware again, and so down to the place of beginning. Sixty years later, Penn's successors were the surveyors of this tract, and, in order to secure as good a bargain as possible, prepared a road for the "walk," provided expeditious means of crossing the intersecting streams, and selected the swiftest pedestrians in the province, that thereby might be accomplished as great a distance as possible within the time limited. The line on the Delaware was not fixed by the treaty, and advantage was taken of the omission to run the course not parallel with the river, but by one which extended north-east for a hundred miles and more, till it struck the Delaware near the mouth of Laxawaxen creek, far above Easton. A million acres of land were thus embraced, when, by a fairer computation, three hundred and fifty thousand would have confined their claim.[1]

This was the largest, but not the least of the frauds which the *Lenapes* had suffered. In the Minnisink country they had also been defrauded. The famous Minnisink patent covered lands which had been purchased from them but never paid for, the purchasers having made the grantors drunk pending the execution of the deed, obtained their signatures when they knew not what they were doing, and then refused the promised compensation on the plea that it had already been given.[2] The Esopus chiefs, and the *Hackinsacks* and *Tappans*, joined in the complaint; the borders of New Jersey and New York, as well

---

[1] *Memoirs Historical Society of Pennsylvania*, v, 68.

[2] "An elderly man who lived in the Highlands, and at whose house I dined on my way from New York some years ago, told me that he lived with or in the neighborhood of one Depuy, and was present when the said Depuy purchased the Minnisink lands from the Indians; that when they were to sign the deed of sale he made them drunk and never paid them the purchase money agreed upon. He heard the Indians frequently complain of the fraud, and declare that they would never be easy until they had satisfaction for their lands."—*Manuscripts of Sir Wm. Johnson*, xxiv, 14. Depuy was probably the agent employed to make the purchase. He was well known to the Moravians, his residence being on the old Mine Road, which they traveled.—*Memorials of Moravian Church*, 1, 46. "The examinant (John Morris) says he often heard the Delawares say that the reason of their quarrelling with and killing the English in that part of the country was on account of their lands which the Pennsylvania government cheated them out of, and drove them from their settlement at Shamokin by crowding upon them, and by that means spoiled their hunting, and that the people of Minnisink used to make the Indians always drunk whenever they traded with them, and then cheated them out of their furs and skins, also wronged them with regard to their lands."—*Colonial History*, vii, 332.

as the wilderness of Pennsylvania, were filled with the threatening protestations of disfranchised proprietors animated by a common determination to hold possession of their ancient homes.

Hitherto their protestations had been without favorable result. The authorities of Pennsylvania, to provide against evil consequences, had appealed to the Five Nations to send delegates to a council at Philadelphia, when they had complained of the "walking" boundaries in 1742. The *Iroquois* delegates heard the complaint, as well as received private presents from the proprietaries. Subsidized by rum and trinkets, they commanded the *Lenapes* to yield possession of the lands. "We conquered you; we made women of you; we charge you to remove instantly; we don't give you liberty to think about it; we assign you two places to go to, either to Wyoming or Shamoking," was their answer, and the debate was closed.

The *Lenapes* had removed as they were bidden, and settled in the valley of Wyoming, but with that removal and settlement the "undisciplined feeling of natural equity" was fully developed in them. Whatever of doubt hung over their right of possession to the lands from which they had been ejected, there was none in regard to those to which they had been assigned. The Five Nations had given them the latter, and they were theirs. In the sale to the Connecticut company these lands were included; in that to the agents of the Pennsylvania proprietaries, their more western hunting grounds were cut off without their consent. Remembering that by precisely similar means they had been despoiled of their former homes, they resolved to fight to the last in defense of their rights; to revenge this last and crowning outrage, and to wipe away with blood the well remembered wrongs which had rankled in their bosoms for years. The chiefs of the east met those of the west in council at Alleghany, rehearsed the wrongs which they had suffered, and declared that wherever the white man had settled within the territory which they claimed, there they would strike him as best they could with such weapons as they could command; and, that the blow might be effectually dealt, each warrior-chief was charged to scalp, kill and burn within the precincts of his birthright, and all simultaneously, from the frontiers, down into the heart of the settlements, until the English should sue for peace and promise redress.¹

The summer was spent in hostile preparations and in establishing alliances. The *Senecas* gave them arms, removed from them the petticoat, and bade them take the hatchet; the " six different nations of French Indians "² plead their cause with the *Mohawks*, and "advised and entreated them" to break the Albany sales, and to "have some consideration for those they called brothers;"³ the council at Onondaga repudiated the offensive contracts. October came, and no sooner had the biting frost reddened the maple and hardened the yellow corn in the husk, than, with their allies, painted black for war, in bands of two or four abreast, they moved eastward with murderous intent, and the line of the Blue mountain, from the Delaware to the Susquehanna, became the scene of the carnival which they held with torch and tomahawk during many coming months. The defenseless settlers were harassed by an unseen foe by day and by night. Some were shot down at the plow, some were killed at the fireside; men, women and children were promiscuously tomahawked or scalped, or hurried away into distant captivity, for torture or for coveted ransom. There was literally a pillar of fire by night and a pillar and cloud by day going up along the horizon, marking the progress of the relentless Indians, as they dealt out death, and pillage, and conflagration, and drove before them, in midwinter's flight, hundreds of homeless wanderers, who scarce knew where to turn for safety or for succor in the swift destruction that was come upon them.⁴

The attacking force appeared in two distinct yet united organizations — that of the eastern *Lenapes*, under the lead of Teedyuscung; that of the western under Shingas.⁵ Both

---

¹ *Thompson's Alienation.*
² These were representatives of the Six Nations who had removed to Canada at the instigation of the French priests.
³ *Colonial History*, vi, 938.
⁴ *Memorials Moravian Church*, 1, 193.
⁵ "*Shingask* was his proper name, which interpreted is a *bog meadow*. This man was the greatest Delaware warrior of that time; were his war exploits on record they would form an interesting document, though a shocking one. His person was small, but in point of courage and activity, he was said never to have been exceeded by any one." (*Heckewelder's Narrative*, 64). Pennsylvania offered £200 for his scalp. His brother, Tamaque, or King Beaver, was also a distinguished warrior and chief.— *Ib.*, 61, 64.

were equal in determination, though perhaps unequal in strength, the western being the most formidable in numbers, in position, and in the direct aid which they could obtain from the French. The defeat of Braddock in July, was the signal for the aggressive action already outlined in general terms. The western organization was first to strike. On the 16th of October they fell upon the whites of John Penn's creek, four miles south of Shamokin. Here they killed or took captive twenty-five persons; and it was only the twenty-third of the month when all the settlements along the Susquehanna, between Shamokin and Hunter's mill, for a distance of fifty miles, were hopelessly deserted. Early in November the Great and Little Cove were attacked and the inhabitants either put to death or taken prisoners, and the settlements totally destroyed.

These blows were promptly seconded by the eastern organization under Teedyuscung. Assembling his allied *Lenape*, *Shawanoe* and *Mahican* warriors at Nescopec, he marked out the plan of the campaign for the coming autumn and winter. Its operations were to be restricted to the "walking purchase," within which it was resolved to chastise the English first, by waging against them a war of extermination. From their lurking places in the fastnesses of the Great Swamp, the wronged warriors, led by Teedyuscung in person, sallied forth on their marauds, striking consternation into the hearts of the settlers. Falling upon the farms along the Susquehanna and Delaware, they fired the harvested grain and fodder in barns and in barracks, destroyed large numbers of cattle and horses, and killed thirteen persons. On the 24th of November the Moravian mission at Gnadenhutten was surprised and ten of its converts scalped, or shot, or tomahawked, or burned to death in their dwellings. This was but the prelude to the tragedy which was to be performed. Along the northern line of the tract which had been so fraudulently surveyed, the tide of devastation rolled its blackening current. Within a month, fifty farm houses were plundered and burned, and upwards of one hundred persons killed on the frontiers on both sides of the Kittatinny, or endless hills. "All our border country," writes a chronicler of the day, "extending from the Potomac to the Delaware, not less than one hundred and fifty miles in length and between twenty and thirty in breadth, has been entirely deserted, its houses reduced to ashes, and the cattle, horses, grain and other possessions of the inhabitants either destroyed, burned or carried off by the Indians; while such of the poor planters who, with their wives, children and servants, escaped from the enemy, have been obliged, in this inclement season of the year, to abandon their habitations almost naked, and to throw themselves upon the charity of those who dwell in the interior of the province."

The *Minsis*, unleashed, performed their part — for each tribal clan, it will be borne in mind, was, by the terms of the compact, required to strike within the territory which they claimed as their

birthright — and on the borders of Ulster and Orange counties in New York, and in the western settlements of New Jersey, were repeated the fearful ravages of the more remote districts of Pennsylvania. Except in the town of Goshen, the settlements here were at considerable distance from each other and much exposed to the surprises of the Indian enemy. The incursions of the Indians were frequent; the people, especially in the northern part of Orange and southern part of Ulster, were kept in almost perpetual alarm and under such " continued military duty as to be rendered incapable of taking care of their private affairs for the support of their families." An extent of country, on the west side of the Wallkill, of fifteen miles in length and seven or eight in breadth, which was "well and thickly settled, was abandoned by the inhabitants, who, for their safety, removed their families to the east side of the river, and became a charge on the charity of their neighbors," while others " removed to distant parts, and some out of the province.[1]

"Fatigues of body, in continually guarding and ranging the woods, and anxiety of mind which the inhabitants could not

---

[1] *New York Manuscripts*, LXXXII, 107, etc.

avoid by their being exposed to a cruel and savage enemy, increased by the perpetual lamentations and cries of the women and children," were not the only evils which the inhabitants suffered. Three men were killed at Cochecton; five men at Philip Swartwout's; Benjamin Sutton and one Rude, two of the Goshen militia, were killed at Minnisink; Morgan Owen was killed and scalped about four miles from Goshen; a woman, taken prisoner at Minnisink, was killed and her body cut in halves and left by the highway; Silas Hulet's house was robbed and he himself narrowly escaped. " From about the drowned lands for fifteen miles down the Wallkill, where fifty families dwelt, all save four abandoned their fields and crops." [1]

Meanwhile General Edward Braddock, whose defeat has been incidentally noticed, had arrived in Virginia with two regiments of English troops, and at a conference with the royal governors, on the 14th of April, had planned four expeditions against the French; the first was to effect the complete reduction of Nova Scotia, the second was to recover the Ohio valley, the third was to expel the French from Fort Niagara and form a junction with the expedition to the Ohio, and the fourth, under the command of Colonel Johnson, was to have for its object the capture of Crown point, for which purpose he was to have the militia of New York, Massachusetts and Connecticut, and the warriors of the Six Nations under his command. To aid in securing the services of the latter, as well as to effect a more complete organization of the Indian alliances, he was appointed superintendent of Indian affairs, with full power to make treaties in the interest of the crown.[2]

Returning from Alexandria, where the conference had been held, Johnson entered upon the work which had been assigned to him. From Mount Johnson, to which he removed the council-fire which had for so many years been kept burning at Albany, he sent a belt to each of the confederate tribes,

[1] " All the families between the deponent's house and Minnisink, to the amount of one hundred and fifty persons, have deserted those settlements and come into four frontier houses, one of which is the deponent's: that deponent's house, which is now a frontier house on that side, and which was, last year, fifteen or sixteen miles within the settlements at Minnisink, is about sixteen miles from Hudson's river."—*Affidavit of James Howell, New York Manuscripts*, LXXXII, 107, etc.

[2] *Colonial History*, VI, 961.

acquainting them of his appointment and asking them to come and meet him. Over a thousand sons of the forest accepted the invitation, and, on the 21st of June, seated themselves before him in council. While ready to do him personal service and honor, they had many complaints to make — were deeply entangled by their pledges to the French as well as to their tribal blood in Canada. Johnson listened to them with patience, and, after answering all their inquiries, delivered to them a ringing appeal to join him. The chiefs listened and applauded; drank the rum which had been provided, accepted the presents, and danced the war dance, but that was all. To march with him to the frontiers they were not prepared, and plead the shortness of the warning, the want of time to call in their scattered people, the disgraceful termination of the contest of 1745, their relations with their Canada brethren; indeed, there was apparently no end to the reasons which they could not assign to conceal their indifference to the English cause and the divisions which existed among themselves.

From this boasted "bulwark" against the French, turn for a moment to the conduct of the nations in the French alliance, led by the flower of the Hudson river tribes. At the call of Vaudreuil three and thirty nations rallied to his ranks. From the rivers of Maine and Acadia, and the wildernesses of Lake Huron and Lake Superior, the martial airs of France were shouted in the many tongues of the allied nations as they pressed with swift destruction upon the border settlements and returned laden with the trophies of the fray.

Hendrik and his *Mohawks*, bound by personal ties to Johnson, with here and there a warrior from the other tribes, to the number of fifty, left Albany with Johnson on the 8th of August. At the "carrying place" some two hundred warriors joined him,[1] giving to him, with the militia, a force of about thirty-five hundred men. The French, marching in about equal force to attack Oswego, were called back and sent, under Baron Dieskau, to the defense of Crown point. Leaving the largest portion of his forces at that Fort, Dieskau pushed on

[1] The French report says: "All the Mohawks were there, some Oneidas, some Tharhkarorin, some Mahicans, and one Onondaga."— *Colonial History*, x, 322.

intending to attack Fort Edward, cut off Johnson's retreat, and annihilate his army. Misled by his guides, he found himself on the road to Lake George and only four miles distant from Johnson's encampment at Ticonderoga. Leaving his position, Johnson detached one thousand men and two hundred Indians to bring on an engagement. The opposing forces met on the 8th of September. Finding the French too powerful, the English fell back to Ticonderoga; the French pursued and resumed the battle under the walls of Johnson's position. After a severe engagement, from twelve until four o'clock, the French retreated. The losses on both sides were heavy, that of the English being one hundred and fifty-eight killed, including King Hendrik and thirty-eight of his warriors, ninety-two wounded and sixty-two missing, while that of the French was between three and four hundred.[1] Johnson was wounded slightly, and Dieskau mortally. The French retreat was unmolested; Crown point was not reduced. Such was the victory which gave to Johnson a baronetcy, and to American history Fort Ticonderoga.

Johnson returned to his residence in November, and was met at Schenectady by a message from the governor of Pennsylvania asking his aid in arresting the depredations of the *Lenapes* in that province. Summoning the chiefs of the Six Nations (Jan. 7th), he informed them that " the *Shawanoes* and *Delawares* and river Indians[2] were committing hostilities in the southern part of New York, as well as in New Jersey and Pennsylvania;" that they had " burned several out settlements and killed many people who had never offended them;" that as the offenders were " looked upon as allies and dependents of the Six Nations," and living within the limits of their country, it was expected that they would reprimand them " for what they had already done, prevent their doing any more mischief, and insist on their turning their arms against the French."[3]

The mission was promptly undertaken by the *Mohawk*, *Oneida* and *Tuscarora* chiefs.[4] They had already sent a belt to the *Lenapes* and their allies desiring that they would not

---

[1] *Life and Times of Sir Wm. Johnson.*
[2] The reference is to Mahican and other clans residing on the Delaware.
[3] *Colonial History*, VII, 44.
[4] These were the only nations represented at the conference.

join with any but the Five Nations;[1] now they would "appoint with them a conference at Tiyoga and endeavor to put a stop to any more bloodshed." The loyal *Seneca* villages[2] exercised their influence in the same direction. Visited by a party of *Lenapes* on their way to Niagara, they tried to persuade them to stop, and called to their aid their most venerable chief; but neither belts nor personal appeals had any effect upon the followers of Shingas. Replying to the loyal *Senecas* they exclaimed: " We have once been women and ashamed to look down at our petticoats, but as you have taken off our petticoats, and encouraged us to begin a quarrel with the English, we are determined never to submit again to that ignominious state while there is one of us alive. It seems to us that you now want to throw all the blame on us, and make peace, which we will not hearken to, but will go to our father the French, who will assist and protect us."[3] Thither they went, and to the commandant at Niagara declared : " Father — We are now at war with the English. When we first began, being very poor, we struck them with billets of wood." In reply, the commandant gave them a hatchet, and arms and ammunition, and lighted afresh the torch of war which they had waved along the borders.

Not more successful were the direct appeals of Johnson's embassadors to Shingas. " Get sober," said they to him, in the metaphorical language of Indian speech ; " Get sober—your actions are those of a drunken man." But the days of yore were gone, when the trembling *Lenape* stood cowering in the presence of the *Mengwe*. Unhesitating submission to the mandates of the tribes that had so long oppressed and insulted his nation, was no longer written on his heart. Of the old confederacy the most powerful part were now his friends, while around him had gathered his grandchildren in formidable numbers. To the words of the embassadors he returned scoff for scoff, and scorn for scorn. " We are men," said he ; " we are men and warriors. We will acknowledge no superiors upon

[1] When speaking of themselves in official transactions Five Nations only were recognized. The Tuscaroras had no territorial rights or authority.
[2] The Onondagas, Cayugas and Senecas preferred neutrality, with the exception of two Seneca villages who remained loyal to the English. As already stated, the great bulk of the Senecas were actively aiding the French.
[3] *Manuscripts of Sir William Johnson*, IV, 131.

earth. We are men, and are determined to be no longer ruled over by you as women. We are warriors, and are determined to cut off all the English save those that make their escape from us in ships. So say no more to us on that head, lest we make women of you as you have done of us."[1]

At Otseningo the embassadors were more successful, the *Lenapes* and their allies there being more immediately under the influence of the *Oneidas*. From thence they returned, on the 27th of December, bearing with them the message that the offending chiefs there had promised to "stop and repent," but as a condition thereto the English must return the captives which they had taken; that they " must see every one of them returned again " or it " would not be well ;" for this they would wait two months, and if the captives were then returned, they would " contrive to make up the matter and settle affairs, and not till then ;" meanwhile they promised that their young men who were on the war path should be called back."[2]

In February, 1756, Johnson again called the attention of his allies to the matter, and reminded them that unless they exerted themselves to "maintain their superiority," they would " not only lose that authority " which had been hitherto acknowledged, but would have the *Lenapes* their enemies. Red Head, the *Onondaga* sachem, replied, that when first requested to do so a message had been dispatched to the *Lenapes*, which had subsequently been "backed with a second message;" that both messages having proved abortive, they had " obtained an interview," through the *Oneidas*, at which the *Lenapes* had promised that hostilities should cease. They would cheerfully renew their efforts, and would appoint a meeting at Otseningo, at which, by a full representation of the tribes, they would endeavor to exercise that influence in which they had hitherto failed.

Pending this new mission, a delegation of friendly *Lenapes* met Johnson in conference, on the 29th of February. The *Oneida* and *Tuscarora* embassadors opened the proceedings, and stated that the *Shawanoes* were on their way to Chugnut[3] where

---

[1] *Thompson's Alienation*, 77 ; *Memoirs Historical Society Pennsylvania*, v, 98.
[2] *Colonial History*, VII, 44, 49.
[3] On the south side of the Susquehanna river, opposite Binghamton. It was a very small portion of the Shawanoes that were represented.

they would live under the protection of the Six Nations; that the *Lenapes* had given the strongest assurances of peace, and that they earnestly desired that a fort might be erected for their protection. Johnson expressed his gratification at the disposition of the chiefs in attendance ; promised that a fort should be built for the protection of the *Lenapes* and that they should be cared for and supplied with arms and ammunition. Adam, on the part of the latter, expressed his appreciation of the kindness which they had received, and promised never to forget it. The visit was of no significance touching the action of the *Lenapes* proper, but appears to have been gotten up to indicate that the *Oneidas* and *Tuscaroras* still had the influence which they claimed.

On the 21st of April, the embassadors of the second mission made their report. They had visited the *Lenapes* and *Shawanoes*, and had succeeded, they said, in " convincing them that they had acted very foolishly and very unjustifiably," and that they had "promised and agreed " to unite with them against the " common enemy ; " but at the same time had expressed the desire that they might have a hearing at Onondaga to convince them that harmony and friendship with them was desired, in which request the embassadors united. Johnson accepted the proposition; he would hold a council at Onondaga twenty days hence, and charged the chiefs, then present with the duty of extending the invitation.

About the same time an important change took place in the *Lenape* government. Tadame,[1] their king, was treacherously murdered, but by whom is not stated, and Teedyuscung, that " lusty, raw-boned man," whose voice had already been heard in the wilderness, became his successor. Enjoying the confidence of his people, as well as possessing great native ability, he had already become a power to be both feared and conciliated. For peace with the English he was ready, but it must be a peace which recognized the rights of his nation ; to no other would he listen, and spurned alike the threats and the blandishments of those who would influence him to a different policy.

[1] We have not met with a more specific reference to this chief. He appears to have been the successor of Allumpanees who died in 1747, after having long out lived his activity.— *Minor's History Wyoming ; Memorials Moravian Church*, 1, 67.

In the meantime, Pennsylvania declared war against the Lenapes and Shawanoes, and sent out a force of three hundred men, under the charge of Benjamin Franklin, to build a fort at Gnadenhütten[1] or Shamokin, and restore the fugitive Moravian Indians and their missionaries to their lands. Johnson doubted the policy of these movements, regarding it as the part of wisdom to have awaited the result of the negotiations which he had inaugurated, and which he believed only awaited the council which he had appointed at Onondaga for their consummation. That council assembled in June, but Teedyuscung did not attend, nor were his subordinate chiefs present in numbers sufficient "to enter upon business and conclude affairs relating to them with proper authority."[2] To entertain and conciliate them special effort had been made. Thirty Indians from the Delaware river, who had been taken prisoners by the English, and whose release had been insisted upon, were taken up in full clothing and armament, as a peace offering, and ample presents were provided for distribution. On the last day of the session Teedyuscung made his appearance, but would do nothing, and the conference was adjourned to Mount Johnson.[3]

The adjourned conference was more successful. Teedyuscung, having satisfied himself that the English were not only sincere in their desire for peace, but had been convinced that the Six Nations, in their present condition, were wholly unable to control his people, made his appearance, and was urged to explain the reason for the hostilities which had been committed, and to enter upon a covenant of peace. But he was not prepared to comply. " I cannot take upon me at this time to give a determinate answer to you," said he, " but I shall punctually deliver your speech to all my nation on my return home, and you shall have our fixed resolutions and positive answers as soon as possible." Dismissing him, Johnson called the confederate

[1] Fort Allen. It was located at the Moravian town of Gnadenhütten, on the Lehigh river, opposite the mouth of the Mahoning, and adjoined the Lenape town of Shamokin where Teedyuscung had his residence. It was built in January, 1756, by Benjamin Franklin.— *Pennsylvania Colonial Records*, VII, 15.

[2] There were only two young warriors of the Delaware nation present.— *Colonial History*, VII, 146.

[3] Neither did the deputation from the Delawares come till that meeting was near upon a conclusion.— *Colonial History*, VII, 153.

chiefs to advise with him what further course to pursue, and it was agreed that the latter should visit Teedyuscung in his tent and persuade him to declare his intentions at the session of the following day. To this the king consented, and, at the appointed time, stated that he could only agree for himself and his people at Tiyoga ; that his brethren on the Ohio must determine for themselves, but for himself and those whose representative he was, he promised to follow the example of the Six Nations — a promise at that time of very doubtful import. Paxinos, the *Shawanoe* king, made similar pledge, and Abraham, on behalf of the *Mahicans* at Otsiningo, united in the assurance of harmony. A formal declaration or covenant of peace and friendship was then made, and the war dance celebrated.

Still Johnson was not altogether satisfied that his work was well done. He knew that the *Lenapes*, and their allies, aspired to if they did not possess the independence which they claimed, and that so long as this was denied, peace would not be possible. The necessities of the English were great,[1] the determination of the *Lenapes* and their allies undisguised. Selfishness became the ally of justice — the diplomacy of Teedyuscung secured the triumph of his people. In the watches of the night Johnson meditated, and on the morning of the 12th of July, after consultation with the sachems of the Six Nations, declared to the *Lenape* king, and the representatives of the *Shawanoes* and *Mahicans*, that, in consideration of the promise they had made, and in full confidence of their future suitable behavior, they were " hereafter to be considered as men," by all their brethren the English, " and no longer as women," and expressed the hope that the Six Nations would follow his example and remove the " invidious distinction." [2] Decking the chiefs with medals, and the kings with silver gorgets, he covered the embers of the council-fire, and sent from his presence a rehabilitated race.

---

[1] The good consequences that will attend the accommodating of this unhappy breach are great. It will give a great turn to the affairs of the present war in North America, and I trust may, by a little time and proper management, enable us to withdraw the Delawares and Shawanese that are settled on the Ohio from the French interest. I doubt their present connections are too strong to hope for this success now.— *Hardy to Lords of Trade*, May 10, 1756.

[2] *Colonial History*, vii, 151, 160.

While the attention of Johnson was mainly devoted to the pacification of the more important Indian nations, the domestic clans of *Minsis* and *Mahicans*, who remained in the valley of the Hudson, were not neglected. To the former, proclamation was made in December, 1755, through the justices of Ulster, inviting them to remove from the "back settlements, where they might be taken for enemies and destroyed," to the "towns where they would be protected and assisted." Accepting these assurances, many of them came forward ; but the promised protection and assistance was not, in all cases, extended. At Wilemantown, in Ulster county,[1] at the house of Charles Stevenson, where a number of them assembled, they were attacked, on the second of March, by a party of armed men, headed by Samuel Slaughter, and a man and his squaw killed. Moving from thence to a wigwam about a mile and a half distant, three Indians, two squaws and two children fell victims to Slaughter's misguided zeal.[2] Those who reached Kingston, while spared hostile attack, were suffered to remain dependent upon such charity as was usually extended to their race. Under the circumstances in which they were placed, they readily accepted the offer which was made to them to remove to the *Mohawk* country. To that end *Mohawk* chiefs were sent to them, with an interpreter, and provision made for their transportation. On the 22d of May they appeared before Johnson, were addressed and assigned to lands in the Schoharie county.[3]

Many of the *Mahicans* of the upper Hudson and *Wappingers* of Dutchess followed in the same direction. On the 28th of May, Johnson writes : " The river Indians whose families are at Fishkill, have had a meeting with the *Mohawk* Indians, and it is agreed that they shall remove and live with the *Mohawks*. Two of those Indians are going down to fetch up their women, children, etc., and I send an interpreter with them. As the removal of these Indians and their incorporation with the *Mohawks* is an affair that will be, I hope, of happy consequence towards the public tranquillity at this juncture, I must desire you

---

[1] Near Walden, Orange county, in the state of New York.
[2] *New York Manuscripts*, LXXXII, 88 ;
[3] *Documentary History of New York*, II, 763, 764.
*Colonial History*, VII, 94, 96, 100, 113.

will give all assistance in your power to the Indians who are going down, and take care that no just cause of dissatisfaction be given to them."[1] When Johnson returned to his residence on the 9th of July, he found, as the fruit of this order, one hundred and ninety-six " *Mohicander* or river Indians," men, women and children, awaiting his pleasure. In the afternoon he clothed the men " from head to foot, gave them ammunition, paint, etc., in the presence of the Six Nations and the *Shawanoes* and *Delaware* kings."[2] They were warmly greeted by their brethren who had left them many years before, and who were then present, as well as by the *Nanticokes*, in whose immediate vicinity they were assigned lands at Otsiningo.[3] Thither they went, and in the subsequent assemblies of the tribes took their place as the allies of the *Senecas*. After serving Johnson faithfully for a time, and especially in his expedition against Crown point, they joined the fortunes of their brethren in the *Lenape* confederation and lost their identity in their subsequent wars.

The peace which Johnson had made with Teedyuscung was only partial. In consenting to it the latter had defined his authority as limited to the territory which he specially represented. For himself, and those who acknowledged his authority, he had promised—the *Lenapes*, *Shawanoes* and *Mahicans* of the Ohio country—he would influence if he could. To attend any peace conference with Johnson, they had refused, as also had the *Minsis*. Said the latter: " We have murdered the English from Canastota to Esopus. Warraghiyagy (Johnson) may pretend to make peace, but peace is not in his power. The governor of Pennsylvania is master this way, and will not listen to peace," and such was the interpretation which Teedyuscung himself

---

[1] *Manuscripts of Sir Wm. Johnson*, IV, 54.

[2] *Colonial History*, VII, 153.

[3] " Last spring," said Jonathan, who represented them at the conference of April 23d, 1757, " last spring, with this belt the Nanticokes took us by the hand and bid us sit down by them. They said to us, ' you Mohikanders and we Nanticokes will be one people and take you Mohikanders by the hand as brethren, and fix you here at Otsiningo, where the Six Nations have lighted a council fire and the Senecas appointed lands for you to cultivate. Call all your dispersed brethren together and sit down here with them as their habitation, and we Nanticokes assure you that whoever shall pinch or hurt you, we shall feel it, and the Six Nations shall do the same.' This belt we propose to send among all our dispersed people; we acquaint you herewith, and whenever you see any of our scattered people passing up the river, you will know they are removing to Otsiningo."—*Colonial History*, VII, 253.

gave to Johnson's jurisdiction. Monakadook,[1] the *Seneca* Half-King, who had been sent to the Ohio *Lenapes* to invite them to Onondaga, was the bearer of a message from them to the governor. On his arrival he found that Teedyuscung had preceded him, and had informed him that he had been empowered by ten nations [2] to conclude a peace, and was prepared to negotiate. Monakadook could give the governor no information on the subject, and was made the bearer to Johnson of the inquiry: " Who is this Teedyuscung who claims to be king of the Delawares ? " coupled with the declaration that his protestations of a desire for peace must be false, "as the Delaware Indians were still murdering " his people.[3]

Johnson professed entire ignorance in regard to the commission which Teedyuscung claimed he had received, and it is not probable that he had any information on the subject. The inference is that the chiefs who were negotiating in his interest, having failed to control the *Lenapes*, had concealed from him their further action in the matter, hoping to effect the end which he sought by other means, with a view to maintain a reputation which they no longer possessed.[4] Johnson promised to make inquiry at Onondaga in regard to the matter. What the result of this inquiry was does not appear; but the governor of Pennsylvania was convinced, and modified his declaration of war, making it applicable only to " implacable and obstinate enemies, and not against any that now are or hereafter may be disposed to hearken to the Six Nations in our favor." By November he

---

[1] So called by the Iroquois.

[2] Including, as subsequently appeared, his own immediate tribes and the Six Nations.

[3] *Colonial History*, VII, 197. The governor sent a more formal message by Captain Newcastle, in October, inquiring into the character and credentials of Teedyuscung, and, it is said was informed by one of the Six Nations that the Delaware chief " did not speak the truth when he told the governor that he had authority from the Six Nations to treat with Onas."

[4] This inference is strengthened by the speech of the Mohawk orator at Lancaster. " In former times our forefathers conquered the Delawares, and put petticoats on them. A long time after that, they lived among you, and, upon some differences between them and you, we thought proper to remove them, giving them lands to plant and hunt on at Wyoming and Juniatta. But you, covetous of land, made plantations there and spoiled their hunting. They complained to us, and we found their complaints true. You drove them into the arms of the French. It is our advice that you send for the Senecas and them, treat them kindly, and give them back some part of their lands, rather than differ with them. It is in your power to settle the difference with them if you please."—*Gallatin*, 78

had fully learned who Teedyuscung was, and at Easton held a formal conference with him. The *Lenape* king stated his complaint boldly and plainly. To the governor's inquiry for specifications in regard to alleged wrongs in the sale of lands, he replied : " I have not far to go for an instance. This very ground under me (striking it with his foot), was my land by inheritance, and is taken from me by fraud. When I say this ground, I mean all the land lying between Tohiccon creek and Wyoming, on the river Susquehanna. I have not only been served so in this government, but the same thing has been done to me as to several tracts in New Jersey, over the river." When asked what he meant by " fraud," he gave instances of forged deeds, under which lands were claimed which were never sold. " This," said he, " is fraud." " Also, when one chief has land beyond the river, and another chief has land on this side, both bounded by rivers, mountains and springs, which cannot be moved, and the proprietaries, ready to purchase lands, buy of one chief what belongs to another, this likewise is fraud." In regard to the lands on the Delaware, he said his people had never been satisfied since the treaty of 1737. The boundary of the land then sold was to have gone only "as far as a man could walk in a day and a half from Nashamony creek," yet the person who measured the ground did not walk but ran. He was, moreover, as they supposed, to follow the winding bank of the river, whereas he went in a straight line. And because the Indians had been unwilling to give up the land as far as the " walk " extended, the governor sent for their cousins, the Six Nations, to come down and drive them from the land. When the Six Nations came down, the *Lenapes* met them for the purpose of explaining why they did not give up the land ; but the English made so many presents to the Six Nations that their ears were stopped. They would listen to no explanations ; and Canasateego[1] had abused them, and called them women. The Six Nations had, however, given to them and the *Shawanoes* the lands upon the Susquehanna and Juniatta for hunting grounds, and had so informed the governor ; but notwithstanding this the white men were allowed to go and settle upon those lands.

[1] A viceroy chieftain who had been set over them by the Six Nations.

Two years ago, moreover, the governor had been to Albany to buy some land of the Six Nations,[1] and had described the boundaries by points of compass, which the Indians did not understand, by which the deeds were made to include lands both upon the Susquehanna and the Juniata which they did not intend to sell. When all these things were known to the Indians, they had declared that they would no longer be friends to the English, who were trying to get all their country away from them. He had come now to smoke the pipe of peace with them, and hoped that justice might be done to his people. [2]

The conference continued nine days, and was the occasion for the display of no little tact and good judgment on the part of Governor Denny, as well as on that of Teedyuscung. The former, as some of the *Iroquois* chiefs expressed it, "put his hand into Teedyuscung's bosom, and was so successful as to draw out the secret, which neither Johnson nor the Six Nations could do;" while tne latter secured a truce at least involving peace on the basis that himself and his people were to remain on the Wyoming lands, and that houses should be built for them by the Pennsylvania proprietaries. He was to go to Johnson's council-fire and explain what had been done, obtain his confirmation and take advice as to the future. Several matters were left unadjusted, Teedyuscung declaring that he was not empowered to consider them, and that the parties interested were not properly represented to make action binding. He proposed that a meeting should be held at Lancaster in the spring, at which all the matters in dispute should be definitely adjusted, and with that understanding the council closed.

But at the meeting which was then appointed, Teedyuscung was not present,[3] and it was not until the 21st of July that the adjourned council was held. On its assemblage the *Lenape* king presented his credentials as the representative of the *Lenapes, Minsis, Mahicans, Shawanoes* and *Nanticokes,* east of the Alleghany mountains, fully empowered by them and by the *Senecas, Onondagas, Cayugas, Oneidas* and *Mohawks,* "to set-

---

[1] At the congress of 1754.
[2] *Life and Times of Sir Wm. Johnson; Colonial History,* VII, 260, etc.

[3] The attendance of the Indians was prevented by the severity of the winter, the snow being too deep to permit them to travel.

tle all differences subsisting between them and their brethren, the English." George Croghan represented Johnson, as superintendent of Indian affairs. A patient, earnest and honest investigation was had. Surrounded by three hundred of his people ; counselled by Paxinos, chief of the *Shawanoes*, and Abraham, chief of the *Mahicans*, and advised by a delegation of Quakers, one of whom, Charles Thompson, acted as his clerk,[1] Teedyuscung conducted his case. " The land is the cause of our difference," said he, " and if I can now prevail with you, as I hope I shall, honestly to do what may be consistent with justice, then will I with a loud voice speak, and the nations shall hear me. The complaint I made last fall, I yet continue. I think some lands have been bought by the proprietor or his agents from Indians who had not a right to sell, and to whom the lands did not belong. I think also when some lands have been sold to the proprietor by Indians who had a right to sell to a certain place, whether that purchase was made by miles or hours' walk, the proprietors have, contrary to agreement or bargain, taken in more lands than they ought to have done, and lands that belonged to others. I therefore now desire that you will produce the writings and deeds by which you hold the land and let them be read in public and examined, that it may be fully known from what Indians you bought the lands you hold and how far your purchase extends. What is fairly bought and paid for, I make no further demands about, but if any lands have been bought of Indians to whom they did not belong, and who had no right to sell them, I expect satisfaction for those lands ; and if the proprietors have taken in more lands than they bought of true owners, I expect likewise to be paid for that. But as the persons to whom the proprietors may have sold those lands which of right belong to me, have made some settlements, I

---

[1] " At this council Teedyuscung insisted upon having a secretary of his own selection appointed, to take down the proceedings in behalf of the Indians. The demand was considered extraordinary and was opposed by Governor Denny. Teedyuscung persisted in his demand, and it was finally acceded to. Charles Thompson, master of the free Quaker School in Philadelphia, was appointed. He was afterwards secretary to the Continental congress, and filled that station for many years. He died in 1824, aged 94 years, full of honors. The Delawares adopted him and gave him a name signifying, the man of truth. — *Life and Times of Sir Wm. Johnson*, II, 14.

don't want to disturb them or force them to leave them, but I expect a full satisfaction shall be made to the true owners for these lands."

The deeds which he questioned, it was proposed should be sent to Johnson to examine; but to this he objected: "We do not know Colonel Johnson; he may be an honest and sincere man. We do understand he treats his Indians very well, but we are sensible that some of the nations are there that have been instrumental to this misunderstanding in selling lands in this province, having in former years usurped that authority and called us women, and threatened to take us by the foretop, and throw us aside as women. But after a long space I believe it is evident, nay there are witnesses present who can prove that it is otherwise. Let the deeds be produced here and put down with the minutes." The governor complied with the request, and the deeds were compared by Thompson, who certified to the correctness of the transcripts which were made. They were five in number.[1] It was agreed that they should be sent to Johnson for transmission to the king, and that awaiting his decision upon the questions which the Indians had raised, there should be peace.

These matters having been made satisfactory, Teedyuscung announced his purpose. "I shall, as I promised," said he, "speak to the different nations with a loud voice. I will faithfully let them know what you have promised, and as we are witnesses that you are wealthy and powerful, and well disposed to assist such as shall come in as brothers, I will let them know it. Those who come to me with hostile intent, I will stop, and if they will not by reasonable terms turn about and join with me, I will then make an end of them or they of me; and if there is a great number, so that I may not be able to withstand them, I will take all prudent steps to let my brethren the English know." "Now," said he, in conclusion, "you

---

[1] 1. A paper copy of the last Indian purchase, July, 28, 1686   2. A release from the Delaware Indians, August 25, 1757.   3. A release from the Five Nations for the lands on the Susquehanna river, October, 11, 1736.   4. A release from the Six Nations of lands eastward to Delaware river, dated October 25, 1736, with another endorsed, " Dated July 9, 1754."   5. A deed of release for Indian purchase, dated August, 22,1749.— *Colonial History*, vii, 313.

may remember I was styled by my uncles, the Six Nations, a woman in former years, and had no hatchet in my hand, but a pestle or hominy pounder. But now, brethren, here are some of my uncles who are present to witness the truth of this. As I had no tomahawk and my uncles were always styled men and had tomahawks in their hands, they gave me a tomahawk; and as my uncles have given me a tomahawk and appointed and authorized me to make peace with a tomahawk in my hand, I take that tomahawk and turn the edge of it against your enemies the French."

The papers which were transmitted to Johnson were immediately sent by him to the lords of trade, accompanied by the statement that "some of the Six Nations were disgusted with the deed which had been given at Albany, while others were conniving at the hostilities which were being committed, and that he conceived the "most effectual method of producing tranquillity," would be the voluntary and open surrender of that deed, leaving the proprietaries to fix with the Indians, in the best manner they could, "the bounds for their settlements." This opinion he had other reasons for entertaining. The Six Nations, whose consequence he never forgot to magnify, would never be satisfied "unless the deeds of the Albany purchase" were "surrendered up, and the claims founded thereon in a great measure set aside;" the *Lenapes* were equally determined, testimony having been furnished him that they had been heard to declare "most solemnly" that "they would never leave off killing the English as long as there was one on their lands; that they were determined to drive them all off their lands, naming Minnisink almost to the North river east (in the provinces of New York and New Jersey); also Bethlehem and the lands on a parallel line to it west," which the English had cheated them out of.[1]

In this conclusion he was most amply justified by the results which had been experienced. Peace had been declared, but no exchange of prisoners had taken place, and while Teedyuscung himself maintained the truce which had been agreed to at Easton, on the Ohio, his allies and kindred spurned the overtures made to them and maintained their alliance with the French. Send-

[1] *Colonial History*, vii, 331.

ing their emissaries eastward, the latter propagated prejudices against the good intentions of the English, magnified the prowess, kindness and generosity of the French, and successfully plead the wrongs which had been committed against them in the sale and occupation of their lands.[1] The *Minsis* were ready listeners to these appeals, and active participants in the hostilities which were continued.[2] Indeed, hostilities were not suspended in any direction. In August, 1757, says Niles,[3] "one James Tidd was scalped in the Minnisinks. About this time, also, one James Watson, with James Mullen, went out on some business and were fired upon by a party of Indians. Watson was found killed and scalped; Mullen was carried off, as was concluded, not being found or heard of. About the 19th of September, Patrick Karr was killed and scalped at a place called Minnisink bridge.

"Some time in the first part of October, in Ulster county, the Indians fired into the furthermost house in Rochester, and killed two women, but were repulsed by two men.[4] Just before the other Indians came up, one of the company that was foremost seized a young woman as she was washing at the door; upon which she screamed out; another woman rescued her, beat off the Indian and shut the door.

"On the 16th of May, 1758, about two clock in the afternoon, about thirteen Indians rushed into the house of one Nicholas Cole, on the frontiers of the Jerseys, if I mistake not. Cole not being at home, they immediately pinioned his wife, and tomahawked their son-in-law, about eighteen years old, and dragged her out of doors, where her eldest daughter, about thirteen years old, lay murdered, and a boy aged eight, and her youngest daughter, aged about four. At last, the poor, helpless

---

[1] *Colonial History*, VII, 87.
[2] *History of the French and Indian War*, Mass. Hist. Soc. Coll., v.
[3] "I am inclined to think the Minnisink Indians who formerly lived on those lands, if not the only are at least the chief perpetrators of those hostilities and ravages which the frontiers of your province and that of New York, have and are daily suffering."— *Johnson to Gov. of New Jersey, July,* 19, 1758.

[4] The official account states that this raid was by a party of Senecas and river (Delaware) Indians. The attack here spoken of, was on the house of Peter Jan, in the south-western part of Rochester. Jan's house was burned and one of his daughters, and two men who acted as scouts, were killed. Jan's wife and two daughters, and himself and two sons who were in the field, escaped.— *Documentary History*, II, 763, 764.

old woman saw the cruel savages thrust their spears into the body of her gasping infant. They rifled the house, and then carried her and her son off, after they had scalped the slain above mentioned.

"Soon after they were joined by two Indians with two German captives they had taken that day, and killed and scalped another, in one Anthony Westbrook's field, near Minnisink, so called, in Susquehanna county, if I mistake not. Not long after Cole returned home; where to his great surprise he found his four children murdered, and his wife and other son missing. Upon which he went to Minnisink (Napanoch) fort, and got a few soldiers to assist him in burying his children and the German. The soldiers joined with some of the neighbors that evening to cross Delaware river at day-light, and waylay the road to Wyoming; and as four of them were going to one Chambers's, about two o'clock at night, they heard the Indians coming down the hill, to cross the Delaware, as was supposed, when one of the four fired on them. They immediately fled, giving a yell after their manner. The woman they led with a string about her neck, and the boy by the hand; who, finding themselves loose, made their escape along the road, and happily met at James McCarty's house, the boy first, and afterward the woman.

"The daughter of one widow Walling, living near Fort Gardiner, between Goshen and Minnisink, going out to pick up some chips for the fire, was shot at by three Indians. Her shrieks alarmed the people. Her brother, looking out at a garret window, and seeing a fellow dispatching and scalping his sister, fired at them, and was pretty certain he wounded one of them. The old woman, during this, with her other daughter and her son, made off and escaped.

"About this time (beginning of June), a sergeant went from Waasing[1] to Minnisink with a party of men, but returned not at the time they were expected. Upon which a larger party went out in search of them, and, at their arrival at Minnisink, found seven of them killed and scalped, three wounded, and a woman and four children carried off. Near about the same time, in

[1] Wawarsing probably.

the frontiers of the Jerseys, a house was beset by a party of Indians, where were seventeen persons, who were killed, as I remember the account. A man and a boy traveling on the road with their muskets were fired on by some Indians in ambush. The man was killed; but the boy escaped, having first killed one of the Indians. Not far from this time—whether before or after I am not certain—the Indians killed seven New York soldiers. This slaughter was committed at a place called Westfalls, in the frontiers of New Jersey."[1]

Such is the imperfect record of these hostilities. That they were not more numerous is due to the erection, by Governor Hardy, in the summer of 1757, of a number of blockhouses along the frontiers of Orange and Ulster county, covering a distance of thirty miles,[2] and affording a refuge to the settlers. At these blockhouses garrisons of regular troops or militia were constantly stationed, and moved to the defense of more exposed situations. They were far from being a perfect protection, however, and, as already shown, were themselves the object of hostile attack.

There was some excuse on the part of the Indians for the continuance of hostilities. The proprietaries of Pennsylvania had manifested no willingness to relinquish their claim to the lands which they had so fraudulently acquired, nor had New Jersey made overtures of restitution. To Johnson's letter to the lords of trade, the proprietaries had entered a remonstrance, denying that any cause of complaint existed in reference to the lands which they held, and at home were unsparing in their

---

[1] A party of Indians lay in ambush to get an opportunity to take the lower fort at Mr. Westfall's. They sent two of their party to espy it, who discovered that there were only two women in the fort. While the two spies returned to inform their party, a small company of soldiers, marching from New Jersey to Esopus, came along and stopped at the fort. They were scarcely seated before the Indians rushed in and fell on the men with their tomahawks. The soldiers fled to the chamber from which they shot at the Indians, and after a desperate fight compelled them to retire, though several of the soldiers were killed.—*History Orange County*, 381.

[2] "From a place called Machakamak to the town of Rochester." (*Gov. Hardy's Message*). Machakamak, is now the village of Port Jervis. The blockhouse at this point was called Col. Jersey fort, and was still standing at the outbreak of the war of the Revolution. The location of the other blockhouses is not marked on Sauthier's map. These blockhouses were joined on the south by those erected by New Jersey of which one was known as Westfall's fort, at the lower neighborhood.

denunciations of the Quakers for having, as they asserted, assisted the Indians against the interests of the province. The papers forwarded by Johnson, however, were too plain a statement of facts to sustain them in their position, and the order was returned directing him to appoint a commission to make an examination of the case. Anticipating the action of this commission, the governor of Pennsylvania appointed a conference with the Indians at Easton, in October, 1758. Teedyuscung attended as the representative of thirteen nations,[1] assumed the position which he had formerly occupied, and sustained himself with eloquence and dignity. Finding that nothing could be done unless the land question was satisfactorily disposed of, the proprietaries came forward and surrendered the confirmatory deed which had been received from the Six Nations at Albany in 1754,[2] and recognized the right of the government to arrange the boundaries of the lands included in the treaty of 1742. A treaty was concluded, after a session of nineteen days. All that Teedyuscung had asked was granted; the boundary lines were agreed to; New Jersey paid the *Minsis* £1,000 for the lands which they claimed in that province, and received a concurrent deed from all the *Lenape* tribes; an exchange of prisoners was agreed to,[3] and peace folded her wing over the long harassed frontiers.

The divisions which existed among the Six Nations, so apparent in the early stages of the controversy with France, increased as the war progressed. In April, 1757, the *Senecas*,

---

[1] The tribes represented were classified as the Mohawks, Oneidas, Onondagas, Cayugas, Senecas, and Tuscaroras, comprising the Six Nations, the Nanticokes, Conoys, Tuteloes, and Chugnuts, of the Susquehannah; the Lenapes, Minsis, Shawanoes, Mahicans, and Wappingers of the Delaware. In the Wappingers will be recognized the families gathered at Fishkill in 1756, and in the Mahicans the clans of that nation whose removal to the Delaware country had commenced in 1730 (*ante*, p. 194).

[2] Not the deed to the Connecticut company. (*Documentary History*, II, 775); also *Colonial History*, VII, 388, where Johnson says: "Brethren, you have been acquainted that at the late treaty at Easton, in Pennsylvania, the proprietary agents, in behalf of their constituents, gave up their claims to the lands on the Ohio, which were sold to the proprietaries in 1754, at Albany, and here I have in my hands the instrument of release and surrender."

[3] It is said that a portion of the prisoners taken by the Lenapes had been given to the Six Nations, but the confederate title is probably used in this as in many other cases when the designation should have been specific to have properly recorded the fact. These prisoners were returned at Canajoharie, April 13, 1759.

*Onondagas*, and *Cayugas*, threw off the disguise of active friendship which they had professed for the English, and sent a large belt to Canada to make peace with the French. " Our promise," said they, " to remain firm to the English was given with the understanding that the war should be prosecuted vigorously ;" now that they saw the French victorious on every side, and the English army retreating as it were, they considered themselves released from all previous obligations and determined to make peace for themselves, and thenceforth to remain neutral. With them the victorious party were desired as friends ; besides, so many of their number were already in the ranks of the French, that those who remained attached to the English had no security from destruction but neutrality.

The advantages of this neutrality were in favor of the French. Although by its terms the English were not deprived of any numerical force, yet the fact that the confederacy was divided in its allegiance had its influence at home as well as among the nations more remote. The *Mohawks* were compromised by it, and became idle spectators to the numerous incursions of the French Indians, while to the Indians of the Ohio country it was an encouragement to continue their revolt. Eventually it drifted into war in behalf of the French ; for the time being it was turned by Johnson to the best advantage possible. " As you have declared yourselves neutrals," said he to the three tribes, " I shall expect you to act as neutrals and not permit either the French or their Indians to pass through your settlements to make war upon the English, and that you do not directly or indirectly give our enemies or their Indians information to our prejudice. Should you violate these rules of behavior, we shall look upon the covenant chain as absolutely broken between us." This promise they gave, and their neutrality was confirmed.

With war rolling its folds of fire on the north and west, and allies within their bosom who were indifferent if not willing spectators to its progress, the English had no mean task before them to retain their supremacy. At one time, indeed, even this seemed hopeless ; [1] but, better counsels prevailing in the pro-

---

[1] " For God's sake," wrote the officer of Massachusetts, in 1757, " exert yourself in command at Albany, to the governor to save a province ; New York itself may

vinces as well as on the part of the home government, the lost ground was recovered and the banners of England floated in undisputed possession of Canada.

In the Ohio country the conflict was continued long after its close at the north, and developed the strength of the ties which had been formed between the western Indians and the French. Usually the first, they were now the last to yield. The *Senecas* joined them; the *Lenapes* saw all their ancient wrongs repeated and riveted upon them in the success of the English. Already had the advanced couriers of the latter penetrated the Ohio valley; here and there in convenient proximity forts had been erected to overawe them and protect their enemies. Every promise which the English had made having been apparently violated, the war-belt of the *Senecas* invited the nations in the French alliance to take up the hatchet in their behalf.[1]

The plot was discovered in time to arrest immediate hostilities, but not to defeat the formation of a more formidable conspiracy. As the tribes felt the chain of English domination drawing closer and closer around them, one among their number, Pontiac, the king of the *Ottawas*, counseled, in the summer of 1762, the formation of a league to drive the English from the continent. The great interior tribes responded. The *Senecas* gave to the movement one thousand warriors; the *Lenapes* and *Shawanoes*, nine hundred; the *Mahicans* and *Wyandots*, two hundred; the Ottawa confederacy under Pontiac a number equal to their allies.[2] Moving quickly to their work, one after another, LeBœuf, Verrango, Presque Isle, Sandusky, St. Joseph, Miami, and Michillimackinac fell into the hands of the conspirators.

---

fall; save a country; prevent the downfall of the British government upon this continent."—*Bancroft*.

[1] "I understood and was told by them (the Delawares) that the breaking out of this war was occasioned by the Seneca Indians who went about with a bloody belt and tomahawk to all the nations engaged in this trouble "—*Manuscripts of Sir Wm. Johnson*, VIII, 14.

[2] The following is Johnson's estimate :

*Friendly Indians.*—*Mohawks*, two villages, 160 warriors; *Oneidas*, two villages, 250; *Tuscaroras*, one village, 140; *Onondagas*, one large village, 150; *Cayugas*, one large village, 200—total, 900 warriors.

*Hostile Indians*—*Senecas*, two villages, 1050; Delawares, of the Ohio, 600; *Shawanoes*, 300; *Wyandots* and *Mahicans*, near Fort Sandusky, 200—total 2150 warriors.—*Manuscripts*, XXIV, 186.

The *Mohawks, Oneidas, Tuscaroras, Onondagas* and *Cayugas* held to their covenant with the English, but only as neutrals. Teedyuscung followed their example, having, in a treaty at Easton, in May, 1762, fully adjusted his dispute with the proprietaries. It was his last treaty. The *Senecas* and the western *Lenapes* were alike offended by his course,[1] and determined to advance their ends by his destruction. Resorting to a mode of warfare favorite among the Indians and especially calculated to serve a double purpose, a party of *Senecas*,[2] ostensibly on a mission of peace, visited Wyoming in April, 1763, and after lingering about for several days, in the night time treacherously set fire to the house of the unsuspecting king, which, with the veteran himself, was burnt to ashes. Remaining on the ground, they inspired the followers of the murdered king with the belief that the work had been done by the Connecticut settlers. Stimulated by these representations, the infuriated *Lenapes* fell upon the unsuspecting whites, on the 14th, and massacred about thirty, drove off their cattle, rifled their stores, and at night applied the torch to dwellings and barns, and lighted up the valley with their destruction.

The fall of Teedyuscung accomplished the purpose which its perpetrators had designed,— the *Lenapes* were consolidated in interest, and the alliances of the *Senecas* made complete. The governor of Pennsylvania sent troops to the scene of conflict,

---

[1] The Indians went away much dissatisfied, especially the Six Nations, *i. e.*, the *Senecas*. The *Shawanoes* and *Delawares* left most of their presents on the road to the Ohio.—*Manuscripts*, VI. 144.

[2] Stone and other writers use the term Iroquois, implying the participation of the confederacy in the transaction, and assuming that they were offended at the growing power of Teedyuscung. Such an interpretation does not correspond with the apparent facts. The Indians were Iroquois it is true, but it is also true that they were *Senecas* or those engaged in stirring up hostilities in the west. Heckewelder says : " Fearing that he might not fall into their measures of joining in a new war against the English, they perhaps concerted the plan of destroying him." Nothing was ever positively known. His successor, *Netawatiewes*, held the throne untill 1776, when by his death, it devolved upon *Coquehagechton*, alias White Eyes, who, during the early part of the Revolution, was distinguished for his friendship to the colonists and for his efforts to keep his people neutral. He died at Tuscorawas (Fort Laurens) of small-pox in 1778. " The person on whom, by lineal descent, the station of head-chief of the nation devolved, being yet young in years, the surviving chiefs *Gelellmand*, alias Killbuck, *Machingwe Pushis*, alias *Large Cat*, and *Tetepachksi* officiated in his stead." The young king was killed in the massacre of peaceable Indians by Williamson at Pittsburg, in 1781.—*Heckewelder's Narrative*, 153, 193, 198, etc.

but the immediate participants in the massacre anticipated their arrival and withdrew to Tioga, while the Moravian Indians, who had taken no part in the transaction, removed to Gnadenhütten. Failing to reach the guilty, a band of lawless whites determined to punish the innocent, and with a hatred born of the pernicious teachings of Church, banded together to exterminate the whole Indian race, "that the saints might possess the land." Sixty in number, these maddened zealots fell upon the *Canestogoes*,[1] a small clan of *Oneida* dependents residing upon their reservation in the most inoffensive manner, hacked their chief in pieces in his bed, murdered three men, two women and a boy, and burnt their houses. But few of the Indians were at home, being absent selling their little wares among the people. On their return the magistrates of Lancaster collected them and placed them in one of the public buildings for protection. Thither they were followed by the fanatics, the building broken open and the massacre commenced. "When the poor wretches saw they had no protection, and that they could not escape, and being without the least weapon of defense, they divided their little families, the children clinging to their parents; they fell on their faces, protested their innocence, declared their love for the English, and that in their whole lives they had never done them any harm, and in this posture they received the hatchet. Men, women and children, infants clinging to the breast, were all inhumanly butchered in cold blood."[2]

The Moravian Indians at Gnadenhütten fled to Philadelphia, and were followed thither by their maddened persecutors, whose numbers now swelled to an insurgent army. The governor called the troops for the protection of the fugitives; the Indians begged that they might be sent to England. An attempt was made to send them to the *Mohawk* country, but after proceeding as far as Amboy, they were recalled. Another season of terror

[1] The Conestogoes are presumed to have been the remnant of the old Susquehannocks, whose destruction was accomplished by the English of Maryland aided by the Five Nations. They were removed from Maryland and settled among the Oneidas until they lost their language, when they were sent to Conestoga. Their name would seem to have been derived from that of the chief under whose charge they were placed.—*Gallatin*, 55.

[2] *Proud*; see also *Life and Times of Sir Wm. Johnson.*

ensued, and the governor hid himself away in the house of Dr. Franklin. The Quakers were alone equal to the occasion, and firmly resisted the intended bloodshed. Persuaded to listen to the voice of reason, the insurgents at length abandoned their murderous purposes and returned to their homes, and the besieged Indians again sought rest in the wilderness.[1]

The combination under Pontiac failed, but not from any lack of courage and determination on the part of the confederates. While maintaining the siege of Detroit, belts, which had been sent in all directions by the French, assured the tribes which had been in alliance with them that their power had departed. The courier who took the belt to the north, offered peace to all the tribes wherever he passed; and to Detroit, where he arrived on the last of October, he bore a letter in the nature of a proclamation, informing the inhabitants of the cession of Canada to England; another addressed to twenty-five nations by name, and particularly to Pontiac, and a third to the commander, expressing a readiness to surrender to the English all the forts of the Ohio and east of the Mississippi.[2] The next morning Pontiac raised the siege, accepted "the peace which his father the French had sent him," and departed with his followers, disappointed but unrelenting.

The *Lenapes* and their allies had, in the meantime, performed their allotted work. Ruined mills, deserted cabins, fields waving with the harvest but without reapers, attested their ruthless warfare east of the Alleghanies, while at Fort Pitt they held successful siege. The Virginia troops under Boquet, who had been sent out against them, barely escaped destruction. At Edge hill, on the 5th and 6th of August, 1763, stratagem alone saved him. Taking advantage of the intrepidity of his assailants, he feigned a retreat. The allies hurried to charge with the utmost daring, when two companies, that had been purposely concealed, fell upon their flank; others turned and met them in front; and the Indians, yielding to the irresistible shock, were routed and put

---

[1] It is a singular fact, that the actors in this strange and tragic affair were not of the lower orders of the people. They were Presbyterians, comprising in their ranks men of intelligence, and of so much consideration that the press did not disclose their names, nor the government attempt their punishment.—*Stone.*

[2] *Bancroft*, v, 133, 164.

to flight. The loss to the English of one hundred and fifteen men, or about one-fourth of their force, attested the bravery of the assailants.[1]

During the winter of 1764, Johnson succeeded in persuading some of the warriors of the neutral nations to unite with a company of militia under his son, John Johnson, for the invasion of the *Lenape* territory. On the 26th of February, a company of insurgents, under command of Captain Bull,[2] was surprised and made prisoners in their encampment near the Susquehanna. The prisoners were removed to Johnson Hall, from whence Bull and thirteen of his warriors were sent to New York and lodged in jail, and the remainder distributed among the confederates. Another *Iroquois* party under Brant, burned the *Lenape* town of Kanestio and six other of their large villages lying on the head waters of the Susquehanna.

Seconding the efforts of Johnson, New Jersey and Connecticut sent out an army of eleven hundred men to attack the *Senecas*, while Pennsylvania and Virginia contributed a greater number to subdue the allies in the Ohio valley. The *Lenapes* fled from their burning villages to the *Senecas*, and the latter, fearing the destruction of their own towns, sent, early in April, a deputation of four hundred of their chief men to Johnson Hall to sue for peace. The overture was taken advantage of by Johnson to gain important concessions. The *Senecas* were required to stop hostilities and engage never again to make war upon the

---

[1] Johnson pays this tribute to the prowess of the Lenapes and their allies: "The Ohio Indians begun on the frontiers of Pennsylvania, Virginia, and the communications to the posts, three of which, Presque Isle, Verrango and La Bœuf, they took immediately. After laying waste all the frontiers they invested Fort Pitt, and reduced the garrison to much danger. Col. Boquet, with six hundred men and a large convoy, marching to its relief, was attacked by only ninety-five of them (for I have the best authorities of white men then with the Indians and of several different Indians, who all agree that that is the true number), who killed about sixty of his people and greatly obstructed his march. In short, to pursue them through their different successful expeditions and depredations would be entering into a tedious detail of facts well known and still sensibly felt here."—*Colonial History*, VII, 962.

[2] "Made them all prisoners to the number of forty-one, including their chief, Captain Bull, son to Teedyuscung, and one who has discovered great inveteracy against the English, and led several parties against them during the present Indian war." (*Johnson, Colonial History*, VII, 611.) In *Memorials of Moravin Church*, I, 252, it is stated that Teedyuscung had three sons, Amos or Tachgokanhelle, the oldest, Kesmitas, and John Jacob." Captain Bull was probably Amos. At that time he was thirty-four years old.

English, deliver up all their prisoners within three months, cede to the crown the Niagara carrying place and allow the free passage of troops through their country, and renounce "all intercourse with the *Delawares* and *Shawanoes*," and assist the English in bringing them to punishment. As hostages, three of their principal chiefs were to await the complete fulfillment of the terms.

When the English under Bradstreet reached Niagara in August, he found no Indians in arms. There the *Senecas* met him, delivered up fourteen prisoners, and asked that the *Lenapes* and *Shawanoes* should be included in the treaty of April,[1] Johnson, who had arrived before Bradstreet, agreed to this on condition that those tribes delivered up their king and Squash Cutter, their chief warrior, and the *Senecas* left with him two of their chiefs as hostages for the fulfillment of the terms. With the *Ottawas*, *Chippewas*, *Hurons*, and other tribes under Pontiac, peace was also made, although Pontiac did not appear. The Indian country was made a part of the royal dominions; its tribes were bound to aid the English troops, and in return were promised assistance and protection; Indian murderers and plunderers were to be delivered up; all captives were to be set free and restored, and the families of English settlers assured of welcome.

Not less successful was the expedition under Boquet. A little below the mouth of Sandy creek, beneath a bower erected on the banks of the Tuscarawas, chiefs of the *Senecas*, the *Lenapes*, the *Shawanoes*, and the *Mahicans*, invited peace. The *Lenapes* delivered up eighteen prisoners, and eighty-three small sticks as pledges for the return of as many more. At the junction of the White Woman and the Tuscarawas, in the centre of the Indian villages, the *Shawanoes* accepted the terms of peace with dejected sullenness, and promised, by their orator, Red Hawk, to collect all captives from the lower towns and restore them in the spring.[2]

On the 27th of April, 1765, the pledges which had been given by the *Senecas* were redeemed by the surrender of the

---

[1] Stone, in his *Life and Times of Sir Wm. Johnson*, gives Bradstreet little credit for his part in this transaction.

[2] Bancroft, v, 210, 221.

*Lenape* king, Long Coat, and his principal warrior, Squash Cutter, who in their turn became hostages for the Susquehanna clans. Captain Bull and two of his warriors were released, and the remaining prisoners, who had been sent to New York for security, were brought up and placed in charge of the commanding officer at Albany until the Susquehanna clans, to whom they belonged, should deliver up their prisoners according to promise. On the 19th of June the latter appeared with twenty-five persons, including even half-breeds, the children of intermarriages with the Indians. The exchange was made; the hostage chiefs departed, and the war of ten years was closed.[1]

The withdrawal of the French brought with it the necessity of treaties with the tribes that had been in alliance with them, as well as changes in the policy of the English. The task was a difficult one. The attachment of the northern and western Indians to the French was strong; the grievances of the *Senecas* and their *Lenape* allies were aggravated by the peace to which they had been compelled and in which they had been forced to concede that their lands were a part of the royal dominions. In regard to their territorial possessions, their decision in 1748 had grown into a positive policy, which the English were obliged to recognize on the very threshold of negotiations, as well as the wide-spread influence which it exerted. To treaties, submissions, and cessions, which recognized any other fact than that they were a free people — that they had independent lands, which were their ancient possessions — they would give no attention, while to proffered protection they replied that they wanted none so much as from the English themselves.[2]

---

[1] The treaty of peace was made with Killbuck or Bemineo, Long Coat or Anindamooky, and Squash Cutter or Yaghkapoose, on the part of the eastern Lenapes, and was ratified and confirmed by Turtle Heart or Aquarsqua, Wieweenoghwa, Tedabajhsika, Lenapes of the Ohio, and Benavissica, Manykypusson, Nanicksah, and Wabysequina, Shawanoes of the Ohio.—*Colonial History*, VII, 738.

[2] *Colonial History*, VII, 958. Colonel Bradstreet, in his "Thoughts on Indian Affairs," gives a different view of the policy of the tribes. He writes: "Of all the savages upon this continent, the most knowing, the most intriguing, the less useful, and the greatest villains, are those most conversant with the Europeans, and deserve most the attention of the government by way of correction, and these are the Six Nations, Shawanoes, and Delawares. They are well acquainted with the defenseless state of the inhabitants who live on the frontiers, and think they will ever have it in their power to distress and plunder them, and never cease raising the jealousy of the Upper Nations against us, by propagating amongst them

To appease their demands Johnson had proposed to them in 1765, to "make a line" which should be recognized alike by themselves and the English as a boundary beyond which neither should pass. The proposition was accepted, but its execution was delayed. Meanwhile the tribes remained morose and jealous and at times ready to take up the hatchet. Hostilities on the western border continued of frequent occurrence; the difficulties in Pennsylvania, were kept alive by the constantly increasing tide of European emigration. Connecticut determined to occupy the Wyoming valley, while the fanatics of the Canestogo massacre shot and scalped with unrelenting zeal the Indian hunters wherever opportunity offered. Smarting under these aggressions, the *Senecas*, in 1768, by a large belt said to the *Lenapes* and *Shawanoes*: " Brethren, these lands [1] are yours as well as ours; God gave them to us to live upon, and before the white people shall have them for nothing, we will sprinkle the leaves with blood, or die every man in the attempt." Finding that the matter could no longer be delayed, a conference was called at Fort Stanwix and the contemplated boundary line established.[2] In the name of the king, Johnson took a deed for the territory south and east of the Ohio. In addition to this deed, William Trent obtained title to a tract between the Kenawha and Monongahela; the proprietaries of Pennsylvania, one of the Wyoming lands, and George Croghan one confirmatory of two grants which the Indians had given him, in 1766,

---

such stories as make them believe the English have nothing so much at heart as the extirpation of all savages. The apparent design of the Six Nations is, to keep us at war with all savages but themselves, that they may be employed as mediators between us and them, at a continuation of expense, too often and too heavily felt, the sweets of which they will never forget nor lose sight of, if they can possibly avoid it. That of the Shawanoes and Delawares is to live on killing and captivating and plundering the people inhabiting the frontiers; long experience has shown them they grow richer, and live better thereby, than by hunting wild beasts."—*Colonial History*, VII, 690.

[1] The reference is to lands then being occupied by the English along the Monongahela, and the Red Stone creek.

[2] This treaty was concluded Nov. 5th, 1768. By its terms all the lands north and west of the Ohio and Alleghany rivers to Kittaning; thence in a direct line to the nearest fork of the west branch of the Susquehanna; thence, following that stream through the Alleghanies, by the way of Burnett's Hills and the eastern branch of the Susquehanna and the Delaware into New York, to a line parallel with Nonaderha creek, and thence north to Wood creek, east of Oneida lake—was recognized as the territorial domain of the Six Nations, *Lenapes, Shawanoes*, etc.— *Colonial History*, VIII, 135.

of thirteen hundred acres on the Alleghany river. The sum of ten thousand dollars in goods and money was paid to the Six Nations and their allies, and their possessions in the valley of the Hudson, as well as of the Delaware, were known to them no more.

Not only was the policy referred to, with its resultant boundary, developed by the war, but the position of the Indian nations was changed. As the representative allies of the English, the confederated tribes still had a name, but in almost all other respects their dominion and authority had shriveled up under the touch of the contending civilizations as certainly as had that of the nations which had earlier fallen under its malign influence. Nominally united when the war closed, and maintaining a recognized deference to the action and wishes of each other, as they had during its continuance, they were nevertheless practically divided. The *Mohawks*, dwelling in the presence of Johnson — his own children swelling their ranks[1] — reflected in their action the wishes of the English government, or stirred up the tribes to mischief with the expectation of rewards as mediators; petted, and perhaps deservedly so, for services which had cost them the loss of their ablest chief and a large number of their best warriors, they were not the less debauched by liquor, enfeebled by disease,[2] and shorn of their prestige; while the *Senecas*, more manly and generous, less contaminated by civilization by their separation from its more immediate influence, dictated the policy and controlled all of active force that remained among their ancient brethren. As a nation they never again appeared in the field as contestants. Power and territory alike fell from their grasp at Fort Stanwix.

Brighter was the record of the *Lenapes*, and their grand-children, the *Shawanoes* and *Mahicans* of the west, judged from the standpoint of the success which had crowned their efforts. Entering upon the struggle as "poor women" striking their oppressors with "billets of wood," they emerged from it "increased in interest and respect," in the opinion of their enemies, "their conduct having restored them to the rank of

---

[1] It is said that Johnson had not less than one hundred children by squaws.

[2] Johnson.—*N. Y. Colonial History*, VII, 957.

men," and given to them an influence not only " very extensive,"[1] but destined in the future to embalm their names as the most formidable of the original Indian nations of Hudson's river. Their prowess vindicated in the field, their diplomacy triumphant in council, their manhood wrung from the unwilling hands of civilized and uncivilized foes, they gave to the conflicts of the west an impetus which made their name national, and grafted it forever upon the politics and history of their native land.

Not lost to the records of this eventful period were the *Mahicans* and *Wappingers* of the Hudson. While floating fragments from their ranks found new homes among the *Mohawks* and *Senecas*, swelled the victorious clans of their brethren in the west, suffered persecution for righteousness' sake at Gnadenhütten, or chanted with Montcalm the war songs of the French, at Westenhuck, in the valley of the Housatonic, their ancient council fire was kept brightly burning and their braves aided to give to the English the supremacy of the continent. The introduction among them of unselfish and devoted ministers of the gospel had restored to them, in a great measure, their ancient character, and made their influence felt in the camp and in the field, so much so, indeed, that the *Mohawks* sent to their schools their children for instruction, and the *Oneidas* were proud to hail them as brothers. When the war came on, Johnson made an effort to raise from their ranks a company to aid in the expedition against Crown point,[2] failing only to permit Governor Shirley to draw off with his expedition " nearly every fighting man among them."[3] After the war they demanded restitution from the *Abenaquis* for the loss of one of their number, and delayed the consummation of peace with them until 1762.[4] After the peace, they revived their claims to lands in Albany county, as well as in Dutchess — in the former, pressing even west of the Hudson, and in the latter, asserting and clearly proving fraud in the sale of the tract now embraced

---

[1] Johnson.—*Colonial History*, VII, 953.
[2] *Johnson Manuscripts*, II, 86.
[3] *Stockbridge, Past and Present.* " They served as a corps in the late war, and are in number about three hundred."—*Tryon,*

*Colonial History*, VIII, 452.
[4] A warrior was finally sent to them by the Abenaquis to compensate them for their loss.—*Johnson Manuscripts*, XXIV, 125.

in the county of Putnam. Failing to secure redress, they attempted the forcible ejectment of the settlers, and compelled the interference of the military. Subsequently, Nimham, the *Wappinger* king, in company with chiefs from the *Mahicans* of Connecticut, visited England and received favorable hearing. Returning to America their claims were thrown into the courts and were there overtaken by the Revolution.

Still clinging to their ancient homes, at the close of the war, were considerable numbers of the *Esopus* and *Mahican* clans, then generally known as " domestic tribes." Of the former " Nachnawachena, alias Sanders, chief sachem, accompanied by sachems Hakawarenim, Qualaghquninjon, and Walagayhin, and twenty-three Indians besides squaws and children," came to conference at Kingston, September 7th, 1771.[1] They were then principally residents of the country back of the Shawangunk mountains, and without special usefulness in the contest which had decided the future rank of their brethren, the *Minsis*, in the west. Not the last, but the closing record of the English administration in reference to them is that by Governor Tryon, in 1774: " The river tribes have become so scattered and so addicted to wandering, that no certain account of their numbers can be obtained. These tribes — the *Montauks* and others of Long island, *Wappingers* of Dutchess county, and the *Esopus, Papagoncks*, etc., of Ulster county — have generally been denominated River Indians and consist of about three hundred fighting men. Most of these people at present profess Christianity, and as far as in their power adopt our customs. The greater part of them attended the army during the late war, but not with the same reputation of those who are still deemed hunters."[2]

[1] *Manuscripts of Sir Wm. Johnson,* XXIII, 4.   [2] *Colonial History,* VIII, 451.

## CHAPTER X.

### The Indians and the War of the Revolution — The Destruction of the Six Nations — The last of the Mahicans.

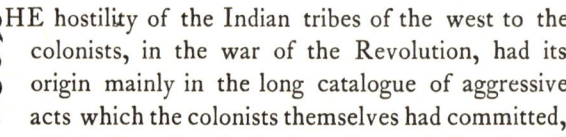HE hostility of the Indian tribes of the west to the colonists, in the war of the Revolution, had its origin mainly in the long catalogue of aggressive acts which the colonists themselves had committed, and against which the tribes had adopted a settled and well understood policy, involving resistance to further encroachments upon territory which they regarded as their especial domain. In their controversies in regard to these encroachments the Indians had learned to distinguish between the king of England and those whom they regarded as their oppressors, and to assume that while the latter were trespassers, the former was a just judge to whom they could appeal. The revision of the Wyoming deeds, and the establishment of the treaty line of 1768, they regarded as having been especially directed by the former, in acknowledgment of the justice of their claims, and this impression was strengthened by the policy which Johnson pursued, as distinguished from that which was sanctioned by colonial authority.[1]

Unfortunately the colonists made not only no effort to remove this impression, but, by their repeated violations of the treaty line, kept alive the irritations which its establishment was de-

---

[1] "His majesty, with great wisdom and discretion, was pleased to direct that (no settlements) should now be made below the great Kanhawa river, with which I acquainted the Indians, agreeable to my orders, but numbers of settlements had been made there previous to the cession. Attempts made since to form others on the Mississippi, and great numbers in defiance of the cession, or the orders of the government in consequence thereof, have since removed not only below the Kanhawa, but even far beyond the limits of the cession, and in a little time we may probably hear that they have crossed the Ohio wherever the lands invite them; for the body of these people are under no restraint, and pay as little regard to government as they do to title for their possessions."— *Johnson, Colonial History* VIII, 460.

signed to remove. The Virginians did not cease to push their pioneers into the Ohio valley, while the Pennsylvanians, under Franklin, although acting with the consent of the tribes in interest, were not the less violators of the spirit of the treaty. The Virginians, however, openly disregarded the compact, and did not scruple to regard the Indians as legitimate prey for their rifles, or to commit a succession of outrages more cruel and unprovoked than any known to savage warfare. Retaliation followed, and what was known as Cresap's war was inaugurated. The immediate causes of this war may be briefly stated. In the spring of 1774, a party of land agents under the lead of Captain Michael Cresap, was sent out by the Virginians to locate and open up farms in the valley of the Ohio, near the present cities of Pittsburg and Wheeling. The Indians remonstrated with Governor Dunmore, but instead of heeding them, the latter sent word to Cresap that he must be prepared for hostilities. Determined to anticipate the Indians in the attack which appeared to be imminent, Cresap, on the twenty-sixth of April, declared war, organized his party and moved towards the Ohio where he killed two Indians, and, on the following day, surprised a party of *Senecas* and inflicted upon them the loss of one man.

Not satisfied with these achievements, the party pushed forward to attack the encampment of Logan, a *Mingoe* chief, near the mouth of Yellow creek. The expedition was abandoned without consummation, only to be transferred to others. Opposite Logan's encampment a trader named Baker had erected a cabin and engaged in the sale of rum. At this cabin a party of flying settlers met, among whom was one Daniel Greathouse who acted as their leader. Logan and his Indians, it is said, had determined to cut off Baker,[1] and that the latter,

---

[1] *Stone's Life and Times of Sir Wm. Johnson*. The attack, however, appears to have been wholly without justification. The following is the account given in *Colonial History*, VIII, 464: "Received information from Captain Crawford and one Mr. Nevill, from Virginia, that on their way to this place they met a number of inhabitants settled below this, moving off, among whom was a party who presented seven Indian scalps, and stated their having taken them in the following manner: That a number of Indians having encamped at the mouth of Yellow creek, they with one Grithouse had collected themselves at the house of one Baker opposite to the said Indian camp, and decoyed the Indian men, and two women over to their side of the river to drink with them, who, upon finding

warned by a friendly squaw to escape, invited the aid of Greathouse, who organized a band of thirty-two men and crossed the river for the purpose of falling upon the Indians; but finding that they were too strong for him, retreated, and, with a show of friendship, invited them to an entertainment. Without suspicion of treachery, part of the Indians accepted the invitation, and while engaged in drinking — some of them in a state of intoxication — were set upon and butchered in cold blood. The Indians who had remained at their encampment, hearing the noise of the treacherous attack, ran to their canoes to rescue their friends. This movement had been anticipated, and sharpshooters stationed in ambuscade, shot numbers of them in their canoes, and compelled the others to return. Logan's mother, brother and sister were among the slain.

These transactions were soon followed by another outrage, which, though of less magnitude, was not less atrocious. An aged and inoffensive *Lenape* chief, named the Bald Eagle, while returning from a visit to the fort at the north of the Kanhawa, was shot while alone in his canoe. Not satisfied with this cowardly act, the perpetrator of the murder seized the canoe, tore the scalp from the head of his victim, placed the body in a sitting posture in the canoe, and sent it adrift down the stream to bear to the friends of the venerated sachem the most exasperating evidence of the hostility which had been committed. At about the same time, Silver Heels, a favorite chief of the *Shawanoes*, was murdered by trespassers upon the Indian territory, and in less than a month forty victims were added to the rapacity of the whites.[1] These acts thoroughly aroused the tribes, and the *Lenapes* and *Shawanoes*, under Cornstalk, and the

them intoxicated, fell upon them and knocked them in the head, and scalped them; that soon after two other Indians came over to see what detained their friends, and were served in the same manner; that after this the Indians appeared uneasy, and six of their men were coming across the river to see, after their people, who approaching near the shore, observed the white people lying in ambush for them, and, attempting to return to their camp, were fired upon and two of them were killed, who dropped into the river, and two others they observed fall dead in the canoe, and the fifth, upon their landing, they could discover very badly wounded so that he could scarce get up the bank."

[1] The very critical situation of Indian affairs, occasioned by the cruelties and murders committed by Cresap, who with some frontier banditti, causelessly murdered near forty Indians on the Ohio.— *Colonial History*, VIII, 471.

*Senecas* and *Mingoes* [1] led by Logan, threw themselves with fire and tomahawk upon the Virginia border.

The war was nominally concluded in October. Immediately on its outbreak Dunmore organized a force of three thousand men and marched to the Ohio country. One of the divisions of this force, under Colonel Lewis, reached the mouth of the Great Kanhawa on the sixth, and was there attacked, on the tenth, by one thousand warriors of the western confederacy, under Cornstalk, who had determined to anticipate his junction with the main army under Dunmore. The battle was a desperate one, and neither party could fairly claim the victory. The Virginians lost their commander, Colonel Lewis, one-half of their commissioned officers and fifty-two privates killed, while the Indians lost, in killed and wounded, two hundred and thirty-three. In the night the Indians retreated. Meanwhile Dunmore had pushed on to the Sciota, with the division under his command, and was there met by a flag of truce from the Indians proposing to treat for peace. Negotiations were opened, and a treaty concluded.[2] But the war did not stop. Boone and Bullit, and other pioneers,[3] provoked fresh hostilities and entailed upon the colonists the animosities which had been engendered in all the long struggle for the possession of the Ohio valley.

The French traders and priests who remained in the Indian country, moreover, contributed in no small degree to keep alive the hostile feeling which they had inculcated from the first hour of their presence in the Ohio valley. In the conflict which they saw was coming, they also saw the hope of a restoration to France of the territory which had been lost. Holding their head-quarters in the Spanish possessions of Louisiana, they in-

---

[1] The *Mingoes* were a mixed people formed mainly by the intermarriage of *Minsis*, *Senecas* and *Shawanoes*. They acknowledged the jurisdiction of, and were ruled by chiefs of the *Seneca* nation. (*N. Y. Colonial History*, VIII, 517). Brodhead states that the "Mingoes were the Andastes, or Gandastogues, or Conestogas who lived at Conestoga creek, where they were settled after their subjugation by the Iroquois" (Gallatin, 55), but such does not appear to be the fact, except as they were made so by the intermarriages of which Johnson speaks.

[2] Cornstalk conducted the negotiations on the part of the Indians. Logan was not present, but sent to the conference the famous speech which Jefferson preserved in his *Notes on Virginia*, and which has made the name of Logan a household word.

[3] Daniel Boone, *Colonial History*, VIII, 395.

vited the northern and western Indians thither and delivered to them speeches " setting forth the danger all their nations were in, from the designs of the English, who, they said, had it in view to possess all their country."[1] From them also came the invitation to the tribes to remove further down the Ohio, with a view to make their organization more compact and formidable, an invitation which Custalaga, a *Lenape* chief, with one hundred of his followers, accepted, and was very soon after followed by larger delegations,[2] animated by a common feeling of resistance. With the alliance of the *Shawanoes* and the *Mahican* clans, the *Lenapes* were now more powerful than the Six Nations themselves,[3] and, no longer taunted as women, but recognized as brothers by them, they prepared to contest the supremacy of the colonists.

The prejudice against the colonists, which was entertained by the western tribes, was, as has been already shown, equally bitter on the part of the *Senecas*, over whom Johnson with great difficulty maintained even a nominal control, and the feeling was largely shared by what were called the Upper nations of the confederacy. The *Mohawks*, *Oneidas* and *Tuscaroras* had less interest in the western controversy. Under the treaty of 1768, they had been paid for the lands which they claimed, not only in Pennsylvania, but for those embraced in the famous Kayaderossera patent on the Hudson,[4] so long a subject of complaint on the part of the *Mohawks*; besides, they were

---

[1] *Colonial History*, VIII, 396, 404, 507.

[2] *Colonial History*, VIII, 396. After the alliance of the colonists with France, this policy was reversed. On the 29th of August, 1779, Count Rochambeau issued to them a proclamation — through a delegation of Oneidas, Tuscaroras and Caughnawagas who visited him at Newport — in the following words : " The king of France, your father, has not forgotten his children. As a token of remembrance, I have presented gifts to your deputies in his name. He learned with concern, that many nations, deceived by the English, who were his enemies, had attacked and lifted up the hatchet against his good and faithful allies, the United States. He has desired to tell you, that he is a firm and faithful friend to all the friends of America, and a decided enemy to all its foes. He hopes that all his children, whom he loves sincerely, will take part with their father in the war against the English."

[3] " The worst circumstance is that these people have of late become more powerful by alliances, and the Six Nations less, so that their authority begins to be disputed at advantage."—*Johnson Manuscripts*, XXII, Nov. 29, 1772.

[4] This patent covered all the land lying between the Hudson and Mohawk rivers, extending from Coic falls, near the junction of those streams, to the third, or as it is now called, Baker's falls, on the Hudson, and contained about seven hundred thousand acres of land.—*Stone's Life of Johnson*, II, 299.

more immediately under the control of the English. The *Mohawks* had a blood alliance with Johnson ; the *Oneidas* and *Tuscaroras* had submitted themselves almost entirely to the guidance of the English ministers who had located among them, and their every-day associations were of a different nature from those of their more westward brethren. Practically, the confederacy was divided, although it still maintained the forms of unity and some of its spirit. While against the authorities of New York the more eastern tribes had no special complaint, their education, from the days of Stuyvesant, had been adverse " to the Bostonians," and the feeling was strengthened by the persistent determination of the Connecticut people to settle at Wyoming in defiance of the treaty of 1768, by which the rights of the proprietaries of Pennsylvania were secured. They hated them, too, upon general principles growing out of the extirminating policy of Church and his followers, and came to sympathize with the Indians in the French alliance and to encourage their hostilities.

The great strength of the control which the English had over them, however, lay in the personal associations of the *Mohawks* with the Johnson family. To create this influence Johnson had become an Indian ; his legitimate children had grown up with theirs, while those by his mistress, Molly Brant, eight in number, were " bone of their bone and flesh of their flesh."[1] Skillfully was this influence wielded by Johnson and the home government. The reduction of Canada had created the necessity for a reorganization of the Indian department. The Canada tribes, as well as those of the west, were too remote for that official intercourse to which they had become accustomed under the French, and required separate superintendence ; but it was also necessary that that superintendence should be conducted on a basis uniform with that which was applied to the confederated tribes. The materials for such an organization were already provided. George Croghan had filled the post of assistant to Johnson ; Daniel Claus and Guy Johnson, the sons-in-law of Johnson, were entirely familiar with the duties to be

---

[1] The children borne to him by Molly Brant, sister of the great chief, were made legitimate by marriage a short time before his death.

performed; their interests were bound up in obedience to the directions of Sir William. To Croghan was assigned the charge of the Ohio country; Col. Claus was sent to Canada, with his head-quarters at Montreal, while Guy Johnson was made deputy in charge of the Six Nations and the neighboring tribes, and remained at Johnson Hall.[1]

That there was plan and purpose in this arrangement, there is no reasonable doubt. It was no idle boast on the part of Johnson, when, in 1771, he wrote that he was confident that "in any event that might happen in Europe or in America," he could, from the measures he had taken and the influence which he possessed, secure and attach to the interests of the crown, " such a body of Indians as if not so numerous as those opposed," to those interests, would "give a severe check to their attempts."[2] Nor were the expectations of the home government disappointed in the result, although the great force of the plan was lost by the death of Johnson in July, 1774.[3] When that event occurred, Guy Johnson at once assumed the duties of superintendent,[4] with all the prestige which his rela-

---

[1] *Colonial History*, VII, 579.

[2] *Documentary History*, II, 983.

[3] Sir William Johnson was born in Ireland, about the year 1714. He was the nephew of Sir Peter Warren, the commodore who was distinguished in the attack on Louisburgh, Cape Breton, 1745. Sir Peter married a lady (Miss Watts) in New York, purchased large tracts of land upon the Mohawk, and about 1734, young Johnson was induced to come to America and take charge of his uncle's affairs in that quarter. He learned the Indian language, adopted their manners, and by fair trade and conciliatory conduct, won their friendship and esteem. He built a large stone mansion on the Mohawk, about three miles west of Amsterdam, where he resided for twenty years, previous to the erection of Johnson Hall at Johnstown, where he resided at the time of his death. He was never given credit for great military skill or personal bravery, and was more expert in intriguing with the Indians, than in leading disciplined troops boldly into action. For his success at Lake George, he was made major general and a knight.

His first wife was a Dutch girl, for whom, it is said, he gave five pounds for payment of her passage money to the captain of the emigrant ship in which she came to this country. By her he had one son, John, and two daughters who married respectively Daniel Claus, and Guy Johnson. When she was on her death-bed, Sir William was married to her in order to legitimate her children. After her death her place was supplied by Molly Brant, sister of Joseph, the Mohawk chief, by whom he had eight children. She was a very sprightly and beautiful squaw when he took her to his mansion as his mistress. Toward the close of his life he married her in order to legitimate her children. He died of disease of the heart, while attending the conference with the Indians stated in the text, July 11th, 1774, aged 60 years.—*Lossing* 1, 232, 287; *Stone's Life and Times of Sir William Johnson, etc.*

[4] He was commissioned to fill the vacancy in September, but performed the duties of superintendent in the interim by virtue of his appointment as deputy.

tionship to his predecessors inspired, combined with the support of Sir John Johnson, who succeeded to his fathers's title and estate, and that of Molly Brant, and Thayendanegea, her brother — the Joseph Brant of the Revolution — then a prominent chief of the upper Mohawk castle, who was made his secretary.

Against these controlling influences the colonists could not only array that which had been acquired by individuals through personal intercourse with the Indians, and that which had been gained by the labors of the Rev. Samuel Kirkland and the Rev. James Dean, missionaries to the *Oneidas* and *Tuscaroras*.[1] The extent of these influences was considerable—especially that exercised by the missionaries named—but nevertheless was entirely inadequate to compensate for that which was wielded by

---

[1] JAMES DEAN.—The history of this individual, and his agency in many of the events transpiring previous to and during the revolutionary war, would form a volume of deeply interesting and most thrilling incidents. He was a native of New England and educated with special reference to missionary labor among the Indians, with whom he lived many years from his youth. At the outbreak of the war he was stationed at Oghkwaga, where he made no attempt to conceal his views from the Indians. In 1774, he was employed by the Continental congress to visit the New York and Canada tribes to ascertain the part they would probably take in the contest. For this purpose he assumed the disguise of an Indian trader and, supplied with goods, accomplished the object of his mission. An adopted son of the Oneidas, and regarded by them with more than parental affection, his influence over them was especially conspicuous. He was subsequently appointed to the office of Indian agent, and during the whole war of the revolution he continued his services to the country in that capacity. A very considerable portion of the war he was stationed at Fort Stanwix, and by virtue of his office, superintended the intercourse with the Indians. At the close of the war the Oneidas granted him a tract of land two miles square, lying on the Wood creek west of Rome, to which he removed in 1784. Here he continued two years, when he effected an exchange with the nation for the tract of land lying in Westmoreland, known as Dean's patent, to which he removed, and where he continued to reside until his death in September, 1832.—*Stone's Life of Brant*, 1, *Appendix*.

SAMUEL KIRKLAND. — This distinguished missionary was born at Norwich, Conn., 1742. After a special education for the work, he was sent to Oneida Castle, in 1766, and continued to labor among that tribe for forty years. During the revolutionary war he was in the pay of the United States, and in 1779, was brigade chaplain in General Sullivan's campaign against the Indians of western New York. After the peace he remained among the Oneidas, and in 1788, assisted at the great Indian council for the extinction of their title to the Genesee country. So sensible was the state government of the value of his services, that in the year 1789, it granted him a tract of land two miles square in the present town of Kirkland, whither he immediately removed, and where he subsequently made a liberal endowment of land for the purpose of founding a school which was originally called Hamilton Oneida Academy, subsequently incorporated under the name of Hamilton College. After a life of much public usefulness, he at length departed this life on the 28th of February, 1808.—*Note, Colonial History*, VIII, 631; *Jones's History of Oneida County*.

the Johnsons. Had Guy Johnson possessed the shrewdness and skill of his predecessor, the result, so far as the Six Nations were concerned, would not have been doubtful; but in that which he gained by his position, he was seriously compromised by the superior diplomacy of the colonists.

Both parties moved with caution. While Johnson was unremitting in his endeavors to preserve the good will and affection of the Six Nations, the colonists lost no time in instructing them in regard to the nature of the controversy, and in advising them to act as neutrals. With a very considerable portion of the Six Nations neutrality had long been an established policy, and gained for the colonists not only an attentive ear, but compelled Johnson to adopt it as the course which he wished them to pursue. To the declarations of Dean and Kirkland, and to the belts which the faithful *Mahicans* sent to all the tribes advising neutrality — that the "dispute did not concern the Indians; that it arose from the crown's endeavors to obtain a large reimbursement for the expenses of the late war, which the colonists could not comply with, and therefore an army was sent to compel them" — Johnson found it necessary to reply that the "dispute was solely occasioned by some people who, notwithstanding the king's law, would not permit some tea to land, but destroyed it;" that the matter was one with which they had "nothing to do," any more than they had "with the foolish people" who talked to them about that "which they themselves did not understand."[1] Thus urged, the Six Nations in general council at Onondaga, resolved to have "nothing to do with the axe, but to support their engagements."

This action left the Johnsons with nothing but their personal influence and official relations, but these they believed, and not without reason, were sufficient to control to a great extent the action of the tribes. The well-founded suspicions of the integrity of the Johnsons, which the colonists entertained, brought the issue to a culmination much sooner than they had intended. The committee of safety of Tryon county, early in 1775, set a strict watch upon their movements, and when, in May, Guy Johnson received secret instructions from General

---

[1] *Colonial History*, VIII, 538, 557.

Gage, requiring him to report himself at Montreal for instructions, he professed alarm for his personal safety and appealed to his retainers among the Indians to induce the Six Nations to take upon themselves his protection. Gathering together a company of tories, among whom John and Walter N. Butler were prominent, and accompanied by Brant and a portion of the *Mohawks*, he fled to Oswego, where he held a conference with the tribes, and from thence pushed on to Montreal, where, in July, he met the Indians of the northren confederacy, seventeen hundred in number.[1] Whether his fears were well founded or not, the movement was an adroit one. Wherever he met the Indians he urged upon their consideration the attack which had been made upon himself, and appealed to the memory of his father-in-law, and to his associations with them, to protect Sir John, and to induce them to become his followers; yet he still insisted that his mission was that of peace, and that the Indians should maintain their neutrality.

Such was the condition of affairs when, in July, the Continental congress resolved to establish three departments of Indian affairs, the northern, middle and southern, "with powers to treat with the Indians in their respective departments, to preserve peace and friendship, and to prevent their taking any part in the present commotion."[2] In accordance with this resolution, the commissioners for the northern department[3] held a council with chiefs of the Six Nations at German Flats on the fifteenth of August, but the attendance being limited, adjourned it to Albany, where, on the twenty-fourth, its proceedings were concluded. At this conference the commissioners recited the grievances of which the colonists complained, and against which they had resolved to take up arms, and advised the Indians to observe neutrality. "This is a family quarrel between us and old England," said they; "you Indians are not concerned in it. We don't wish you to take up the hatchet against the king's

[1] *Colonial History*, VIII, 636.
[2] It was not until a year later that congress authorized the employment of Indians. Those who acted with the colonial forces prior to that time were enlisted by the colonies in their independent capacity.
[3] The commissioners for the northern department were Gen. Philip Schuyler, Major Joseph Hawley, Turbot Francis, Oliver Wolcott and Volkert P. Douw. The department included the Six Nations and all other tribes to the northward of them.

troops; we desire you to remain at home, and not join either side, but keep the hatchet buried deep. In the name and behalf of all our people, we ask and desire you to love peace and maintain it, and to love and sympathize with us in our trouble, that the path may be kept open with all our people and yours, to pass and repass without molestation."

"You told us it was a family quarrel," said Abraham, the venerable chief of the upper Mohawk castle,[1] in reply; "and that we should sit still, and mind nothing but peace. Our great man, Colonel Johnson, did the same at Oswego; he desired us to sit still likewise. You likewise desired us that if application should be made to us by any of the king's officers, we would not join them. Now, therefore attend, and apply your ears closely. We have fully considered this matter. The resolutions of the Six Nations are not to be broken or altered.[2] When they resolve, the matter is fixed. This chain is the determination of the Six Nations not to take any part, but as it is a family affair, to sit still and see you fight it out. We beg you to receive this as infallible, it being our full resolution; for we bear as much affection for the king of England's subjects on the other side of the water, as we do for you upon this island. It is a long time since we came to this resolution. It is the result of mature deliberation. It was our declaration to Colonel Johnson. We told him we should take no part in the quarrel, and hoped neither side would desire it. The resolutions of the Six Nations are not to be broken." [3]

While there can be no reasonable doubt that the determination of the Six Nations was fairly expressed by the speaker, its announcement was not without qualifications. The Wyoming lands, he insisted, the tribes regarded as belonging to the proprietaries of Pennsylvania, and desired that the settlement which

---

[1] Abraham was the brother of Hendrik (*Colonial History*). He originally represented the lower Mohawk castle, and was known as Little Abraham. On the death of Hendrik, he became chief sachem of Canajoharie or the upper Mohawk castle; Young Abraham, as he was called, succeeded to the lower Mohawk castle, and Seth became chief of the Schoharies (*Colonial History*, VII, 115). He subsequently followed the fortunes of the Johnsons, but died soon after the opening of the Revolution.

[2] Referring to the action of the council at Onondaga.— *Colonial History*, VIII, 556.

[3] Proceedings of conference.— *Colonial History*, VIII, 605, etc.

they had made in 1768 should be held as valid against the Connecticut people.[1] The commissioners had expressed the determination of the colonists " to drive away, kill and destroy all who appeared in arms " against them. " We beg you to take care what you do," said Abraham; " there are many around us who are friends to the king. As to your quarrels to the eastward along the sea coasts, do as you please. But it would hurt us to see those brought up in our bosoms ill-used. In particular we would mention the son of Sir William Johnson.[2] He was born among us, and does not intermeddle in public disputes. We would likewise mention our father the missionary who resides among the *Mohawks*. The king sent him to them, and if he was removed, they would look upon it as taking away one of their own body." Then the people of Albany had taken from them two pieces of land, " without any reward, not so much as a single pipe;" they should be restored. " If you refuse to do this, we shall look upon the prospect to be bad; for if you conquer, you will take us by the arm and pull us all off."

Whatever may have been the precise character of the instructions which Guy Johnson received from General Gage, there is no doubt in regard to those which were issued to him by the ministry, and which he received after his arrival in Montreal. These instructions were under date July 5th and July 24th. In the former he was advised to inform the Indians that in consequence of the " unnatural rebellion" which had broken out, the " immediate consideration" of the grievances of which they

[1] Connecticut claimed by virtue of the boundaries of its original charter. The deed which they had received was set aside in the agreement of 1768.

[2] John Johnson was the son of Sir William by his first wife. He was born in 1742, and succeeded his father to his title and estates in 1774. He was not as popular as his father, being less social and less acquainted with human nature. His official relations to the parent government, and his known opposition to the rebellious movements of the colonies, caused him to be strictly watched, and, as we have noted in the text, not without just cause. Expelled from his estate, his property confiscated, his family in exile, he became an uncompromising enemy to the patriots, and exerted his influence against them until the close of the war. Soon after the close of the war he went to England, and, on returning in 1785, settled in Canada. He was appointed superintendent and inspector general of Indian affairs in North America, and for several years he was a member of the legislative council of Canada. To compensate him for his losses, the British government made him several grants of lands. He died, at the house of his daughter, Mrs. Bowers, at Montreal, in 1830, aged 88 years.—*Lossing*, 1, 285.

had complained was defeated, but that they should ultimately be protected and preserved in all their rights ; while in the latter he was told that, as they had already "hinted that the time might possibly come when the king, relying upon the attachment of his faithful allies, the Six Nations, might be under the necessity of calling upon them for their aid and assistance," that time had now come ; that he should " lose no time in taking such steps" as might be necessary " to induce them to take up the hatchet against his majesty's rebellious subjects," and that he should " engage them in his majesty's service" upon such plan as would be suggested to him by General Gage. The course to be pursued in carrying out this plan was left to Johnson, but with the specific instruction that he should " not fail to exert every effort to accomplish it, and to use the utmost dilligence and activity in the execution of the order."[1]

Entering upon the duties assigned to him with a zeal sharpened by the seizure of his property in the Mohawk valley, Johnson nevertheless found his efforts to control the Six Nations obstructed by the action of the council of Onondaga in favor of neutrality, as well as by the success of the colonists in the reduction of Ticonderoga and Crown point, and although Brant and his *Mohawks* still adhered to him, his recruits were principally confined to enlistments from the Canada tribes. When Montgomery attacked Quebec, he claimed to have had over four hundred Indians in encampment, but of that number only ninety were participants in the engagement. The retreat of the Americans and the subsequent capture of Ethan Allen inspired his recruits for a short time, but by the middle of October scarce one of his dusky followers remained.

Even Brant was lukewarm and indifferent. The pledge of the tribes was sacred and could not be easily broken, even by one so firmly bound to the fortunes of the Johnsons. Besides, he was thoroughly schooled in the selfish politics of his predecessors, and would have positive assurances of compensation for his services. In this emergency, the plan resorted to in 1710 was adopted. Brant was sent to England ; was there feasted and honored as his predecessors had been, and like

[1] *Colonial History*, VIII, 596.

them returned to the tribes pledged to do the bidding of his royal master. Reaching Canada in the winter of 1776, he at once entered upon the work of organizing a force of Iroquois[1] to operate upon the borders of New York and Pennsylvania, in conjunction with the operations of the western confederacy. The field had been as well prepared for him as possible. Sir John Johnson, the last of the patrons of his family, had fled from his parole of honor, and taken refuge in Montreal, and whatever regard the confederates had for his father had been fully aroused, while the tories had been active in prejudicing the colonists.

In the spring of 1777, Brant appeared at Oghkwaga with a retinue of warriors. He had not yet committed any act of hostility within the borders of New York, yet none doubted his intentions. In June he ascended the Susquehanna to Unadilla, with about eighty warriors, and requested an interview with the Rev. Mr. Johnstone of the Johnstone settlement. He declared that his object was to procure food for his famished people, and that if it was not furnished, the Indians would take it by force. Mr. Johnstone sounded him in regard to his purposes, and the chief told him, without reserve, that he had made a covenant with the king, and was not inclined to break it. The people supplied him with food, but the marauders not satisfied, drove off a large number of cattle, sheep, and swine. As soon as they departed, not feeling safe in their remote settlement, the whites abandoned it, and took refuge in Cherry Valley. Some families in the neighborhood of Unadilla fled to the German Flats, and others to Kingston and Newburgh on the Hudson.

For the purpose of obtaining more positive information in regard to the intentions of the Indians, General Herkimer was instructed to visit Brant at Unadilla. Herkimer took with him three hundred Tryon county militia, and invited Brant to meet him. This the chief agreed to. It was a week after Herkimer arrived at Unadilla, however, before Brant made his

---

[1] "Joseph, since his arrival from England, has showed himself the must zealous and faithful subject his majesty can have in America, in Indian matters, and deserves to be noticed as such."— *Colonel Claus, Colonial History*, VIII, 724.

appearance. He came accompanied by five hundred warriors. Neither party had confidence in the other, and it was finally agreed that their accompanying forces should encamp within two miles of each other, and that the principals to the conference should, with a few of their followers, meet in an open field. These preliminaries being adjusted, the conference was opened. In reply to Herkimer's inquiries, Brant declared, " that the Indians were in concert with the king, as their fathers had been; that the king's belts were yet lodged with them, and they could not violate their pledge; that Herkimer and his followers had joined the Boston people against their sovereign; that although the Boston people were resolute, the king would humble them; that General Schuyler was very smart on the Indians at German Flats,[1] but at the same time was not able to afford them the smallest article of clothing; and finally, that the Indians had formerly " made war on the white people when they were all united, and as they were now divided, the Indians were not frightened." He also told Herkimer that a path had been opened across the country to Esopus, for the tories of Ulster and Orange to join them."[2]

A few days after this conference, Brant withdrew his warriors from the Susquehanna, and joined Sir John Johnson and Colonel John Butler, who had collected a body of tories and refugees at Oswego,[3] preparatory to a descent upon the Mohawk and Schoharie settlements. There Guy Johnson, and other officers of the British Indian department, summoned a

[1] The conference of July, 1775.
[2] *Campbell's Annals of Tryon County.* Claus tells the brazen story that Herkimer " had three hundred men with him and five hundred more in the distance," and that " Brant, who had not two hundred men, after resolutely declaring that he was determined to act for the king," obliged Herkimer to retreat "with mere menaces, not having twenty pounds of powder among his party." (*Colonial History,* VIII, 720.) It was by such stories that the Indian ring managed to give a consequence to the Six Nations which they did not possess.
[3] In 1722, under the direction of Governor Burnet, a trading house was erected at Oswego, on the east side of the river. In 1726, in order to prevent the encroachments of the French, Governor Burnet erected old Fort Oswego, on the west side of the river. In 1755, Fort Ontario was constructed, on the east side of the river, under the direction of Governor Shirley. On the 14th of August, 1756, both these forts, with a garrison of 1600 men, and a large quantity of ammunition, were surrendered to the French, under Montcalm. The forts were returned to the English under the treaty of peace of 1763. They were surrendered to the United States, by the British government, under the treaty of 1794.

grand council of the Six Nations, who were invited to assemble " to eat the flesh and drink the blood of a Bostonian;" in other words, to feast on the occasion of a proposed treaty of alliance against the patriots, who were denominated Bostonians as a special appeal to the prejudices of the Indians. There was a pretty full attendance at the council, but a large portion of the sachems adhered faithfully to their covenant of neutrality, and it was not until the British commissioners appealed to their avarice that their sense of honor was overcome. The contract was closed by the distribution of scarlet clothes, beads, and trinkets, in addition to which each warrior was presented a brass kettle, a suit of clothes, a gun, a tomahawk and a scalping knife, a piece of gold, a quantity of ammunition, and a promise of a bounty upon every scalp he should bring in.[1] Brant was acknowledged as a war captain, and soon after commenced his career of blood upon the borders.

Meanwhile the attention of the colonists had not been entirely devoted to the Six Nations. In April, 1774, the Provincial congress of Massachusetts sent a message to the *Mahicans* and *Wappingers*[2] at Westenhuck, apprising them of the gathering tempest, and expressing a desire to cultivate a good understanding with them. In reply, Captain Solomon Wa-haun-wan-waumeet visited Boston on the eleventh of April, and delivered the following speech:

" Brothers: We have heard you speak by your letter; we thank you for it; we now make answer.

" Brothers: You remember when you first came over the great waters, I was great and you was very little, very small. I then took you in for a friend, and kept you under my arms, so that no one might injure you; since that time we have ever been true friends; there has never been any quarrel between us. But now our conditions are changed. You are become great

---

[1] *See Life of Mary Jamison.* This pamphlet was written in 1823, and published by James D Bemis, of Canandaigua, N. Y. She was taken a captive near Fort Duquesne (now Pittsburg) when a child, and was reared among the Indians. She married a chief and became an Indian in every particular, except birth. At the council here spoken of she was present with her husband.— *Lossing's Field Book of the Revolution,* I, 239.

[2] This message was addressed "To Captain Solomon Ahhannuauwaumut, chief sachem of the Moheakounuck Indians." He died in 1777.

and tall. You reach the clouds. You are seen all around the world, and I am become small, very little. I am not so high as your heel. Now you take care of me, and I look to you for protection.

"Brothers: I am sorry to hear this great quarrel between you and old England. It appears that blood must soon be shed to end this quarrel. We never till this day understood the foundation of this quarrel between you and the country you came from.

"Brothers: Whenever I see your blood running, you will soon find me about to revenge my brother's blood. Although I am low and very small, I will gripe hold of your enemy's heel, that he cannot run so fast, and so light, as if he had nothing at his heels.

"Brothers: You know I am not so wise as you are, therefore I ask your advice in what I am now going to say. I have been thinking, before you come to action, to take a run to the westward, and feel the mind of my Indian brethren, the Six Nations, and know how they stand — whether they are on your side or for your enemies. If I find they are against you, I will try to turn their minds. I think they will listen to me, for they have always looked this way for advice, concerning all important news that comes from the rising of the sun. If they hearken to me, you will not be afraid of any danger behind you. However their minds are affected you shall soon know by me. Now I think I can do you more service in this way, than by marching off immediately to Boston, and staying there; it may be a great while before blood runs. Now, as I said you are wiser than I; I leave this for your consideration, whether I come down immediately or wait till I hear some blood is spilled.

"Brothers: I would not have you think by this that we are falling back from our engagements. We are ready to do any thing for your relief, and shall be guided by your councils.

"Brothers: One thing I ask of you, if you send for me to fight, that you will let me fight in my own Indian way. I am not used to fight English fashion, therefore you must not expect I can train like your men. Only point out to me where your enemies keep and that is all I shall want to know."

Two days afterwards the congress made the following reply:

"Brothers: We this day, by the delegate from Stockbridge, first heard of your friendly answer to our speech to you by Captain William Goodrich, which answer we are told you made to us immediately by a letter, which we have not yet received. We now reply.

"Brothers: You say that you were once great, but that you are now little; and that we were once little and are now great. The Supreme Spirit orders these things. Whether we are little or great, let us keep the path of friendship clear, which our fathers made and in which we have both traveled to this time. The friends of the wicked counselors of our king fell upon us, and shed some blood soon after we spake to you last by letter. But we, with a small twig killed so many, and frightened them so much, that they have shut themselves up in our great town called Boston, which they have made strong. We have now made our hatchets, and all our instruments of war, sharp and bright. All the chief counselors, who live on this side the great water, are sitting at the grand council-house in Philadelphia; when they give the word, we shall all as one man, fall on, and drive our enemies out of their strong fort, and follow them till they shall take their hands out of our pouches, and let us sit in our council-house, as we used to do, and as our fathers did in old times.

"Brothers: Though you are small yet you are wise. Use your wisdom to help us. If you think it best, go and smoke your pipe with your Indian brothers toward the setting sun, and tell them of all you hear and all you see; and let us know what their wise men say. If some of you young men have a mind to see what we are doing, let them come down and tarry among our warriors. We will provide for them while they are here.

"Brothers: When you have any trouble, come and tell it to us, and we will help you."

The occasion for the services of the *Mahicans* was not long delayed. When the alarm came up from Lexington, a year later, they took the field, and participated in the battle of Bunker Hill on the seventeenth of June. From thence Captain Solomon, or Captain Hendrik as he was subsequently known, repaired with his warriors to the council at German

Flats, and, at its adjourned session at Albany, renewed the pledge of his people in language most eloquent. "Depend upon it," said the noble chieftain; "depend upon it we are true to you, and mean to join you. Wherever you go, we will be by your sides. Our bones shall die with yours. We are determined never to be at peace with the red coats, while they are at variance with you. We have one favor to beg. We should be glad if you would help us to establish a minister amongst us, that when our men are gone to war, our women and children may have the advantage of being instructed by him. If we are conquered, our lands go with yours; but if you are victorious, we hope you will help us to recover our just rights."[1] Wherever the influence of the *Mahicans* could reach, it was exerted among their brethren of the west. Their fugitive clans at Oghkawaga, and their associates from the Esopus tribes,[2] refused for a time to take up the hatchet against the colonists, and held the *Tuscaroras* to neutrality; while those among the *Lenapes*, east of the Alleghanies, as well as the domestic *Lenape* clans, joined them in an earnest support of the patriots. At White Plains, in October, 1776, their united war-cry, " Woach, Woach, Ha, Ha, Hach, Woach!" rang out as when of old they had disputed the supremacy of the Dutch, and their blood mingled with that of their chosen allies.[3]

Active hostilities brought sifting time to the Six Nations. Notwithstanding the efforts of the Johnsons and the pleadings of Brant, they were not united in the alliance with the British,

---

[1] The *Mahicans* claimed several tracts of land, extending even west of the Hudson. Their principal claim, however, was for a portion of the Livingston patent and for lands at Westenhuck. The latter they claimed to have leased to the whites for a term of years, but had lost the papers. The matter has been before the legislature of New York several times, but like the claim of the Wappingers, has never been adjusted.

[2] " We, the head of this place, with our brethren the *Tuscaroras* and some of the *Onondagas* and *Mahicanders*, being assembled. * * We hope you will give no heed to the false reports that are going about, for we assure you, brothers, that we are sincerely disposed to keep our covenant of peace with you our brethren." (*Letter to Justices of Kingston signed by chiefs of Tuscarora and Esopus Indians*). See *Proceedings Provincial Convention of New York*, I, 803, 805; II, 301, 419, 424. To what extent these Indians were compromised with Brant is not known, but it is quite certain that a large number of the Esopus Indians became his obedient followers.

[3] The Indians were stationed on Chatterton's hill, under Colonel Haslet, and were in the heaviest of the engagement on the 28th of October.— *Lossing's Field Book*, II, 822.

although Brant doubtless drew recruits from all the tribes. The *Oneidas* and *Tuscaroras* consistently refused to join him; the *Onondagas* were not at first warmly enlisted in the movement; the *Mohawks* were divided.[1] So far as recognized tribal action was concerned, however, it soon became an established fact, that the *Mohawks*, *Cayugas*, *Onondagas*, and *Senecas*, had attached themselves to the king. Of the entire confederacy not more than eight hundred warriors took the field, under the British, at any time; but this number, added to those from the Canada tribes, and those whose hostilities in the west had never been suspended, constituted no inconsiderable portion of their forces. Could they have been regularly enrolled and disciplined, or could their services have been depended upon at any time, they would have constituted an effective body of men; but their modes of warfare would not admit of discipline, and their habits of living would not permit their attendance, in any considerable numbers, except at certain seasons of the year. That they were a scourge to the frontier settlements, is unquestioned; yet in no instance does it appear that they constituted the entire attacking force, but on the contrary that they were invariably led by tories, whose deeds of cruelty outrivaled savage ingenuity, and whose numbers, in most instances, was greater than that of the Indians.

The principal campaign in which the British Indians were engaged was that undertaken in 1777, to determine the control of the Hudson river. Sweeping down from Canada with his powerful army, Burgoyne recaptured Crown point and Ticonderoga, while his auxiliaries, the Indians and tories, attacked the defenses more remote from his route. Of these Fort Schuyler[2] was the first, against which Colonel Butler marched

---

[1] The reference is *not* to the lower Mohawk castle of which Little Abraham was chief sachem while his brother Hendrik lived, but to that known as the Praying Mohawks, at the mouth of Schoharie creek, which maintained at least a nominal alliance with the colonists, or rather observed the neutrality to which they had pledged themselves. General Sullivan, however, believed that they "were constantly employed in giving intelligence to the enemy, and in supporting their scouting parties when making incursions," and that "when the Mohawks joined the enemy," they were "left to answer those purposes, and keep possession of the land" of the tribe. By his direction they were subsequently taken prisoners and removed to Albany.—*Stone's Life of Brant*, II, 40.

[2] Originally Fort Stanwix. The present city of Rome, Oneida county, now covers

from Oswego with a motley crew of whites and Indians,[1] under the commands of John Johnson, Claus, and Brant, and united with the forces under St. Leger.[2] The siege commenced on the fourth of August, when a few bombs were thrown into the fort, while the Indians, concealed behind trees and bushes, wounded several men who were engaged in raising the parapets. Similar annoyances occurred on the fifth, but formidable operations were held in abeyance pending an attack upon a force of colonists who were approaching, for the relief of the fort, under General Herkimer. To meet this force Butler and Brant were dispatched, and at Oriskany was fought the desperate engagement in which the heroic Herkimer gave up his life.

Meanwhile a successful sally from the fort had carried consternation and disgrace into the British ranks. So impetuous was this sally, that the camp of John Johnson and his Royal Greens was seized; its valorous commander fleeing without his coat, and his tory confederates following at his heels. Twenty-one wagon-loads of spoil, five British standards, the baggage and papers of Johnson, and the clothing of his Indian allies,[3] rewarded the victors. The siege was continued until the twenty-second, when an incident occurred which showed the unreliability of the Indians, and defeated its further prosecution. A half idiot, named Hon Yost[4] Schuyler, a nephew to General Herkimer, who had been taken to Canada by Walter Butler, burst into the British camp almost out of breath, and delivered the story that the Americans, in numbers like the forest leaves, were approaching; that he himself had barely escaped with his life, in testimony of which he appealed to his coat which

its site. The old fort was erected during the French and Indian war of 1755, and subsequently became a point of much importance in transactions with the Six Nations.

[1] Johnson's Royal Greens.
[2] St. Leger's detachment was sent to Oswego, there to unite with Butler's refugees and Brant's Indians, and with them to penetrate the country from that point, capture Fort Schuyler, sweep the valley of the Mohawk, and join Burgoyne at Albany.
[3] Colonel Claus (*Colonial History*, VIII, 721) gives the following particulars:

"During the action (at Oriskany), when the garrison found the Indians' camp (who went out against their reinforcements) empty, they boldly sallied out with three hundred men and two field pieces, and took away the Indians' packs, with their clothes, wampum and silver work, they having gone in their shirts, or naked, to action. The disappointment was rather greater to the Indians than their loss, for they had nothing to cover themselves with at night, against the weather, and nothing in our camp to supply them."

[4] *Jan Joost*, John Justus.

bore the marks of several bullets. The Indians were thoroughly alarmed. St. Leger tried to pacify them, but, mourning the loss of over seventy of their number at Oriskany, and apprehensive of further disaster, they broke and fled towards their boats on Oneida lake, killing on their way thither many of their tory allies, and obliging St. Leger to write that they were "more formidable than the enemy they had to expect."[1]

But, while conducting the siege, they took occasion to chastise the *Oneidas* who had refused to unite with them. After the battle of Oriskany, Brant and a party of his warriors fell upon the old Oneida castle, burned the wigwams, destroyed the crops, and drove away the cattle of his former confederates. No sooner had he retreated, however, than the *Oneidas* retaliated. The residence of Molly Johnson, at the Upper Mohawk castle, was ravaged, herself and family driven from home, and her cash, clothing and cattle taken. From thence the avengers visited the Lower castle, and drove the followers of Little Abraham, one hundred in number, to refuge in Montreal, laying waste their plantations. Molly fled to Onondaga, and besought vengeance for the indignities which she had suffered, but to her possessions she was never restored; the indignant *Oneidas* had blotted out forever the seats of power from whence her tribe had swayed the destinies of a once powerful people.[2]

In the meantime the battle of Bennington had been fought with disastrous results to Burgoyne, not the least of which was the pall which it threw over the spirits of his dusky allies, who now began to find their way back to Canada in large numbers. With his defeat at Stillwater, they were as thoroughly demoralized as they were at Fort Schuyler when frightened by an idiot boy. Within three days after that battle, one hundred and fifty warriors made their peace with General Gates, accepted the war-belt, partook of the feast, and joined the Americans. When the final surrender of the British army came, not an

---

[1] The story of Hon Yost is well told in *Lossing's Field Book*. Having lost their shirts the Indians evidently feared that they might lose their skins.

[2] *Colonial History*, VIII, 725. Johnson says (*ibid.*, 727), the destruction of the Mohawk castles occurred after the battle of Bennington, and that the fugitives fled to Burgoyne, but the account by Claus is the most probable.

Indian was found in its ranks. For their conduct Johnson and Claus had many excuses to offer. The latter charged that their "harsh and indiscreet treatment" by Major Campbell, caused the greatest part of them to quit Burgoyne; Johnson assumed that at Oriskany they were not adequately supported by St. Leger, and that had they been they "would have rendered more material service;" but the fact would seem to be that they had acted in precise accordance with the course which they had pursued in the previous war with France, and were ready at all times to court the favor of the party which, for the time being, appeared the most successful. The evidence of their moral greatness is yet wanting.

For border warfare, however, the Indians under Brant, who were principally composed of *Senecas, Onondagas, Cayugas* and *Mohawks*, were still a power in the hands of the tories, as their subsequent ravages in the Mohawk valley, and at Wyoming and Minnisink, in 1778-9, sufficiently attest. The path which Brant had opened to the Esopus country, in the spring of 1777, became indeed a path of blood. Rallying such warriors as could be induced to continue in the service of the crown, Colonel John Butler succeeded, in the spring of 1778, in organizing a force of five hundred Indians and six hundred tories, and with these made his appearance on the Susquehanna. At Wintermoot's fort, on the third of July, the colonial militia, in inferior numbers, under Colonel Zebulon Butler, opposed his progress in a desperate conflict. Retreating from thence to Fort Forty, and unable to rally the flying inhabitants to its defense, terms of capitulation were agreed to by which the valley of Wyoming was surrendered to the mercy of savage white men and half-civilized Indians. Foremost in the frightful orgies which followed, was Catharine Montour, the Queen Esther of the *Senecas*, a half-breed,[1] who assumed the office of executioner, and, using a maul and a tomahawk, passed around the

[1] She was a native of Canada, and her father one of the French governors, probably Frontenac. She was made a captive during the wars between the Hurons and the French and the Six Nations, and was carried into the Seneca country, where she married a young chief who was signalized in the wars against the Catawbas. He fell in battle, about the year 1730. Catharine had several children by him, and remained a widow. Her superior mind gave her great ascendancy over the Senecas, and she was a queen indeed among them.—*Lossing*, 1, 257.

ring of prisoners, who had been arranged at her bidding, deliberately chanted the song of death and murdered her victims to its cadences in consecutive order. Forts, houses, barns, grain and cattle were destroyed. When Butler and his tories withdrew, the homes of five hundred settlers had been laid waste, their occupants made fugitives, their dead left unburied. Shielding their bloody work, with the name of Brant, and throwing the cause of the attack on the disaffection of the Indians at the occupation of the valley by the whites, Butler and his tories have been floated on the page of history as endeavoring to restrain the ravages which they had instigated. Stripped of their disguise, they now stand as the spoilers of an exposed settlement, without the excuse which a regularly constituted army might offer of harassing an enemy.[1]

Although Butler withdrew his followers from the valley almost immediately after the massacre, he nevertheless left behind him those who had personal grievances to avenge and mercenary rewards to secure. These were mainly fugitives from the Esopus clans at Oghkwaga, and tories, who, availing themselves of the withdrawal of Count Pulaski and his legion of cavalry from Minnisink, where they had been stationed for the protection of the frontier, made a descent, on the fourth of May, 1779, upon the settlers at Fantinekil in western Ulster, killing six of the settlers and burning four dwelling houses and five barns. Colonel Cortlandt's regiment, then stationed at Wawarsing, went in pursuit of the authors of the mischief, but without success. Scarcely had he turned back, before the town of Woodstock was attacked and several houses destroyed.

Reinforced by Brant in person, the war raged along the entire border. In July, Fantinekil was again visited, and the widow

[1] The story of Wyoming has been told in all its details by Minor and Stone, and others, and is repeated by Lossing in his *Field Book*. Notwithstanding the persistent efforts of the poet Campbell and that of the English historians to escape censure by blackening the name of Brant, the fact is pretty well established that he was almost entirely innocent of the excesses which were committed. Nor is there better ground for associating with the transaction the old dispute of the Lenapes. That question was satisfactorily settled by the treaty of 1768. The only question in dispute was that between the Connecticut company and the proprietaries of Pennsylvania, in which the Indians had no part, except as they were influenced by the contestants. The truth of Wyoming can only be written by an analysis of the actors in the massacre and their association with the proprietaries of Pennsylvania.

of Isaac Bevier and her two sons, and Michael Socks and his father, mother, two brothers, wife and two children, were massacred, and the house which they occupied given to the flames. At the house of Jesse Bevier the assailants were successfully resisted, although the building was set on fire and its inmates exposed to a terrible death. Alarmed, it is said, by a faithful dog, settlers two miles distant came to the relief of their friends. The tories fled without completing their work, only to reappear at Napanoch, where they burned the only house standing on the site of the present village of Ellenville. From thence they moved to Minnisink, where, on the night of July 19th, Brant, with sixty of his Indians, and twenty-seven tories disguised as savages, stole upon the little town, and, before the people were aroused from their slumbers, fired several dwellings. With no means of defense, the inhabitants sought safety in flight to the mountains, leaving all their worldly goods a spoil to the invaders. Their small stockade fort, a mill, and twelve houses and barns were burned ; several persons were killed and some taken prisoners. Orchards and farms were laid waste, cattle were driven away, and booty of every kind carried to Grassy brook on the Delaware, where Brant had his headquarters.

Alarmed by fugitives, Lieutenant Colonel Tusten, of Goshen, issued orders to the officers of his regiment to meet him at Minnisink the next day, with as many men as they could muster. In response to this call one hundred and forty-nine men were gathered in council with him the following morning. Tusten regarded the force as too small to attempt the pursuit of the invaders, but he was overruled, and the line of march taken up. On the twenty-first, Colonel Hathorn, of Warwick, joined the pursuers with a small additional force, and assumed the command. On the twenty-second, Hathorn pushed on to the high hills overlooking the Delaware, near the mouth of the Lackawaxen, where the enemy was discovered. Brant, who had watched the movement, ordered the main body of his warriors to an ambuscade in the rear of Hathorn's force, and when the latter, not finding his foes in front as he expected, attempted to return from the plain which he had reached, he was met by the fire of his wily antagonist. A long and bloody conflict ensued. Brant had the advantage of position and superior numbers; one-third of Hathorn's small force became detached; closer and closer the Indians and their white allies drew their circle of fire until Hathorn was hemmed within the circumference of an acre of ground, upon a rocky hill that sloped on all sides, where he maintained the conflict until the sun of that long July day went down. With the gathering twilight the ammunition of the militia was exhausted, and, placing themselves in a hollow square, they prepared their last defense with the butts of their muskets. Broken at one corner, the square became a rout, and the flying fugitives were shot down without mercy. Behind a rock on the field, Tusten dressed the wounds of his neighbors, while its shelter was also made the point from which a constant fire was kept up by a negro without his knowledge. As the last shot fell from this retreat, the Indians rushed to the spot, killed Tusten and the wounded men in his charge, seventeen in number, and completed the bloody work which they had commenced. Of the whole number who went forth to chastise the invaders, only about thirty returned to relate the scenes through which they had passed, and to graft forever their traditions of the carnage from which they had escaped upon the history of Orange county.

The attack upon Wyoming and the devastation which threatened the borders determined the action of congress. In the spring of 1779, and while yet the incursions upon the frontiers of Ulster county were in progress, an expedition was organized to invade the Seneca country, in which the tories and Indians held their headquarters, with a view to chastise and disperse them. This expedition moved in two divisions, the first under General Sullivan by the way of the Susquehanna and Wyoming; and the second under General James Clinton through the valley of the Mohawk. The expedition was entirely successful. At Tioga the divisions were united, and from thence moved into the heart of the Indian country, and marked their pathway with blazing Indian villages and blackened harvest fields. " The Indians shall see," said Sullivan, " that we have malice enough in our hearts to destroy everything that contributes to their support," and faithfully was that determination executed. Catharine Montour received in part the punishment she merited in the destruction of her residence at Catharinestown; Kendaia was swept from existence; Kanadaseagea, the capital of the *Senecas*, near the head of the lake which bears their name, with its sixty well built houses and fine orchards; Kanandaigua, with its "twenty-three very elegant houses, mostly framed, and, in general, large," and its fields of corn and orchards of fruit, and Genesee castle, the capital of the *Onondagas*, with its "one hundred and twenty-eight houses, mostly large and very elegant," were alike destroyed. Forty Indian towns were burned; one hundred and sixty thousand bushels of corn in the fields and in granaries, were destroyed; a vast number of the finest fruit trees were cut down; gardens covered with vegetables were desolated; the proud Indians, who had scarce felt the touch of the colonists except in kindness, were driven into the forests to starve and be hunted like wild beasts; their altars were overturned, their graves trampled upon by strangers, and their beautiful country laid waste.

The punishment administered by Sullivan was indeed terrible, but was it just? That the projectors of the expedition, including Washington, so regarded it, is well known; that four of the tribes had broken their pledge of neutrality and carried forward their revenges and prejudices to the account of the innocent, is also known. That they were the victims of the wiles of designing men — had learned their lessons of hatred in the earlier controversies between the contending civilizations — was as strongly urged in their behalf then as it can be now. Had they been without warning, the destruction of their towns would have been without justification; but they had been both warned and entreated. In December, 1777, congress had addressed to them an earnest and eloquent appeal to preserve their neutrality, and refrain from further hostilities, to sit under the shade of their own trees and by the side of their own streams and "smoke their pipe in safety and contentment;"[1] but they

---

[1] This address recognized the division which then existed in the confederacy. To the four hostile tribes, it said:

"Brothers, Cayugas, Senecas, Onondagas and Mohawks: Look well into your hearts, and be attentive. Much are you to blame, and greatly have you wronged us. Be wise in time. Be sorry for your faults. The great council, through the blood of our friends who fell by your

would not listen, and grew bold in the supposed impossibility of being reached by the government. The visitation which they had provoked was a necessity.

The scourging army passed by the towns of the *Oneidas* and *Tuscaroras*, and struck its blows where chastisement was most deserved. A single village of the *Mohawks* was spared,[1] consisting of four houses, the occupants of which were made prisoners ; but the torch was stayed by the entreaties of homeless frontier settlers who begged that they might occupy them until they could procure others, and to them was also given the grain, horses and cows, the stores and furniture, of the remaining followers of Little Abraham, who had found opportunity to make themselves obnoxious as informers, if not as active participants in the English cause. The council-seat of the traditional Atotarho was thrown down, and the council-fire of the nation, which had so long been kept burning at Onondaga, was put out never to be rekindled on its ancient hearth.

The offending tribes were astounded. The *Onondagas* flew to the *Oneidas* for relief; the *Senecas* and *Cayugas* joined the

tomahawks at the German Flats, cries aloud against you, will yet be patient. We do not desire to destroy you. Long have we been at peace; and it is still our wish to bury the hatchet, and wipe away the blood which some of you have so unjustly shed. Till time shall be no more, we wish to smoke with you the calumet of friendship at Onondaga. But, brothers, mark well what we now tell you. Let it sink deep as the bottom of the sea, and never be forgotten by you or your children. If ever again you take up the hatchet to strike us, if you join our enemies in battle or council, if you give them intelligence, or encourage or permit them to pass through your country to molest or hurt any of our people, we shall look upon you as our enemies, who, under a cloak of friendship, cover your bad designs, and like the concealed adder, only wait for an opportunity to wound us when we are most unprepared. Believe us who never deceive. If, after all our good counsel, and all our care to prevent it, we must take up the hatchet, the blood to be shed will lie heavy on your heads. The hand of the thirteen United States is not short. It will reach to the farthest extent of the country of the Six Nations ; and while we have right on our side, the good Spirit, whom we serve, will enable us to punish you, and put it out of your power to do us farther mischief."

To the Oneidas and Tuscaroras no such warning words were necessary. "Hearken to us," said the address to them : "It rejoices our heart that we have no reason to reproach you in common with the rest of the Six Nations. We have experienced your love, strong as the oak ; and your fidelity, unchangeable as truth. You have kept fast hold of the ancient covenant chain, and preserved it free from rust and decay, and bright as silver. Like brave men, for glory you despise danger ; you stood forth in the cause of your friends, and ventured your lives in our battles. While the sun and moon continue to give light to the world, we shall love and respect you. As our trusty friends, we shall protect you, and shall at all times consider your welfare as our own."— *Stone's Life of Brant*, 1, 292, etc.

[1] The castle of the Praying Maquas at the mouth of Schoharie creek.

*Mohawks* at Fort Niagara.[1] Humbled, the former sent their chiefs to Fort Stanwix and asked, "Was the destruction of our castle done by design, or by mistake? If by mistake, we hope to see our brethren, the prisoners; but if our brethren, the Americans, mean to destroy us also, we will not fly — we will wait here and receive our death." "I know the agreement made four years ago with the Six Nations," replied Colonel Van Schaick; "I also know that all of them, except the *Oneidas* and *Tuscaroras*, broke their engagements and flung away the chain of friendship. The *Onondagas* have been great murderers; we have found the scalps of our brothers at their castle. They were cut off, not by mistake, but by design — I was ordered to do it, and it is done." Trembling, the fugitives at Niagara, appealed to Haldiman, the governor of Canada: "The great king's enemies are many, and they grow fast in number. They were formerly like young panthers; they could neither bite nor scratch; we could play with them safely; we feared nothing they could do to us. But now their bodies are become big as the elk, and strong as the buffalo; they have also got great and sharp claws. They have driven us out of our country for taking part in your quarrel. We expect the great king will give us another country, that our children may live after us, and be his friends and children as we are."[2]

At Fort Niagara they perished in large numbers from diseases caused by the absence of accustomed food, and the exposures to which they were necessarily subjected. But their hatreds grew with their misfortunes. Red Jacket plead with them to make peace, without avail; against the name of Washington they wrote that of Annatakaules, the destroyer of towns. Still powerful for predatory warfare, they organized anew during the winter, and, with Corn-Planter in command of the *Senecas*, fell upon the *Oneidas* and *Tuscaroras*; burned their castle, church, and village, and drove the offenders down upon the

---

[1] Fort Niagara was erected by the French in 1725, and was for many years the seat of the French missionaries. The English captured it in 1759, when it was rebuilt and regarrisoned. During the revolution, it was held by the British, and became the head-quarters of the Indians and tories. It was surrendered to the United States in 1794.

[2] The authenticity of this document has been disputed. The portion quoted, however, is a statement of facts, if not by the Indians themselves.—*Appendix* Stone's *Life of Brant.*

white settlements for protection.[1] In May, in detached parties they renewed their attacks upon the borders of Ulster county, plundered the houses of Thomas and Johannes Jansen, in the town of Shawangunk; killed a Miss Mack and her father, as well as a young woman from New York then residing with them, in one of the mountain gorges, and subsequently reached the Hudson in an attack upon the settlement at Saugerties, where they made prisoners of Captain Jeremiah Snyder and his son Isaac, who were taken to Fort Niagara and from thence to Montreal. The convenient instruments of the tories, they followed their footsteps wherever they were bidden.

In the meantime, Sir John Johnson, at the head of a band of refugees and Indians, five hundred in number, stole through the woods from Crown point and appeared at Johnson Hall. His purpose was to remove the treasure which he had buried on the occasion of his first flight, and to punish some of his old neighbors. In both he was successful. Two barrels of silver coin, the fruits of his father's honest traffic with the Indians, rewarded him; his attendants lighted up the surrounding neighborhood with blazing dwellings, and murdered the defenseless people. The village of Caghnawaga[2] was given to the flames, and along the Mohawk valley for several miles every building, not owned by a loyalist, was burned, the cattle killed, and all the horses that could be found taken away. With many prisoners and much booty, Johnson made good his retreat.

During the autumn more formidable operations were undertaken. Sir John Johnson, with three companies of refugees, one company of German Yagers, two hundred of Butler's Rangers, and one company of British Regulars, with Brant and

---

[1] The fugitives collected together near Schenectady, where they remained until after the war, in active alliance with the colonists.

[2] This village took its name from that of the ancient Mohawk village called Caudaonague; by the French, Onengioure, and by the Dutch, Kaghnewage. It was in this village that Father Jogues was so badly treated during eighteen months of captivity. Its site is now covered by the village of Fonda, Montgomery county. The Mohawks who originally occupied it were proselyted by the Jesuits and induced to remove to Canada, where they were established at a mission called by themselves, in remembrance of their ancient village, Caghnawaga. (*Brodhead*, II, 129, 299. *Ante*, p. 97). At the time of its destruction it was occupied principally by German families from the Palatinate.

Corn planter and five hundred of their warriors, entered the Schoharie valley, and although not successful in reducing the block-houses which had been erected, nevertheless spread destruction along their pathway. Not a house, barn, or grain-stack known to belong to a whig, was left standing; one hundred thousand bushels of grain were destroyed in a single day. The houses of the tories were spared, but no sooner had the enemy retired than the exasperated whigs set them on fire, and all shared the common fate. The valley of the Mohawk was next visited. At Caghnawaga the buildings which had been left standing at the previous visitation, as well as those which had been rebuilt, were destroyed, and every dwelling on both sides of the river, as far up as Fort Plain, was burned. Murder and rapine attested alike the hatred of Johnson for his former neighbors and the vengeance of his dusky allies.

But the marauders were not permitted to again escape without molestation. Governor George Clinton, having received information from two *Oneidas*, of their movements, promptly marched to the relief of the district. A strong body of *Oneida* warriors, led by their chief, Louis Atyatoronghta,[1] who had been commissioned a colonel by congress, joined him on his way. Near Fort Plain the opposing forces met; Brant and his Indians, in a thicket of shrub oaks, were supported by Johnson, while the right of the patriot line was held by the *Oneidas*. The defiant war-whoop of the opposing chiefs was echoed by their followers; supported by the militia, the *Oneidas* dashed forward; Brant gave way and fled, wounded in the heel, to the fording place near the old upper Indian castle, crossed the river and found refuge in the rear of the reserve forces of his friends. Johnson immediately made hasty retreat to his boats on Onondaga lake, and escaped to Canada by the way of Oswego, shorn of whatever prestige he had gained on his former raid.

Similar were the events of 1781. The devastations of the invading bands commenced again on the borders of Ulster. In August, a body of three hundred Indians and ninety tories fell

---

[1] It is said that he was the representative of three nations, having in his veins the blood of the French, the Indian, and the negro. His bravery was unquestioned.

upon the settlers in the Wawarsing valley and "burned and destroyed about a dozen houses, with their barns," and killed one of the inhabitants, "the rest having fled." Colonel Hardenburgh, with a force of only nine men, hastened forward to the aid of the settlers, and, throwing his men into a small stone house, checked the advance of the enemy. In their repeated attempts to dislodge him, thirteen of their number were left dead upon the field. Colonel Paulding's regiment of state levies, together with the militia, was soon on the ground, but not in time to punish the marauders, although they were pursued for seven days.

In October the Mohawk valley was visited by Major Ross and Walter N. Butler at the head of about one thousand troops, consisting of regulars, tories and Indians. The settlement known as Warren Bush was broken into so suddenly that the people had no chance for escape. Many were killed and their houses plundered and destroyed. Colonel Willett, informed of the incursion, marched with about four hundred men, including *Oneida* warriors, to the defense of the valley. He was joined by Colonel Rowley with the Tryon county militia, and the plan of attack agreed to. Rowley was sent to fall upon the enemy in the rear, while Willett was to attack them in front. The belligerents met a short distance above Johnson Hall, and a battle immediately ensued. Willett's militia broke and fled to the stone church in the village, but at that moment Rowley attacked the rear and soon compelled the enemy to retreat, leaving forty of their number killed and wounded and fifty prisoners. The pursuit was not taken up until the next morning, when it was continued until evening before the enemy were reached. A running fight then ensued; Butler's Indians became alarmed at the havoc in their ranks and fled; a brisk fire was kept up for some time by the tories, until Butler, who was watching the fight from behind a tree, exposed his head and fell under a quick ball from an *Oneida*, who knew him and who was watching his motions; his troops fled in confusion; the *Oneida* bounded across the stream that separated the contestants, and while Butler, yet living, cried for quarter, finished the work which he had commenced, tore from his head the reeking trophy which he sought, and bore it as a banner in the onward charge

of his comrades. So perished Walter N. Butler, the most heartless of all the tories who engaged in the border wars; so closed the attacks upon the frontier settlements of New York.

The gallantry of the *Oneidas* and *Tuscaroras* during the war was only exceeded by that of the *Mahicans* and *Wappingers*. Active in the campaign of 1777, the latter joined Washington again in the spring of 1778, and were detached with the forces under Lafayette to check the depredations of the British army on its retreat from Philadelphia. At the engagement at Barren hill they defeated a company of British troops, but not precisely in the manner of creditable warfare. Stationed in a wood at a considerable distance from the main army, they met the attack of the enemy by discharging their muskets and uttering their hideous battle-cry. "The result," says Sparks, "was laughable; both parties ran off equally frightened at the unexpected and terrific appearance of their antagonists."[1]

But such was not their record in Westchester county, where they first met the British, and where they were stationed soon after the engagement at Barren hill. In July, while Simcoe and Tarleton were making some examinations of the country, the *Mahicans* formed an ambuscade for their capture, and very nearly succeeded in their purpose, the party escaping by changing their route.[2] Their most distinguished service, however, was performed in August. While on a scouting expedition on the thirtieth, Lieutenant Colonel Emerick met a body of them under Nimham, the king of the *Wappingers*, and in the engage-

---

[1] *Sparks*, VII, 547.   [2] *Simcoe's Military Journal.*

ment which followed was compelled to retreat. On the following morning the whole of the British force at Kingsbridge was ordered out and the largest portion placed in an ambuscade, while Emerick was sent forward to decoy his assailants of the previous day. The plan failed, but an engagement was brought on, by Emerick's corps, on what is now known as Cortland's ridge, in the present town of Yonkers, which was one of the most severe of the war. The Indians made the attack from behind the fences, and in their first fire wounded five of their enemies, including Simcoe. Falling back among the rocks they defied for a time the efforts to dislodge them. Emerick offered them peace and protection if they would surrender; four of their number accepted the terms only to be hewn in pieces as soon as they reached his lines. The engagement was renewed; Emerick charged the ridge with cavalry in overwhelming force, but was stoutly resisted. As the cavalry rode them down, the Indians seized the legs of their foes and dragged them from their saddles to join them in death. All hope of successful resistance gone, Nimham commanded his followers to fly, but for himself exclaimed: "I am an aged tree; I will die here." Ridden down by Simcoe, he wounded that officer and was on the point of dragging him from his horse when he was shot by Wright, Simcoe's orderly. "The Indians fought most gallantly," is Simcoe's testimony; but the number engaged is not stated. Emerick reported that "near forty" of them "were killed or desperately wounded." If his previous statement is correct, that the number who had "just joined Washington" was "about sixty," over one-half must have fallen in the engagement.[1]

To their services in that and in other engagements the testimony of Washington is added.[2] Literally did they redeem the pledge which they had given at Albany, the pledge of Ruth: "Whither

[1] Near forty of the Indians were killed or desperately wounded, among them Nimham, a chieftain who had been to England, and his son (*Simcoe's Journal*). Bolton states that eighteen bodies were recovered from the field and buried in one pit. The loss of the British is said to have been five; but it was rare indeed that they made a correct return, and the number may have been much greater.

[2] "Head Quarters, Bergen Co., September 13, 1870.
To the President of Congress:
Sir: This will be presented to your excellency by Captain Hendriks Solomon of Stockbridge. He and about

thou goest I will go, and where thou lodgest I will lodge; thy people shall be my people, and thy God my God; where thou diest will I die, and there will I be buried." The privations which the patriots suffered, they shared without a murmur; in their devotion they never wearied. When the tattered banners of the struggle were folded away, they returned to their ancient seats, and at the head waters of the Hudson again met the white men, now their brothers by a holier covenant, as they had met them in 1609, the sole representatives of the Indian tribes of Hudson's river.

By the treaty of peace between the United States and Great Britain — which was without stipulation in regard to the Indian allies of the latter government — " the ancient country of the Six Nations, the residence of their ancestors from the time far beyond their earliest traditions, was included within the boundaries granted to the Americans." Nor was this their only loss; in their social and political condition they had been great sufferers by their unfortunate alliance. The great body of the *Oneidas* and *Tuscaroras* had been severed from the confederacy; the " eastern door " of their " Long House " had been broken in and its ancient keepers, the *Mohawks*, made fugitives from the seats of their fathers; the alliance of the four tribes with the crown had divested them of the respect of the victors; their towns had been destroyed and their fields wasted by the scourging army of Sullivan. When the war closed, the *Oneidas* and *Tuscaroras* returned to their possessions, assured of the protection of their American allies; the *Mohawks*, after brooding awhile over their misfortunes, retired to the banks of the Ouise

twenty of his tribe have been serving as volunteers with the army since the beginning of July. They have been generally attached to the light corps, and have conducted themselves with great propriety and fidelity. Seeing no immediate prospect of any operation in this quarter, in which they can be serviceable, they are desirous of returning home after receiving some compensation for the time, during which they have been with us, and after having made a visit to Philadelphia, I have thought it best to gratify them, not only on account of being agreeable to them, but because I have it not in my power to furnish them with such articles of clothing as they request, and which they would prefer to money. Congress will, I doubt not, direct such a supply as they shall think proper. Captain Solomon, with part of these people was with us in the year 1778. The tribe suffered severely during that campaign, in a skirmish with the enemy, in which they lost their chief and several of their warriors.

I have the honor to be

Yours, etc.,

GEO. WASHINGTON."

or Grand river, under the protection of the crown,[1] prepared to renew the struggle whenever they should be bidden by those whom they served; the *Senecas* relighted their council-fire, broken, dispirited and divided.

New York was disposed to complete the work of disintegration and dispersion, which the war had developed, by expelling the *Senecas, Onondagas* and *Cayugas* from all the country within its bounds which had not been ceded by them under the treaty of 1768; but congress adopted a more liberal policy, nevertheless one involving punishment. Commissioners on the part of the United States met the representatives of the tribes at Fort Schuyler in October, 1784, prepared to negotiate a treaty based on a concession of territory. The *Mohawks* were not represented; the *Senecas* asked delay until the tribes on the Ohio could be summoned, but the commissioners would not consent, nor would they recognize a unity that did not exist. Red Jacket opposed the burial of the hatchet, while Cornplanter counseled peace, regarding the loss of territory, on the terms offered, as far better than the hazards of further war. The efforts of the latter prevailed, and, on the twenty-second, a treaty was signed by which the United States gave peace to the *Mohawks, Senecas, Onondagas* and *Cayugas*, and received them under their protection, on condition that all the prisoners in their possession, white and black, should be delivered up. The *Oneidas* and *Tuscaroras*, as well as all the tribes, were secured in the possession of the lands they were then occupying, with power to sell and relinquish, but at the same time gave up all claims to the territory not in absolute occupation west of a line beginning at the mouth of the Oyonwayea creek, flowing into Lake Ontario four miles east of Niagara, thence southerly, but preserving a line four miles east of the carrying path, to the mouth of Tehoseroron or Buffalo creek; thence to the north boundary of Pennsylvania; thence south along the Pennsylvania line to the Ohio.

Had the tribes been permitted to follow their own inclinations, this treaty would perhaps have been conclusive; but the Eng-

---

[1] At the close of the war the Mohawks were temporarily residing on the American side of the Niagara river, in the vicinity of the old landing place above

lish in Canada, and especially the tories, professing to believe that the contest between the colonies and the mother country had been postponed, not determined,[1] disseminated discontent and hastened to revive in the hearts of their allies the sacredness of the boundary line of 1768, and the policy upon which it had been based. The *Lenapes* and *Shawanoes* were encouraged to revolt; Corn planter was driven from power by Red Jacket. Brant assumed the task of organizing formidable and active hostilities, and for that purpose visited England in 1785. On his return the tribes in interest opened communications with the American government, suggested that a grand council should be called, and that, pending its assemblage, and determination, surveyors and settlers should be restrained from passing beyond the Ohio.

The government, anxious to prevent hostilities, replied by sending instructions to General St. Clair, then governor of the north-western territory, to inquire particularly into the temper of the Indians, and if he found them hostile, to endeavor to hold as general a treaty with them as he could convene, and, if possible, satisfactorily extinguish their title to lands as far westward as the Mississippi. Under these instructions St. Clair concluded at Fort Harmer, on the ninth of January, 1789, two separate treaties; the first, with the sachems of the Five Nations, the *Mohawks* excepted; the second, with the sachems of the *Lenapes*, *Wyandots*, *Ottawas*, *Chippewas*, and other western clans represented. These treaties recognized the boundary line of 1784, but at the same time modified that treaty by conceding the right of the Indians to compensation for lands east of the line as far as the boundary of 1768.

At the negotiation of these treaties the fact became strikingly apparent that the confederate tribes were without agreement upon any line of policy,[2] Brant openly denouncing many of his

---

the fort. The governor of Canada subsequently assigned them lands on the Grand river about forty miles above Niagara Falls.—*Stone*, II, 239.

[1] Great Britain, it will be remembered, refused to negotiate a commercial treaty with the United States, or to surrender certain forts within the northern boundary of the territory which had been relinquished. It was not until 1794, that a treaty was ratified covering these points, meanwhile the encouragement of the officers of the crown to the Indians was not disguised. See Johnson's letter in *Stone's Life of Brant*, II, 267.

[2] St. Clair writes: "A jealousy sub-

late allies as having " sold themselves to the devil."[1] Failing to unite and wield the tribes to his purposes, he appealed to the *Lenapes* and *Shawanoes* to take the offensive, with himself and his associates as followers. The latter accepted the belt, and began hostilities along the western border, then covering an extent of four hundred miles. To restrain and punish the insurgents General Harmer was sent out, in the autumn of 1790, with a force of fifteen hundred men, but suffered disaster in a conflict near the junction of the St. Joseph and St. Mary rivers; and General St. Clair, with an expedition for a similar purpose, was defeated and severely punished in November of the following year.[2]

Encouraged by these successes, the *Lenapes* and their allies resisted the overtures for peace which Captain Hendrik Aupaumut, the *Mahican* chief, conveyed to them, and, in council at Miami Rapids, on the 13th of August, 1793, issued the declaration, that to them the money which the United States offered for their lands was of no value, to most of them unknown; that no consideration whatever could induce them to sell that from which they obtained sustenance for their women and children; that if peace was desired, justice must be done, and to that end the money which was offered them should be divided among the settlers who had invaded their country and they be bidden to withdraw; that they never made any agreement with the king by which their lands followed the fortunes of his wars, nor would they now make a treaty which denied to them the right to make " bargain or cession of lands whenever and to whomsoever they pleased;" peace with them could be had only on the basis that the Ohio should remain the boundary line beyond which the white man should not come. " We can retreat no further, because the country behind hardly affords food for its present inhabitants; we have therefore

---

sisted among them, which I was not willing to lessen by considering them as one people. They do not so consider themselves; and I am persuaded their general confederacy is entirely broken. Indeed, it would not be very difficult, if circumstances required it, to set them at deadly variance."—*Am. State Papers*, IV, 10.

[1] In other words, to the Yankees, against whom he manifested at all times the most intense hatred.

[2] *Stone's Life of Brant*, II, 308, etc.; *Gallatin*, 50, 51, 68.

resolved to leave our bones in this small space, to which we are now consigned."

Thirteen tribes, the *Lenapes, Shawanoes, Minsis, Mahicans,* of the Delaware, *Nanticokes* and *Conoys,* the seven nations of Canada, the *Wyandots, Miamis, Chippeways* and *Pottawattamies,* and the *Senecas* of the Glaize, signed the declaration, and on the thirtieth of June following, sealed it with the blood of their bravest warriors in battle against General Wayne on the ground where St. Clair had been so disastrously defeated in 1791.[1] From that field they retired crushed and broken, while fire and sword followed them in their retreat, and blazing villages and ruined fields convinced them that however just their cause, there was a limit to their powers of resistance. Ruined in estate, and deserted by their English allies, with whom the United States had finally concluded definite treaty, they came up to a conference with Wayne, at Greenville, on the third of August, 1795, and accepted the terms of their conquerors.[2]

Full of interest as are the details of this struggle, they do not strictly pertain to the purpose of this work, the general facts sufficiently indicating the events attending the retreating footsteps of the once powerful occupants of the western valley of the Hudson. Leaving the *Lenapes* and their grandchildren on the banks of the Mississippi, the warriors of the Six Nations, who, in small number, had participated in the contest, returned to the reservations which had been set apart for them by the legislature of New York, which in part they still occupy.[3] From their ancient dominions the *Mahicans* at Westenhuck removed, in 1785, on the invitation of the *Oneidas,* to a tract six miles square in the present towns of Augusta, Oneida county, and Stockbridge, Madison county. Here they resided until 1821, when, with other Indians of New York, they purchased of the *Menominees* and *Winnebagoes,* a tract of land on the Wisconsin and Fox rivers in Wisconsin, and took up their residence there.[4]

---

[1] *Stone's Life of Brant,* ii, 382, etc.
[2] The loss inflicted upon the Americans during this war is officially stated at over two thousand men.
[3] *Census of New York,* 1855, appendix.

Only a comparatively small portion of the original reservations now remain in their possession.
[4] *Stockbridge, Past and Present.*

And there were other settlements. A band of *Montauks* of Long Island, *Mohegans* of Connecticut, and *Pequots* and *Narragansetts* of Massachusetts, under the leadership of Samson Occum, a *Mohegan* missionary, took up their residence in the Oneida country in 1788, and were confirmed on a reservation two miles in length by three in breadth, in the present town of Marshall, Oneida county, where, having no language in common, they adopted the English, and received the name of Brothertons. They subsequently removed to the west and settled in Wisconsin.

Similar was the course of the domestic clans of *Raritans*. From an early period a remnant of the tribe had occupied a reservation in the county of Burlington, New Jersey, where they were known as Brothertons. In 1802, they accepted an invitation from the *Mahicans* to unite with them, and, obtaining consent from the legislature, sold their lands and removed to the reservation of the latter. They were officially met by the authorities of New Jersey for the last time in 1832, when, reduced to about forty souls, they applied to the legislature for remuneration on account of their rights of hunting and fishing on unenclosed lands, which they had reserved in their various agreements with the whites, and the legislature promptly directed the payment to them of two thousand dollars in full relinquishment of their claims.[1]

[1] The application was made by *Shawuskukhkung* or Wilted Grass, a chief of the Delawares, who had been educated at Princeton at the expense of the Scotch Missionary Society. At the time of making the application he was seventy-six years of age. His address to the legislature, on the occasion, was as follows:

"My Brethren.—I am old, and weak, and poor, and therefore a fit representative of my people. You are young, and strong, and rich, and therefore fit representatives of your people. But let me beg you for a moment to lay aside the recollection of your strength and of our weakness, that your minds may be prepared to examine with candor the subject of our claims.

"Our tradition informs us, and I believe it corresponds with your records, that the right of fishing in all the rivers and bays south of the Raritan, and of hunting in all unenclosed lands, was never relinquished, but on the contrary was expressly reserved in our last treaty, held at Crosswicks, in 1758.

"Having myself been one of the parties to the sale, I believe in 1801, I know that these rights were not sold or parted with.

"We now offer to sell these privileges to the state of New Jersey. They were once of great value to us, and we apprehend that neither time nor distance, nor the non-use of our rights, has at all affected them, but that the courts here would consider our claims valid were we to exercise them ourselves, or delegate them to others. It is not, however, our

On a small reservation on Long island the *Montauks* have still a representation, though with scarce a member of pure blood. On the third of March, 1702, they made an agreement with the English in which the rights of each were definitely fixed, and resided in peace with their neighbors until after the revolution, when they made claim to lands which they had previously ceded, but without success. The first to welcome Hudson's wandering bark, they are now the last representatives of the tribes which once held dominion on Sewanhackie.

Domestic clans or families of *Minsis* and *Mahicans* lingered

wish thus to excite litigation. We consider the state legislature the proper purchaser, and throw ourselves upon its benevolence and magnanimity, trusting that feelings of justice and liberality will induce you to give us what you deem a compensation."

The whole subject was referred to a committee, before whom Hon. Samuel L. Southard voluntarily and ably advocated the claim of the Delawares; and at the conclusion of his speech remarked: "That it was a proud fact in the history of New Jersey, that every foot of her soil had been obtained from the Indians by fair and voluntary purchase and transfer, a fact that no other state in the union, not even the land which bears the name of Penn, can boast of." The committee reported in favor of an appropriation of $2,000, which the legislature at once confirmed. This was the crowning act of a series in which justice and kindness to the Indians had been kept steadily in view; and was thus acknowledged by the veteran chief in a letter to the legislature dated "Trenton, March 12, 1832:

"Bartholomew S. Calvin (his English name), takes this method to return his thanks to both houses of the state legislature, and especially to their committees, for their very respectful attention to, and candid examination of, the Indian claims which he was delegated to present.

"The final act of official intercourse between the state of New Jersey and the Delaware Indians, who once owned nearly the whole of its territory, has now been consummated, and in a manner which must redound to the honor of this growing state, and, in all probability, to the prolongation of the existence of a wasted, yet grateful people. Upon this parting occasion, I feel it to be an incumbent duty to bear the feeble tribute of my praise to the high-toned justice which, in this instance, and, so far as I am acquainted, in all former times, has actuated the councils of this commonwealth in dealing with the aboriginal inhabitants.

"Not a drop of our blood have you spilled in battle — not an acre of our land have you taken but by our consent. These facts speak for themselves, and need no comment. They place the character of New Jersey in bold relief and bright example to those states within whose territorial limits our brethren still remain. Nothing save benisons can fall upon her from the lips of a *Lenni Lenape*.

"There may be some who would despise an Indian benediction; but when I return to my people, and make known to them the result of my mission, the ear of the Great Sovereign of the universe, which is still open to our cry, will be penetrated with our invocation of blessings upon the generous sons of New Jersey.

"To those gentlemen, members of the legislature, and others who have evinced their kindness to me, I cannot refrain from paying the unsolicited tribute of my heart-felt thanks. Unable to return them any other compensation, I fervently pray that God will have them in his holy keeping — will guide them in safety through the vicissitudes of this life, and ultimately, through the rich mercies of our blessed Redeemer, receive them into the glorious entertainment of his kingdom above."—*See note by W. J. Allinson, New Jersey Historical Collections.*

around their ancient seats for some years after the close of the revolution, but of them one after another it is written, "they disappeared in the night." In the language of Tamenund at the death of Uncas: "The pale faces are masters of the earth, and the time of the red men has not yet come again. My day has been too long. In the morning I saw the sons of *Unami* happy and strong ; and yet, before the night has come, have I lived to see the last warrior of the wise race of the *Mahicans*."

# APPENDIX.

# APPENDIX.

### I. BIOGRAPHICAL SKETCHES.

THE personal history of the early Indian kings and chiefs who held dominion in the valley of the Hudson, is involved in even greater obscurity than that which attaches to their contemporaries in other parts of the new world. Of MASSASOIT, MIANTONOMOH, UNCAS, PHILIP, and other New England chiefs, and of POWHATTAN and POCAHONTAS of Virginia, there is some definite information; but of those who welcomed the emigrants from Holland, names alone survive. MONEMIUS and UNUWATS, whose castles Hudson visited, have no record except in the deed which they gave to their lands, while AEPJIN, king of the *Mahicans*, and GOETHALS, king of the *Wappingers*, float in an uncertain twilight which is scarcely relieved on the part of their contemporaries, KAELCOP and SEWACKENAMO of the *Minsis*, WYANDANCE, of the *Montauks*, and ORITANY of the *Hackinsacks*, by the stirring scenes in which they were participants. Even as late as 1710, when more definite records came to be written, there is no preservation of the lines of kings, nor is there positive identification of the *Mahican* and *Iroquois* sachems who then visited England. True, it is said that HENDRIK of the *Mohawks*, was one of the latter, and that ELOW-OH-KAOM, of the *Mahicans*, left a daughter who became the wife of UMPACHENEE, a chief subsequently known to the missionaries of Stockbridge; but as a rule, the declaration is not the mere creation of the poet SPRAGUE, that

> "The doomed Indian leaves behind no trace,
> To save his own or serve another race,
> With his frail breath his power has passed away,
> His deeds, his thoughts, are buried with his clay.
>   His heraldry is but a broken bow,
>   His history but a tale of wrong and woe,
>   His very name must be a blank."

On the part of the *Lenapes* the name of TAMANY, or TA-MANED has been preserved in a halo of traditionary glory. He was one of their sachems or kings, and lived possibly as late as 1680. Heckewelder says: "The fame of this great man extended even among the whites, who fabricated numerous legends respecting him, which I never heard, however, from the mouth of an Indian, and therefore believe to be fabulous." He is said to have been a resident of the present county of Bucks, in Pennsylvania, and that he was buried near a spring about three and a half miles west of Doylestown, in that county. Heckewelder adds, that when Colonel George Morgan of Princeton, visited the western Indians, by order of congress, in 1776, he was so beloved for his goodness that the *Lenapes* gave to him the name of their venerated chief. Morgan brought back to the whites such glowing accounts of the qualities of the ancient chief, that, in the revolutionary war, he was dubbed a saint, his name was placed on some calendars, and his festival celebrated on the first day of May in every year. " On that day a numerous society of votaries walked together in procession through the streets of Philadelphia, their hats decorated with bucks' tails, and proceeded to a handsome rural place out of town which they called a wigwam, where, after a long talk or Indian speech had been delivered, and the calumet of friendship and peace had been smoked, they spent the day in festivity and mirth. After dinner Indian dances were performed on the green in front of the wigwam, the calumet was again smoked, and the company separated." " After the war," adds Thatcher, " these meetings were broken up ; but since that time Tammany societies have sprung up in Philadelphia and New York, which have excited no little influence in political circles."

ALLUMMAPEES, or *Sassoonan*, is the first ruling king of the *Lenapes*, known to the records. He was the associate, perhaps the successor of *Tamany*. In 1718, he headed the deputation of Indian chieftains at Philadelphia, who signed an absolute release to the proprietaries for the lands " situate between Delaware and Susquehanna, from Duck creek to the mountains on this side Lechay, which lands had been granted by their ancestors to William Penn." In 1728, he had removed "from on Delaware to Shamokin." Conrad Weisser, the Indian interpreter, writes in 1747: "The Delaware Indians last year intended to visit Philadelphia, but were prevented by ALLUMMAPEES' sickness, who is still alive, but not able to stir. They will come down this year, some time after harvest. ALLUMMAPEES has no successor in his relations, and he will hear of none so long as he is alive, and none of the Indians care to meddle in the affair. *Shikellimy*[1] advises that the government should name ALLUMMAPEES' successor, and set him up by their authority, that at this critical time there might be a man to apply to, since ALLUMMAPEES has lost his senses and is incapable of doing anything." In 1747, the old chief took part in a treaty with the Moravians concerning the erection of a smithy at their town. In the fall of that year he deceased. Whatever he may have been in his earlier years, he was but little more than an intemperate imbecile at the time of his death. Weisser writes: " ALLUMMAPEES would have resigned his crown before now, but as he had the keeping of the public treasure (that is to say of the council-bag), consisting of belts of wampum, for which he buys liquor, and has been drunk for these two or three years almost constantly, it is thought he won't die so long as there is one single wampum left in the bag."[2]

TADAME was the successor of *Allummapees*. He held the crown until 1756, when he was " treacherously murdered, but by whom or for what cause," says Minor, " we find no record."[3] The probabilities are, however, that as he was active in the hostilities which had then been inaugurated with the English, his death was caused by some wretch of his own tribe for the purpose of obtaining the price which the governor of Pennsylvania had offered for his scalp.

TEEDYUSCUNG, the most distinguished of the modern *Lenape* kings, was the successor of *Tadame*. Major Parsons writes that he was " a lusty, raw-boned man, but haughty and very desirable of respect and command." Reichel, in his *Memorials of the Moravian Church*, adds : " According to his own state-

---

[1] *Shikellimy* was one of the viceregent Oneida chiefs, residing at Shamokin. He died in 1748.

[2] *Memorials of the Moravian Church*, i, 67.

[3] *History of Wyoming*.

ment, he was born about the year 1700, in New Jersey, east of Trenton, in which neighborhood his ancestors of the *Unamis* had been seated from time immemorial. Old Captain Harris, a noted *Delaware*, was his father. The same was the father also of Captain John of Nazareth, of young Captain Harris, of Tom, of Jo, and of Sam Evans, a family of high-spirited sons who were not in good repute with their white neighbors. The latter named them, it is true, for men of their own people, and TEEDYUSCUNG they named Honest John; yet they disliked and then feared them, for the Harrises were known to grow moody and resentful, and were heard to speak threatening words as they saw their paternal acres passing out of their hands, and their hunting-grounds converted into pasture and plowed fields." When the Moravians appeared at Bethlehem, TEEDYUSCUNG came to hear them; soon after professed conversion and was baptized. His conversion, however, was not proof against the wrongs which his people had suffered, and when the offer of the crown was made to him he readily accepted it, and became their leader. At the conferences which he attended, says the writer last quoted: " TEEDYUSCUNG stood up as the champion of his people, fearlessly demanding restitution of their lands, or an equivalent for their irreparable loss, and in addition the free exercise of the right to select, within the territory in dispute, a permanent home. The chieftain's imposing presence, his earnestness of appeal, and his impassioned oratory, as he plead the cause of the long-injured *Lenape*, evoked the admiration of his enemies themselves. He always spoke in the euphonious *Delaware*, employing this Castilian of the new world to utter the simple and expressive figures and tropes of the native rhetoric with which his harangues were replete, although he was conversant with the white man's speech. It would almost appear, from the minutes of these conferences, that the English artfully attempted to evade the point at issue, and to conciliate the indignant chieftain by fair speeches and uncertain promises. The hollowness of the former he boldly exposed, and the latter he scornfully rejected; so that it was soon perceived that the Indian king was as astute and sagacious, as he was unmovable in the justice of his righteous demands. This conviction forced itself upon his hearers, and then they yielded to the terms he laid down." He was the hero of the war of 1755, for while *Hendrik* boldly demanded the simple distribution of presents, TEEDYUSCUNG wrung the liberties of his people from both his civilized and uncivilized enemies.

In the spring of 1758, TEEDYUSCUNG removed to Wyoming, where, agreeably to his request and the conditions of treaty, a town had been built for him and his followers by the government of Pennsylvania. Here he lived not unmindful of his long cherished object, and here he was burned to death on the night of the 19th of April, 1763, while asleep in his lodge. "The concurrent testimony of his time agrees in representing him as a man of marked ability, a brave warrior, a sagacious counsellor and a patriot among his people. Although he was governed by strong passions, and a slave of that degrading vice which was the bane of his race, he was not devoid of feeling, but susceptible of the gentler influences of our nature. Numerous are the anecdotes extant, illustrating his love of humor, his ready wit, his quickness of apprehension and reply, his keen penetration, and his sarcastic delight in exposing low cunning and artifice." Stone adds: "In regard to the character of TEEDYUSCUNG, the sympathies of Sir William Johnson were with his own people; yet in his correspondence, while he labored somewhat to detract from the lofty pretensions of the *Delaware* captain, the baronet conceded to him enough of talent, influence, and power among his people, to give him a proud rank among the chieftains of his race. Certain it is, that TEEDYUSCUNG did much to restore his nation to the rank of MEN."

NETAWATEES, the successor of *Teedyuscung*, is spoken of in the highest terms by Loskiel and Heckewelder. Loskiel says: "This wise man spared no pains to conciliate the affection of all his neighbors. He sent frequent embassies to his grandchildren, admonishing them to keep the peace, and proved in truth a wise grandfather to them. He used to lay all affairs of state before his counsellors for their consideration, without telling them his own sentiments. When they gave him their opinion, he either approved of it, or stated his objections and amendments, always stating the reasons of his disapprobation.

Thus he kept them active, and maintained great respect. When the war of the revolution came on he did every thing in his power to preserve peace among the Indian nations. He, however, received a message from the *Hurons*, "that the *Delawares* should keep their shoes in readiness, to join the warriors." This message he would not accept, but sent several to the *Hurons* admonishing them to sit still, and to remember the misery they had brought upon themselves by taking share in the late war between the English and the French. These belts were carried to the chiefs of the *Hurons* in Fort Detroit, but as it was necessary to deliver them in the presence of the English governor, the latter, "to fulfill his duty, cut them in pieces, cast them at the deputies' feet, and commanded them to depart." He died at Pittsburg in 1776. Loskiel adds : "Ever since his sentiments changed in favor of the Gospel, he was a faithful friend of the brethren, and being one of the most experienced chiefs of his time, his council proved often very serviceable to the mission. The wish he uttered as his last will and testament, that the *Delaware* nation might hear and believe the word of God, preached by the brethren, was frequently repeated in the council by his successors, and then they renewed their covenant to use their utmost exertions to fulfill this last wish of their old, worthy and honored chief. Upon such an occasion Captain White Eyes, holding the Bible and some spelling books in his hands, addressed the council with great emotion and even with tears. My friends, said he, you have now heard the last will and testament of our departed chief. I will therefore gather together my young men and their children, and kneeling down before that God who created them, will pray unto him, that he may have mercy upon us and reveal his will unto us. And as we cannot declare it to those who are yet unborn, we will pray unto the Lord our God, to make it known to our children, and children's children." Heckewelder says : " All the surrounding nations appeared to have been sensible of his worth. While living, he often encouraged his people to adopt the way of living by agriculture, and finally become civilized. His ideas were, that unless the Indians changed their mode of living they would in time dwindle to nothing."

## APPENDIX.

Captain WHITE EYES, or *Coquehageahton*, distinguished for his friendship for the Americans in the early stages of the revolution, was the successor of *Netawatwees*, but held the government only two years. On his death, in 1778, a regency took the direction during the minority of the lineal heir to the throne. On the death of the latter, in 1781, GELELEMAND, alias Killbuck, became king by election.

One of the earliest chiefs of the *Shawanoes*, of whom record has been preserved, was PAXINOS or *Paxinosa*, who came to the Minnisink country in 1692, and who appears, in the records of New York, as chief of the Minnisinks. He subsequently fell back with his people to the Delaware country, and next appears in the difficulties which grew out of the removal of the *Lenapes* to Wyoming. With a desire to strengthen themselves at the latter place, *Teedyuscung* and PAXINOS visited the "believing Indians" at Gnadenhütten, in 1752, and desired them to remove to the lands which they had selected, repeating as the order of the Six Nations : " They (the *Iroquois*) rejoice that some of the believing Indians have removed to Wyoming ; but now they lift up the remaining *Mahicans* and *Delawares* and settle them down in Wyoming, for there a fire is kindled for them, and there they may plant and think on God." About eighty of the converts accompanied the parties to Wyoming, but the remainder refused to do so, under the advice of the missionaries. In the spring of 1754, PAXINOS again appeared in the settlement, accompanied by twenty-three warriors and three *Iroquois* embassadors, and added to the order already quoted, that if the invitation was not heeded, " the great head (the *Iroquois*) would come down and clean their ears with a red-hot poker." Says Loskiel : " PAXINOS then turned to the missionaries, earnestly demanding of them not to hinder the Indians from removing to Wajomick, for that the road was free, therefore they might visit their friends there, stay with them till they were tired, and then return to their own country." On the 11th of February, 1755, PAXINOS " demanded an answer to the message he had brought last year," and was told that " the brethren would confer with the Iroquois themselves, concerning the intended removal of the Indians at Gnadenhütten to Wajomick." Loskiel adds: "PAXINOS, being only an embassador in this business, was satisfied, and even formed a closer acquaintance with the brethren. His wife, who heard the gospel preached daily, was so overcome by its divine power, that she began to see her lost estate by nature, and earnestly begged for baptism. Her husband, having lived thirty-eight years with her in marriage, to mutual satisfaction, willingly gave his consent, prolonged his stay at Bethlehem, was present in the chapel, and deeply affected when his wife was baptized by Bishop Spangenberg." The Indians did not remove, and, soon after PAXINOS' last visit, the Moravian settlement near Shamokin was attacked, and fourteen persons killed. On the 24th of November, Shamokin shared the same fate. Several persons were killed, and eleven belonging to the mission were burned alive; and, on New Year's day the work of destruction was completed. What connection PAXINOS had with these hostilities does not appear, but it is said that he sent his two sons to rescue brother Kiefer, if he should be in the hands of the enemy, and that that missionary was conducted by them to Gnadenhütten, showing that he must have been aware that the attack was contemplated. He was present at the treaty with Johnson in 1756, and at Easton with *Teedyuscung* in 1757, on which latter occasion he was addressed by Governor Denny as "our hearty friend and a lover of peace." Reichel says he removed with his family to the Ohio country in 1758, and that he was the last *Shawanoe* king east of the Alleghanies. At the time of his removal he was an old man, and was doubtless soon after gathered to his fathers. His son *Kolapeka* or *Teatapercaum*, alias Samuel, was a distinguished chief in the war of 1764.

Although perhaps not strictly a part of the history of the Indians of Hudson's river, the connection of the *Shawanoes* with the *Minsis* will permit the introduction of one or two of their more prominent chiefs. BENEVISSICA represented them in the treaty at Fort Stanwix in 1764, and again in 1765. In 1774, it is said that a belt was sent to NERERAHHE, a *Shawanoe*, "but he being a sachem, sent it to the chief warrior of his nation, SOWANOWANE." Although it does not positively appear, there is some ground for the presumption that the latter was none other than the famous CORNSTALK, who stood at the head of the western confederacy in that year, and who held the command in the engagement with the forces under Dunmore and Lewis at Point Pleasant. He was a man of more than ordinary nerve and power, as well as one of the most eloquent of his race. Says Stone: "Col. Wilson who was present at the interview between the chief and Lord Dunmore, thus speaks of the chieftain's bearing on the occasion: 'When he arose, he was in no wise confused or daunted, but spoke in a distinct and audible voice, without stammering or repetition, and with peculiar emphasis. His looks, while addressing Dunmore, were truly grand and majestic, yet graceful and attractive. I have heard the first orators in Virginia, Patrick Henry and Richard Henry Lee; but never have I heard one whose powers of delivery surpassed those of CORNSTALK.'" After his treaty with Dunmore he became a friend to the English, and to that friendship gave up his life. Learning that his people were determined to make war upon the English, he visited the latter in 1777, at the fort which they had erected at Point Pleasant to take advice. The commandant of the fort detained him as a hostage, and while thus detained he was joined by his son *Ellinipsico*. Soon after the arrival of the latter, a white man named Gilmore was killed near the fort. The cry of revenge was raised, and a party of ruffians assembled, under the command of Capt. Hall, who, instead of pursuing the guilty, fell upon the hostages in the fort. Seeing that there was no escape for him, the old chief addressed his son: "My son, the Great Spirit has seen fit that we should die together, and has sent you to that end. It is his will, and let us submit." CORNSTALK fell, perforated with seven bullets, and died without a struggle, while his son met his fate with composure and was shot on the seat upon which he was sitting. "Thus," says Withers in his *Indian Chronicles*, "perished the mighty CORNSTALK, sachem of the *Shawanoes*, and king of the northern confederacy in 1774, a chief remarkable for many great and good qualities. He was disposed to be at all times the friend of the white man, as he was ever the advocate of honorable peace. But when his country's wrongs summoned him to battle, he became the thunderbolt of war, and made his enemies feel the weight of his arm. His noble bearing, his generous and disinterested attachment to the colonies, his anxiety to preserve the frontier of Virginia from desolation and death, all conspired to win for him the esteem and respect of others ; while the untimely and perfidious manner of his death caused a deep and lasting feeling of regret to pervade the bosoms, even of those who were enemies to his nation, and excited the just indignation of all towards his inhuman murderers."

The most distinguished chief of the *Shawanoes*, of more modern times, was TECUMSEH, who, as Parton justly writes, " though not the faultless ideal of a patriot prince that romantic story represents him, was all of a patriot, a hero, a man, that an Indian can be." He was a cross-breed, the son of a *Shawanoe* by a *Creek* woman, and at a very early age gave evidence of superior abilities in the wars which were terminated by the treaty of 1794. Thoroughly indoctrinated in the policy of his people, and a willing student of the schools which demanded a line beyond which the whites should not advance to the hunting grounds of the west, the sale of the lands of his tribe on the Wabash, soon after Mr. Jefferson came into power, gave him great offense. About this time *Hendrik*, of the *Mahicans*, conceived the plan of uniting the tribes of the west for the better protection of their interests. TECUMSEH seized the idea quickly and perverted its purpose to the accomplishment of an organization which should have for its object the entire destruction of the whites, after the plan of his great prototype, King *Philip*. From tribe to tribe he passed, declaring : " The Great Spirit gave this great island to his red children ; he placed the whites on the other side of the big water ; they were not contented with their own, but came to take ours from us. They have driven us from the sea to the lakes ; we can go no further. They have taken upon them to say this land belongs to the *Miamis*, this to the *Delawares*, and so on ; but the Great Spirit intended it as the common property of us all." For four years he was engaged in the work of preparing the tribes for a general war. A silent man in the ordinary circumstances of life, he could employ more than the eloquence of Logan, and when descanting upon the Indian's wrongs, and the white man's encroachments. General Harrison, who was long his patient and forbearing adviser, and then his conqueror, speaks of him as "one of those uncommon geniuses which spring up occasionally to produce revolutions, and overturn the established order of things. If it were not for the vicinity of the United States, he would, perhaps, be the founder of an empire, that would rival in glory Mexico or Peru. No difficulties deter him. For four years he has been in constant motion. You see him to-day on the Wabash, and in a short time hear of him on the shores of Lake Erie or Michigan, or on the banks of the Mississippi; and wherever he goes he makes an impression favorable to his purposes." Failing to accomplish his purpose, he accepted the overtures of the British and brought to their aid, in the war of 1812, two thousand warriors — an alliance more powerful than that which that government had ever been able to command even in the palmiest days of the Five Nations. On the banks of the Thames, on the 5th of October, in an engagement which will forever occupy a prominent place in American history from its association with his fate, he gave up his life in endeavoring to promote the cause of those in whose selfish purposes he had no interest, but in whom he found what he believed to be the avengers of the wrongs of his people. He is described as a person of erect, athletic frame, of noble, commanding appearance, and the air of a king. When he arose before his savage audiences, his imposing manner created a feeling of awe; but when he kindled with his great subject, he seemed like one inspired. His eye flashed fire, his swarthy bosom heaved and swelled with imprisoned passion, his whole frame dilated with excitement, and his strong untutored soul poured itself forth in eloquence, wild, headlong, and resistless. When not addressing his clans, he was cold and haughty. "His withering sarcasm," says Headley, "when Proctor proposed to retreat from Walden; his reply to the interpreter, who, offering him a chair in the presence of Harrison, said, 'Your father wishes you to be seated,'—' My Father! the sun is my father, and the earth my mother; I will rest on her bosom'— reveal a nature conscious of its greatness." And Parton adds: "If to conceive a grand, difficult, and unselfish project, to labor for years with enthusiasm and prudence in attempting its execution; to enlist in it by the magnetism of personal influence great multitudes of various tribes; to contend for it with unfaltering valor longer than there was hope of success; and to die fighting for it to the last, falling toward the enemy covered with wounds, is to give proof of an heroic cast of character, then is the *Shawanoe* chief TECUMSEH, in whose veins flowed no blood that was not Indian, entitled to rank among heroes."[1]

The Six Nations were not without their great men, of whom King HENDRIK, or *Soi-en-ga-rah-ta*, who stood for so many years at the head of the *Mohawks*, was one. It is said that he was born in 1680, and that he was one of the chiefs who visited England in 1710.[2] His father was a *Mahican* chief, called by his people The Wolf, who, either by captivity and adoption became a member of the *Mohawk* family, or was attracted thither by the fair charmer who became his wife, herself the daughter of a king. In the right of his mother, HENDRIK became king. When about twenty years of age, and for half a century or more subsequently, he represented his people in council and in camp, coming down to the present time as a model of Indian courage and the embodiment of Indian eloquence. His greatest service to the English appears to have been performed in the battle under Johnson, at Lake George, in 1755, where he lost his life, and his greatest speech that which he delivered before the conference at Albany in 1754. That the reader may judge of its merits, without the trouble of reference, its most important parts are copied:

"Brethren: We return you all our grateful acknowledgments for renewing and brightening the covenant chain. This chain belt is of very great importance to our united nations, and all our allies; we will therefore take it to Onondaga, where our council-fire always burns, and keep it so securely that neither thunder nor lightning shall break it; there we will consult over

---

[1] *Parton's Life of Jackson; Headley's Second War with England; Drake's Life of Tecumseh; Montgomery's Life of Harrison.*

[2] The statement of Governor Hunter (*Colonial History*, v, 358), leaves no room to doubt that Hendrik was one of the chiefs named as parties to this expedition.

it, and as we have lately added two links to it, so we will endeavor to add as many more links to it as lies in our power; and we hope when we show you this belt again, we shall give you reason to rejoice at it, by your seeing the vacancies in it filled up. In the meantime we desire that you will strengthen yourselves, and bring as many into this covenant chain as you possibly can.

"We do now solemnly renew and brighten the covenant chain with our brethren here present, and all our other absent brethren on the continent.

" Brethren : As to the accounts you have heard of our living dispersed from each other, 'tis very true. We have several times endeavored to draw off those of our brethren who are settled at Oswegatchie but in vain, for the governor of Canada is like a wicked deluding spirit ; however, as you desire we shall persist in our endeavors.

" You have asked us the reason of our living in this dispersed manner. The reason is, your neglecting us for these three years past. You have thus (taking a stick and throwing it behind his back), thrown us behind your back, and disregarded us, whereas the French are a subtle and vigilant people, ever using their utmost endeavors to bring our people over to them.

"Brethren : It is very true as you told us that the clouds hang heavy over us, and 'tis not very pleasant to look up, but we give you this belt to clear away all clouds, that we may all live in bright sunshine, and keep together in strict union and friendship; then we shall become strong and nothing can hurt us.

" Brethren : This is the ancient place of treaty, where the fire of friendship always used to burn, and 'tis now three years since we have been called to any public treaty here. 'Tis true there are commissioners here, but they have never invited us to smoke with them ; but the Indians of Canada come frequently and smoke here, which is for the sake of their beaver ; but we hate them. 'Tis your fault, brethren, that we are not strengthened by conquest, for we would have gone and taken Crown point, but you hindered us ; we had concluded to go and take it, but we were told it was too late, and that the ice would not bear us ; instead of this, you burnt your own fort at Saratoga and run away from it, which was a shame and a scandal to you. Look about your country and see; you have no fortifications about you, no, not even to this city; 'tis but one step from Canada hither, and the French may easily come and turn you out of your doors.

"Brethren: You desire us to speak from the bottom of our hearts, and we shall do it. Look about you and see all these houses full of beaver, and the money is all gone to Canada, likewise powder, lead and guns, which the French now make use of at Ohio.

"Brethren: The goods which go from hence to Oswego, go from thence to Ohio, which further enables the French to carry on their designs at the Ohio.

"Brethren: You were desirous that we should open our minds, and our hearts to you; look at the French, they are men, they are fortifying everywhere; but, we are ashamed to say it, you are all, like women, bare and open without any fortifications."

At the same conference, in subsequent session, he spoke as follows:

"Brethren: There is an affair about which our hearts tremble and our minds are deeply concerned; this is the selling of rum in our castles. It destroys many, both of our old and young people. We request of all the governments here present, that it may be forbidden to carry any of it amongst the Five Nations.

"Brethren: We are in great fears about this rum; it may cause murder on both sides. We don't want it to be forbid to be sold to us at Albany, but that none may be brought to our castles. The *Cayugas* now declare in their own name, that they will not allow any rum to be brought up their river, and those who do so must take the consequences.

"Brethren: We, the *Mohawks* of both castles, have also one request to make, which is, that the people who are settled round about us, may not be suffered to sell our people rum; it keeps them all poor, makes them idle and wicked; if they have any money or goods they lay it all out in rum; it destroys virtue and the progress of religion amongst us. We have a friendly request to make to the governor and all the commissioners here present, that they will help us to build a church at Canajoharie, and that we may have a bell in it, which, together with the putting a stop to the selling of rum, will tend to make us religious and lead better lives than we now do."

Comparisons, it is said, are odious; in this case they are not necessary in order to strip from history the high coloring which has been given to the eloquence of HENDRIK. Nor can it with truth be added that Aupaumut "for capacity, bravery and vigor of mind, and immovable integrity united, he excelled all the aboriginal inhabitants of whom we have any knowledge." Concede to him all that even charity demands for his race, he yet failed to rise to the greatness of *Massasoit*, *Uncas*, *Philip*, *Teedyuscung*, *Aupaumut*, *Pontiac*, or *Tecumseh*. He was less eloquent than *Logan* the *Oneida*, than *Aupaumut* the *Mahican*, than *Cornplanter* or *Red Jacket* of the *Senecas;* his bravery and his integrity were alike tarnished by his selfishness. That he was a great man among his people, " esteemed the bravest of the brave, among the *Iroquois*," is true. The concurrent testimony of every traditionist awards to him great natural talents, judgment and sagacity. His death was heroic; his life, a criticism on the debasing influences of civilization upon his race.

THAYENDANEGA, or *Joseph Brant*, who is regarded as the successor of King *Hendrik*,[1] is said to have been the son of a *Mohawk* woman by a chief of the *Onondagas*, although there have been those who have regarded him as one of the illegitimate children of Sir William Johnson. He was born, says Stone, in the Ohio country, in 1742, where his father and mother were

---

[1] Speaking of the succession of kings, Schoolcraft remarks: "The son of the chief's oldest sister was the chief presumptive. Such was the Iroquois rule when King Hendrik fell at the battle of Lake George; he had a son of mature age, who made use of the memorable expression, on hearing his father's death, " No, he is not dead, but lives here," striking his breast. Yet he did not succeed his father in the Mohawk chieftaincy. It fell to his sister's son, Little Abraham, a mild and politic chief, who died at the era of the opening of the American revolution. On this, there was a vacancy which was supplied by the election of Joseph Brant, an entirely new man in the line of chiefs. It was the wise policy of Sir Wm. Johnson and his son, to lay the greatest stress on his tribal authority, and to strengthen it by every means, as the best and most direct way of exercising an influence over the tribes." (*Hist. Indian Tribes*, part IV, 481). In *Colonial History*, VIII, 53, Abraham is said to have been the great Hendrik's brother, not a son of the sister of that chief, as stated by Schoolcraft. But he was not the less the legitimate successor to the throne.

then temporarily residing, and where his father soon after died. His mother, on her return to Canajoharie, married an Indian called Carrihogo, or News Carrier, whose Christian name was Barnet or Bernard, which was subsequently contracted into Brant, by which name his step-son was also known, being first called Brant's Joseph, and subsequently, by inversion, Joseph Brant. His position as chief was mainly due to his associations with the Johnsons. His sister, Mary or Molly, was the concubine of Sir William, and as her brother was perhaps necessarily much in her company, Johnson sent him to Dr. Wheelock's school, and subsequently employed him as his secretary as an agent in public affairs. Throughout the revolution he was engaged in warfare chiefly upon the border settlements of New York and Pennsylvania, in connection with the Johnsons and Butlers. After the war he devoted himself to the social and religious improvement of the *Mohawks*, who were settled upon the Ouise or Grand river, in Upper Canada, upon lands granted to them by the governor of that province. He translated the Gospel of St. Mark into the *Mohawk* language ; and in many ways his exertions for the spiritual and temporal welfare of his people were eminently successful, and endeared him to his nation. He was far from being a great or an able chief, many of his contemporaries being his peers in courage and in native ability. His education and his association with the Johnsons gave him in prominence what he lacked in distinctive merit. He died at his residence at the head of Lake Ontario, November 24th, 1807, aged 65 years. One of his sons (John) was an officer in the British service, on the Niagara frontier in the war of 1812. (*Lossing*, 1, 257). Schoolcraft repudiates the claim set up by Stone that Brant was made the war chieftain of the confederacy. He asserts that no such office existed, and that Brant was simply a chief of the third and lowest class. (*Notes on the Iroquois*, 496). The authority which he exercised was undoubtedly by virtue of his commission from the British government. At no time was his course approved by the united voice of the confederacy in council at Onondaga.

LOGAN, who was regarded by Jefferson as the most eloquent of all the aborigines, " was the son of *Shikellimy*, alias *Swatane*, an *Oneida* chief of the *Oquacho* or Wolf tribe of Indians, who was in 1728, acting representative of the Five Nations, in business affairs with the proprietary government, and who was appointed their vicegerent, and in this capacity administered their tributaries within the province of Pennsylvania, with Shamokin for his seat.[1] His father was one of the earliest to encourage the introduction of Christianity by the Moravians. He was a great friend of the celebrated James Logan, who accompanied Penn on his last voyage to America, and who subsequently became distinguished in the colony for his learning and benevolence. Hence the name of his son. LOGAN married a *Shawanoe* woman and removed from his father's lodge to the Ohio country where he became a chief, and, from the fact of his intermarriage with the *Shawanoes*, a *Mingoe*. He was a friend of the white men, by education and association, and one of the noblest of his race, not only by right of birth, but in consideration of his own character. During the Indian wars connected with the contest with France, he took no part save in the character of a peace-maker. In the spring of 1774, a company of land agents and traders on the Ohio came in collision with the Indians, and in retaliation for the loss of two of their men, succeeded in killing LOGAN's entire family, including his youngest brother and his sister. For this and similar acts, LOGAN placed himself at the head of a band of Ohio *Senecas*, and, in company with the *Lenapes* and *Shawanoes* under *Cornstalk*, invaded the Virginia border with fire and tomahawk. At the treaty of peace with Dunmore, LOGAN was not present. On being visited for the purpose of securing his assent to the terms, he delivered the famous speech which Jefferson has preserved in his *Notes on Virginia*, and which has become familiar wherever the English language is spoken : " I appeal to any white man to say if he ever entered LOGAN's cabin hungry, and he gave him not meat ; if ever he came cold and naked and he clothed him not. During the course of the last long and bloody war, Logan remained idle in his cabin, an advocate for peace.

[1] *Memorials Moravian Church*, I, 83. *Shikellimy* is called a Cayuga chief, by some writers, and his son a Mingoe, but the testimony of Reichel seems clear that both were full-blooded Oneidas. Shikellimy had three sons, *John, James Logan,* and *John Petty*. He died in 1749.— *Loskiel*, II, 119.

Such was my love for the whites, that my countrymen pointed, as they passed, and said, 'Logan is the friend of the white men.' I had even thought to live with you, but for the injuries of one man. Colonel Cresap, the last spring, in cold blood and unprovoked, murdered all the relations of Logan, not even sparing my women and children. There runs not a drop of my blood in the veins of any living creature. This called on me for revenge. I have sought it; I have killed many; I have fully glutted my vengeance. For my country, I rejoice at the beams of peace; but do not harbor a thought that mine is the joy of fear. Logan never felt fear. He will not turn on his heel to save his live. Who is there to mourn for Logan? Not one." Soon after the treaty at which this speech was delivered, LOGAN became intemperate, and on his return from one of his visits to Detroit was murdered in the woods.

Among the distinguished men of the Five Nations at an earlier period was GARANGULA, who was called "the pride of the *Onondaga* tribe," and whose speech in reply to M. de la Barre, the governor of Canada, in 1684, is quoted by Thatcher and Drake. At the time of its delivery he was an old man, and disappears from history soon after. A man of more activity was the warrior called by the English, BLACK KETTLE. Colden speaks of him as a "famous hero;" but few of his exploits have come down to the present time. "It is only known," says Thatcher, "that he commanded large parties of his countrymen, who were exceedingly troublesome to the French. In 1691, he made an irruption into the country around Montreal, at the head of several hundred men. "He overran Canada (say the French annalists), as a torrent does the low lands, when it overflows its banks, and there is no withstanding it. The troops of the stations received orders to stand upon the defensive; and it was not until the enemy were returning home victorious, after having desolated the French possessions, that a force of four hundred soldiers was mustered to pursue them. BLACK KETTLE is said to have had but half that number with him at this juncture, but he gave battle and fought desperately. After losing twenty men slain, with some prisoners, he broke through the French ranks and escaped, leaving a considerable number of his enemies wounded and killed." The story is no doubt exaggerated, but the courage and daring of the famous chief is well attested. At a later period the names of SKENANDO, CORNPLANTER and RED JACKET are prominent in Indian annals. The former was of the *Oneidas*, and the author of this famous reply: "I am an aged hemlock; the winds of an hundred winters have whistled through my branches; I am dead at the top. The generation to which I belonged has run away and left me." He was one of the converts to the missionary, Kirkland; was a warm friend of the Americans during the revolution, and died in 1816, at the age of one hundred and ten years. CORNPLANTER was a *Seneca* half-breed, his father being a Dutch trader. RED JACKET was a full-blooded *Seneca*. Both were distinguished for their eloquence, and both were engaged in the border wars of the revolution as inveterate enemies of the colonists. The former died in 1836, at the age of one hundred and one years, and the latter in 1830, aged about ninety years.

PASSACONNAWAY, who was at the head of the *Pennacooks* at the time of the discovery, was one of the most distinguished men of the Indian nations. "His name," says Schoolcraft, "is indicative of his warlike character —*Papisseconewa*, as written by himself, meaning The Child of the Bear." We first hear of him in 1627 or 8. Thomas Morton, in his *New English Canaan*, thus speaks of him, being in this country at that time: "That Sachem or Sagamore is a Powah of great estimation amongst all kind of salvages, there hee is at their Revels which is the time when a greate company of salvages meete from several parts of the country, in amity with their neighbors), hath advanced his honor in his feats or jugling tricks (as I may right tearme them), to the admiration of the spectators, whom hee endeavored to perswade that hee would goe under water to the further side of a river to broade for any man to undertake with a breath, which thing hee performed by swimming over and deluding the company with casting a mist before their eyes that see him enter in and come out; but no part of the way he has bin seene; likewise by our English in the heat of all summer, to make ice appear in a bowle of faire water, first having the water set before him, hee hath begunne his incantation according to their usual custom, and before the same hath bin ended, a thick cloude has darkened the aire, on a sodane a thunder clap hath bin heard that has amazed the natives; in an instant hee hath showed a firme peece of ice to flote in the middest of the bowle in the presence of the vulgar people, which doubtless was done by the agility of Satan his consort."

But he was something more than a juggler; his ability as a warrior and as a ruler is acknowledged. Gookin wrote of him in 1675: " He lived to a very great age, as I saw him alive at Pawtucket when he was about one hundred and twenty years old." Schoolcraft argues that the time when Gookin saw him was in 1648, and hence that he was one hundred years old when the English first purchased land from him. He was converted by Eliot in 1648, and continued a professing Christian until the time of his death. In 1660, when about one hundred and thirty years old, he called his tribe around him and delivered his farewell speech. " The occasion," says Schoolcraft, " filled all with sorrow, in spite of Indian stoicism. PASSACONNAWAY was deeply affected, and his voice, tremulous with age and emotion, still was musical and powerful — a splendid remnant of that whose power and beauty, in the fullness and vigor of manhood, had soothed or excited the passions of assembled savages, and moulded them to suit the purposes of the speaker.

"Hearken," said he, " to the words of your father. I am an old oak, that has withstood the storms of more than an hundred winters. Leaves and branches have been stripped from me by the winds and frosts — my eyes are dim — my limbs totter — I must soon fall! But when young and sturdy, when no young man of the *Pennacooks* could bend my bow — when my arrows would pierce a deer at an hundred yards, and I could bury my hatchet in a sapling to the eye — no weekwam had so many furs, no poll so many scalp-locks as Passaconaway's! Then, I delighted in war. The whoop of the *Pennacook* was heard upon the Mohawk — and no voice so loud as Passaconaway's. The scalps upon the pole of my weekwam told the story of *Mohawk* suffering.

" The English came, they seized our lands ; I sat me down at Pennacook. They followed upon my footsteps; I made

# APPENDIX.

war upon them, but they fought with fire and thunder; my young men were swept down before me when no one was near them. I tried sorcery against them, but still they increased and prevailed over me and mine, and I gave place to them, and retired to my beautiful island of Natticook. I, that can make the dry leaf turn green and live again; I, that can take the rattlesnake in my palm as I would a worm, without harm; I, who had communion with the Great Spirit, dreaming and awaking; I am powerless before the pale faces. The oak will soon break before the whirlwind, it shivers and shakes even now; soon its trunk will be prostrate, the ant and the worm will sport upon it. Then think, my children, of what I say; I commune with the Great Spirit. He whispers me now. 'Tell your people, peace, peace is the only hope of your race. I have given fire and thunder to the pale faces for weapons; I have made them plentier than the leaves of the forest, and still they shall increase! These meadows they shall turn with the plough, these forests shall fall by the axe, the pale faces shall live upon your hunting-grounds, and make their villages upon your fishing places.' The Great Spirit says this, and it must be so. We are few and powerless before them. We must bend before the storm. The wind blows hard! The old oak trembles! Its branches are gone! Its sap is frozen! It bends! It falls! Peace, peace with the white man is the command of the Great Spirit, and the wish — the last wish of Passaconnaway."

The old chief did not die at that time, but his activity was so impaired that he abdicated his throne to his son *Wannalancet*. He died between 1663 and 1669 — the oldest, most learned, and most eloquent of his race.

SOQUANS and MINICHQUE appear as representatives of the *Mahicans* on the Hudson in 1700. The first was a speaker of more than ordinary merit, as his public addresses attest. MINICHQUE is called the "great sachem" of his people, and great he certainly was in forgiving, upon his death-bed, his murderers, and praying that they might be spared the punishment due for the offense which they had committed. There is a moral grandeur in this, the crowning act of his life, which appeals to every reasonable mind. It is to be regretted that so little is known of his history. There is no doubt he was one of the leaders of the *Mahicans* at the time the *Mohawks* appealed to the governor of Canada, to protect them against his nation,[1] and that he subsequently became firmly attached to the English government. He was an intemperate man, but in this was no exception to his race; he was beloved by his people for his greatness as a savage; his dying wish associates with his memory one of the "attributes of the gods."

The "oldest man" among the *Mahicans*, when the New England missionaries first visited them, was Captain JOHN KONAPOT. He was one of the signers to the deed to Parsons and his associates in 1724, and subsequently became an influential member of the mission church at Stockbridge. Hopkins says of him: "KONAPOT, the principal man among the *Muhhekanok* of Massachusetts, was strictly temperate, very just and upright in his dealings, a man of prudence and industry, and inclined to embrace the Christian religion;" and Sergeant adds: "He is an excellent man, and I do believe has the true spirit of Christianity in him." He had from Gov. Belcher a commission as captain, and served his people and the Massachusetts government well and faithfully. His son, JOHN KONAPOT, Jr., is said to have been the grandson of old King *Hendrik* of the *Mohawks*. The date of his death is not given, but it probably occurred about 1750.

The most distinguished man of the *Mahicans* was Captain HENDRIK AUPAUMUT, subsequently known as Captain HENDRIK, who appears to have sustained the most important relation to his tribe and to the nation for nearly half a century.[2] Of his birth and parentage nothing is known. He is first

---

[1] *Brodhead*, II, 161.

[2] In 1771, Benjamin Kok-ke-we-naunaut, called King Benjamin, being 94 years of age, resigned his office of sachem, and requested his people to elect a successor. Solomon Un-haun-nau-waun-nutt was chosen. He was acting in that capacity at the outbreak of the revolution and was addressed by the Massachusetts Convention. He died in February, 1777, while Benjamin lived until 1781, dying at the advanced age of 104 years. After the death of King Solomon, the government, it is said, devolved upon Joseph Quanau-kaunt (pronounced, by the English at least, Quinney-hong, and now generally spelled Quinney), who divided his power more equally with his counsellors — Peter Poh-quon-nop-peet (pronounced Ponknepeet), Captain Hendrik Aupaumut and Captain John Konapot, Jr. The wife of Captain Hendrik and the wife of King Solomon, were the sisters of King Joseph.—*Stockbridge, Past and Present*.

## APPENDIX.  321

introduced as the speaker in the conference with the *Mohawk* embassadors during the war of 1746. At the conference in Albany, in 1754, he represented his tribe, and in response to the governor, delivered the following address:

"Fathers: We are greatly rejoiced to see you all here. It is by the will of Heaven that we are met here, and we thank you for this opportunity of seeing you altogether, as it is a long time since we have had such an one.

"Fathers: Who sit present here, we will just give you a short relation of the long friendship which hath subsisted between the white people of this country and us. Our forefathers had a castle on this river. As one of them walked out he saw something on the river, but was at a loss to know what it was. He took it at first for a great fish. He ran into the castle and gave notice to the other Indians. Two of our forefathers went to see what it was, and found it a vessel with men in it. They immediately joined hands with the people in the vessel and became friends. The white people told them they should not come any further up the river at that time, and said to them they would return back whence they came and come again in a year's time. According to their promise they returned back in a year's time, and came as far up the river as where the old fort stood. Our forefathers invited them on shore and said to them, here we will give you a place to make you a town; it shall be from this place to such a stream, and from the river back up to the hill. Our forefathers told them, though they were now a small people they would in time multiply and fill up the land they had given to them. After they went ashore some time, some other Indians who had not seen them before, looked fiercely at them, and our forefathers observing it, and seeing the white people so few in number, lest they should be destroyed, took and sheltered them under their arms. But it turned out that those Indians did not desire to destroy them, but wished also to have the white people for their friends. At this time, which we have now spoken of, the white people were small, but we were very numerous and strong. We defended them in that low state, but now the case is altered. You are numerous and strong; we are few and weak; therefore we expect you to act by us in these circumstances as we did by you in those we have just now related. We view you now as a very large tree which has taken deep root in the ground; whose branches are spread very wide. We stand by the body of this tree and we look around to see if there be any who endeavor to hurt it, and if it should so happen that any are powerful enough to destroy it, we are ready to fall with it.

"Fathers: You see how early we made friendship with you. We tied each other in a very strong chain. That chain has not yet been broken. We now clean and rub that chain to make it brighter and stronger, and we determine on our part that it shall never be broken, and we hope you will take care that neither you nor any one else shall break it. And we are greatly rejoiced that peace and friendship have so long subsisted between us.

"Fathers: Don't think strange at what we are about to say. We would say something respecting our lands. When the white people purchased from time to time of us, they said they only wanted to purchase the low lands; they told us the hilly land was good for nothing, and that it was full of wood and stones; but now we see people living all about the hills and woods, although they have not purchased the lands. When we inquire of the people who live on these lands what right they have to them, they reply to us, that we are not to be regarded, and that these lands belong to the king; but we were the first possessors of them, and when the king has paid us for them, then they may say they are his. Hunting now has grown very scarce, and we are not like to get our living that way. Therefore we hope our fathers will take care that we are paid for our lands that we may live."[1]

In the war which followed, HENDRIK served the English faithfully, and returned to his people with honor. In 1774, he represented his tribe at the Albany conference held by the commissioners of the Continental Congress, and there delivered one of the most eloquent speeches in the English language. "Depend upon," said he, "we are true to you, and mean to join you. Wherever you go, we will be by your sides. Our bones shall

[1] *Colonial History*, vi, 881.

lie with yours. We are determined never to be at peace with the red coats, while they are at variance with you. We have one favor to beg: we should be glad if you would help us to establish a minister among us, that when our men are gone to war, our women and children may have the advantage of being instructed by them. If we are conquered, our lands go with yours; but if you are victorious, we hope you will help us to recover our just rights." And in this spirit himself and his people fought to make a free nation for white men.

Welcoming the missionaries among his people, HENDRIK impressed upon them a recognition of his worth even while refusing to unite with them, and in all his intercourse with them and with the authorities, won, by his demeanor and his integrity, the tribute due to royalty. Says his biographer: "He was often employed as an interpreter, and in this capacity his strong memory, his clear, lucid manner, and his mind-illumed face, as he conveyed the thoughts of a preacher to his people, are highly praised. His public speeches are spoken of as always remarkable for perspicuity and sound sense. 'I have,' says our informant, 'seen many Indian chiefs, but never his equal;'" testimony which is the more valuable, coming as it does from one who had no personal ends to serve by magnifying the consequence of the people among whom he labored, and who at one time had "the Great Hendrik" of the *Mohawks* among his pupils.

After the war of the revolution HENDRIK was frequently employed by the government on missions to the western Indians, and was an important agent in the negotiations with them. In 1810, says his biographer, Captain HENDRIK [1] was on the

---

[1] Captain Hendrik was employed in this capacity at the suggestion of the Rev. Mr. Kirkland, who wrote to General Knox, then secretary of war (April 22, 1791), as follows: "As I deprecate an Indian war from every principle of humanity and policy, permit me, sir, to suggest the idea of sending Captain Hendrik, one of the chiefs of the Stockbridge tribe to the westward. This tribe had formerly more influence with the Miamies, Shawanoes, Delawares and Chippewas, than all the Six Nations. Captain Hendrik is well acquainted with their customs and manners, and has since the war received several invitations to make them a visit. As you are in a measure a stranger to Captain Hendrik, allow me to say, from long personal acquaintance with him, that he is very little inferior to Cornplanter, who himself has a high esteem for the Stockbridge chief."— *Sparks' Life of Kirkland.*

White river, with his son Abner, and designed to have settled on the land given the *Mahicans* by the *Miamis*. Here he formed the plan of collecting all the eastern Indians in that region at a place where they might live in peace with the whites, and in fellowship with each other. Before *Tecumseh* began his labors, HENDRIK had sent a speech to his people on the subject, and was anxiously waiting for a reply, when his work was overtaken by the former and diverted into a gospel of hate. Then it was that the government paid to HENDRIK the highest compliment that could be given, by appointing him as the man most fit of all others to meet the eloquent chief of the *Shawanoes* on his own ground. For three years he followed the footsteps of *Tecumseh* and his brother, and so well and thoroughly did he combat their eloquence and their sophistry, that, had not the war of 1812 intervened, and the seductive influences of the British been given to the aid of the *Shawanoes*, they would have been powerless for evil. Of his labors in this field the Rev. John Sergeant writes : " It appears that through the judicious arrangements of Captain HENDRIK, the influence of the prophet is nearly at an end." His biographer adds : " Captain HENDRIK himself says that the head men of the various tribes do not join the prophet, but only the ignorant and unwary; that the message of the *Delawares* had already shut his mouth, and he believed that in the course of the next summer he would ' be brought down from the Wabash, to the ground from which his ancestors were created,' and so it proved. We find nothing, in the public histories of those times respecting Captain HENDRIK, but we do find that the battle of Tippecanoe was hazarded because the already waning power of *Tecumseh* required some desperate act; and the eloquence of Captain HENDRIK, his influence as a Muh-he-ka-neew chief with the western Indians, and the information communicated by Mr. Sergeant, take us ' behind the scenes,' and show us at least one great cause of that waning. All due honor to the ' hero of Tippecanoe ; ' but let not the faithful *Mahican*, who, by sapping and mining, prepared the way for that victory, be forgotten." [1]

*Stockbridge, Past and Present; Stone's Life of Brant*, II, 307.

## APPENDIX.          325

In the war of 1812, Captain HENDRIK joined the American army, was favorably noticed, and promoted to office. In all his public duties he never for a moment forgot his people, and one of his last acts was to write a history of his nation. In 1829, he removed to Green Bay, Wisconsin, where he was gathered to his fathers, the "noblest Roman of them all." What his namesake was to the English government, Captain HENDRIK was to the United States; what his namesake was not to his people, Captain HENDRIK was: an example of unselfish devotion and purity of character.

OCCUM, a *Mahican*, was the first educated and ordained Indian minister. He attended Dr. Wheelock's school at Lebanon, about the middle of the eighteenth century, embraced Christianity and was baptized by the mame of SAMSON. He began his labors as a teacher and evangelist among the *Montauks* on Long island, where he kept a school for some years. He was afterwards ordained by the Presbytery to preach the gospel, and became an efficient means of introducing Christianity to the Indian bands located at separate places in New England and New York. In 1755-56, he visited England, in company with the Rev. Mr. Whitaker, in order, by personal appeals, to solicit funds for the support of Dr. Wheelock's school. Not only was his mission successful, but, as he was the first Indian minister who had visited that country, he attracted special attention, and wherever he went crowds gathered to hear him. About 1786, he went to the country of the *Oneidas*, taking with him several Indians of kindred blood, who clung to him as their leader. He was subsequently joined by a number of *Mohegans* from the sea-coast of New England, and a few *Nanticokes*, *Narragansetts* and *Pequots*. Differences existing in their dialects, they agreed to drop them altogether, and adopt the English, taking the name of Brothertons. He continued to devote himself to the interests of his people till age incapacitated him, and younger laborers stepped in. During his old age, he went to live with his kindred at New Stockbridge, where he died in 1792. Schoolcraft adds: "It is expressly stated by the New England clergy, to whom we are indebted for these notices, that his Christian and ministerial character were well approved, and that he was deemed to possess a peculiar fluency and aptness in teaching the Indians, over whom he exercised a happy influence. It is inferable, but not distinctly said, that the first or early period of his ministry formed the one of his most active usefulness; but his whole life, after his conversion, is to be regarded as a triumphant evidence of the power and endurance of the gospel truth in the Indian heart. Nor am I aware that we have a superior, if an equal, instance of an individual of the pure Indian blood having been ordained to the ministry who has left behind him so excellent a testimony of consistent usefulness. The foundation of the tribe of the Brothertons is a work due to his enterprise, foresight and exertions. The practical working of the plan which he introduced was excellent. The Brothertons continued to dwell together at their first location in Oneida county till they had well advanced in elementary education and the arts. At this period of their history, they sent delegates to Wisconsin to procure a cession of territory from the indigenous Indians of Fox river of that state, on the borders of Winnebago lake. Having disposed of their possessions in Oneida county, they in due time migrated to that location, where they now reside. By an act of congress, the Brothertons of Wisconsin were admitted to all the rights of citizens of the United States. They were also admitted, by a state act, to the rights of citizens of Wisconsin. The problem of their triple emancipation from barbarism, idleness, and political defranchisement, is thus completely worked out; and worked out in a practical way, in which the experience and wisdom of Occum and his clerical teachers of the olden time predicted, it could only be done." During his later years Occum's reputation passed under a cloud, and before his death he relapsed into some of the worst habits of his tribe; but this fact cannot detract from his personal worth or the excellence of his earlier life. Men can be found in all nations, whose record is marred by the weaknesses of age. "It is not conceived necessary to digress or deny the fact that Noah got drunk."[1]

[1] *History of Indian Nations*, part v, 518, etc.

## APPENDIX.

The Moravian missionaries have preserved in their records the names and services of many of the Indian chiefs with whom they were associated, but none whose character is brighter than that of the *Mahican* chieftain, WASAMAPAH, or *Tschoop*, who, after his conversion was called *John*. He was the ruling chief at Shekomeko, in the present county of Dutchess. When first met by the missionary Rauch, he is described as the "greatest drunkard" among his people, and as being crippled by his vices. He became not only a convert, but an interpreter and a preacher of the word of life. Most eloquent is his own account of his conversion: "Brethren, I have been a heathen, and have grown old among the heathen, therefore I know how the heathen think. Once a preacher came and began to explain to us that there was a God. We answered: 'Dost thou think we are so ignorant as not to know that? Go back to the place from whence thou camest?' Then, again, another preacher came and began to teach us and to say, 'You must not steal, nor lie, nor get drunk,' etc. We answered: 'Thou fool, dost thou think we don't know that? Learn first thyself, and then teach the people, to whom thou belongest, to leave off these things; for who steal and lie, or who are more drunken than thine own people?' and thus we dismissed him. After some time, Brother Christian Henry Rauch came into my hut and sat down by me. He spoke to me nearly as follows: 'I come to you in the name of the Lord of heaven and earth. He sends me to let you know that he is willing to make you happy, and to deliver you from the misery in which you are at present. To this end he became a man, gave his life as a ransom for man, and shed his blood for him.' When he had finished, he lay down upon a board, being fatigued with his journey, and fell into a sound sleep. I then thought, 'What kind of a man is this? There he lies and sleeps; I might kill him and throw him into the woods, and who would regard it? But this gives him no concern! However, I could not forget his words. They constantly recurred to my mind. Even when I slept I dreamed of that blood which Christ shed for us. This was something different from what I had ever before heard, and I interpreted Christian Henry's words to the other Indians."

WASAMAPACH removed from Shekomeko to the Delaware, in August, 1745. Here he acted as interpreter in the service held for the Indians on Sunday afternoon ; he also gave instruction in Mahican to a number of brethren and sisters who were designed for missionaries. On the organization of the refugees from Shekomeko into a Christian congregation, at Friedenshütten, on the 24th of July, 1746, he was appointed their teacher. Soon after the small pox broke out, and he became one of its victims, after an illness of seven days, during which he gave evidence of the thoroughness of his conversion. His death took place on the 27th of August, and his funeral on the 28th. Loskiel writes : "John was one of the first fruits. As a heathen he distinguished himself by his heathen and sinful practices, and as his vices became more seductive, on account of his natural wit and humor, so as a Christian he became a most powerful and persuasive witness of our Saviour among his nation. His gifts were sanctified by the grace of God, and employed in such a manner as to be the means of blessing both to Europeans and Indians. Few of his countrymen could vie with him in point of Indian oratory. His discourses were full of animation, and his words penetrated like fire into the hearts of his countrymen ; his soul found a rich pasture in the gospel, and whether at home, or on a journey, he could not forbear speaking of the salvation purchased for us by the sufferings of Jesus, never hesitating a moment, whether his hearers were Christians or Indians. In short, he appeared chosen by God to be a witness to his people, and was four years active in this service. Nor was he less respected as a chief among the Indians, no affairs of state being transacted without his advice and consent." And Bishop Spangenberg adds : "In his mien was the majesty of a Luther, a man whose mind grappled as by intuition the glorious mysteries of the gospel of Christ, and whose strength of will, inspired and sanctified by Christianity, at once triumphed over the vilest passions and most hideous vices by which the human heart can be deformed."

SHABASCH, the associate of *Wasamapah*, is also favorably spoken of by Loskiel. He became a convert and was baptized under the name of Abraham. He was appointed elder of the

## APPENDIX. 329

congregation at Shekomeko, and discharged its duties with credit. He subsequently accepted the chieftaincy of the *Mahicans* of the Delaware country and represented them in the conferences with Johnson, and also with the governor of Pennsylvania. He died in 1762, " much respected on account of his wisdom and grave deportment."

The *Wappingers* were not without their hero in the person of DANIEL NIMHAM, who, in 1765, is described as "a native Indian and acknowledged sachem or king of a certain tribe of Indians known and called by the name of *Wappingers*." He appears to have taken up his residence at Westenhuck in 1746, and to have subsequently taken part in the war of that period and also of that of 1754. The proceedings to which he was a party for the recovery of the lands of his people, would occupy a volume. The facts stated in the case, as reported by the lords of trade, on the hearing of NIMHAM, who visited England, for that purpose, are " that the tract of land, the property and possession whereof is claimed by these Indians, and their title disputed, is situated between Hudson's river and the line which divides the province of New York from that of Connecticut, extending in length from east to west about twenty miles, and in breadth from north to south about sixteen miles, and containing about two hundred and four thousand and eight hundred acres of land; that they continued in the uninterrupted possession of these lands, and in the actual improvement and settlement of the same, by themselves and their tenants, until the commencement of the late war (1755), when the head sachem, accompanied by all the males of that tribe able to bear arms, went into your majesty's service under Sir William Johnson, and the residue removed to Stockbridge, for their greater convenience and accommodation; that whilst the said sachem and his people were fighting under your majesty's banner, all this tract of land was taken up by persons claiming under a grant thereof made by the governor of New York to one Adolph Phillipse in 1697, and afterwards purchased by him of the ancestors of the said Indians, which purchase they allege, was not a purchase of the whole tract comprehended in the grant of 1697, but only of a small part of it;[1] that finding themselves by these claims likely to be dispossessed of their patrimonial lands, they chose a guardian of their rights, and proceeded to try their claim in various suits and actions in the courts of law of New York; that judgment having been given against them on those several suits and actions (in the trial of which they state great prejudice and partiality), they applied by petition in February, 1765, to the lieutenant-governor and council, and had a hearing upon their case; that in the proceedings before the lieutenant governor and council they were treated with great supercilious neglect, the claims of their adversaries countenanced and supported with apparent partiality, and a decision given against them upon the evidence of a deed of purchase of these lands from their ancestors, which deed they suggest to have been fraudulent and counterfeit." It subsequently appeared that Phillipse obtained his patent five years before he made his purchase, in violation of the laws of the province, and there is very little reason to doubt that he then obtained it from self-constituted proprietors to cover a most nefarious transaction. That NIMHAM and the *Wappingers* were unlawfully deprived of the lands embraced in the present county of Putnam, may be regarded as certain.[2]

NIMHAM'S tragic death, in Westchester county, has already been referred to. The following account of the engagement in which he sealed his devotion to the cause of the colonists with his life, is from the pen of those against whom he fought,[3] American historians refusing, apparently, to do justice to the memory of one who was wronged in his life and in his death:

"Lieut. Col. Simcoe, returning from head-quarters, the 30th of August, heard a firing in front, and being informed that Lieut. Col. Emerick had patrolled, he immediately marched to his assistance. He soon met him retreating; and Lieut. Col.

---

[1] The reference is to the Canopus' lands included in the manor of Cortlandt.
[2] Phillipse did not live to enjoy his ill-gotten lands. On his death they became the property of his father, and afterwards of his heirs. John Jacob Astor subsequently purchased the reversionary interest of the heirs, for $100,000, and ten years afterwards received from the state of New York $500,000 in six per cent stocks for the title which he had acquired.
[3] *Simcoe's Military Journal.*

Emerick being of opinion the rebels were in such force that it would be advisable for him to return, he did so. Lieut. Col. Simcoe understood that NIMHAM, an Indian chief, and some of his tribe, were with the enemy; and by his spies, who were excellent, he was informed that they were highly elated at the retreat of Emerick's corps, and applied it to the whole of the light troops at Kingsbridge. Lieut. Col. Simcoe took measures to increase their belief; and, ordering a day's provisions to be cooked, marched the next morning, the 31st of August, a small distance in front of the fort, and determined to wait there the whole day, in hopes of betraying the enemy into an ambuscade. His idea was, as the enemy moved upon the road, to advance from his flanks ; and he meant to gain the heights in the rear of the enemy, attacking whomsoever should be within reach by his cavalry and such infantry as might be necessary. In pursuance of these intentions, Lieut. Col. Emerick with his corps was detached from the Queen's Rangers and Legion, as Lieut. Col. Simcoe thought fully instructed in the plan; however, he most unfortunately mistook the nearer house for the one at a greater distance, the names being the same, and there he posted himself, and soon after sent from thence a patrol forward upon the road, before Lieut. Col. Simcoe could have time to stop it. This patrol had no effect, not meeting the enemy; had a single man of it deserted, or been taken, the whole attempt had, probably, been abortive. Lieut. Col. Simcoe, who was half way up a tree, on the top of which was a drummer boy, saw a flanking party of the enemy approach. The troops had scarcely fallen into their ranks when a smart firing was heard from the Indians, who had lined the fences of the road, and who were exchanging shots with Lieut. Col. Emerick, whom they had discovered. The Queen's Rangers moved rapidly to gain the heights, and Lieut. Col. Tarleton immediately advanced with the Hussars and the Legion of cavalry ; not being able to pass the fences in his front, he made a circuit to return further upon their right ; which, being reported to Lieut. Col. Simcoe, he broke from the column of rangers, with the grenadier company, and, directing Major Ross to conduct the corps to the heights, advanced to the road, and arrived without being perceived, within ten yards of the Indians. They had been intent on the attack on Emerick's corps and the Legion; they now gave a yell and fired upon the grenadier company, wounding four of them, and Lieut. Col. Simcoe. They were driven from the fences; and Lieut. Col. Tarleton, with the cavalry, got among them, and pursued them rapidly down Cortlandt's ridge. That active officer had a narrow escape; in striking at one of the fugitives, he lost his balance and fell from his horse; luckily the Indian had no bayonet, and his musket had been discharged. Lieut. Col. Simcoe joined the battalion and seized the heights. A captain of the rebel light infantry and a few of his men were taken; but a body of them, under Major Stewart, who afterwards was distinguished at Stony Point, left the Indians and fled. Though the ambuscade, its greater part, failed, it was of consequence. Near forty of the Indians were killed or desperately wounded; among others NIMHAM, a chieftain who had been to England, and his son; and it was reported to have stopped a large number of them, who were excellent marksmen, from joining General Washington's army. The Indian doctor was taken; and he said that when NIMHAM saw the grenadiers close in his rear, he called out to his people to fly, 'that he himself was old and would die there.' He wounded Lieut. Col. Simcoe, and was on the point of dragging him from his horse, when he was killed by Wright, his orderly Hussar. The Indians fought most gallantly; they pulled more than one of the cavalry from their horses. French, an active youth, bugle-horn to the Hussars, struck at an Indian, but missed him; the man dragged him from his horse, and was searching for his knife to stab him, when, loosening French's hand, he luckily drew out a pocket pistol, and shot the Indian through the head, in which situation he was found. One man of the Legion Cavalry was killed, and one of them and two of the Hussars, wounded."

The battlements of the Hudson,—

"The mountain columns
With which earth props heaven,"—

the early home of the patriot chief, are the monuments to his memory; the eternal flow of the Mahicanituk his requiem.

## II. LANGUAGE.

THE early Dutch writers resolved the various dialects which they met among the Indians into "four distinct languages, namely: *Manhattan, Minqua, Savanos,* and *Wappanoos.*" With the *Manhattan* they included the dialect spoken in the neighborhood of Fort Amsterdam, "along the North river, on Long island, and at the Neversink; with the *Minqua,* the *Senecas* and other inland tribes." The *Savanos* was the dialect of the south, and the *Wappanoos* that of the east. The progress of the inquiry resulting in this classification was slow. Wassanaar writes, in 1621: "'Tis worthy of remark, that so great a diversity of language exists among the numerous tribes. They vary frequently not over five or six miles; forthwith comes another language; they meet and can hardly understand one another. There are some who come sixty miles from the interior, and cannot well understand those on the river." Michaëlius, writing in 1628, says: "Their language methinks is entirely peculiar. Many of our common people call it an easy language, which is soon learned, but I am of a contrary opinion. For those who can understand their words to some extent and repeat them, fail greatly in the pronunciation and speak a broken language, like the language of Ashdod. For these people have different aspirates and many guttural letters which are formed more in the throat than by the mouth, teeth, and lips, which our people not being accustomed to, guess at by means of their signs, and then imagine that they have accomplished something wonderful. It is true, one can learn as much as is sufficient for the purposes of trading, but this occurs almost as much by signs with the thumb and fingers as by speaking. It also seems to us that they rather design to conceal their language from us than to properly communicate it, except in things which happen in daily trade; saying that it is sufficient for us to understand them in those: and then they speak only half their reasons with shortened words; and frequently call a dozen things and even more by one name ; and all things which have only a rude resemblance to each other they frequently call by the same name. In truth it is a made up childish language : so that even those who can best of all speak with the Indians and get along well in trade, are nevertheless wholly in the dark and bewildered when they hear the Indians speaking with each other by themselves." Another writer says: "The language of this people is very various; they are very difficult for strangers to learn as they are spoken without any principles." And Van der Donck, writing in 1656, concludes : "Their languages and dialects are very different, as unlike each other as the Dutch, French, Greek and Latin are. Their declensions and conjugations have an affinity with the Greek and accord to it. Their declensions, augmentations, cases and adverbs, are like the Greek ; but to reduce their language to any of ours, would be impossible, for there is no resemblance between the same. Before we have acquired a knowledge of any of their languages or dialects, we know no more of what they say than if a dog had barked."

While these sturdy Dutch linguists were plodding over the subject, the Rev. John Eliot, of Massachusetts, had grasped the hidden key of the language and proclaimed that it had principles and form ; that even that which Michaëlius denominated "shortened words" was made in accordance with rules, and that in the observation of that writer of the fact that they frequently called " a dozen things and even more by one name," he had simply failed to note the inflections which constituted an important principle of the language. But notwithstanding the publication of Eliot's grammar in 1666, and the observations of the Jesuit and Moravian priests, it was not until 1819 that Du Ponceau, after a thorough comparison of the writings of his predecessors, was enabled to announce the proposition : " That the American languages in general use are rich in words and in grammatical forms, and that, in their complicated construction, the greatest order, method, and regularity prevail."

It remained, however, for subsequent writers, and especially for Gallatin [1] and Schoolcraft, to elucidate fully the grammatical

---

[1] *A Synopis of the Indian Tribes within the United States east of the Rocky Mountains, etc., by Hon. Albert Gallatin,* 1836.

structure of the languages and define the characteristic features of the several dialects.

According to these writers there were but two generic Indian languages, the *Algonquin* and the *Iroquois;* but these two were divided into tribal dialects and groups with distinctive characteristics. While each *Iroquois* tribe had its dialect, the generic language, as spoken by the Five Nations of New York, differed in many respects from that spoken by the southern and western *Iroquois* families. The *Algonquin* was represented by equally distinct tribal and general types. Edwards says that the *Mahican* was spoken " by all the Indians throughout New England ; " that though each tribe had "a different dialect," the language was "radically the same." Yet the *Algonquin* of the *Mahicans* was essentially different from the *Algonquin* of the *Lenapes.* Loskiel explains this more fully : " Though the three tribes of the *Delawares* have the same language, yet they speak different dialects. The *Unamis* and *Wunalachtikos,* who formerly inhabited the eastern coast of Pennsylvania and New Jersey, nearly agree in pronunciation ; but the dialect of the *Monsys,* who formerly lived in Menissing, beyond the Blue mountains, differs so much from the former, that they would hardly be able to understand each other, did they not keep up a continual intercourse. The language of the *Delawares* has an agreeable sound, both in common conversation, and public delivery. The dialect spoken by the *Unamis* and *Wunalachtikos* is peculiarly grateful to the ear, and much more easily learnt, by an European, than that of the *Monsys,* which is rougher and spoken with a broad accent. However, the *Monsy* dialect is a key to many expressions in the *Unamis* and *Wunalachtikos.* The latter have a way of dropping some syllables, so that, without a knowledge of the former, it would be impossible either to spell their words or guess their meaning.

" Several other languages derive their origin from the *Delaware,* and this proceeds chiefly from the vicinity or connections of the different nations and tribes. For instance, the language of the *Mahikans* is nearly related to the *Monsy* dialect, these two nations having formerly been neighbors in the province of New York. The *Shawanose* is also related to the *Monsy,* but more to the *Mahikan;* only the former generally place the accent upon the last syllable. The *Ottawa* is nearly related to the *Shawanose,* but the *Chippewa* more immediately to the *Delaware.* The language of the *Twichtwees* and *Wawiachtanos* resembles the *Shawanose;* in dialect the *Kikapus, Tukachohas, Moshkos,* and *Karhaski,* differ from the *Delaware* in proportion to their distance from each other, but all are nearly related."

The *Algonquin* dialects spoken in the valley of the Hudson, at the time of the discovery, were at least six in number : The *Manhattan,* the *Wappanoo,* the *Mahican,* the *Minsi,* the *Unami* and the *Unalachtin.* It is stated that the *Mahicans* conquered the territory which they occupied, mixed with their own the dialect of the people whom they had subdued and formed that subsequently spoken by themselves. It is also said that the *Wappanoos* overran the old *Manhattans* and created another mixed dialect, while the third type was found among the natives of Long Island, in which perhaps many of the essential features of the *Manhattan* were preserved. Of the three types on the west, the *Unami* and the *Unalachtin* are classed as *Delaware* as distinguished from the *Minsi.* The *Mahican* has been preserved, partially at least, as has also to some extent the Long Island,—the latter extending along the east side of the river as far as the Highlands, where it met the *Wappanoos,* which has been preserved as spoken by its more eastern families in the *Massachusetts;* but the dialects on the west, as they were modified by association with those on the east, and the dialects of the east as modified by association with those on the west, are lost except as they live in geographical names, which resist established rules of interpretation, or are approximately preserved as they were spoken elsewhere, modified by different associations. How widely they differed, can be inferred from Loskiel's statement that the *Minsi* of the Hudson resembled the *Mahican* and the *Shawanoe* and was scarce understood by its more western families — how widely they differ in the imperfect forms in which they have been preserved, a few words from each will sufficiently illustrate. Man, in Long Island, is *run; wonnun* (white man) in Wappinoo or Massachusetts, *wosketomp;* in Mahican *neemanoo;* in Delaware and Minsi, *lenno.* Mother, in Long Island, is *cwca;* in Massachusetts, *okaooh;*

in Mahican, *okegan*; in Minsi, *guy*; in Delaware, *gahowes*. Stone, in Long Island, is *sun*; in Massachusetts, *hussun*; in Mahican, *thaunaumka*; in Minsi, *achsun*; in Delaware, *akhsin* (stone), *pemapukhk* (rock). Earth, in Long Island, is *keagh*; in Massachusetts, *ahke*; in Mahican, *akek*; in Minsi, *achgi*; in Delaware, *aki, akhki*.

But while the peculiar dialects of the valley have been lost, or have at best an imperfect preservation, the principles upon which they were based have been written. Gallatin says: " The fundamental characteristics of the Indian languages of America appear to be a universal tendency to express in the same word, not only all that modifies or relates to the same object, or action, but both the action and the object ; thus concentrating in a single expression a complex idea, or several ideas among which there is a natural connection. All the other features of the language seem to be subordinate to that general principle. The object in view has been attained by various means of the same tendency and often blended together: a multitude of inflections properly so called ; a still greater number of compound words, sometimes formed by the coalescence of primitive words not materially altered, more generally by the union of many such words in a remarkably abbreviated form, and numerous particles, either significative, or the original meaning of which has been lost, prefixed, added as terminations, or inserted in the body of the word." An extreme illustration of this principle is furnished by Mather, in the compound phrase " Kummogkodonattoottummooetiteaongannunnonash," which is presumed to imply, " our question." Edwards illustrates it in a simpler form in the *Mahican*. "If a man hold out *his* hand to an Indian to know the name, he may receive the answer " knish " — *thy* hand ; but if he touches the hand of the *Indian*, he is told " nnisk " — *my* hand ; and in either case he will infer that he has received the Indian word for hand, simply, when there is no such word in the language." Schoolcraft, in his treatise,[1] explains this principle more fully and defines the idioms and structure of the language. From this treatise the annexed synopsis is made, presuming that those having occasion to do so,

---

[1] " *An Essay on the Grammatical Structure of the Algonquin Language.*" —*History of Indian Tribes*, part II, 353, etc.

or whose curiosity prompts them to the study, will consult the original.

### Grammar of the Algonquin Language.

1. *Alphabet.* The *Algonquin* possesses all the vowel sounds as heard in far, fate, fall ; met, meet ; shine, pin ; not, note, move ; put, nut. It has two labials, *b* and *p*; five dentals, *d, t, s, z,* and *j* or *g,* soft ; two nasals, *m* and *n;* and two primary gutturals, *k* and *g,* hard. The letters *f, r, v,* are wanting. The sound of *x* is also believed to be wanting in all the *Algonquin* dialects but the *Delaware* and *Mahican* of the Hudson valley, in which it is fully heard in Coxsackie, and in a few of the earlier geographical terms of New Jersey, the sound of *r* is represented in *ah*. Thus an alphabet of five vowels and thirteen consonants is capable of expressing, either simply or in combination, every full sound of the *Algonquin* language. In this estimate of primary sounds, the letters *c,* and *q,* and *y* as representing a vowel sound, are entirely rejected. The soft of *c* is *s,* the hard, *k.* The sound of *g* is always that of *k.* In the formation of words the vowelic, diphthongal and mixed sounds are syllabic. The following table represents the elementary syllables on the primary vowel sounds :

| (1) | | (2) | | (3) | | (4) | |
|---|---|---|---|---|---|---|---|
| AI as A in Fate. | | A as in Father. | | A as in Fall. | | A as in Hat | |
| | | | | | | only uttered with a consonant following. | |
| Aib | Bai | Ahb | Bah | Aub | Bau | | |
| Aid | Dai | Ahd | Dah | Aud | Dau | Ab | |
| Aig | Gai | Ahg | Gah | Aug | Gau | Ad | |
| Aih | Hai | Ah | Hah | Auh | Hau | Ag | |
| Aik | Kai | Ahj | Jah | Auj | Jau | Ah | |
| Ail | Lai | Ahk | Kah | Auk | Kau | Aj | |
| Aij | Jai | Ahl | Lah | Aul | Lau | Ak | |
| Aim | Mai | Ahm | Mah | Aum | Mau | Al | |
| Ain | Nai | Ahn | Nah | Aun | Nau | Am | |
| Aip | Pai | Ahp | Pah | Aup | Pau | An | |
| Ais | Sai | Ahs | Sah | Aus | Sau | Ap | |
| Ait | Tai | Aht | Tah | Aut | Tau | As | |
| Aiw | Wai | Ahw | Wah | Auw | Wau | At | |
| Aiz | Yai | Ahz | Zah | Auz | Yau | Au | |
| Aizh | Zhai | | | Auzh | Zhau | Az | |

## APPENDIX.

| (1) | (2) | (1) | (2) |
|---|---|---|---|
| EE as in me | E as in met | I as in Fine. | I as in Pin. |
| Eeb Bee | Eb | Bi | Ib |
| Eed Dee | Ed | Di | Id |
| Eeg Gee | Eg | Gi | Ig |
| Eeh He | Eh | Hi | Ih |
| Eej Jee | Ej | Ji | Ij |
| Eel Lee | Ek | Ki | Ik |
| Eek Kee | El | Li | Il |
| Eem Mee | Em | Mi | Im |
| Een Nee | En | Ni | In |
| Eep Pee | Ep | Pi | Ip |
| Ees See | Es | Si | Is |
| Eet Tee | Et | Ti | It |
| Eew Wee | Eu | Wi | Iw |
| Eez Zee | Ez | Yi | Iz |
|  |  | Zi |  |

| (1) | (2) | (4) |  |
|---|---|---|---|
| O as in Note | O as in Move. | O as in Not. | U as in But. |
| Bo | Oob  Boo | Ob | Ub |
| Do | Ood  Doo | Od | Ud |
| Go | Oog  Goo | Og | Ug |
| Ho | Ooh  Hoo | Oh | Uh |
| Jo | Ooj  Joo | Oj | Uj |
| Ko | Ook  Koo | Ok | Uk |
| Lo | Ool  Loo | Ol | Ul |
| Mo | Oom  Moo | Om | Um |
| No | Oon  Noo | On | Un |
| Po | Oop  Poo | Op | Up |
| So | Oos  Soo | Os | Us |
| To | Oot  Too | Ot | Ut |
| Wo | Oow  Woo | Ow | Uz |
| Yo | Ooy  Yoo | Oy |  |
| Zo | Ooz  Zoo | Oz |  |

Diphthongal sounds are heard in limited classes of words, ending in *ia*, *io*, and *ou*. The nasal sounds, which abound in the language, are chiefly confined to the letter *n*, and the combination *ng*. The gutturals are mostly formed by the letters *gh* and *kh*. The hard sound of *g* has its expression in the half utterance of *k* by which it is followed, as in the attempt to pronounce *gk*. The combinations of *ch*, *sh*, and *zh*, are common, as are also those of *bw*, *dw*, *gw*, and *hw*. *Ai* expresses the sound of *a* as in fate; *ah* the sound of *a* as in father; *au*, as in fall, auction, and *au* in law; *ee* is the sound of *e* as in feel; *ia*, as the sound of *i* in media; *oi*, the sound of *o* in voice; *aiw*, *ouw* and *eow* appear in converting verbs indicative into different moods; *ih*, the sound of *i* suddenly stopped off; *ooh*, the sound of *o* suddenly stopped off; *uh*, the sound of *u*, roughly aspirated, and also *ugh*; *ch*, as in English, also, *sh* and *zh*; *bw* as in bwoin; *gw* as in gwiuk; *hw* as in mohwa; *kw* as in wewukwun; *mw* as in wa-mwa; *ny* as in nyau; *tshw* as in tshwe—tshwees-ke-wa, a snipe.

2. *Substantives.* In a general survey of the language there is perhaps no feature which obtrudes itself so constantly to view, as the principle which separates all words, of whatever denomination, into animates and inanimates, as they are applied to objects in the animal, vegetable, or mineral kingdom. This principle has been grafted upon most words, and carries its distinctions throughout the syntax. It is the gender of the language; but a gender of so unbounded a scope, as to merge it in the distinctions of a masculine and feminine, and to give a two-fold character to the parts of speech.

Nouns animate embrace the tribes of quadrupeds, birds, fishes, insects, reptiles, crustacea, the sun, moon, and stars, thunder, and lightning; for these are personified, and whatever possesses animal life, or is endowed, by the peculiar opinions and superstitions of the Indians, with it. In the vegetable kingdom their number is comparatively limited, being chiefly confined to trees, and those only while they are referred to as whole bodies, and to the various species of fruits, seeds, and esculents. It is to be remarked, however, that the names for animals are only employed as animates, while the objects are referred to as whole and complete species; but the gender must be changed when it becomes necessary to speak of separate members. Man, woman, father, mother, are separate nouns, so long as the individuals are meant; but hand, foot, head, eye, ear, tongue, are inanimates. Buck is an animate noun, while his entire carcase is referred to, whether living or dead; but neck, back, heart, windpipe, take the inanimate form. In like manner eagle, swan, dove, are distinguished as animates; but beak, wing, tail, are arranged with inanimates. So oak, pine, ash, are animates; branch, leaf, root, inanimates.

No language is perhaps so defective as to be totally without number. But there are few which furnish so many modes of indicating it as the *Algonquin*. There are as many modes of forming the plural as there are vowel sounds, yet there is no distinction between a limited and an unlimited substantive plural; although there is, in the pronoun, an *inclusive* and an *exclusive* plural. Whether we say man or men, two men or twenty men, the singular *inin-e*, and the plural *ininewug*, remain the same. But if we say we, us or our men (who are present), or we, us, or our Indians (in general), the plural we, and us, and our — for they are rendered by the same form — admit of a change to indicate whether the objective person or persons be *included* or *excluded*. This principle forms a single and anomalous instance of the use of particular plurals; and it carries its distinctions, by means of the pronouns, separable and inseparable, into the verbs and substantives, creating the necessity of double conjugations and double declensions, in the plural forms of the first person. Thus the term for Our Father, which, in the inclusive form, is *Kosinaun*, is, in the exclusive, *Nosinaun*.

The general plural is variously made. But the plurals making inflections take upon themselves an additional power or sign, by which substantives are distinguished into animates and inanimates. Without this additional power, all nouns plural would end in the vowels *a*, *e*, *i*, *o*, *u*; but to mark the gender, the letter *g* is added to animates, and the letter *n* to inanimates, making the plurals of the first class terminate in *ag*, *eeg*, *ig*, *og*, *ug*, and of the second class in *an*, *een*, *in*, *on*, *un*. Ten modes of forming the plural are thus provided, five of which are animate, and five inanimate plurals. A strong and clear distinction is thus drawn between the two classes of words, so unerring indeed, in its application, that it is only necessary to inquire how the plural is formed to determine whether it belong to one or the other class.

Where a noun terminates with the vowel in the singular, the addition of the *g*, or *n*, shows at once both the plural and the gender. In other instances, as in *peena*, a partridge ; *seebe*, a river ; it requires a consonant to precede the plural vowel, in conformity with a rule previously stated. Thus *peenai-wug;* and *seebe-wun.* Where the noun singular terminates in the broad instead of the long sound of *a*, as in *ogimau*, a chief ; *ishpatinau*, a hill, the plural is *ogim-aug*, *ishpatinaun.* But these are mere modifications of two of the above forms, and are by no means entitled to be considered as additional plurals.

Comparatively few substantives are without number. There is, however, one exception from the general use of number. This exception consists of the want of number in the *third person* of the declensions of animate nouns, and the conjugation of animate verbs. Not that such words are destitute of number, in their simple forms, or when used under circumstances requiring no change of these simple forms — no prefixes and no inflections. But it will be seen, at a glance, how very limited such an application must be in a transpositive language.

Distinctions of number are founded upon a modification of the five vowel sounds. Possessives are likewise founded upon the basis of the vowel sounds. There are five declensions of the noun to mark the possessives, ending, in the possessive, in *am*, *eem*, *im*, *om*, *um*, *oom*. Where the nominative ends with a vowel, the possessive is made by adding the letter *m*, as in *maimai*, a woodcock, *ne maimaim*, my woodcock, etc. Where the nominative ends in a consonant, as in *ais*, a shell, the full possessive inflection is required, making *nin dais-im*, my shell. In the latter form, the consonant *d* is interposed between the pronoun and noun, and sounded with the noun, in conformity with a general rule. Where the nominative ends in the broad, in lieu of the long sound of *a*, as in *ogimau*, a chief, the possessive is *aum*.

It is a constant and unremitting aim in the Indian languages, to distinguish the actor from the object ; partly by prefixes, and partly by inseparable suffixes. That the termination *un* is one of these inseparable particles, and that its office, while it confounds the number of the third person, is to designate the object, appears probable, from the fact that it retains its connection with the noun, whether the latter follow or precede the verb, or whatever its position in the sentence may be.

In tracing the operation of the rule through the doublings of the language, it is necessary to distinguish every modification of sound, whether it is accompanied, or not accompanied, by a modification of the sense. The particle *un*, which thus marks the *third person and persons*, is sometimes pronounced *wun*, and sometimes *yun*, as the euphony of the word to which it is suffixed may require. But not the slightest change is thereby made in its meaning.

Substantives require, throughout the language, separable or inseparable pronouns, under the form of prefixes. Inflections of the first and second persons, which occupy the place of possessives, and those of the third person, resembling objectives, pertain to words which are either primitives, or denote but a single object, as moose, fire. There is, however, another class of substantives, or substantive expressions, and an extensive class — for it embraces a great portion of the compound descriptive terms — in the use of which no pronominal prefixes are required. The distinctions of person are, exclusively, supplied by pronominal suffixes. Of this class are the words descriptive of country, place of dwelling, field of battle, place of employment, &c. Thus, *Aindaud*, home or place of dwelling, in the substantive singular; is *Aindauyaun*, my home; *Aindau-yun*, thy home; *Aindau-d*, his home. And the substantive plural is *Aindau-yaun-in*, my homes; *Aindau-yun-in*, thy homes; *Aindau-yaung-in*, our homes, &c.

Substantives have modifications by which locality, diminution, a defective quality, and the past tense are expressed; by which various adjectives and adverbal significations are given; and finally the substantives themselves converted into verbs. Such are, also, the modes of indicating the masculine and feminine (both merged in the animate class), and those words which are of a strictly *sexual* character, or are restricted in their *use* to males or females.

That quality of the noun which, in the shape of an inflection, denotes the relative situation of the object by the contiguous position of some accessory object, is expressed, in the English language, by the prepositions *in, into, at* or *on*. In the Indian they are denoted by an inflection. Thus the phrase, in the box, is rendered, in the Indian, by one word, *mukukoong;* the termination *oong* denoting the locality, not of the box, but of the object sought after. Generally, the inflection is employed when there is some circumstance or condition of the noun either concealed, or not fully apparent. The principal local inflections are *ing* and *oong*, which become *aing* and *eeng* as the terminal vowel of the noun may require. *Ishkodai,* fire; *Ishkod-aing*, in or on the fire; *Sebe*, river; *Sebeeng*, in or on the river; *Kon*, snow; *Kon-ing*, in or on the snow; *Azhibik*, rock; *Azhibik-oong*, in or on the rock, &c.

The local form pertains either to such nouns of the animate class as are in their nature inanimates, or at most possessed of vegetable life. There is another variation of the local form of the noun, indicative of locality in a more general sense. It is formed by *ong* or *nong*, frequent terminations in geographical names. Thus, from *Ojibwai* (Chippewa) is formed *Ojibwainong*, place of the Chippewas. The termination *ing* is also sometimes employed, as *Monomonikaun-ing*, in the place of wild rice, &c.

The diminutive forms of the noun are indicated by *ais, ees, os,* and *aus*, as the final vowel of the word may require. Thus, *Ojibwai*, a Chippewa, becomes Ojibw-*ais*, a little Chippewa; *Amik*, a beaver, Amik-*os*, a young beaver; *Minnis*, an island, Minnis-*ais*, a small island; *Shomin*, a grape, Shomin-*ais*, a little grape; *Ossin*, a stone, Ossin-*ees*, a small stone; *Sebe*, a river, Seb-*ees*, a small river; *Negik*, an otter, Negik-*os*, a small otter; *Wakiegun*, a house, Wakieg-*aus*, a small house. These diminutives, as far as they can be employed, supersede the use of adjectives, and are happily employed by the Indian in expressing ridicule or contempt. When applied to animals, or to inorganic objects, their meaning, however, is very nearly limited to an inferiority in size or age. Sometimes both the local and diminutive inflections are employed. Thus the word *minnisain-sing* signifies, literally, in the little island.

The syllable *ish*, when added to a noun, indicates a bad or dreaded quality, or conveys the idea of imperfection or decay.

The sound of this inflection is sometimes changed to *eesh*, *oosh*, or *aush*. Thus *Eckwai*, a woman, becomes Eckwai-*wish*, a bad woman ; *Nebi*, water, becomes Nebe-*esh*, strong water ; *Webeed*, a tooth, becomes Webeed-*aush*, a decayed or aching tooth. The rule is nearly universal that the final sound of *sh*, in any of its forms, is indicative of a faulty quality.

Substantives have, therefore, a *diminutive* form, made in *ais*, *ees*, *os*, or *aus* ; a *derogative* form, made in *ish*, *eesh*, *oosh*, or *aush* ; and a *local* form, made in *aing*, *eeng*, *ing*, or *ong*. By a principle of accretion, the second and third may be added to the first form, and the third to the second.

While substantives have their primitive and derivative forms, they also appear as compounds. Among the primitives may be found dissyllables and possibly trisyllables ; but as a principle, all polysyllabic words, all words of three syllables, and most words of two syllables, are compounds.

3. *Adjectives.* It has been remarked, that the distinction of words into animates and inanimates, is a principle intimately interwoven throughout the structure of the language, constituting indeed its fundamental principle. In the plural only of the substantive is the adjective indicated. One set of adjective symbols express the ideas peculiarly appropriate to animates, and another set is exclusively applicable to inanimates. Good and bad, black and white, great and small, handsome and ugly, have such modifications as are practically competent to indicate the general nature of the objects referred to, whether provided with, or destitute of, the vital principle. And not only so, but by the figurative use of these forms, to exalt inanimate masses into the class of living beings, or to strip the latter of the properties of life.

Examples illustrating this principle are quoted, and explained in complex and simple forms. Of the latter, it is said : Ask a Chippewa the name for a rock, and he will answer, *auzhebik*. Ask him the name for red rock, and he will answer, *miskwaubik* ; for white rock, *waubaubik* ; for black rock, *mukkuddawaubik* ; for bright rock, *wassyaubik* ; for yellow rock, *ozahwaubik* ; for green rock, *ozahwushkwaubik*; for smooth rock, *shoishkwaubik*, etc., compounds in which the words, red, white, black yellow, etc., unite with *aubik*.

Let this mode of interrogation be continued, and extended to other adjectives, or the same adjectives applied to other objects, and results equally regular and numerous will appear. *Minnis*, we shall be told, is an island ; *miskominnis*, a red island ; *mukkuddaminnis*, a black island, etc. *Annokwut*, is a cloud ; *miskwaunakwut*, a red cloud ; *waubahnokwut*, a white cloud, etc. *Neebe* is the specific term for water, but is not generally used in combination with the adjective. The word *goma*, like *aubo*, appears to be a generic term for water or potable liquids. Hence, *gitshee*, great, *gitshig-guma*, great water ; *minno*, good, *minwau-guma*, good drink, etc. *Baimwa* is sound ; *baimwawä*, the passing sound ; *minwäwä*, a pleasant sound ; *mudwayausshkau*, the sound of waves dashing on the shore. These examples might be continued ad infinitum. Every modification of circumstances, almost every peculiarity of thought, is expressed by some modification of the orthography. Enough has been given to prove that the adjective combines itself with the substantive, the verb, and the pronoun ; that the combinations thus produced are numerous, afford concentrated modes of conveying ideas, and oftentimes happy terms of expression.

Varied as the adjective is in its changes, it has no comparative inflection. A Chippewa cannot say, that one substance is hotter or colder than another ; or of two or more substances unequally heated, that this or that is the hottest or coldest, without employing adverbs or accessory adjectives. And it is accordingly by adverbs and accessory adjectives that the degrees of comparison are expressed. *Pemnaudizziwin* is a very good substantive expression, indicating *the tenor of being or life*. *Nem bimmaud-izziwin*, my tenor of life ; *Ke bimmaud-izziwin*, thy tenor of life. To form the positive degree, *minno*, good, and *mudjee*, bad, is introduced between the pronoun *d* and the verb, thus : *Ne minno pimmaud-izziwin*, my good tenor of life ; *Ne mudjee pimmaud-izziwin*, thy bad tenor of life. To c nstitute the comparative degree, *nahwudj*, more, is prefixed to the adjective. When the adjective is preceded by the adverb, it assumes a negative form.

4. *Pronouns.* Pronouns are buried, if we may so say, in the structure of the verb. In tracing them back, to their primitive

forms, through the almost infinite variety of modifications which they assume in connection with the verb, substantive, and adjective, it will facilitate analysis to group them into preformative and subformative classes; terms which have already been made use of, and which include the pronominal prefixes and suffixes. They admit of the further distinction of separable and inseparable pronouns. By separable is intended those forms which have a meaning by themselves, and are thus distinguished from the inflective and subformative pronouns, and pronominal particles; significant only in connection with another word.

Of the first class are the personal pronouns *nee* (I), *kee* (thou), and *wee*, or *o* (he or she), which are declined, to form the plural persons, by *neen owind*, *keen owau*, *ween owau*. The plural of the possessive mine, or my, in the inclusive, is made by *k* the pronominal sign of the second person, and the usual substantive inflection in *win*, with a terminal *d*. The letter *o* is a mere connective, without meaning. The second person is rendered plural by the particle, *au* instead of *win*. The third person has its plural in the common sign of *w*. The examples cited embrace the mode of distinguishing the person, number, relation, and gender — or what is deemed its technical equivalent, i. e., the mutations words undergo, not to mark the distinctions of sex, but the presence or absence of vitality; and also the inflections which the pronouns take for tense, or rather, the auxiliary verbs, have, had, shall, will, may, etc. This class embraces the preformative or prefixed pronouns.

The inseparable suffixed or subformative pronouns are: *yaun*, my; *yun*, thy; *id* or *d*, his or hers; *yaung*, our (ex.); *yung*, our (in.); *yaig*, your; *waud*, their. These pronouns are exclusively employed as suffixes; and as suffixes to the descriptive substantives, adjectives, and verbs. Relative pronouns are very limited. Demonstrative pronouns, both animate and inanimate, are found in many forms

The *Algonquin* language is in a peculiar sense a language of pronouns. Originally there appear to have been but three terms, answering to the three persons, I, thou, or you, and he or she. By these terms, the speaker or actor is clearly distinguished; but they convey no idea of sex, the word for the third person in which we should suspect it, being strictly epicene. In a class of languages strongly transitive, the purposes of precision required another class of pronouns, which should be suffixed to the end of verbs, to render the object of the action as certain as the actor is. The language being without auxiliary verbs, their place is supplied by the tensal syllables, *ge*, *gah*, and *guh*, which have extended the original monysyllables into trisyllables. This is the first step on the polysyllabical ladder. To make the suffixed or objective pronouns, they appear to have availed themselves of a principle which they had already applied to nouns — namely, the principle of indicating, by the letters *g* or *n* added to the plural terms, the two great divisions of creation, on which the whole grammatical structure is built — namely, the genderic classes of living or inert matter. As these alphabetical signs, *g* and *n*, could be applied to the five terminal vowel sounds of all nouns and all verbs (for they must, to be made plural or conjugated, be provided with terminal vowels, where they do not, when used disjunctively, exist), there is naturally a set of five vital or animate and five non-vital or inanimate plurals. Ten classes of nouns and ten classes of verbs are thus formed. But as the long vowels in *au* and *oan* require three more varieties of numerical inflection in each of these vowels, the respective number of plural terms is eight, and the total sixteen — sixteen modes of making the plural, and sixteen conjugations for the verb. This is productive of a variety of terminal sounds, and appears at the first glance to be confused, but the principle is simple and easily remembered; so easily, that a child need never mistake it. The terminal *g* or *n* of each word denotes *in all positions*, the two great genderic classes of nature, which are the cardinal points of the grammar.

Agreeably to data furnished, the regular plurals are respectively *ag*, *eg*, *ig*, *og*, *ug*, and *ain*, *een*, *in*, *on*, *un*, with the additional *aug*, *eeg*, and *oag*, in the vital, and *aun*, *een*, and *oan*, for the long vowels, in the non-vital class. Only two ideas are gained by thirty-two numerical inflections, namely, that the objects are vital or non-vital.

The pure verbs, the noun-verbs, the adjective-verbs, and the propositional, adverbial, and compound terms and declensions, are made plural precisely as the nouns, regard being always had to the principles of euphony, in throwing away or adding a letter, or giving precedence to an adjective inflection. The suffixed pronouns are required to be put at the end of these plurals, where they will not always coalesce without inserting them before the sign of the epicene or anti-epicene.

These suffixed plural inflections, as before indicated, are *yaun*, *yun*, *id*, or simply *d*—*I*, *you*, *he*, *she;* which are changed to plurals personal by the usual inflections of the letter *g*, making them *yaung*, we, us, our (ex.); *yung*, we, us our (in.), and *yaig* for ye. The vital particle are, is placed before *d* for the pronoun they.

As the pronouns are made plural precisely as the nouns, for distinction's sake, the numerical inflections *aig*, *aug*, *eeg*, *ig*, *og*, *oog*, *ug*, may be employed to express the various senses of we, they, them, and us, ours, theirs. These fourteen suffixed pronouns enable the speaker to designate the objective transitive persons, and to designate the reflex action in the first plural, which is uniform.

The anti-epicene suffixed pronouns for the same persons, are *ain*, *een*, *in*, *on*, *aun*, *un*, *aim*, *eem*, *im*, *om*, *oam*, *um;* with such changes in their adjustment as usage and the juxtaposition of consonants have produced.

5. *Verbs.* The whole stock of verbs in the Indian vocabulary is grouped with five epicene and five classes of anti-epicene conjugations. The conjugations embrace not only the natural verbs in common use, but they provide for all the nouns and noun-adjectives of every possible kind; for these, it must be remembered, can all be converted, under the plastic rules of the language, into verbs.

With a formidable display of vocal terms and inflective forms, there is, therefore, a very simple principle to unravel the lexicography, namely, fidelity to the meaning of primary and vowelic sounds. If we compare this principle to a thread, parts of which are white, black, green, blue and yellow, the white may stand as the symbol of five vowelic classes of words in *a*, the black in *b;* the green in *c;* the blue in *d;* and the yellow in *e*. It creates no confusion to the eye to add, that there is a filament of red running through the whole series of colored strands, whereby five additional distinctions are made, making ten in all. These represent the two great classes of sounds of the *Algonquin* grammar, denoting what has been called the epicene and anti-epicene scheme.

If we would know to what class of conjugations a word belongs, we must inquire how the plural is made. It will be borne in mind that all verbs, like all substantives, either terminate in a vowel sound, or, where they do not, that a vowel sound must be added in making the plural, in order that it may serve as a coalescent for the epicene *g* or the anti-epicene *n*. Thus man, *inine*, is rendered men, *ininewug*, not by adding the simple epicene plural *ug*, but by throwing a *w* before it, making the plural in *wug*. So *paup*, to laugh, is rendered plural in *wug*, and not *ug;* whilst *minnis*, an island, *sebens*, a brook, and all words ending in a consonant, take the regular anti-epicene plural in *un*. The rule that in syllabication a vowel should follow a consonant is indeed universal.

The arrangement of the vowelic classes is so important to any correct view of the grammar of the language, and is, at the same time, so regular, euphonious, and philosophical, that it will impress it the better on the mind, by presenting a tabular view of it.

### Corresponding Classes of Verbs.

*Epicene Substantives.*

|   |   |   | Plural Inflections. |
|---|---|---|---|
| 1. Words ending in | a | | äg |
| 2. " " " | e | | ëg |
| 3. " " " | i | | ïg |
| 4. " " " | o | | ög |
| 5. " " " | u | | üg |

*Anti-epicene Substantives.*

| 1. Words ending in | a | | än |
| 2. " " " | e | | ën |
| 3. " " " | i | | ïn |
| 4. " " " | o | | ön |
| 5. " " " | u | | ün |

APPENDIX. 351

*Epicene Verbs.*

CLASS OF CONJUGATIONS.

1. Verbs ending in . . ä or äg . . . in class a
2. " " " . . ë or ëg . . . " e
3. " " " . . ï or ïg . . . " i
4. " " " . . ö or ög . . . " o
5. " " " . . ü or üg . . . " u

*Anti-Epicene Verbs.*

1. Verbs ending in . . ä or än . . . in class a
2. " " " . . ë or ën . . . " e
3. " " " . . ï or ïn . . . " i
4. " " " . . ö or ön . . . " o
5. " " " . . ü or ün . . . " u

6. *Radices.* The *Algonquin* language is founded on roots or primary elements having a meaning by themselves. As *waub*, to see; *paup*, to laugh; *wa*, to move in space; *bwa*, a voice. The theory of its orthography is to employ these primary sounds in combination, and not as disjunctive elements, which has originated a plan of thought and concords quite peculiar. It is evident that such particles as *ak*, *be*, *ge*, were invested with generic meanings before they assumed their concrete forms of *ak-e*, earth; *ne-be*, water; *ge-zis*, sky. Without attention to this theory of radices, and to the word-building principle of the language, — to this constant capacity of incremental extension, and to the mode of doubling, triplicating, and quadruplicating ideas, it is impossible to analyze it — to trace its compounds to their embryotic roots, and to seize upon those principles of thought and utterance, by attention to which, there has been created in the forests of America, one of the most polysyllabic and completely transpositive modes of communicating thought that exists.

Humboldt applies the term "agglutinated" in defining the structure of the language. If by agglutination be meant accretion, and the adhesive principle be its syntax, the term is certainly appropriate. Whatever is agglutinated in the material world requires gluten to attach piece to piece, and its analogy in the intellectual process of sticking syllable to syllable, and word to word, is the accretive principle; and this syllabical gluten is precisely that to which the closest attention is required to trace its syntax.

7. *Word-Building.* The accretive system upon which the language is based is most clearly illustrated by analysis. *Waub* is, apparently, the radix of the verb, to see, and of the word, light. *Waubun* is the east, or sunlight, and, inferentially, place of light. *Aub* is the name of the eye-ball, hence *ai-aub*, to eye, or to see with the eye-ball. *Ozh* appears to be the root of every species of contrivance designed to float on water. *Wa-mit-ig-ozh*, the people of the wooden-made vessel — this is the *Algonquin* term for a Frenchman. *Ozh*, vessel; *mitig*, trees or timbers, and *wa*, a plural phrase indicative of persons. It is said the Indian must have had a term for grape, before he made the compound term for wine, since the meaning of the latter is grape-liquor. *Aubo* in the *Algonquin*, means a liquid or liquor. *Shomin*, is a grape — but this is itself a dual compound. *Min*, in the same language, means a berry. The primordial root of the word is *Sho*. Hence the terms:

| A Radix | . . . . *Sho* . . . . | . A grape. |
|---|---|---|
| A Radix, | . . . *Min*. | . . A berry. |
| Undecided, | . . . *Aubo* | . . . A liquor. |
| A compound of four syllables. | Shominaubo. | Wine, that is grape-berry liquor. |

The word *Mishimin* means an apple. It is compounded from *Mish*, the primordial root, and *Min*, a berry, with the short sound of *i* thrown in for euphony. The principle of euphony requires a vowel to be interposed where two short words meet, which would bring two consonants (as in this case) together, and a consonant in expressions which would bring two vowels together. The enlargement of the word into the class of trisyllables, in all these cases, brings only *sound* into the new compound, without any enlargement of the sense. By joining the word *aubo* to this dualistic term, we have the Indian name for cider.

| Radix, | . . . . . *Mish* . . . Apple. |
|---|---|
| Connective, | . . . . . *i* |

# APPENDIX.

| Radix, | *Min* | . Berry. |
|---|---|---|
| Undecided, | *Aubo* | . Liquor. |
| Compound of four syllables. | *Mishiminaubo.* | Apple-berry liquor. |

The term for rum is *ishkoda wabo*. Ishkoda is itself a compound word, *koda* signifies a plain or valley, and *ish*, fire, and is employed perhaps to denote quality and prostration; *w* is a coalescent and *aubo*, liquor — five syllables, fire-liquor. The word for mechanical, and all classes of implements, is *Jĕgun*. To break up (any inanimate substance), is *Pegoobidön*. Land or earth is *Akki; Akkum*, surface of the earth. Hence, *Pegookumibeéjegun*, a plough or breaking-up-land instrument. *Wassaau* is light; *Biskoona*, flame. Hence, *Was-ko-nen-jegun*, a candle or light flame instrument.

Not only verbs and substantives are thus compounded and lengthened out in their syllabical structure, but adjectives admit of similar forms. Thus from the adjective radix *misk*, there is formed a variety of dual and trial compounds, which are in daily vocal use.

| *Misquee,* | Blood. | From *misk*, red, and *nebee*, water. |
|---|---|---|
| *Misqueewon,* | Bloody. | " " *won*, a substance. |
| *Misqueengua,* | A blush. | " " *equa*, a female. |
| *Misquawauk,* | Red cedar. | " " *auk*, a tree. |

From the word *Minno*, good, is derived.

| *Minnomonedo,* | . . A good God; or an heavenly spirit. |
|---|---|
| *Minnoinnini,* | . . A good man. |
| *Minnoequa,* | . . . A good woman. |

From the word *Mudjee*, or *Matchee*, as it is usually written, is formed:

| *Matcheemonedo,* | . . . . A bad spirit of demon of evil. |
|---|---|
| *Matcheinnini,* | . . . A bad man. |

One of the most striking sources of Indian compounds is that derived from men's and women's names. The open firmament of heaven is the field from which these names are generally derived. They are, consequently, sublime or grandiloquent in phraseology; sometimes poetic, always highly figurative, and often bombastic or ridiculous. The following examples of the personal names of each sex will denote this:

| | |
|---|---|
| Au be tub gee zhig, | Centre of the sky. |
| Baim wa wa, | The passing thunder. |
| Cheeng gaus sin, | The noise of wind. |
| Esh ta nak wod, | Clear sky or cloudless sky. |
| Mo kau ge zhig, | The sun bursting from a cloud. |
| Ning au be un, | The westerly wind. |
| O zhau wus co ge zhig, | The blue sky. |
| Pa bau ge me wong, | The showers. |
| Sa sa gun, | Hail. |
| Waub un nung, | The morning star. |

Males have two and sometimes three names, but generally two, one of which may be called his baptismal name, and the other that which he has acquired from some incident or circumstance. The former is studiously concealed, and never revealed by the Indian bearing it; the latter is the familiar cognomen. It is characteristic of female names, that they denote the gender in their terminal syllable *qua*. The following will sufficiently illustrate the manner in which they are compounded:

| | |
|---|---|
| Au zhe bik o qua, | Woman of the rock. |
| Baim wa wa ge zhig a qua, | Woman of the thunder-cloud. |
| Cheeng gosh kum o qua, | Woman of the sounding footsteps. |
| Ke neance e qua, | Little rose-bud woman. |
| Mau je ge zhik o qua, | Woman of the zenith. |
| O gin e bug o qua, | Woman of the rose. |
| O buh bau mwa wa ge zhig o qua, | Woman of the murmuring of the skies. |

The formation of geographical names is no exception to the rule. *Wombi*, in the Natick, or Massachusetts dialect,— which the *Wappingers* are presumed to have spoken,— means white; *ic*, or *ik*, is a termination for *azhebik*, a rock or solid formation of rocks. Hence Wombic, the Indian name for the White mountains of New Hampshire. In the Algonquin, *monaud* signifies bad; *nok* and *nac*, in the same language, is a term indicative of rock or precipice. Hence Monadnock, a detached mountain of New Hampshire, whose characteristic is thus denoted to consist in the difficulty or badness of its ascent. The Delawares denominate their river *Lenapehituk*. Of this term *Lenape* is their own proper name, *ituk* is a local phrase. The Mahicans gave to their river a name similarly constituted in *Mahicanituk*. The particle *na* in the Chippewa, indicates, in compounds, "fairness, abundance, excellence, something surpassing."· *Amik*, is a term for a beaver, and *ong* denotes place. Thus *Namikong*, the name for a noted point on Lake Superior, means a surpassing place for beavers. The name *Housatonick* is a trinary, which appears to be composed of *wassa*, bright, *atun*, a channel or stream, and *ick* from *azhebic*, rocks; i. e., "Bright stream flowing through rocks." While it is perhaps impossible to translate many of the local and geographical names which are found in the valley of the Hudson, from the fact that the language was a mixture of Algonquin, Manhattan, Wappenackie, Mahican, Minsi and Iroquois, their formation was in accordance with the concrete principle, and in many cases the root terms are easily detected.

Connected with this branch of his subject, the author introduces a plan of a system of geographical names, founded on the aboriginal languages, which gives to the investigation a practical form, and, if adopted, would enrich our own language as well as preserve the original. He says:

"It is found that many aboriginal terms which are graphically descriptive in the native dialects, fail in the necessary euphony and shortness necessary to their popular adoption. The principles of the polysynthetic languages embrace the rule of concentrating, in their compounds, the full meaning of a word upon a single syllable, and sometimes a single letter. Thus in Alonquin, the particle *be* denotes water; *wa*, inanimate motion; *ga*, personal action; *ac*, a tree; *hic*, a rock or metal. The syllable *ti*, in Iroquois, constantly means water; *tar*, a rock; *on*, a hill; *nec*, a tree. In the Natick or Massachusetts dialect, as given by Mr. Eliot, the negative form of elementary words is *matta;* the local inflection *ett;* the adjective great, *missi;* black, *mooi*; white, *wompi*.

"The Indian languages also contain generic syllables or particles in the shape of inflections to nouns and verbs; in the Algonquin, *abo*, a liquid; *jegun*, or simply *gun*, an instrument; *jewun*, a current; *wunzh*, a plant; *ong* or *onk*, a place, &c.

"By these concentrations, descriptive words become replete with meanings; but it requires a very nice collocation and adjustment of syllables to attain the requisite degree of euphony, for the adoption of such compounds by foreign ears. Generally, words of three syllables recommend themselves to the English ear for quantity, in geographical names adopted from an Indian language, as heard in Oswego, Chicago, Ohio, Monadnock, and Toronto. In the terms suggested in the following lists of words, intended to be introduced into our geographical nomenclature, the principles of elision and concentration referred to, have been applied. The root-forms carry the entire signification to which they are entitled, in the elementary vocabulary, after they have been divested, by analysis, of their adjuncts. Thus, in the Algonquin, the syllable *ac* stands for land, earth, ground, soil; *be*, for water, liquid; *bic*, for rock, stone, metal, hard mineral; *co* for object; *ke* for country, precinct, or territory; *os* for pebble, loose stone, detritus; *min*, good; *ia*, the term for a beautiful scene; *na*, a particle, which, in compound words, denotes excellence; *oma*, a large body of water; *non*, a place; *gan*, a lake; *coda*, a plain or valley; *oda*, a town, village, or cluster of houses, &c.

"By adding the primary syllable of a word, as conveying the entire signification of the word, and employing it as a nominative to other syllables, which are also made use of in their concentrated forms, a class of words is formed, which are generally shorter than their parent forms, more replete in their meanings, and securing, at the same time, a more uniformly euphonious pronounciation. Quantity and accent being thus at command by these elisions and transpositions, the number of syllables of which a new class of words shall consist, is a question to be predetermined. Expletive consonants, harsh gutturals, and double inflections, the pests of Indian lexography, are dropped, and the selections made from syllables which abound in liquid and vowel sounds. For it should be the object to preserve, as

APPENDIX. 357

new elements in this peculiar branch of American literature, not the harsh and barbarous, but the soft and sonorous sounds.

1. *Terms from the Algonquin.* " As a basis for these terms, we take, from the vocabulary of analyzed words, the primary terms *ad, ab, os, wud, pat, mo, at, seeb, gon, pew, chig, naig, ag, mon, tig, cos, pen, mig, won;* meaning respectively deer, home, pebble, mountain, hill, spring, channel or current, river, clay-land, iron, shore, sand, water's edge, corn, tree, grass, bird, eagle, rose-bud. Subjecting these nominatives to the adjective expression *ia,* signifying beautiful, fair, admirable, and placing the particle *nac,* land, earth, soil, in the objective, and changing the latter for *gan* a lake; *bee,* water; *min,* good; *na,* excellent; *ma,* large water; *ock,* forest; we have the following trisyllabic terms:

| | | |
|---|---|---|
| Deer, | *Ad* | *Ad ia nac.* |
| Home, | *Ab* | *Ab ia nac.* |
| Pebble, | *Os* | *Os ia nac.* |
| Mountain, | *Wud* | *Wud ia nac.* |
| Hill, | *Pat* | *Pat ia nac.* |
| Spring, | *Mo* | *Mo ia nac.* |
| Current, | *At* | *At ia nac.* |
| River, | *Seeb* | *Seeb ia nac.* |
| Clay-land, | *Gon* | *Gon ia nac.* |
| Iron, | *Pew* | *Pew ia nac.* |
| Shore, | *Chig* | *Chig ia nac.* |
| Sand, | *Naig* | *Naig ia nac.* |
| Beach, | *Ag* | *Ag ia nac.* |
| Corn, | *Mon* | *Mon ia nac.* |
| Tree, | *Tig* | *Tig ia nac.* |
| Grass, | *Cos* | *Cos ia nac.* |
| Bird, | *Pen* | *Pen ia nac.* |
| Eagle, | *Mig* | *Mig ia nac.* |
| Rose-bud, | *Won* | *Won ia nac.* |

" By reversing the action of the verb, or noun nominative, a new set of phrases is created, by which the meaning is changed from deer-land, home-land, &c., to land of deer, land of home, &c. The number of the objective syllables is as various as the objects in nature. The whole class of animals, birds, reptiles, insects, fishes; the wide-spread phenomena of the heavens, of the forests and of the waters, supply words which are susceptible of being employed in the construction of new terms. Not only can the objective be exchanged for the nominative, but the qualifying word admits of many euphonious exchanges, and it may itself be employed as an objective, and the nominative itself thrown in the body of the terms as a qualifying syllable; producing a set of words like those heard in Peoria and Kaskaskia, where the terminal syllable, *ia*, denotes fair or beautiful. In these terms the syllable *os*, denoting pebble or drift, is the adjunct noun.

*Adósia* . . . Fair deer land, . . From *Adic*.
*Abósia*, . . Fair home land, . . " *Abia*.
*Patósia*, . . Fair hill, . . . . " *Ishpatina*.

" If the terminal *ome* or *oma*, as it is heard in Gitchig-oma, be employed, we have a set of terms denoting water prospects.

*Min-ó-ma*, . . . . . . Good water.
*Mos-ó-ma*, . . . . . Moose water.
*Mon-ó-ma*, . . . . . . Spirit water.
*Mok-ó-ma*, . . . . . Spring water.
*Ac-ó-ma*, . . . . . . Rock water.

" The particle *na* as heard in Namikong, denotes excellent, abundant, surpassing. By taking this for the objective syllable, and retaining the same nominative, and the same qualifying syllable made use of above, the resulting terms are as follows:

*Min-iá-na*, . . . . Good, fair and excellent.
*Ack-iá-na*, . . . .   "      "    land.
*Tig-iá-na*, . . . .   "      "    trees.
*Mon-iá-na*, . . . .   "      "    spirits.

2. *Terms from the Iroquois.* The syllables *co*, a cascade; *ti*, water; *tar*, rock; *on*, hill; *asto*, a defile, are selected as exhibiting the transpositive capacities of this language.

" Termination in *atea*, a valley or landscape.

*Co-at-at-ea*, . . . Valley below falls.
*Ti-at-at-ea* . . . Well watered valley.

*Tar-at-at-ea,* . . . Rocks of the valley.
*On-at-at-ea,* . . . Hills of the valley.
*As-to-at-ea,* . . . Narrow pass of a river in the valley.

"Terminations in *oga*, a place, change these terms to "place of water and rocks," "place of hills and rocks," "place of the watery vale," etc. Terminations in *io*, beautiful: Co-i-o, beautiful falls; Te-i-o, beautiful waters; On-ti-o, beautiful hills; Tar-i-o, beautiful rocks; Os-i-o, beautiful view."

Examples of transpositions and elisions are abundantly furnished, but sufficient have been quoted to illustrate the principle and direct attention to the subject. Instead of Smith's corners, Johnson's mills, and a class of local terms without significance, might be introduced Na-pee-na, abounding in birds; Al-gan-see, water of the plains; I-ós-co, water of light; I-é-nia, wanderer's rest; Was-sa-han-na, bright river; Sho-min-ac, grape-land; Mon-á-kee, spirit land; Tal-lú-la, leaping waters; Os-sé-go, beautiful view; Bis-có-da, beautiful plain, terms of appropriate and permanent import. For private residences or country seats, no class of terms could be applied more expressive or more American. The titles of the old world certainly need not be copied when those that are fresh and fragrant await adoption.

### Dialectic Vocabularies.

Dialectic vocabularies, while not without their value for comparative purposes and for supplying primitive terms, afford but little aid in other respects. As a general rule, those which have been preserved are composed of words spoken in different localities and at different periods, and frequently mislead the inquirer. Those having occasion to do so, will consult them in their most complete form in *Schoolcraft's History*, and in *Gallatin's Synopsis*. The table annexed is introduced as simply illustrative.

## Comparative Vocabulary.

| | OLD ALGONQUIN. | LONG ISLAND. | MASSACHUSETTS. | MAHICAN. | DELAWARE. | MINSI. | SHAWANOES. | CHIPPEWAY. | MOHAWK. |
|---|---|---|---|---|---|---|---|---|---|
| God, | Kitchi manitoo, | manto, | manittoo ; manit, | {manito—a spirit,. pautaumonvoh,} | manitto, | | wishemenetou, | ketche manito, | lawaneeu. |
| Man, | alissinap, | run, | wosketomp, | neemanaoo, | *liinnu ; lenno, | lenno, | illeni, | | oonguich. |
| Woman, | ickweh, | squah, | mittamwosses, | pghainoom, | *hokkua²a², okhqueh, | ochqueu, | equiwa, | | o-oonhechlien. |
| An Indian, | | ichun, | aberginian, | | lenape, | | elanematthalene, | | guihhoonwih. |
| House, Hut, | wikiwam, | weecho, | wekit ; wetu, | weekuwuhm, | wiquõám, | wichquoam, | wiggewoam, | wakyigun, | canuchsha. |
| Fire, | skootay, | shut, | nootae ; nootau, | stauw, | *taande ; tendeu, | tendeu, | scoote, | ishkodai, | ocheerle. |
| Water, | nipi, | nup ; niep, | nippe, | nbey, | *bee ; mbi, | niby, | neppee ; nipee, | neebi, | oochnekanus. |
| Earth, | ackey, ackwin, | keagh, | ohke, | akek, | *ha²a²kke ; aki ; akhki, | achgi, | assiskee ; ake, | ahke, | oohunjah. |
| River, | sipin, | seepus, | sepu, | sepoo, | *kittuun ; sipu, | sipu, | sepi, | seebi, | kaihunhatate. |
| Stone, | assin, | sun, | qussuk ; hussun, | thaunaumku, | akhsun, | achsün, | iregonah, | {ossin-(stone), azhibik-(rock),} | oonoyah. |
| Tree, | meteeh, | peuoye, | mehtug, | machtok, | mihktuk, | michtuk, | toauane, | metik, | kerlitle. |
| White, | wabi, | wampayo, | wompi, | waupaaeek, | *opeek ; wa)e ; wapsu, | opeh, | opee, | {wawhishkaw-(inan), wawbizze-(animate)} | curlagu. |
| Black, | mackatey, | shickayo, | moo-i, | n'sikkayóoh, | *siitke ; ne:gissit, | nesgeek, | mukkoote, | mukkudiawa, | cahoonge. |
| Red, | miskwey, | squayo, | mishque, | m'chgaju, | *mokkee ; makhget, | machksu, | m'shwáhwee, | miskwa, | ooqunchtarla. |
| Valley, | | | {ooneuhkoi; oonouwohkoai,} | | {*indatatakushaak; pakhsajek,} | | natikgúee, | tahwattenaug, | chechuloom wakko. |
| Hill, | | | wadchuemes, | gh'aukoock, | {*kuitahuun; wakhtshut.t,} | | moqueghke, | ishpatinah, | onondate. |
| Mountain, | | | wudchue ; wadchu, | w'chu, | *ohee ; wakhtshu, | | missiwagewee, | wudju, | yoonoondoo waunuh. |
| Island, | minnis, | | menohhannet, | mnauhan, | *menatey ; menokhtey, | Minnis, | menathee, | minnis, | cawaynoote. |
| Beaver, | amik, | | tummunk, | amisque, | *nakuee ; ktemaque, | | amaquah, | ahmik, | chinnectoo. |
| Bear, | mackwah, | | mosq, | mquoh, | mak'hk, | | mawquah, | mukwah, | ooguharlee. |
| Wolf, | mahingan, | | {mukquooshim ; mukquoshim,} | | {tumme ; m'tummeu ; wiekhtuheu,} | | m'wáiwah, | mieengun, | ahguohhoo. |
| Partridge, | pileysiwey, | apacus, | nahenan, | pahpahcogh, | *pupikuiis ; popocus, | | kokolahıothah, | pinai. | oohquaizun. |
| Turkey | nahiam, | | | | tshikenum, | | pelewa, | mezissa, | skaihwurlowurnee. |
| Fish, | kikons, | operamae, | nahmos, | namáassak, | *namiis ; namoes, | namees, | amatha, | kikon. | keiyunk. |

* West New Jersey dialect as distinguished from Pennsylvania.

APPENDIX. 361

### III. Geographical Nomenclature and Traditions.

IN addition to the geographical terms which have been given in the body of this work, there are many to which reference may very properly be made, as well as traditions "which take the form of history," from their very general acceptance as such. It is to be regretted that the orthography of most of the Indian geographical terms is so badly rendered in the official records as to make interpretation almost impossible, even where the dialect has been preserved, and especially is it to be regretted that the dialects themselves have not been preserved with more of their original character. As an almost universal rule, however, the statement may be accepted as a fact that the Indians had little of poetry in their composition, and that, while many of their terms can be made poetical, they were originally of the plainest and simplest descriptive equivalents. A black hill or a red hill, a large hill or a small one, a small stream of water or a larger one, or one which was muddy or stony, a field of maize, or of leeks, overhanging rocks or dashing waterfalls (*patternack*),— almost invariably denoting some physical peculiarity, or some product of the soil. Their commemorative terms were few.

*Manhattan* has already been explained as signifying island, or, in its plural form, islands; as applied to the people, "the people of the islands." The extreme point of land between the junction of East and North rivers, of which the battery is now a part, was called *Kapsee*, and is still known to many persons as the Copsie point. The term appears to have denoted a "safe place of landing," formed by eddy waters. *Sappokanikan*, a point of land on the Hudson below Greenwich avenue, is supposed to indicate, "the carrying place," from *sipon*, river, and *ounigan*, a portage. The Indians carried their canoes either over the point or across the island to East river, at this place, to save the trouble of paddling down to the foot of the island and then up the East river. (*O'Callaghan*). Corlear's hook was called *Naghtognk*, according to Benson. The name is also given as *Rechtauck;* from *reckwa,* sand. A tract of meadow land on the north end of the island, near Kingsbridge, was called *Muscoota,* that is "meadow or grass land." (*Benson.*) *Warpoes* was a term bestowed on a piece of elevated ground, situated above and beyond the small lake or pond called the *kolck;* the latter occupying several acres in the neighborhood of the present halls of justice in Centre street. Many of the streets of the city are laid out upon the old Indian paths. This is true of Broadway from the battery to the Park, where the Indian paths forked, one running east to Chatham square, and the other west to Tivoli garden, etc. This would lead to *Warpoes* by paths on the east and west side of the kolck. At or beyond *Warpoes* the paths again forked, one leading to *Sappokanikan* on the Hudson, and the other to *Naghtognk* or Corlear's hook. The island was not a place of permanent abode of the Indians, but was only occupied during certain seasons. It was sold to Minuet, the first director-general of the Holland government, in 1624, and was then estimated to contain about twenty-two thousand acres. The price paid to the Indians was sixty guilders, or about twenty-four dollars.

Staten island bears different names in different deeds. In the deed to Michael Pauw, in 1631, it is called *Matawucks,* and in that to Capellen, in 1655, *Eghquaous.* DeVries says that it was called *Monocknong,* and that the clan occupying it were *Monatons.* The deed to Capellen states that it was jointly owned by the *Raritans* and the *Hackinsacks.* Governor's island was called by the Indians, *Pagganck;* Bedloe's island, *Minnisais;* Ellis' island, *Kioshk;* and Blackwell's island, *Minnahanock,* the latter signifying "at the island," or "the island home." "The word is a compound of *Menahan,* an island, and *uck,* locality." (*O'Callaghan*).

On the point of land now occupied by Fort Schuyler is located a tradition which Judge Benson relates in his *Memoirs of New York.* Directly opposite the fort are the famous stepping stones,[1] consisting of a number of rocks which project

---

[1] On a map descriptive of the battle near Lake George, in 1755, Stepping Stones is also applied to the palisades on the Hudson.—*Documentary History,* IV, 259.

in a line from the Long Island shore, and show their bare tops at low water. " An Indian origin," says Benson, " is asserted for this name, and a tradition vouched as authority." It is said, that at a certain time the evil spirit set up a claim against the Indians, to Connecticut, as his peculiar domain; but they being in possession, determined, of course, to try to hold it. The surface of Connecticut and Long Island were then the reverse of what they are now. The latter was covered with rocks; Connecticut was free from them. The Indians first tried to negotiate with his majesty; offering to retire from the land, provided they were permitted to girdle the trees and remove their property. No answer was made to the proposition, and both parties appealed to arms. The arch-leader took the field alone; and being an overmatch for the Indians in skill and spirit, he at first advanced on them; but, they having provided there should be constant reinforcements on their march, thereby preserving their corps entire, and harassing him incessantly, giving him no rest night nor day, he was obliged finally to yield to vigilance and perseverance, and fall back. He retired collected, and, as usual, gave up the ground only inch by inch; and though retiring, still presenting a front whenever attack threatened. He kept close to the sound to secure his flank from attack on that side; and having reached the point, and the water becoming narrow, and the tide running out, and the rocks showing their heads, he availed himself of them, and stepping from one to the other effected his retreat to Long Island. He at first betook himself, silent and sullen, to Coram, in the middle of the island; but it being in his nature not to remain idle long, and rage being superadded, soon roused him and ministered to him the means of revenge. He collected all the rocks in the island in heaps at Cold Spring, and throwing them in different directions, to different distances across the sound in Connecticut, covered the surface of it with them as we now see it."

This tradition was given to the first settlers at Cold Spring, and the last Indians who remained there not only undertook to show the spot where his majesty stood, but insisted that they could still discern the prints of his feet. A projecting point of land on the neck is still called Satan's Toe.

Among the natural curiosities of Long Island is *Ronconcoa lake*, lying upon the boundary line which divides the four towns of Smithtown, Setauket, Islip, and Patchogue. This lake is of great depth and for a long time was supposed to be unfathomable. It has an ebb and flow in its waters at different periods ; and was early made the theme of Indian story and tradition. They regarded it with a species of superstitious veneration, and although it abounded in a variety of fish, they, at the early settlement, refused to eat them, believing they were superior beings and placed there by the Great Spirit.

About thirty miles from Brooklyn and midway between the north and south sides of the island, is a hill known as *Manetta*, a corruption of the original name, which was *Manitou*, or the hill of the Great Spirit. The tradition is, that many ages since, the aborigines residing in those parts suffered extremely from the want of water. Under their suffering they offered up prayers to the Great Spirit for relief. That in reply to their supplications, the Great Spirit directed their chieftain should shoot his arrow in the air, and on the spot where it fell they should dig, and would assuredly discover the element they so much desired. They pursued the direction, dug, and found water. There is now a well situated on this rising ground ; and the tradition continues to say, that this well is on the very spot indicated by the Good Spirit. The probabilities are that the hill takes its name from the fact that it was used as the place of general offering to the Great Spirit.

*Canoe Place*, on the south side of the island, near Southampton, derives its name from the fact, that more than two centuries ago a canal was made there by the Indians, for the purpose of passing their canoes from one bay to the other, that is across the island from *Mecox* bay to *Peconic* bay. Although the trench has been in a great measure filled up, yet its remains are still visible, and partly flowed at high water. It was constructed by *Mongotucksee*, or Long Knife, who then reigned over the nation of *Montauk* — a chief of gigantic form, proud and despotic in peace, and terrible in war. But although a tyrant of his people, he protected them from their enemies, and commanded their respect for his savage virtues. He sustained his power not less by the resources of his mind than by the vigor of his arm. An ever watchful policy guided his councils. Prepared for every exigency, not even aboriginal sagacity could surprise his canton. To facilitate communication around the seat of his dominion — for the purpose not only of defense but of annoyance — he constructed this canal, which remains a monument of his genius. The praises of *Mongotucksee* are still chanted in aboriginal verse to the winds that howl around the eastern extremity of the island.

Long Island, as already stated, was called *Sewanhackey*. Among the localities, *Occopoque* (Riverhead), takes its name from *accup*, a creek. The Indian village of *Accopogue* was situated on the creek which enters Little Peconic bay on the north side. *Nepeage* was the name of the peninsula which unites Montauk to the western part of East Hampton, and is supposed to mean "water land," from *nepe*, water, and *eage*, earth or land. (*O'Callaghan.*) *Montauk*, the name for the east end of the island, is from *mintuck*, a tree, in the Narragansett dialect. The place abounded with trees, according to Thompson. (*Ibid.*) *Namke*, from *namaas*, fish and *ke*, place was the name of the creek near Riverhead. (*Ibid.*) *Mereyckawick* (Brooklyn), is from *me*, the article in the Algonquin; *reckwa*, sand, and *ick*, locality, "the sandy place." The name was probably applied, at first, to the bottom land or beach. Wallabout bay was called "the boght of Mareckawick." (*Ibid.*) *Huppogues*, in Smithtown, is an abbreviation of *sumhuppaog*, the Narragansett word for beavers. (*Rhode Island Historical Collections*, I, 95.)

Bolton, in his *History of Westchester County*, has preserved many of the Indian names in that district. To the Spuyten Duyvel creek he assigns the term, *Papirinimen*. O'Callaghan gives the same name to a tract " on the north end of the island of Manhattans," about 228th street, between Spuyten Duyvel creek on the west and Harlem river on the east. Saw mill creek was called *Neperah*, from *nepe*, water, and gave its name to the Indian village of *Nappeckamak*, which stood on the site of the present village of Yonkers, literally "the rapid water settlement." In an obscure nook on the Hudson, west of the *Neperah*, is a large rock which was called *Meghkeekassin*, or

*Amackassin*,[1] or "the great stone," to which it is said the Indians paid reverence as an evidence of the permanency and immutability of their deity.

No Indian name more frequently occurs in the history of the county than that of *Weckquaesgeek*, nor one the precise location of which there is more difficulty in determining. O'Callaghan says: "This tract is described as extending from the Hudson to the East river. The name is from *wigwos*, birch bark, and *keag*, country —" the country of the birch bark." Bolton gives the name to an Indian village which occupied the site of Dobbs' ferry, which he denominates "the place of the bark kettle." In *Albany Records*, III, 379, is this entry: "Personally appeared *Sauwenare*, sachem of Wieckqueskeck, *Amenameck* his brother, and others, all owners, etc., of lands situated on North river called *Wieckquaeskeck*, and declared that they had sold the same to Wouter Van Twiller in 1645." In a deed to Frederick Phillipse, April 12, 1682, the bounds of the tract conveyed are given as, "southerly to a creek or fall called by the Indians Weghquegsike," and in another deed the tract is described as "a piece of land lying about *Wighquaeskeek*," and in still another the creek is called *Weghqueghe*. Bolton says the creek was called *Wysquaqua*.

The Indian name for Tarrytown was *Alipconck*, "the place of elms." Sing-Sing takes its name from an Indian village called *Ossing-sing*, from *ossin*, a stone, and *ing*, a place, the "place of stones," or "stone upon stone." (*Bolton*.) In a deed to Philip Phillipse, 1685, it is said, "a creek called *Kitchawan*, called by the Indians *Sinksink*." Bolton, however, gives the name of *Kitchawonck* to the Croton river. The site of the present village of Peekskill was called *Sackhoes* and was occupied by an Indian village known by that name. Teller's point was called *Senasqua*. Tradition weaves the story that the forms of the ancient warriors still haunt the surrounding glens and woods of this district, and the Haunted Hollow, and the sachems of Teller's point, have become household words in the neighborhood. Another tradition tells us that a desperate conflict was

---

[1] In one of the Phillipse Deeds, it is described as "a great rock called by the Indians *Sigghes*."

once held here by the *Kitchawongs* against their enemies, and that the mound near the entrance to Teller's point was erected over the dead who fell on that memorable occasion.

Anthony's nose was called *Kittatenny*, a Delaware term signifying "endless hills."[1] *Poconteco* river, called also *Pekanteco* or *Pereghanduck*, is presumed to express in its name the dark river; from *pohkunni*, dark, inde. *pecontecue*, night. The stream may have been densely overshadowed by trees. (*O'Callaghan*.) Bolton says the name signifies "a run between two hills." The Dutch styled it "Sleepy Haven kil," hence the origin of the present term Sleepy Hollow applied to the valley. *Sacrahung*, or mill river, takes its name from *sacra*, rain. Its liability to freshets after heavy rains, may have given origin to the Indian name. (*Ibid.*) *Quinnahung*, a neck of land at the mouth and west side of the Bronck river,— from *quinni*, long, and *unk*, locality. (*Ibid.*) *Aquehung*, "the place of peace,"— from *aquene*, peace,— was the name given to the place occupied by Jonas Bronck in commemoration of the peace which was there concluded with the Indians in 1643. (*Ibid.*) The Indian name for the Bronck tract, however, was *Ranachque* or *Raraque*. The tract commonly called by the English the "White Plains," was known to the Indians as *Quaroppas*. Verplanck's point was called *Meahagh*, and the lands immediately east, *Appamaghpogh*. *Poningo*, the name of the residence of one of the chiefs of the *Siwanoys*, embraces the tract of land now included in the towns of Rye and Harrison. Rye Neck was called *Apawquammis*. The town of Morisania was known as *Ranachque* or *Raraque*. The towns of New Castle and Bedford occupy a tract called *Shappequa*, a name now applied to the Shappequa hills, and destined to be remembered from its recent association with the name of Mr. Horace Greeley. The west neck adjoining New Rochelle was called *Magopson*. The Byram river was known by the name of *Armonck*, and the meadows bordering it *Haseco* and *Miosehassaky*. Harlem river was called *Muscoota*; Blind brook, *Mockquams*, and the high ridge east of it, *Enketaupuenson*; Beaver dam or Stony Brook, *Pockestersen*, and Delancey's neck, *Waumainuck*. A tract called *Rippowams*

[1] The name is applied to the entire range both in New Jersey and New York.

fell to the share of the people of Stamford, Conn., in 1655. It extended eighteen miles north and south, and eight miles east and west.

In the town of Carmel, in the county of Putnam, is located Lake *Macookpack*, now *Mahopack*, a term probably signifying simply a large inland lake, from *ma* large water and *aki* land. The same name was applied to what is now known as Copake lake in Columbia county. The lake is nine miles in circumference, and is situated about eighteen hundred feet above the level of the sea. On one of the islands of the lake is what is called the Chieftain's rock, on which was held, according to tradition, the last council of the tribe. This council was for the purpose of considering the proposition of the English to buy their lands and remove the tribe to the far west. Canopus, the aged sachem of the tribe, urged his followers to reject the proposal; to rally to the defense of their empire, and the graves of their fathers. His impassioned eloquence determined the council against the proposition. JOHN W. LEE, Esq., of New York, has thrown this legend into the following verse:

" Once the airy curtain lifted, and the shadows rolling back,
Shadows of the years that hover o'er the lake of Mahopac —
Showed me Indian warriors gathered in the wooded island dell,
Which the rocks, all worn and moss-clad, and the waters guarded well.
\* \* \* \* \* \* \* \* \* \*

Then upon the ledge above them, rose an aged, yet stalwart form,
Like some monarch of the forest, bending never to the storm,
Rose the CHIEFTAIN OF THE ISLAND, with that bearing of a king,
Which the pride of birth may strive for, but the SOUL alone can bring.

Turned his eagle gaze upon them, and with voice as clarion clear,
Waked the dreamers, and the waiting, wearied MAIDEN sleeping near:
" Rouse, Mahicans! sons of heroes! keep your ancient honor bright!
I have seen you in the battle — ye were lions in the fight.

" I have seen you in the council, when the watch-fire lit the glen,
And the clouds of war hung o'er us — ye were all undaunted then;
When the faggots blazed around you, all defiant in your pain;
I have heard you chant your death-song — chieftains, NOW be men again!

"Snake or traitor hissed that whisper: 'Sell your forests, there is rest
On the banks of the Mississippi, on the prairies of the west.'
Who the craven counsel uttered? Let him in the fire-light stand!
Nay, he dares not. Crouching coward! palsied be thy trembling hand!

"When the pale-face, rushing on thee, grasps thy hatchet and thy bow!
Hark, the Spirit! 'Stand, Mahicans; guard your forests, meet the foe!'
By the memory of our empire; by the mounds along the bank,
Where our fathers hear the moaning of the river Kicktawanc!

"Brothers! gird ye for the struggle; breast to breast, and eye to eye,
Let us swear the oath of glory — one to conquer, one to die!
Sound once more your ancient war cry! Sound it from the mountain's steep,
Where the eagle hath her eyrie, and the rocks their vigils keep.

"Twice ten thousand shouts shall answer from the river to the sea!
Dare, nor falter! Fear is failure. Craven-hearted, will ye flee?
Go! yet on the darkening future, read the sentence of your doom,
As, in letters of the lightning, traced upon a scroll of gloom!

"Go! the western tribes shall meet you, ye will be an handful then,
And shall perish in your weakness — perish from the minds of men!
Like yon rushing highland river, in its mountains wild and free,
In the ocean lost forever. Thus shall be your destiny."

The Highlands of the Hudson were not called Matteawan mountains, as stated by Moulton. The Indians had no names for mountain ranges, but designated different parts or peaks by different names. In the patent known as the Little Nine Partners, one of the more eastern peaks of the Highland range is called *Weputing*, from *Weepitung*, literally tooth mountain, probably from its resemblance to a molar tooth. The nearest approach to a name for the range was that which the Indians sometimes applied to themselves — *Wequehachke*, or "the people of the hill country."[1] The Dutch used Hoogland or Hogeland in speaking of the range, and, like the Indians, gave names to particular peaks, as Anthony's Nose, Dunderberg, Buttaberg, etc.

---

[1] Hogeland, or Hoogland, Dutch for Highlands, a name applied to the Highlands of New York. The Indians called them *Wequehachke*, the hill country.— *Memorials Moravian Church*, 1 ,6.

*Matteawan* was the Indian name for what is now called Fishkill creek; but which the early settlers denominated the "Fresh kil or creek." The meaning of the word has been defined as "good furs," and Moulton has endeavored to associate it with the incantations of Indian priests, but on no positive authority. *Matta*, in the Massachusetts dialect, is the elementary form of negative words, and generally used for *no*; *wa* is inanimate motion. This interpretation applied to the creek, would be "no water" or "little water or motion." Another classification would be *ma*, large water; *tea*, valley or landscape; *wan*, inanimate motion — literally "the large water in the valley," *wan* perhaps referring to that portion of the creek near its confluence with the Hudson.

What is now known as Wappinger's creek, while appropriately preserving the name of its aboriginal owners, was not so called by them, but by the very beautiful name, *Mawenawasigh*. The precise meaning of the phrase cannot be given. *Ma* is the Algonquin for large water; *we* is also water; *na* is excellence, fairness, abundance, something surpassing; *wasigh* is apparently a corrupt rendering of *wassa*, light or foamy water. A large stream of excellent water, or a large waterfall, would seem to cover the original definition. Such names are beautiful without interpretation, and far more appropriate than many English geographical terms. Wappinger's Falls, the name of the village near the locality from which it takes its name, might well be changed to *Mawenawasigh*.

*Apoquague* was the Indian name of what is now called Silver lake, in Fishkill. The name signifies "round pond." *Wiccopee* was the Indian name of the highest peak in the Fishkill mountains on the south border of East Fishkill, and also of the pass or gorge in the mountains through which the Indian trail formerly ran. An Indian castle is traditionally located here, and another at *Shenandoah*. It is said that at Fishkill hook remains of an Indian burial ground have been found, and also that apple trees planted by them were still bearing within the memory of the earlier inhabitants.

An explanation of *Wappingers* may be proper in this connection. Although passed irrevocably into history, the term is a corruption of *wabun*, east, and *acki*, land which, as applied by the Indians to themselves, may be rendered Eastlanders, or Men of the East. The French preserved the original very nearly in *Abenaqué*, and Heckewelder in *Wapanachki* (note, ante p. 45). The Dutch historians are responsible for *Wappingers*, perhaps from their rendering of the sound of the original word, and perhaps as expressing the fact that they were, in the Dutch language, *wapen* or half-armed Indians.

Fourteen miles west of the Hudson and a few miles north of Poughkeepsie was *Querapoquett*, from whence the boundary of the Sackett tract ran north-east to a tree on the east side of the *Wesiack* subsequently known as Ten Mile river. Of the Indian name, O'Callaghan says: " *Wissayck*, rocky country," from *qussuk*, a rock, and *ick*, a locality." A more correct explanation is probably derived from *wassa*, light, and *ick*, locality — the light or bright waters. It was in this district that the Moravians found their fields of labor in the villages of *Shecomeco*, *Wechquadnach* and *Pachgatgoch*. The former name is preserved in that of the stream upon which the village stood, while the second is applied to the lake now called Indian pond.

A tract of meadow land "lying slanting to the Dancing Chamber," north of Wappinger's creek, had for its eastern boundary a creek called *Wynogkee*. Schoolcraft defines Poughkeepsie as signifying safe harbor, from *apokeepsing*; but the interpretation is open to question. In early documents the name is variously spelled. In a deed to Arnot Veil, 1680, covering the tract, the boundaries are described as " beginning at a creek called *Pacaksing*, by the river side ;" in a petition from Wm. Caldwell the orthography is *Pogkeepke*; in an affidavit by Myndert Harmense, it is *Pokeepsinck*; in other papers the prevailing orthography is *Poghkeepke*, and finally it is found applied to a pond of water, lying in the vicinity of the city, and its signification given; or muddy pond, an explanation which accords with the accepted interpretation of *Ramepogh* — a simple generic term for pond, or ponds, modified by locality or character. West of Poughkeepsie, and constituting the boundary of the Veil tract was *Matapan* fall or creek. In the geographical terms of this district *ma*, *mata* and *matea*, frequently occur.

Crum Elbow creek was called *Equorsink*, and the lands adjoining, on the Hudson, *Eaquaquanessink;* so given in a patent to Henry Beekman, the bounds of which ran from the Hudson "east by side of a fresh meadow called *Mansakin* and a small creek called *Mancapawimick*." In a patent to Peter Falconier and others the lands are called *Eaquaquannessinck*, the meadow *Mansakin*, the small creek *Nancapaconick*, and the Crum Elbow *Eaquarysink*. The boundary line of the "Great Nine Partners patent" began "at the creek called by the Indians *Aquasing* and by the Christians Fish creek." The Christians spoken of made free use of the word Fish, no less than three streams emptying into the Hudson being given that name. The signification of the Indian name, however, is not involved in the Dutch designations. In this case *Aquasing* apparently indicates stony, from *qusuk*. Roeloff Jansen's kil was the dividing line between the *Mahicans* and the *Wappingers*, a fact which has not only been already stated but which the reader will recognize in the change in dialect shown in the geographical terms. The creek was called *Sankpenak*. In the Livingston patent, of which it formed the southern boundary, the names of a number of localities are given, and, in some cases, their signification. In his first purchase were "three planes" or tracts of "flat lands" called *Nekankook*, *Kickua*, and *Wicquaskaka*, lying on the Hudson between "a small creek or kil" lying over against Katskill, called *Wackanhassack*, and a place called by the Indians *Swaskahamuka*. His second, or *Taghkanick* tract, began at a place called *Minissichtanock;* thence west along a small hill "to a creek" called *Quissicheook ;* thence "to a high place" called *Skaanpook*, which, "a little lower down" is called *Twastawekah ;* then south along the foot of the high mountains "to the path that goes to *Wawijchtanok*, "to a hill called by the Indians *Mananosick ;*" then west to "a creek" called *Nachawawachkano*, "which creek empties into the *Twastawekah*," the place "where the two creeks meet being called *Mawichnanck*." His third purchase began at a creek called *Wachankasigh ;* thence to a place called *Wawanaquassick*, "where the heaps of stones lye," near the head of a creek called *Nanapenahekan*, "which comes out of a marsh lying near unto the said hills of the said heaps of stones upon which the Indians throw another as they pass by, from an ancient custom among them;" then to the "northernmost end of the hills that are to the north of *Tacahkanick*, known by the name of *Ahashewaghkick;*" then "along the said hills to the southernmost end of the same, cailed *Wichquapakkat*." In the line of the boundaries "a rock or great stone" is called *Acawaisik*, and " a dry gully at Hudson's river," *Sackahampa*. *Taghkanick*, the name now applied to the entire range of hills forming the eastern boundary of the manor lands, was originally local, as appears not only from the names given to the north and south ends respectively, but from the fact that the Indians had no titles for entire mountain ranges. The name is pronounced Toh-kon-ick, and is said to have been given to a spring on the west side of the mountains in Copake. Copake lake was called *Kookpake*. (See *Mahopac*.) *Scompamuck* was the name of the locality now covered by the village of Ghent.

*Wawanaquassick*, "where the heaps of stones lye;" has its plural in *wa-wa*; *na* signifies good; *quas* is stone or stones, and *ick* locality. The name is without commemorative character. Of the custom referred to in the quotation, the Rev. Gideon Hawley writes: "We came to a resting place, and breathed our horses, and slaked our thirst at the stream, when we perceived our Indian looking for a stone, which having found, he cast to a heap, which for ages had been accumulating by passengers like him, who was our guide. We inquired why he observed that rite. He answered that his father practised it and enjoined it on him. But he did not like to talk on the subject. I have observed in every part of the country, and among every tribe of Indians, and among those where I now am in a particular manner, such heaps of stones or sticks collected on the like occasion as the above. The largest heap I ever observed, is that large collection of *small* stones on the mountain between Stockbridge and Great Barrington. We have a Sacrifice rock, as it is termed, between Plymouth and Sandwich, to which stones and sticks are always cast by Indians who pass it. This custom or rite is an acknowledgment of an invisible being. We may style him the unknown

God, whom this people worship. This heap is his altar. The stone that is collected is the oblation of the traveler, which, if offered with a good mind, may be as acceptable as a consecrated animal. But perhaps these heaps of stones may be erected to a *local* deity, which most probably is the case."

There has always been manifested a disposition to invest the unexplained customs of the Indians with suppositions and superstitions. Mr. Hawley's description is marred in this respect. The custom referred to had nothing of worship in it, nor was it in recognition of an " unknown God," or of a " local deity." The stone heaps were always by the side of a trail or regularly traveled path, and usually at or near a stream of water. The Indians paused to refresh themselves, and, by throwing a stone or a stick to a certain place, indicated to other travellers that a friend had passed.

*Twastawekak*, was the name of what is now known as Klaverack creek. *Machackoesk* was the name of a tract lying on both sides of Kinderhook creek ; *Pomponick* that of another tract in the same vicinity, and *Kenaghtequak* that of a small creek. The New England path, one of the routes of travel between the Indians of the Hudson and those of the east, ran along a portion of the boundary line of the Kinderhook patent. Kinderhook is Dutch of course, but is said to have had its origin in the fact that the point was a favorite place for the children of the Indians to practice their games, and perhaps the only point at which they could be observed from vessels passing on the river, as the Dans-Kammer was the only point at which devil worship was similarly observed. There is a fragrance in the fact that makes the name more palatable than most of the Dutch geographical terms.

*Schodac*, to which tradition assigns the important position of the capital of the *Mahicans* at the time of the discovery, is now covered by the village of Castleton. The name is from *skootag*, fire, and *ack*, place.

*Sannahagog* is the name given for the tract of land extending on the east side of the river from Beeren island to Smack's island. Beeren island was called *Passapenock* and subsequently, Mahican island. It was occupied by the *Mahicans* until the war of 1689, when they were "persuaded to goe and live at Katskill," where they would be in greater readiness for the public service. *Cachtanaquick* is described as an island over against Beeren island. The island opposite Albany known as Smack's, was called " *Schotack* or Aepjen's island." *Poetanock* was the name for Mill creek, opposite Albany, and *Semesseeck* that for a tract through which it passed. Another tract adjoining took its name from its owner, *Paep-Sikenekomtas*, abbreviated to *Papsickenekas*. *Petuquapoen* and *Tuscumcatick* are names applied to what is now Greenbush. *Keeseywego* was the name of a kil opposite Albany, described as being " 1200 rods from Major Abram Staets's kil." *Paanpaack* was the name of the tract now covered by the city of Troy. *Taescameasick* and *Sheepshack* are now covered by Lansingburgh, and *Popquassick*, which is described as " a piece of woodland on the east side of the river near a small island commonly known as whale fishing island," is also supposed to be a part of the town of Lansingburgh. *Panhoosick* was the name of a tract north of Troy, and is still preserved in that of one of the towns of Rensselaer county and in Hoosick river. A small stream flowing into the Hoosick from the south was called *Tomhenack* creek, and one from the north bore the name of *Poquampacak*. Further east the *Wallomschock*, after taking in several tributary mountain streams from Vermont, adds its waters in considerable volume. The Indian village of *Schaticook* which stood at the confluence of the Hoosick and Hudson, has already been referred to. *Dionondahowa* is given as the Indian name for the falls on the Batten kil below Galesville, Washington county, and *Tioneendogahe* to the kil itself. (*Patent to Schuyler.*) The same name was also applied to the outlet of Lake George, now called *Ticonderoga*, by which it is known in its many historic associations. It is a generic term and appears under different orthographies and interpretations. " *Tionderoga*, meaning the place where two rivers meet. The French called it Carillon, on account of the noise of the waterfall at the outlet." (*Brodhead.*) " *Tsinondrosie*, or *Cheonderoga*, signifying brawling water, and the French name, Carillon, signifying a chime of bells, were both suggested by the noise of the rapids." (*Ga-*

*zetteer.*) "*Dionderoga,* 'place of the inflowing waters;' *Ticonderoga,* from *ti,* water; *on,* hills; *dar,* precipitous rocks, and *oga,* place." (*Schoolcraft.*) *Quequicke* was the name of the falls on the Hoosick east of the bounds of Schaticook, now known as Hoosick Falls. In answer to the claim that the Hoosick takes its name from Abraham Hoosac, one of the early settlers, is the positive assertion, in one of the first patents, that a tract, "twenty-five English miles north-east of the city of Albany," was "known by the Indian name of *Hoosack.*" The name is from *hussun,* stone, and *ack,* place — literally "stony country." A strata of round stones, such as are used for street pavements, apparently underlies the entire valley.

On the west side of the Hudson and the harbor of New York are the *Neversink* hills. The name, according to Schoolcraft, is from *onawa,* water, between the waters, and *sink,* a place; but this interpretation appears to be forced. The word probably signifies a place abounding in birds. Hudson found the Indians there "clothed in mantles of feathers. *Amboy,* according to Heckewelder, is from *emboli,* and signifies a place resembling a bowl or bottle. *Epating,* in the rear of Jersey city, is from *ishpa,* high, and *ink,* a place — hence *Ishpatink,* or *Espating,* a high place, supposed to be Snake hill. (*O'Callaghan.*) Schoolcraft applies the same term to "the high sandy bank now known as Brooklyn Heights." *Arissheck* was the name of Paulus Hook, now Jersey City. *Hobokenhacking* was the name of the tract now embraced in the site of Hoboken, and is said to have meant tobacco pipe. The term was frequently used to express crookedness, and in this instance was applied to the form of the river shore. *Raritan,* a forked river; *Passaic,* from *Pakhsajek,* a valley; *Gamoenapa,* the aboriginal for Communipau; the Raritan Great Meadows were called *Man-kack-ke-wachky; Wiehacken* is still preserved in the name of Wehawken; Hackinsack river perpetuates the name of the Hackinsacks and is the modern rendering of the original *Ack-kin-kas-hacky.* The name is said to mean, "the stream that unites with another in low level ground." *Haquequenunck,* sometimes spelled *Aquackanonk,* was the name for the ract now covered by the city of Patterson, and *Totama* the name of the falls — a word signifying to sink, to be forced down under weight by water. *Watchtung* — literally mountain — was the name of a range of hills lying some twelve miles west of the Hudson; *Ramspook* or *Ramapo*, a river into which empties a number of round ponds; *Pompton*, "crooked mouth," referring to the manner in which the Ringwood and Ramapo rivers pass down and discharge themselves into the *Pompton*.

It is said that the *Tappans* derived their name from *Tuphanne*, a cold stream, signifying the people of the cold stream. *Kumochenack* was the name for Haverstraw bay. A small stream flowing into the Ramapo river was the *Chesekook*, a name also applied " to a tract of upland and meadow " embraced in and known as the " Chesekook patent," which covered a large portion of the original county of Orange, now Rockland. A small stream emptying into the Hudson just below Stony point, was called *Minnisconga*, from *minnis* an island, *co* or *con*, object, and *ga* a place, referring without doubt to Stony point itself which was then an island. The site of the present town of Orangetown was called the *Narrasunck* lands as late as 1769, a name which probably has its signification in *na* and *unk*, " good land." Verdrietig hook, or Tedious point, as the Dutch called it from the fact that it was generally so long in sight from their slow-sailing sloops, was called *Quaspeck*, from *qusuk*, a stone.

Opposite Anthony's Nose, was a " small rivulet called by ye Indians *Assinnapink*," or " the stream from the solid rocks." South of this rivulet was *Tongapogh* kil, and north of it *Pooploop's* kil, the latter apparently the name of an Indian owner. Buttermilk falls were called the Prince's falls, evidently from their ownership by a prince of " the people of the hill country." Plum point, north of the Highlands, was called *Cowonham's* hill, and the rocky island lying opposite, *Poleber's* island, which has been corrupted into Pallopel's island, and invested with a Dutch tradition which is not its own.

That which has been known as the Murderer's creek, from a period anterior to Van der Donck's *Map of New Netherland* (1656), enters the Hudson at Cornwall, and originally formed the starting point for the line which divided the counties of Orange and Ulster. That its name was derived from some unexplained event or hostile action on the part of the Waoranecks appears to be conclusively established from the fact that it was applied to it only until it reached the castle of that chieftaincy on the north spur of *Schunemunk* mountain, about seven miles from its mouth. Tradition affirms in explanation, that at an early period a company of traders entered the creek with their sloop and were enticed on shore, where they were murdered on a hill still known as Sloop hill in commemoration of the event; and this explanation is strengthened by the fact that the name of the hill is coexistent with that of the creek. It is here that Paulding locates his beautiful story of *Naoman*, so generally accepted as history:

"Little more than a century ago, the beautiful region watered by this stream was possessed by a small tribe of Indians, which has long since become extinct, or incorporated with some other savage nation of the west. Three or four hundred yards from where the stream discharges itself in the Hudson, a white family, of the name of Stacy, had established itself in a log house, by tacit permission of the tribe, to whom Stacy had made himself useful by a variety of little arts, highly estimated by the savages. In particular, a friendship existed between him and an old Indian, called Naoman, who had often came to his house and partook of his hospitality. The Indians never forgive injuries nor forget benefits. The family consisted of Stacy, his wife, and two children, a boy and a girl, the former five, and the latter three, years old.

"One day Naoman came to Stacy's hut in his absence, lighted a pipe, and sat down. He looked very serious, sometimes sighed very deeply, but said not a word. Stacy's wife asked him what was the matter — if he was sick. He shook his head, sighed, but said nothing, and soon went away. The next day he came again and behaved in the same manner. Stacy's wife began to think strange of this, and related it to her husband, who advised her to urge the old man to an explanation, the next time he came. Accordingly, when he repeated his visit, the day after, she was more importunate than usual. At last the old Indian said: 'I am a red man, and the pale faces are our enemies; why should I speak?' 'But my husband and I are your friends; you have eaten salt with us a hundred times, and my children have sat on your knees as often. If you have anything on your mind, tell it me." "It will cost me my life if it is known, and the white-faced women are not good at keeping secrets," replied Naoman. "Try me and see." "Will you swear, by your Great Spirit, that you will tell none but your husband?" "I have none else to tell." "But will you swear?" "I do swear, by our Great Spirit, I will tell none but my husband." "But if my tribe should kill you for not telling?" "Not if your tribe should kill me for not telling."

"Naoman then proceeded to tell her, that, owing to some encroachments of the white people below the mountains, his tribe had become irritated, and were resolved, that night, to massacre all the white settlers in their reach; that she must send for her husband, inform him of the danger, and as speedily and as secretly as possible, take their canoe and paddle with all haste over the river for safety. "Be quick, and do nothing that may excite suspicion," said Naoman, as he departed. The good wife sought her husband, who was on the river fishing, told him the story, and, as no time was to be lost, they proceeded to their boat, which was unluckily filled with water. It took some time to clean it out, and meanwhile, Stacy recollected his gun which had been left behind. He proceeded to the house and returned with it. All this took up considerable time, and precious time it proved to this poor family. The daily visits of old Naoman, and his more than ordinary gravity, had excited suspicion in some of the tribe, who had, accordingly paid particular attention to the movements of Stacy. One of the young Indians, who had been kept on the watch, seeing the whole family about to take to the boat, ran to the little Indian village about a mile off, and gave the alarm. Five Indians collected, ran down to the river where their canoes were moored, jumped in and paddled after Stacy, who, by this time, had got some distance out in the stream. They gained on him so fast that twice he dropped his paddle and took up his gun. But his wife prevented his shooting, by telling him that, if he fired, and they were afterwards overtaken, they would meet with no mercy from the Indians. He accordingly refrained, and applied his paddle till the sweat rolled in big drops from his forehead. All would not do; they were overtaken within a hundred yards from the shore, and carried back, with shouts of yelling and triumph.

"When they got ashore, the Indians set fire to Stacy's house, and dragged himself, his wife and children to their village. Here the principal old men, and Naoman among them, assembled to deliberate on the affair. The chief men of the council stated, that some one of the tribe had, undoubtedly, been guilty of treason, in apprizing Stacy, the white man, of the designs of the tribe, whereby they took the alarm, and well nigh escaped. He proposed to examine the prisoners, to learn who gave the information. The old men assented to this, and Naoman among the rest. Stacy was first interrogated by one of the old men, who spoke English and interpreted it to the others. Stacy refused to betray his informant. His wife was then questioned, while at the same moment, two Indians stood threatening the two children with tomahawks, in case she did not confess. She attempted to evade the truth, by declaring that she had a dream the night before, which alarmed her, and that she had persuaded her husband to fly. 'The Great Spirit never deigns to talk in dreams to a white woman,' said the old Indian. 'Woman, thou hast two tongues and two faces. Speak the truth or thy children shall surely die. The little boy and girl were then brought close to her, and the two savages stood over them ready to execute his bloody orders.

"'Wilt thou name,' said the old Indian, 'the red man who betrayed his tribe? I will ask three times.' The mother answered not. 'Wilt thou name the traitor? This is the second time.' The poor woman looked at her husband, and then at her children, and stole a glance at Naoman, who sat smoking his pipe with invincible gravity. She wrung her hands, and wept, but remained silent. 'Wilt thou name the traitor? 'Tis the third and last time.' The agony of the mother waxed more bitter; again she sought the eye of Naoman, but it was cold and motionless. The pause of a moment awaited her reply, and the tomahawks were raised over the heads of the children, who besought their mother not to let them be murdered.

"'Stop!' cried Naoman. All eyes were turned upon him. 'Stop!' repeated he, in a tone of authority. 'White woman thou hast kept thy word with me to the last moment. I am the traitor. I have eaten of the salt, warmed myself at the fire, shared the kindness of these Christian white people, and it was I that told them of their danger. I am a withered, leafless, branchless trunk; cut me down if you will; I am ready.' A yell of indignation sounded on all sides. Naoman descended from the little bank where he sat, shrouded his face with his mantle of skins and submitted to his fate. He fell dead at the feet of the white woman by a blow of the tomahawk.

"But the sacrifice of Naoman, and the firmness of the Christian white woman, did not suffice to save the lives of the other victims. They perished — how, it is needless to say; and the memory of their fate has been preserved in the name of the pleasant stream, on whose banks they lived and died, which, to this day, is called the Murderer's creek."

Six miles west of the scene of this tradition is the mountain range called *Schunemunk*, or, as in the early deeds, *Skonnemoghky*, on the northern spur of which, and near its base was the castle or village of the clan to whom it refers, and where they continued to reside until after considerable settlements had been made around them. The name is also spelled *Skonanoky*, and is apparently derived from *Shunna*, sour, and *na* excellent, *nuk*, local — probably referring to the abundance of wild grapes found there. On the east side of the mountain, in the town of Cornwall, and near the centre of the Wilson patent, was an Indian burial grond, so designated in a survey by General James Clinton. In its vicinity on the north is a hill which was called *Winegtekonk*, now known as Woodcock mountain. Further west, in the town of Goshen, what is called Run-bolt's-run, preserves in its name and source, the name and place of residence of *Rombout*, one of the chiefs who signed the deed for the Wawayanda tract, whose wigwam stood beside the spring from which the stream flows. A modern tradition associates the name of *Wawastawa*, another of the grantors of the tract, with the stream, through his daughter, to whom a Frenchman named Boltez made love. The maiden rejected his suit and fled towards her father's cabin. Just then her father's shrill whistle was heard, and she paused in her flight and exclaimed, " Run, Bolt, Run ! " an exclamation which, when the story came out, was applied to the streamlet. On Sugar Loaf mountain, in Chester, was an Indian village and burial ground some time after the advent of the whites. It is said that the chieftaincy located here paid tribute to the Senecas as late as 1756. *Mistucky*, a locality in Warwick, is probably an abbreviation of *Miskotucky*, a compound word implying red hills or red plains. *Pochuck*, a name applied to one of the streams of that town as well as to the district known as Florida, seems to retain the root term for bog or muddy land.

*Jogee Hill*, in the town of Minisink, takes its name from and preserves the place of residence of *Keghgekapowell* alias *Joghem*, one of the grantors of lands to Governor Dongan in 1684. A considerable canton is said to have resided in the vicinity at an early period, and that *Joghem* remained an occupant of this hill long after his brethren had departed for the west. Arrowheads and small images of various kinds have been found here, and among other articles an Indian tomahawk the whole of which is a pipe, the pole being the bowl, and the handle the stem. *Minnisink* is from *Minnis*, an island, and *ink*, locality, and not from *Minsis*, the name of the wolf tribe of the Lenapes. The name has a very general application to lands, in Pennsylvania as well as New York, known as the Minnisink country. It had its origin in the tradition that the land was covered with water before the Delaware broke through the mountain at the water gap, or Pohoqualin, and is said to mean the land from which the water is gone.

Entering the Hudson south of Newburgh is *Quassaick* creek. The name is from *qussuk*, a stone, and the signification stony brook. Partly in Newburgh and partly in New Windsor is what is called *Muchattoes Hill*, a name apparently derived from *Muhk*, red ; *at*, near or by, and *os*, small — a small red hill near the river.

North of Newburgh the rocky peninsula known as *Dans-Kammer* point is a feature in the landscape as well as in the history of the river. It was at this place that the Indians held their worship of the devil, on one occasion four or five hundred being seen here engaged in that service. There were two grassy plots on which the dances and other orgies were held, the one called the large Dans-Kammer, and the other the little Dans-Kammer. The first is now occupied by the Armstrong house; the second was on the rocky point which retains the name. The place has its story as well as its history.

"Hans Hansen," the story says, "was the son of Jacobus Hansen, one of the first settlers in the vinicity of Albany, and, except an occasional skirmish with the Indians, had enjoyed undisturbed peace and honor in the small circle that constituted his settlement. He had now arrived at such an age that the affairs of his farm were too fatiguing for his declining years; and Hans being the eldest son, the superintendency necessarily devolved on him; but so important a station could not be properly filled without the assistance of a *vrouw*. Hans accordingly looked among the fair of his acquaintances, and, with the consent of his parents, paid his addresses to Miss Katrina Van Vrooman, whose residence was but a mile from his own habitation. Those were "matter of fact" days, and the girl consented, without any flirtations, to become his wife. The wedding day was appointed, and the neighbors invited; but before the ceremony could be performed, it was necessary to obtain a license from the governor, whose residence was in New York.

"Hans accordingly prepared to go thither for his license, and a party of his young friends, as well as his prospective bride, determined to accompany him. Katrina invited to the excursion an old squaw named Leshee, to whom she was much attached, but who was regarded by some as having intercourse with the Evil One, and was often consulted even in matters of importance by the superstitious Dutchmen. The day of the departure was marked by a severe storm, from which Leshee boded ill-luck; but the party were impatient of delay, and proceeded on their journey.

"The affianced pair, after three days' journey, reached the house of the governor, obtained the necessary license, and then proceeded without delay homeward. On the evening of the sixth day they reached the Dans-Kammer. The place was known to them, and the company resolved to stop there and partake of some refreshments. Leshee remonstrated against visiting the scene of the rites and sacrifices of her tribe, and repeated the old prophetic lines —

> For none that visit the Indian's den
> Return again to the haunts of men ;
> The knife is their doom, oh, sad is their lot ;
> Beware! beware of the blood-stained spot.

But the evening was beautiful, the place attractive, the Indians at peace, their war-whoop hushed and their sacrificial fires extinguished ; hence they resolved to land. Drawing up their boats on the sandy beach, they seated themselves on the site of the Indians' place of worship — partook of their refreshments, joined in the dance, smoked the pipe and told the story.

"In company with one of his friends, Hans wandered over the plain, and on turning espied the sparkling of an eye in a thick cluster of bushes. Knowing that it was no one of his party, he proceeded cautiously, without appearing to observe it, until he came near enough to see it was an Indian, when, raising his rifle and taking deliberate aim, he directed his companion to make close search. Finding but one, they bound him and took him to the company, who were preparing to leave, and some of whom were already in their boats. Hans soon recognized the Indian as one with whom he had recently had trouble. He questioned him closely, but he refused to explain his presence or his purposes. Finding his efforts fruitless, Hans prepared to embark, when the Indian broke the silence by a shrill yell.

"The result was soon manifest. A company of warriors, who had concealed themselves and their canoes above the point, were seen darting forward with appalling velocity. Hans' only hope of escape was his boats. The Indians drew nearer and nearer — they were within an arrow's flight, and yet Katrina and two others were on shore. Hans faltered a moment when he saw the danger to which Katrina was exposed ; but it was momentary. Placing his knife at the breast of his captive, he shouted to the Indians, that if they approached a step, their chief should die; but if they permitted the company to embark, their chief was free. The Indians knew the determination of Hans, and stopped; the females were got on board, and Hans had stepped to shove off the boat. Just then the quick voice of the chief was heard, commanding his warriors to proceed. They hesitated until a reproach from their chief, when they again came forward with the rapidity of thought.

"Death now seemed the immediate doom of the party; but Hans, always ready in emergency, was prompt in this. He placed the chief before him and proceeded in this manner on board his boat. As he expected, the Indians dared not risk their chieftain's life, for they well knew the quick arm of Hans would place him between the arrow and its intended victim. Just at the point of safety, the Indians separated so that they could kill their enemy without endangering the life of their chief. Hans again raised his knife, and proclaimed that the first arrow that flew the chief should die. But the enmity of the chief was stronger than his love of life. He gave the war-whoop — a cloud of arrows darkened the air — the glittering knife descended and the chief was no more. Wounded, Hans stepped on board his boat and shoved off. The Indians flew to their canoes; the pursuit was speedy and the arm of Hans weak from loss of blood. He was soon overtaken and carried back in company with Katrina and her friends. Speedily the bridal pair were tied to trees and tortured in all the ways savage barbarity could devise. Then gathering the materials for the fire, they kindled the flame and celebrated the dance of death around their victims in fiendish glee, until the forms of Hans and his fair bride were mingled with the ashes of the pyre — their embrace of love was at the stake of death.

"The remaining captives were treated more humanely, and were subsequently ransomed by their friends." Such is the tradition.

There is no more familiar name, in Orange county, than that of *Wawayanda*, nor one the significance of which is less clearly known. It first appears in 1703, in a petition from Dr. Staats in which he states that a tract which he had purchased, called

*Wawayanda,* or *Woerawin,* was "altogether a swamp." Its next use is in the deed and patent of Wawayanda, granted in 1703, while yet Staats's petition was under consideration. Staats's purchase was never definitely located, but that it covered a portion of the Drowned lands is known from the fact that the Wawayanda patent included the lands which he claimed. In the deed from the Indians, and in the patent, the description implies that the name embraced more than one tract, the language being "called by the name or names of *Wawayanda;*" while the deed to Staats is apparently located by the name of *Woerawin,* a term which may be derived from *woreco,* handsome, or *wooreecan,* good, or from *wewocan,* from *wewau,* waters, and *wocan,* barking or roaring, a term descriptive of the roaring of waters at a high fall, or in a rushing rapid stream in a flood. The distinction between the terms more clearly appears when considered in connection with the use of local and general terms in other patents. In the deed to Governor Dongan for the Evans patent the language is, "comprehending all those lands, meadows and woods called" by specific names, "together with the hills, valleys, woods," etc., surrounding and adjoining or within a district defined by certain natural boundaries, while *Minnisink* embraced an undefined territory. The explanation would seem to be that *Woerawin* was the name of a particular part of the tract, while *Wawayanda* was a *district* embracing several well known and occupied lands, or a *village* and its dependencies. This explanation accords with the name itself. *Wa,* according to Schoolcraft, is a reflective plural and may mean *he* or *they,* or, by repetition, *we;*[1] it has no descriptive significance whatever. *Aindau-yaun* is my home; *Aindau-yun,* thy home; *Aindau-aud,* his or her home; *da,* town or village. From these terms we have *Wa-wa-yaun-da,* signifying "our homes or places of dwelling," or "our village and lands." Accepting the last, we find on the tract a Long house, situated on what is still called Long house creek, which was undoubtedly the seat or castle of the canton.

---

[1] Substantives are generally combined with inseparable possessive pronouns prefixed. The duplication *nana, wawa, wawall,* distinguishes the double plural, or combination of both the noun and possessive pronoun in the plural ('our fathers').—*Zeisberger's Grammar.*

The stream of water now known as the Tinbrook,—from the German Tinn Brock, or thin brook,—was called by the Indians *Arackhook*, or *Akhgook*, the Delaware term for snake, the reference no doubt being to the extremely sinuous course of its flow, which resembles the contortions of a snake when thrown upon a fire. In 1701, Robert Sanders[1] filed a petition for a patent to a tract of land described as " beginning at a fall (*i. e.*, a stream of water) called *Arackhook* and running thence *northerly* on the *east* side of the Paltz creek until it comes to a place called *Kackawawook*, and from thence due east four miles into the woods, and from thence parallel to Paltz creek until a due west line shall touch the aforesaid fall." He stated that he had held the land since June 4th, 1689 ; that all the Indians formerly owners were dead, and asked that a patent be issued to himself, his son Thomas, and Johannes Bush, William, Sharpas, and Joseph Cleator. He renewed the petition, April 18th, 1702, calling the tract *Oghgotacton*, and stated that his title was derived from a loan which he had made to the Indian proprietor, who, as well as all his relations, were then dead. In confirmation of his claim he presented the following paper :

" Whereas, *Pungnanis* is indebted to Robert Sanders the value of seventy pounds, and being ten years gone to the *Ottowawas*, and his brother *Corpowin*, now going to the war, desires that ye said Robert Sanders may keep the land of his brother, called *Oghotacton*, till his brother pays him the said sum of seventy pounds,[2] Robert Sanders comes to me to ask for leave to take this land from the said *Corpowin*, and I do give him authority to take," etc., etc. Signed by Gov. Dongan, June 4, 1689.

A patent was issued to Sanders under this petition, but, for some reason which does not appear, was not taken up by him.

---

[1] Robert Sanders, of Albany, was a distinguished and intelligent Indian trader. He became well versed in the languages, both of the Mohawks and the River Indians, and acted as interpreter between them and the English on several occasions. He enjoyed the confidence of the Indians to a high degree, and was made governor of Schenectady, occupying that post at the time of the massacre. He was particularly designated, by Mr. Miller, as a proper person to furnish the government information in regard to the condition of Canada. He rendered himself so obnoxious to the French governor there, in consequence of his opposition to the Jesuit missionaries among the Five Nations, that he was the subject of special complaint to Governor Dongan in 1687.—*Munsell's Annals of Albany*.

[2] Less then seventy dollars of United States currency.

On the 30th of June, 1712, a patent was issued to Henry Wileman covering the same tract but extending its boundaries west to the falls in the Walkill at Walden, the inference doubtless being that the word "fall" in Sanders' boundary had reference thereto. The Tinbrook enters the Walkill on the east about half a mile from the falls at Walden.

Much has been written in explanation of the word *Shawangunk*, and yet the solution of the term is far from satisfactory. The Rev. CHARLES SCOTT, in a paper read before the Ulster Historical Society,[1] remarks very properly that the interpretation by Schoolcraft, so extensively copied, that the word means white rocks, from *shawan*, white, and *gunk*, rock — alluding to the white cliffs which face the mountains west of Tuthiltown, is not sustained by any known vocabulary of Indian dialects. The word comes down to us in two principal forms, *Shawangunk* and *Chawangong*, the first in the Dutch records of the Esopus wars, and the second in some of the early English patents. In the deed to Governor Dongan, in 1684, it is specified as a certain tract of land, the language being, "all those lands, meadows and woods called Nescotack, Chawangon," etc. The patent to Thomas Lloyd, Feb. 22, 1686, is described as at the place called by the Indians *Chawangong*. Says Mr. SCOTT of the latter: "This tract of land was situated on the west side of Shawangunk kil, and north of what is now known as McKinstry's tannery. The next locality, to the north, was named by the Indians *Nescotonck*. On the south was *Schanwemisch*, or as the Dutch pronounced it, *Wishauwemis*, the beech woods, or place of beeches." In this manner he localizes the application of the name. He continues:

"This fixes with some accuracy the bounds of the original Indian Shawangunk. It was a section of fine low land, situated mainly on the west side of Shawangunk kil, for about five miles, from near the mouth of the Mary kil, to the mouth of the Dwars kil. Two miles to the west, and near the foot of the mountain, was a flat called *Weighquatenheuk*, the place of willows; and about two miles east, on the Wallkill, another fine region of meadow and maize fields, which they designated

[1] Vol. I, part III, 229, etc., of *Proceedings*.

*Wanoksink*, or the place of sassafras. It was the seat of the main settlement of the Esopus tribe, on the east side of the mountains, and had, on its southern border, the village, or castle, which was destroyed by the Dutch in September and October, 1663. This, and nothing else, was the Shawangunk of the red man. From thence the name began to spread, when the country was opened to European settlement, until it became widely used. First, the kil was made to assume it, instead of its appropriate *Achsinink;* then the settlers along the kil for miles were said to have it for their home; then the mountains or high hills running from Rosendale to Minnisink, were thus designated; and finally the precinct and afterwards the township. And here let it be remarked that the name belongs in no sense whatever to the mountains now bearing it. The Evans patent calls them the high hills of *Pitkiskaker* and *Aioskawosting*. In local records, they are for years termed simply the high hills or the steep rocks.

After a careful analysis of the word, he concludes:

"I venture to interpret: *Shawangum* — south water. Shawangunk, etc., the place on or at the south water, water being referred to generically, and not specifically, as the proper name of the kil. But to what kil and to what locality is Shawangunk relatively south? Take the map of Ulster county, and notice the position, in respect to each other of the Rondout and of the Shawangunk kils; and remember that the Indian paths from one valley to the other, ran almost due north and south, and one good reason is manifest. The warrior and the hunter passed either from the north part of Shawangunk proper through the traps, to Marbletown, or from the south part of the same, by Awosting lake — the Long pond — to the Kerhonkson. Stand upon the mountain top and glance down either path, to the winding streams, and upon their corn fields, and the meaning of the north water or the south water, can be easily understood. Again, at either terminus of the Aioskawosting, or southern path, were Indian villages and settlements of cultivated fields. The one was on the north water and the other on the south, for in truth they thus stood towards those opposite points of compass. The above mentioned villages became afterwards the sites of the old fort and the new fort, mentioned in the second Esopus war."

While Mr. Scott's investigation has brought out many facts of interest, it is not clear that he is correct in locating the name, or in explaining its meaning. If the name relates to a particular tract of land, then in that tract must be found its explanation; if in any stream of water, as the south water, its explanation must be sought there. The solution may be in one of the paths or trails which he describes as crossing the mountain and extending into the southern country, one of which was taken by the Long Island Indians who accompanied Kregier's expedition, in 1663, being the shortest route to their homes. This trail continued across the present county of Orange, where it formed one of the boundary lines of the lands of Christopher Denn, and is described in one of his deeds as the Chauwungonk path. It connected with the main trail which ran from Hackinsack to the Minnisink country, partially described in the *Journal of Arent Schuyler* in 1694. Whether called the north or south trail it led to and took its name apparently from one particular locality. This locality would seem to be indicated in the word itself. The first part or noun of the word, *shawan* or *chawan*, would seem to be from *jewan*, swift current or strong stream; *onk* or *gonk*, a place, literally the country of the strong stream, or the rapid water settlement, or if interpreted in connection with some part of the Wallkill, as indicating a specific portion of the Chawangong trail, the reference may be to a place where the shallowness of the current gave to it rapidity and yet afforded a fording or crossing place. To precisely such a place the trail in question led and the ford there established was not only used by the Indians and the early settlers, but is still used as such. Another interpretation is derived from *shong'*, the Algonquin for mink, and *um* or *oma*, water, or *onk*, a place or country. This would give the mink river, or the mink country. Still another is derived from *cheegaugong*, the place of leeks, and has no little force in the abundance of wild onions which are still found in that section of country. Indeed, so universal is this pest of the farmer there, that they might well have given their name to the stream, the valley, and the mountains.

The name of the Indian castle destroyed by Kregier, and which is described "as being situated at the head of the Kerhonkson," has not been preserved, unless it has that preservation in the name of the creek itself. It is altogether probable that such is the fact as it would accord with Indian custom, as illustrated in the case of the *Pakadasank*, to which reference will be made hereafter. In regard to this fort, as well as that called the New fort, Mr. Scott, in another paper, says :

" From the Delaware to the Hudson there once existed two great pathways of Indian travel. The one started from the mouth of the Neversink or Mahakemack, at Port Jervis, and passing by the ancient Peenpack, and through Mamakating hollow, struck the Rondout at Napanoch. Thence following that stream through Wawarsing and Rochester, it passed over in Marbletown to the Esopus, and skirted the latter to its mouth at Saugerties. The other crossed the mountain range at Minnisink, to the eastern valleys, and followed the Shawangunk, the Wallkill and the Rondout to the Hudson. The first may be distinguished as the Mamakating, and the second as the Shawangunk trail. From trail to trail the cross paths may yet be traced, and in some places have been marked upon the mountain rocks by the passing footsteps of ages."

It was on the Mamakating trail, about twenty-three miles south-west of Kingston, that he locates the Old fort, or that destroyed by Kregier on the 31st of July, and designates its site as being " on the south side of the Kerhonkson, near the line between Rochester and Wawarsing, just north of what is called Shurker's hill, and about three miles from the mouth and at the head of the Kerhonkson." The New fort, or that destroyed on the 4th of October, he says, " was in the town of Shawangunk, on the east bank of the Shawangunk kil, and twenty-eight miles from Kingston." He adds: " Whatever doubts there may be as to the Kerhonkson village, or the Old fort, there can be none as to that situated on the Shawangunk. From the first settlement of the country the place has been called The New Fort. The village which was found abandoned on the 4th of October, was in the vicinity of Burlingham. An Indian burial ground marks the spot, and a path led from thence to the hunting house at Wurtsboro." The site of the New fort, and the trails are described as follows :

"The mouth of the Shawangunk kil is six miles away, and most of that distance is occupied by fine and fertile lowlands. From the water rises an abrupt declivity, of irregular formation, reaching, it may be, an elevation of 75 or 80 feet, and then spreading out into a beautiful sandy plateau of twenty or thirty acres. The hill side is covered with the original forest, and broken up into what seem to be artificial mounds. On the edge of the plain overlooking the creek, the fort was situated, and the wigwams a little distance below. To the north, along the kil, extends a flat of moderate dimensions ; but on the opposite side are some of the finest lowlands in Ulster county. Here the Indians planted their maize, and one spot is yet distinguished as Basha's cornfield. The plateau is covered with flints and arrow-heads, which every ploughing turns up to the hands of those who prize them. From this village a pathway, yet preserved, led across the mountains to Wawarsing and the Kerhonkson settlement, just twelve miles to the north. This was the Wawarsing trail, so well known to all the early inhabitants of Shawangunk and Rochester. Another trail bore off to the traps, and through the clove to Marbletown. And yet a third passed eastward to the Hudson, through Montgomery and New Windsor, and branching, near the Wallkill, to the south, gave access from the Esopus clans, to the wigwams of the Haverstraws and Hackinsacks."

That the valley of the Wallkill was thickly peopled at the time of the discovery, there is no question. Along its banks and tributary streams imperfect but conclusive evidence is found of occupation both by permanent and temporary villages, and in the old patents are many names of localities which investigation would clothe with interest. Skirting along the eastern base of the Shawangunk mountains is a stream called the *Pakadasank* which took its name from an Indian village or castle at its head. The location of this village entered into the discussion in defining the boundaries of the Evans patent, and is referred to, in a paper bearing date in 1756, as follows :

"But what proves that point past contradiction is the description given of the western bounds of Evans's first purchase, which expressly says it extended all along said hills, etc., and the river Pakadasank southerly to a pond called *Mallolausly* (Maretange), lying on the top of the said hills. Nothing could more plainly point out where that pond lies, and which is the right pond, than the river Pakadasank which takes its rise at the foot of the said hills, opposite the said pond and extends *northerly* along the foot of the said hills from a place called Pakadasank, where the Indians who sold the land had a large settlement, and from that place to the head of the said river, and nowhere else, the said river is called by that name. And the said Indian settlement called Pekadasank is said to be included in the first purchase, but the line run from Stony point excludes that land for it is southward of their pond."

The Pakadasank has its source or head in Maretange pond on what was formerly called the *Alaskayering mountains* or Minnisink hills, flows north through the western part of the town of Crawford, and empties into the Shawangunk kil. Another stream, called the Little Pakadasank has similar source and outlet. There is reason for supposing that the Indian village, from which both streams took their name, was in the present town of Crawford, Orange county.

One of the boundaries of the Paltz patent, now known as Paltz point, was called and known by the Indians, *Maggrnapogh*. In the Ulster records is this certificate: "These are to certify that the inhabitants of the towns of New Paltz, being desirous that the first station of their patent named Moggonck might be kept in remembrance, did desire us, Joseph Horsbrook, John Hardenburgh, Roeleft Eltinge, Esq., justices of the Peace for the county of Ulster, to accompany them, and there being Ancrop, the Indian, then brought us to the High Mountain which he named *Maggrnapogh*, at or near the foot of which hill is a small run of water and a swamp which he called Moggonck, and the said Indian Ancrop affirms it to be the right Indian names of the said places as witness our hands this nineteenth day of December, 1722." Ancrop was at that time sachem of the Esopus Indians.

Schoolcraft has preserved a pictographic inscription on the Esopus rocks, "which, from its antiquity and character appears to denote the era of the introduction of fire-arms and gunpowder among the tribes inhabiting that section of the valley of the Hudson."[1] He says:

"The location of the inscription is on the western bank of the Hudson, at Esopus landing. Other indications have been reported, at sundry times, of the skill of these ancient Indians in inscribing figures on rocks. Tracks of human feet are among these objects; but the progress of building in that vicinity, and the existence of but little curiosity on that head, appears to have destroyed these interesting traces of a people who now live only in history. The traditions of Ulster county do not refer to a period when this inscription was not there. The inscription may be supposed, if the era is properly conjectured, to have been made with metallic tools. The lines are deeply and plainly impressed. It is in double lines. The plumes from the head denote a chief, or man, skilled in the Indian medico-magical art. The gun is held at rest in the right hand; the left appears to support a wand. It is in the rampant Indian style. Such an inscription, recording the introduction of the gun, would not be made when that era had long past and lost its interest. Indians never resort to historical pictography when there is nothing new to tell. Thus the Indian pictography throws a little light on the most rude and unpromising scene; and if the sources of these gratifications are but small, we are indebted to them for this little. No attempt of rude nations to perpetuate an idea is ever wholly lost."

*Atkarkarton*, the Indian name for Kingston, was not the name of an Indian village, but for a tract called by the Dutch the Great Plot, or meadow on which the Indians raised corn and beans. *At* is equivalent to *at* or *by* the waters.

Nutten Hook, at Katskil, was called by the Indians *Kockhachchingh*; a place known to the Dutch as the Flying corner, was called by the Indians, *Machawanick*; a small stream which enters "the creek called the Kats kil" on the south, was called *Quatawichnaak*; Silvester Salisbury, in 1678,

---
[1] *History of the Indian Tribes of the United States*, part iii, 73. *Ante*, p. 157.

## APPENDIX. 395

obtained "five great flats or plains" called *Wachachkeek*, *Wichquanachtekok*, *Pachquyak*, *Assiskowachkok*, and *Potick*; a tract sold to Jacob Lockerman was bounded on the south by a creek called *Canasenix*, " east on the river in the Great Imbocht where Loveridge leaves off, called by the Indians *Peoquanackqua*, and west by a place called by the Indians *Quachanock*;" and Henry Beekman had a tract "under the great mountains called Blue hills, by a place called *Kiskatameck*." The *Mahican* village known as *Potick*, was apparently located west of Athens, where the name is preserved in Potick hill and Potick creek, the latter forming the west line of the town. It may be added that the term Katskil was applied by the Dutch as descriptive of the totemic emblem of the Indians, a wolf.

Wanton island, a short distance north of Katskill landing, is the site of a traditionary battle between the *Mahicans* and the *Mohawks*. Like other traditions which are woven into history, the issue involved in the conflict is a pure fiction. The tradition is related by Stone, in his *Life of Brant*, as follows:

"Brown, in his *History of Schoharie*, gives a singular tradition in regard to the kings of the *Mohawks*, of which I have found no other mention. The *Mohawks* and *River Indians* were once bitter enemies, the former becoming the terror and scourge of the latter. Brown states that the last battle between the *Mahicans* and *Mohawks* took place on Wanton island, in the Hudson river, not far from Katskil. The question between them was, which should have the honor of naming their king, or which should have the tribute of the river tribes. Both nations collected their utmost strength upon that island, for the purpose of a final decision, and fought a pitched battle, which continued during the whole day. Towards night, the *Mohawks*, finding that the *Mahicans* were likely to prove an overmatch for them, deemed it necessary to resort to stratagem, for which purpose they suddenly took to flight, and gained another island in the evening. They here kindled a great number of fires, and spread their blankets on some bushes, gathered and disposed around them for that purpose, as though they themselves had encamped by their fires as usual. The

*Mahicans* following on, landed upon the Island in the depth of night, and were completely taken in by the deception. Supposing that the *Mohawks* were sleeping soundly beneath their blankets, after their fatigue, the *Mahicans* crept up with the greatest silence, and pouring a heavy fire upon the blankets, rushed upon them with knives and tomahawks in hand, making the air to ring with their yells as they fell to cutting and slashing the blankets and bushes instead of Indians beneath them. Just at the moment of their greatest confusion and exultation, the *Mohawks*, who had been lying in ambush flat upon the ground at a little distance, poured a murderous fire upon their foes, whose figures were rendered distinctly visible by the light of their fires, and rushing impetuously upon them, killed the greater part and made prisoners of the residue. A treaty was then concluded, by which the *Mohawks*, were to have the king and the *Mahicans* were to hold them in reverence, and call them Uncle. Hendrik was the king first named such by the *Mohawks*, after this decisive victory, " who lived to a great age," says Brown, " and was killed at the battle of Lake George under Sir William Johnson."

The boundary line of the Coeymans tract began at a point on the west shore of the Hudson called *Sieskasin*, described as " opposite the middle of the island called by the Indians *Sapanakock*." *Caniskeck* is also the name for a tract in the town of Coeymans about ten miles south of Albany. *Coxackie* or *Kuxakee* has had several interpretations. Schoolcraft defines it as "the place of the cut banks," where the current deflected against the western shore had gradually worn away the land. O'Callaghan says that the word is a corruption of the Algonquin Kaaks-*aki*, from *Kaak*, a goose, and *aki*, locality, " the country of the wild goose." Another interpretation is *Cooksockuy*, signifying owl-hoot. The most satisfactory explanation will be found perhaps in *co*, object, and *aki*, land, the reference being to the clay banks which rise there to the height of 100 feet, and form a conspicuous object in the river scenery. *Neweskeke* or *Naveskeek*, about ten miles south of Albany, is described as being a corner or neck of land having a fresh water river running to the east of it.

Coeyman's Hollow was called *Achquetuck*, and the creek, *Oniskethau*. Another creek is still known by the Indian name, *Hahnakrois*.

Coeyman's Creek.

*Sunckhagag* is recorded as the name of the tract from Beeren island to Smack's island.[1] The boundaries extended two days' journey into the interior. *Tawalsontha* was the *Mahican* name of the creek now called Norman's kil, in the town of Bethlehem, and *Tawassgunshee* that of the mound on which Fort Orange was erected. Schoolcraft gives *Tawasentha* as the orthography of the former term and regards it as signifying "the place of the many dead," adding that the *Mohawks* once had a village there, and that in excavating the road to Bethlehem an Indian burial ground was opened. But the Mohawks never had a village there, and the interpretation is in apparent violalation of the custom of the Indians in bestowing names. We have yet to find the name of an Indian burial ground, and especially a stream of water and a burial ground bearing the same name.

[1] The name appears on both sides of the river, *ante*, p. 374.

Schenectady[1] is said to signify "beyond the plains." Schoolcraft gives *Con-no-harrie-go-harrie* as the original name of the site of that city, and says "the name is in allusion to the flood wood on the flats." Another authority gives *Oron-nygh-wurriegughre* as the name of the region immediately around the city, but it has been very wisely dropped notwithstanding its signification, maize lands. *Canastagione*, a tract in Albany county, is said to mean the great maize land, from *onuste* (Mohawk) maize, and *couane*, great. It is added that *Niskayunah*, the present name of this tract, is only a variation of *Canastagione*, and is derived from *onatschia* another Iroquois word for maize, the *o* and *t* being dropped. (*O'C.*)

*Saratoga* is said to be derived from *soragh*, salt, and *oga*, a place, the place of the salt springs. Schoolcraft says the word is from *assarat*, sparkling waters, and *oga*, a place, but evidently bases his interpretation on the hypothesis that Saratoga springs are referred to. The name was first applied, however, to the site of the present village of Schuylerville on the Hudson, and in that connection is said to signify swift water. On Sauthier's map the name is given to a lake west of Schuylerville. Gov. Dongan endeavored to reclaim the Mohawk converts from Canada and settle them here in 1687. He writes: "I have done my endeavors and have gone so far in it that I have prevailed with the Indians to consent to come back from Canada on condition that I procure for them a piece of land called *Serachtague* lying upon Hudson's river about forty miles above Albany, and there furnish them with priests." A fort was subsequently erected there and a settlement formed. In the war of 1745, the fort was destroyed by the French, together

---

[1] The Iroquois name for the spot where Albany now stands was *Skenectadea*. In regard to this and other Iroquois geographical names in that vicinity, Dr. Mitchill, in answer to an inquiry from the Rev. Dr. Miller, in 1810, on information from John Bleecker, for many years an interpreter of the Iroquois, as well as from the Oneida chief, Louis, and other Indians, writes that *Canneoganakalonitàde* was their name for the Mohawk river; *Skenectadèa,* the city of Albany; *Ohnowalagàntle*, the town of Schenectady; *Càhohàtatèa*, the north or Hudson river; *Tioghsáhronde*, the place or places where streams empty themselves. "What their etymologies are," he adds, "I have not been able to ascertain, except as to *Skenectadèa*, Albany, which signifies the place the natives of the Iroquois arrived at by travelling through the pine trees."—*Collections of the New York Historical Society*, I, 43.

with about twenty houses; thirty persons were killed and scalped, and about sixty taken prisoners.[1] The Indians were not occupants of the place at the time of this occurrence. Waterford, Saratoga county, was called *Nachtenack*, and the island, known as Long Island, near Waterford, *Quahemiscos*. There is apparently a mixture of the *Mahican* and *Mohawk* dialects in some of the names in this section of the state.

*Cohoes*, a term still preserved in the falls of the Mohawk, was not the name of the falls but of the island below them, and, from its diminutive termal *oes*, is presumed to mean simply a small island. Regarding *co* as expressing object, the first syllable may have reference to the falls, in which case the rendering would be, the island at the falls; or applied to the falls, would class them as *small* compared with Niagara. The term is *Mahican*, and is applied in another form to a district in New Hampshire, the *Coos* country. Van der Donck says of the falls, as they appeared in 1656: " The water glides over the falls as smooth as if it ran over an even wall and fell over the same. The precipice is formed of firm blue rock; near by and below the falls there stand several rocks, which appear splendid in the water rising above it like high turf-heaps, apparently from eight, sixteen, to thirty feet high; very delightful to the eye. The place is well calculated to exalt the fancy of the poets. The ancient fabulous writers would, if they had been here, have exalted those works of nature, by the force of imagination, into the most artful and elegant descriptive illusions. The waters descend rapidly downwards from the falls, over a stony bottom, skipping, foaming and whirling boisterously about the distance of a gun-shot or more."

[1] *Ante*, p. 205.

# ERRATA.

Page 9, 9th line, for *then*, read than.
" 9, 19th line, for *hospitality, so*, read hospitality. So he.
" 18, 11th line, for *Agassis*, read Agassiz.
" 24, 9th line, for *make*, read also.
" 27, 21st line, for *sacrifice and fires*, read sacrificial fires.
" 27, 22d line, for *Kitzinacka* read Kitzinacka.
" 27, 29th line, for *were*, read where.
" 29, 26th line, for *presents be*, read presents were.
" 29, 27th line, for *it*, read was.
" 32, 5th line, for *called*, read asked.
" 63, 3d line, for *at*, read above.
" 66, 14th line, for *causes,,* read cause.
" 87, 10th line, for 1680, read 1630.
" 154, 24th line, for *soon he*, read soon as he.
" 172, 27th line, for *concede*, read accede.
" 176, 13th line, for *permanent*, read their.
" 187, 11th line, for *others* read other.
" 197, 26th line, for *Totaltk*, read Potatik.
" 253, 4th line, for *Mahicans*, read Mohegans.
" 261, 1st line for *predecessors*, read predecessor.

Errors in uniformity of orthography not noted.

# INDEX.

Abenaquis, a Mahican nation, 41; murder Mohawk chiefs, 156; English agree not to assist, 159; made peace with the Iroquois, 183; make peace with the Mahicans, 252; Iroquois refuse to renew war with, 193
Abraham, or Schabash, a Mahican chief, converted by Moravians, 197; made captain by Mahicans, 89; assistant at Gnadenhütten, 89; elected chief sachem of Mahicans of the Delaware, 197
Little, sachem of Lower Mohawk castle, 264; brother of King Hendrik, 313; succeeds King Hendrik, 264
Abrahamsen, Isaac, rescues an Indian boy, 107
Ackhough, sachem of Weckquaesgeeks, 79
Adair, James, theory of, concerning origin of American Indians, 16
Adogbegnewalquo, a Mohawk chief, address of, 141
Aepjin, chief sachem of Mahicans, 58; party to treaty of 1645, 118; totemic signature of, 119; council fire at Schodac, 58; authorized to treat for Esopus Indians, 137
Aepjin's island, 375
Agassiz, theory of, 17
Analysis of tribes and chieftaincies, 71
Andastes, war with the Iroquois, 55
Andros, Governor, offers lands to fugitive Indians, 177; invites Pennacooks to settle at Schaticook, 63
Andriaensen, Maryn, in command at massacre at Corlear's Hook, 106
Ankerop, sachem of Esopus Indians, 201
Ann Hoock, alias Wampage, a chief of Siwanoys, 81
Ann Hutchinson, murder of, 112; daughter of, returned from captivity, 118

Albany, Fort Nassau erected at, 99; Fort Orange erected at, 99; Dutch make treaty with Mahicans and Iroquois at, 54; surrendered to the English, 158; English establish council fire at, 161; council fire removed from, to Mount Johnson, 222; commissioners of congress hold council with Iroquois at, 263; aboriginal name of, 398
Algonquin language, 64; grammar of, 338
Aix la Chapelle, conditions of treaty of, 208
Algonquin nations, 56, 64
Allegewi, tradition concerning, 45
Alliances, how formed, 32
Alliance, nature of, between the Dutch and the Iroquois, 145; of Dutch with Long Island chieftaincies, 124; of English with Iroquois and Mahicans, 158
Ampamit, address of, to Gov. Burnet, 191
Appamanskoch, sachem of Raritans, 90
Aquackanonks, location of, 91
Armies, how composed, 30
Ashhurst, Sir John, buys lands of Waoranecks, 93
Assiapam, sachem of Matinecocks, 74
Assinapink creek, 92, 377
Atkarkarton, Kingston so called, 125, 394
Attention in sickness, 23
Atyataronghta, Louis, captain of Oneidas, aids the Americans, 284
Aupamut, see Hendrik, Captain
Barren Hill, Mahicans in battle of, 286
Bald Eagle, a Lenape chief, death of, 256
Beeren, or Mahican island, 85, 374
Bellomont, Gov., description of an Indian conference, 186
Bennington, battle of, 275
Biographical Sketches, 299
Abraham, Little, sachem of Lower Mohawk castle, 264

## 402    INDEX.

Biographical Sketches, continued —
 Allummapees, chief sachem of Lenapes, 300
 Aupaumut, or Captain Hendrik, chief sachem of Mahicans, 320
 Benevissica, chief sachem of Shawanoes, 306
 Black Kettle, a war-captain of the Five Nations, 316
 Chambers, Captain Thomas, 138
 Corn-planter, a sachem of the Senecas, 317
 Cornstalk, a war-captain of Shawanoes, 306
 Dean, Rev. James, 216
 Garangula, an Onondaga chief, 316
 Johnson, Sir John, 265
 Johnson, Sir William, 260
 Kirkland, Rev. Samuel, 261
 Konapot, John, Captain, a Mahican, 320
 Kryn, war-captain of Caghnawagas, 180
 Logan, a Mingoe chief, 314
 Minichque, a Mahican sachem, 185, 319
 Montour, Catharine, 276
 Nererahhe, chief sachem of Shawanoes, 306
 Netawatwees, chief sachem of Lenapes, 303
 Nimham, Daniel, chief sachem of Wappingers, 329
 Occum, Rev. Samson, a Mahican, 325
 Passaconnaway, chief sachem of Pennacooks, 317
 Paxinos, chief sachem of Shawanoes, 305
 Red Jacket, a Seneca chief, 317
 Saunders, Robert, 357
 Shabasch, or Abraham, a Mahican chief, 328
 Shingas, a Lenape war captain, 219
 Skenando, an Oneida chief, 317
 Soiengarahta; or King Hendrik of the Mohawks, 310; portrait of, 70
 Soquans, a Mahican sachem, 184, 319
 Tadame, chief sachem of Lenapes, 301
 Tamany, chief sachem of Lenapes, 300
 Tecumseh, a Shawanoe chief, 308
 Teedyuscung, chief sachem of Lenapes, 301
 Thayendanega, or Joseph Brant, 313

Biographical Sketches, continued —
 Wasarnapah, or Tyschoop, a Mahican chief, 197, 327
 White Eyes, Captain, chief sachem of Lenapes, 305
Block-houses constructed in Minnisink country, 240
Bloom, Domine, description of Esopus massacre, 147
Boone, Daniel, 257
Bouwensen, Thomas, roasted and eaten by Mohawks, 100
Boquet, Col., expedition of, 246, 248
Braddock, General, 220, 222
Bradstreet, Col., expedition of, 248; opinion of, concerning Iroquois, 249
Brainerd, Rev. David, missionary labors, 196, 198
Brant, Molly, 259, 261, 275
 Joseph, 261, 265; sent to England, 265; accepts war-belts of the crown, 266; organizes warriors in English service, 267; Herkimer holds conference with, 267, 268; descent of, on Wyoming valley, 276; commits depredations in Orange and Ulster, 277; Minnisink, commands massacre at, 278, 279; defeated at Fort Plain, 284; flight of, at Fort Schuyler, 274; efforts of, to arouse western tribes, 290; biographical sketch of, 313
Bull, Captain, son of Teedyuscung, 247
Burgoyne, Gen., expedition of, 273
Burnet, Governor, address to Mahicans, 191
Butler, John, accompanies Guy Johnson, 263
 Walter N., accompanies Guy Johnson, 263; commands in expedition against Mohawk valley settlements, 283; killed by an Oneida warrior, 285
Caghnawaga, Mohawk village of, 61, 97; attacked by Mahicans, 97; destroyed by the French, 97; Dutch embassadors visit, 132; converted by Jesuits, 179, 211; Dutch village at, destroyed by John Johnson, 283
 Nation, or Praying Indians, 179, 211
Calmet, theory of, 16
Canada, settlement of, commenced, 53
Canestogaes, massacre of, 245
Canassatiego, an Iroquois viceroy, speech of, 69
Canopus, sachem of Nochpeems, 80

# INDEX. 403

Captains, war chiefs so called, 31
Captahem, sachem of Aquackanonks, 91
Carnarsees, location of, 72
Cartwright, Col. George, makes treaty with Iroquois, 158
Castles, mode of constructing, 25
Catholic priests, labors of, 166, 168; law in relation to, 176
Cayugas, one of the Iroquois nations, 35; village of, 98; accept the war belts of the English, 273
Chambers, Thomas, Capt. settles at Esopus, 125; biographical sketch of, 133
Champlain, discovers Lake Champlain, 53 aids the Hurons, 53; encourages conversion of Indians, 156
Chaatity of females, 22
Chesekock tract, 83, 377
Chegonoe, sachem of Rockaways, 73
Chekatabut, a Massachusetts Mahican chief, 61
Child birth, 23
Claus, Daniel, 259; appointed superintendent of Canada, 260
Claverack, village of, 63; creek, name of, 63
Clinton, Governor, appeal of, to the Iroquois, 205
DeWitt, theory of, 16
   Gen. James, commands in expedition against Iroquois, 279
   Gov. George, commands in expedition for relief of Schoharie valley, 284
Coginiquant, sachem of Nesaquakes, 74
Colden, Lieut. Gov., 57
Coleman, John, killed by the Indians, 9
Colonists, efforts, of, to secure neutrality of Indian tribes in Revolution, 261
Communipau, aboriginal name of, 90, 376
Conarhanded, sachem of Weckquaesgeeks, 79
Connecticut, agents purchase lands at Wyoming, 216; determine to occupy, 150, 259
Conflict with Indians, at Stony Point, 11; at Shorackappock, 11, 77
Conference at Albany, 1754, 212, at Albany, 1776, 263
Congress, Continental, established three Indian Departments, 263; organizes expedition against the English Indian allies, 279; address of, to Iroquois, 280; treaty of, with Iroquois, 289
Corchaugs, location of, 74
Corlear's Hook, massacre of Indians at, 106, 108; aboriginal name of, 361

Cornbury, Gov., attends conference at Albany, 184.
Cornstalk, commands Lenapes and Shawanoes, 256; biographical sketch of, 307
Corn-planter, a Seneca chief, leads an attack on Oneidas, 282; driven from power by Red Jacket, 290; noticed, 317
Cortland's Ridge, Mahicans in battle of, 287
Couwenhoven, negotiates with Esopus Indians, 151, 154
Cralo, Fort, at Greenbush, 149
Cresap's War, causes of, 255
Croton, traditional sachem of Kitchawongs, 79
Croton river, aboriginal name of, 79, 366
Croghan, George, commissioner to treat with Western Indians, 209; assistant to Sir Wm. Johnson, 250, 259; superintendent of Ohio country, 260
Crown Point, expedition for capture of, failure of, 224
Custalaga, a Lenape chief, removal of, 258
Dans-Kammer, devil worship at, 29, 94; boundary line at the, 93; Couwenhoven at the, 151; tradition of the, 382
Dean, Rev. James, labors of, among Oneidas and Tuscaroras, 261; biographical notice of, 261
Declarations of war, 31
Deeds, explanation of signatures to, 93
DeHart, Balthazar, purchases lands, 92
Denotas, or bags for measuring corn, 26
DeVries, David Pietersen, plantation of, on Staten Island, destroyed, 102; locates among the Tappans, 91; endeavors to prevent massacre of fugitive Indians, 106; plantation of, spared by Indians, 109; negotiates treaty of peace, 109; plantation destroyed, 113
Dieskau, Baron, commands French expedition for reduction of Oswego, 223; mortally wounded in battle at Ticonderoga, 224
Dobb's Ferry, aboriginal name of, 78
Dongan, Gov., purchases lands on the Hudson, 93, 95; endeavors to defeat the operations of the French, 169; gives medals to the Iroquois, 169; appeals to James II, to maintain alliance with Iroquois, 169; asks for Catholic priests, 169

# 404　　INDEX.

Dress, of an Indian belle, 21; Hudson's description of, 8; Verazzano's description of, 19
Dwellings and mode of construction, 24
Du Bois, Mrs. Louis, captured by the Esopus Indians, 153; tradition concerning, 153
Dunmore, Gov., 257
Dutch, neutrality of, in Indian wars, 54; treaty of, with Mahicans, etc., 54; send embassadors to the Mohawks, 132; responsible for the Manhattan wars, 119; responsible for the Esopus wars, 134; surrender province to the English, 158
Eelkins, Jacob, imprisons chief of the Sequins, 100
Emerick, Col., account of battle of Cortland's Ridge, 286, 287
English capture Fort Amsterdam, 158; treaty with the Iroquois, 55, 158; treaty with Mahicans, 158, 160; laws regulating intercourse with the Indians, 162; treaty of Esopus, 163
Eskmoppas, sachem of Rockaways, 73
Esopus, derivation of term, 94; first settlement at, 125; settlers at, abandon lands, 112, 123; first war at, 120; Stuyvesant solicited to protect, 125; buildings destroyed at, 125; new village established at, 128; second war of, 133, 134; torture of prisoners at, 135; village held in siege, 135; peace established at, 142; renewal of hostilities at, 147; new village, destroyed, 147; description of massacre at, 147; peace re-established at, 155; inscription on rocks at, 157, 394
Esopus Indians, chieftaincies of, 94, 95; make peace with the Senecas, 68; first war with the Dutch, 120; sachems solicit peace, 128; Stuyvesant holds conference with, 129; Indians massacred at, 133; renew hostilities, 135; treaty of peace with (1660), 142; Stuyvesant sends chiefs into slavery, 138; demand renewal of treaty, 146; second war with, 147; treaty of peace with (1663), 155; treaty of, with the English, 163; a portion of, remove to Oghawaga, 201, 272; conference with domestic clans, 201; friendly, invited to remove from back settlements, 230; friendly, massacred near Walden, 331; friendly, remove to Ticonderoga, 97, 230; condition of, 1768, 253

Evert Pels, a Dutch prisoner, escapes torture by adoption, 144
Fantinekil, attack on, 277
Festivals, 27, 116
Five Nations, see Iroquois
Fletcher, Gov., 175; hastens to the relief of the Mohawks, 175
Food and mode of preparation, 24
Fort Amsterdam held in siege by the Indians, 113, 123 : surrendered to the English, 158; Nassau, construction of, 99; Necessity, Washington erects, 211; Niagara, erected by the French, 282 ; headquarters of Indians and Tories in war of Revolution, 282; Orange, construction of, 99; Plain, battle of, 284; Schuyler, siege of, 273
Franklin, Benjamin, commands expedition to build Fort at Gnadenhütten, 228
French, employ Catholic missionaries, 168 ; secure treaty of neutrality, with Duke of York, 169; make prisoners of Iroquois chiefs by treachery, 171 ; at war with the Senecas, 171; yield to the demands of the Iroquois, 172; Indian war of 1689, 172; preparation for war, 189; Iroquois and Mahican converts aid, 187; tribes in alliance with, 190; interpretation of treaty of Aix-la-Chapelle, 208 ; erect monuments in Ohio valley, 208 ; Washington defeats near Great Meadows, 210; compel Washington to evacuate Fort Necessity, 211; liberality of, to Indian allies, 211 ; surrender possession of Canada, 243 ; changes in relation with Indian tribes caused by withdrawal of the, 249; residents of the Ohio valley encourage hostilities against the English, 257; Mohawks agreement of, with Iroquois, 204
Frontenac, Count de, governor of Canada, 173; plans expeditions against the English, 173; invades the Mohawk country and destroys their castles, 175 ; invades the Onondaga country, 176
Galissonière, commissioned to occupy Ohio valley, 208
Gallatin, Hon. Albert, statement of, concerning subjugation of Mahicans, 56
Garangula, a chief of Onondagas, 316
Gardiner, Lion and David, 76
German Flats, commissioners of congress held conference with Iroquois at, 263

# INDEX. 405

Gil, sachem of Seatalcats, 74
Gist, Christopher, commissioned to treat with Western tribes, 209
Geographical nomenclature, 361
  Accopogue, village of, Long Island, 365
  Alipconck, Tarrytown, 366
  Appamaghpogh, near Verplanck's Point, 367
  Aquehung, or Byram river, 367
  Apawquammis, Rye Neck, 367
  Armonck, Byram river, 367
  Apoquague, Silver Lake, Dutchess county, 370
  Assinnapink creek, Orange county, 377
  Arackhook, Tinn Brock, Orange county, 387
  Alaskayering mountains, Orange county, 393
  Ackkinkashacky, Hackinsack, 396
  Amboy, New Jersey, 376
  Arissheck, Paulus Hook, 376
  Atkarkarton, Kingston, 394
  Achquetuck, Coeyman's Hollow, 397
  Achsinink, Shawaugunk kill, 389
  Aioskawosting, Shawangunk, Ulster county, 389
  Chesekook, Rockland county, 377
  Cowonham's hill, Plum point, 377
  Cachtanaquick island, 375
  Caniskeck, Coeymans, 396
  Coxackie, Greene county, 396
  Canastagione, Niskayunah, 398
  Cohoes Falls, 399
  Dionondahowa, falls on Batten kil, 370
  Equorsink, Crum Elbow, 372
  Gamoenapa, Communipau, 376
  Huppogues, Smithtown, Long Island, 365
  Hobokenhacking, Hoboken, 376
  Haquequenunck, Patterson, 376
  Hannakrois creek, 397
  Hoosack, Rensselaer county, 376
  Ishpatinck, Brooklyn Heights, 376
  Jogee Hill, Orange county, 382
  Kapsee, Copsie Point, New York, 361
  Kitchawonck, Croton river, 366
  Kittatenny, Anthony's nose, 367
  Kookpake Lake, Columbia county, 373
  Keeseywego, creek opposite Albany, 375
  Kockhachchingh, Nutten Hook, Katskill, 394

Geographical nomenclature, continued—
  Kiskatameck, Katskill, 395
  Kumochenack, Haverstraw bay, 377
  Kackawawook, Orange county, 387
  Kerhonkson, Ulster county, 391
  Kaunaumeek, Massachusetts, 86
  Manhattan, New York, 361
  Muscoota, New York, 362
  Matawucks, Staten Island, 362
  Manetto hill, Long Island, 364
  Mecox bay, Long Island, 364
  Mereyekawick, Brooklyn, 365
  Meghkeekassin, a rock, Yonkers, 365
  Montauk, Long Island, 365
  Meahagh, Verplanck's point, 367
  Magopson, New Rochelle, 367
  Muscoota, Harlem river, 367
  Mockquams, Blind Brook, 367
  Mahopak lake, Putnam county, 368
  Matteawan creek, Dutchess county, 370
  Mahicanituk, Hudson's river, 42
  Mankackkewachky, Raritan meadows, 376
  Minnisconga, Stony point, 377
  Mistucky, Warwick, Orange county, 382
  Minnisink, Orange county, 382
  Muchattoes Hill, Orange county, 382
  Matapan creek, Dutchess county, 371
  Machackoesk, Kinderhook, 374
  Maggrnapogh, New Paltz, Ulster county, 393
  Machawanick, Katskill, 394
  Naghtognk, Corlear's Hook, New York, 361
  Nepeage, Long Island, 365
  Namke Creek, Long Island, 365
  Namke creek, Long Island, 365
  Neperah, saw mill creek, 365
  Nappeckamak, Yonkers, 365
  Narrasunck, Haverstraw, 377
  Neversink Hills, New Jersey, 376
  Neweskeke, Albany county, 396
  Nescotonck, Shawangunk, Ulster county, 388
  Nanapenahekan creek, Columbia county, 372
  Occopoque, Riverhead, Long Island, 365
  Ossingsing, Sing Sing, 366
  Oniskethau, Coeymans creek, 397
  Peconic bay, Long Island, 364

# INDEX.

Geographical nomenclature, continued—
Papirinimen, Spuyten Devil creek, 365
Poconteco river, Westchester county, 367
Poningo, Westchester county, 367
Pockestersen, Stony Brook, 367
Pachgatgoch, Schaticook, 195
Pompton river, New Jersey, 377
Pooploop's kil, Orange county, 377
Poleber's Island, Pallopel's Island, 377
Pochuck, Warwick, Orange county, 382
Pakadasank, Orange county, 392
Poghkeepke, Poughkeepsie, 371
Passapenock, Beeren Island, 374
Poetanock, Mill creek, opposite Albany, 375
Petuquapoen, Greenbush, 375
Paanpaack, Troy, 375
Panhoosick, north of Troy, 375
Passaic river, New Jersey, 376
Potick, Athens, Greene county, 385
Pitkiskaker, Shawangunk, Ulster county, 389
Quinnahung, Westchester county, 367
Quaroppas, White Plains, 367
Querapoquett, Dutchess county, 371
Quaspeck, Verdrietig Hook, 377
Quassaick creek, Newburgh, 382
Quequicke, Hoosic Falls, 376
Rechtauck, New York, 362
Ronconcoa lake, Long Island, 364
Ranachque, Morisania, 367
Rippowams, Stamford, Ct., 368
Ramapo river, 377
Raritan river, 376
Sappokanikan, New York, 361
Sewanhackey, Long Island, 365
Sackhoes, Peekskill, 366
Senasqua, Teller's Point, 366
Sacrahung, Mill river, 367
Shappequa, Westchester county, 367
Shenandoah, Dutchess county, 370
Shecomeco, Dutchess county, 86, 371
Schunemunk mountain, Orange county, 381
Shawangunk, Ulster county, 388
Sankpenak, Roeloff Jansen's kil, 372
Scompamuck, Ghent, Columbia county, 373
Schodac, Columbia county, 58, 374
Schotack, Aepjin's Island, 375
Sieskasin, Coeymans, 396

Geographical nomenclature, continued—
Sunckhagag, Albany county, 87, 397
Schenectady, Albany, 398
Saratoga, Saratoga county, 398
Seepus, Esopus river, 94
Sannahagog, opposite Albany, 374
Sheepshack, Lansingburgh, 375
Schanwemisch, Ulster county, 388
Sackahampa, Columbia county, 373
Totama, Passaick Falls, 376
Tuphanne, Rockland county, 377
Tongapogh kil, Orange county, 377
Taghkanick mountains, Columbia county, 373
Twastawekah, Klaverack creek, 372, 374
Taeseameasick, Lansingburgh, 375
Tioneendogahe, Batten kil, 375
Ticonderoga, 375
Tawalsontha, Norman's kil, 99, 397
Tawassgunshee, Fort Orange, Albany, 397
Warpoes, New York, 362
Wanoksink, Ulster county, 389
Wawijchtanok, Columbia county, 85, 86, 372
Wnahktakook, Westenhuck, 62, 86
Weckquaesgeek, Westchester Co., 78, 366
Wysquaqua, Wicker's creek, 78
Waumainuck, Delancey's neck, 367
Weputing, Dutchess county, 369
Wicopee, Dutchess county, 370
Wappingers Falls, Dutchess Co., 370
Wechquadnach, Conn., 371
Wynogkee creek, Dutchess county, 371
Wiehacken, Wehawken, New Jersey, 376
Wachtung mountains, New Jersey, 376
Winegtekonk mountain, Orange county, 381
Wawayanda, Orange county, 385
Wawanaquassick, Columbia county, 372
Wallomschock river, Bennington, Vt., 375
Willehoosa, Port Jervis, Orange county, 96
Gnadenhütten, Moravians settle at, 198; Mahican converts remove to, 198; attacked by Lenapes, 220; converts fly to Pennsylvania for protection against Presbyterians, 245

## INDEX.    407

Goethals, sachem of Wappingers, 84, 299; solicits peace on behalf of Esopus Indians, 136
Goharius, sachem of Weckquaesgeeks, 79
Gouwarrowe, sachem of Matinecocks, 74; security for Hackinsacks and Tappans, 117
Government and laws, 29
Greenbush, Mohicans ravage, 60
aboriginal name, 375
Haaskouaun, an Iroquois chief, 172
Hackinsacks, location of, 90; Van der Horst settles among, 104; a warrior of, robbed, 104; complaint of, regarding presents, 111; young men clamor for war, 111; take part in war of 1643, 110; propose an exchange of prisoners, 123; negotiate on behalf of Esopus Indians, 139
Harmer, Gen., commands expedition against Lenapes and Shawanoes, 291
Hathorn, Col., commands in battle of Minnisink, 278
Haverstraw, location of 92; bay, aboriginal name of, 377
Hendrik, chief sachem of Mohawks, visits England, 188; addresses conference at Albany, 213; takes part in expedition against Crown Point, 223; killed in battle at Lake George, 224; biographical sketch of, 310;
Hendrik, Captain, a Mahican chief, 271; speech of, at Albany, 272; biographical sketch, 320
Herkimer, Gen., holds conference with Brant, 267; mortally wounded at Oriskany, 274
Hiawatha, the story of, 36
Hoosic French capture fort at, 204; aboriginal name of, 375, 376
Hoosic falls, aboriginal name of, 376
Horikans, location of, 85
Housatonic river, neutral boundary line, 62
Hudson, Henry, 7; conflict of, with Indians at Stony Point, 11; conflict of, with Indians at Shorackappock, 11, 77; discovers the Mahicanituk, 7; intoxicates Indians at Castleton, 10; traditions respecting his visit, 12; visits Indians at the Narrows, 8; visits Indians at Castleton, 9
Hunter, Gov., attends conference at Albany, 189
Hutchinson, Ann, killed by Weckquaesgeeks, 112; daughter of, returned from captivity, 118

Indian villages and localities, 34, 361
Albany county, 85, 87, 96, 397
Columbia county, 85, 88, 372
Dutchess county, 83, 369
Greene county, 95, 394
Long Island, 72, 364
New Jersey, 89, 376
New York, 361
Orange county, 93, 377
Putnam county, 80, 368
Rensselaer county, 85, 374
Rockland county, 91, 377
Staten Island, 91, 362
Saratoga county, 59, 398
Ulster county, 94, 388
Westchester county, 77, 365
Iroquois confederacy, 35; territory of, 35; tradition respecting origin, 35; tribal divisions, 36, 96; totemic emblems, 49; tradition respecting organization of confederacy, 36; called the Five Nations, 36, 39; form of government, 39; organization of confederacy, 39; national council, 40; political supremacy, 52; wars with the Hurons, 53; defeated by Champlain, 53; territory invaded by the French, 54; make treaty with the Dutch, 54; treaties with the English, 53, 55, 158; French determine to destroy, 171; chiefs made prisoners by treachery, 172; Mahicans in alliance with, 160, 172; capture Montreal, 173; threaten Quebec, 173; losses sustained in the war of 1689, 179; refuse to break their treaty with the Abenaquis, 192; hold conference with New England commissioners, 192; Six Nations, so called, 190; strength of, in 1750, 202; refuse to take part in war of 1744, 203; decline in prowess of, 203; grand conference at Albany, 206; practical division of confederacy, 207, 259; chiefs visit England, 188; French priests convert, 179, 211; condition in 1768, 251; action in regard to the war of the Lenapes, 224; reply to invitation to embark in war of 1765, 223; resolve to remain neutral in war of Revolution, 262, 264, 266; debauched by the English, 267; divided in alliance in war of the Revolution, 273; strength in the British alliance, 273; territory invaded by expedition under Gen. Sullivan, 279; condition under treaty of peace with Great Bri-

Iroquois, continued —
tain, 288 ; treaty with, in 1784, 289
Jesuits, labors of the French, 166, 168
Johnson, Sir William, 17 ; commissioned to invite Iroquois to conference, 212 ; appointed superintendent of Indian affairs, 222 ; commissioned to organize expedition for capture of Crown Point, 222; removes council fire to Mount Johnson, 222; holds conference with Iroquois, 223 ; commands in battle of Lake George, 224 ; endeavors to suppress hostilities in Pennsylvania, 224; holds conference with Lenapes, etc., 228, 229; removes petticoats from Lenapes, 229 ; efforts of, to hold Indian tribes in alliance with the crown, 259 ; biographical notice of, 260
Johnson, Sir John, 260; commands Royal Greens in siege of Fort Stanwix, 274 ; removes his father's treasures, 283 ; commands expedition against Schoharie settlements, 284; biographical notice of, 265
Johnson, Guy, deputy superintendent of Iroquois, 260; holds conference at Oswego, 263 ; appeals to Iroquois to take up arms, 263 ; second conference at Oswego, 268 ; receives instructions from Gen. Gage, 262
Johnson Hall, battle of, 285
Joselyn, John, 16
Juet, Hudson's mate, visits Indians at Castleton, 9
Jumonville, death of, 210
Kalebackers, Indians having guns, 136
Katskills, location of, 95 ; loving men of, 9, 95
Katsban, a village of the Katskills, 177
Katonah, sachem of Siwanoys, 82
Kayingehaga, Mohawks so called, 35
Kayaderossera patent, 258
Keeperdo, a Mahican chief, territory of, 194
Kieft, director, attempts the collection of tribute, 101 ; urges war measures, 102 ; proclaims a public fast, 109 ; solicits aid from New England, 113 ; solicits mediation of Mohawks and Mahicans, 117
King, Thomas, chief of the Oghakawagas, 201
King, Philip, winter quarters near Albany, 62 ; influence of his teachings, 203
Kingston, first settlement at, 125 ; a village palisaded at, 128 ; aboriginal name of, 394

Kinte-Kaying, an Indian dance, 28, 115
Kitchawongs, location of, 79
Kitchawong, sachem of Kitchawongs, 79
Kitzanacka, Indian priest, 27
Kirkland, Rev. Samuel, missionary labors of, 261
Konapot, sachem of Mahicans, 89 ; commissioned captain, 196
Kregier, Martin, journal of second Esopus war, 60 ; commands expedition against Esopus Indians, 149
Krieckbeck, commandant at Fort Orange, joins war party of Mahicans, 100 ; killed by the Mohawks, 100
Kryn, chief of the Caghnawagas, 180
La Barre, governor of Canada, 169
Lafayette, Mahicans under command of, 286
Lake George, battle of, 224
Language, 333 ; Algonquin, origin of name, 64 ; Algonquin, grammar of the, 338 ; dialectic vocabularies, 359 ; general reference, 333 ; geographical names, formation of, 354 ; word building, 352
Lawrence, Dr., 17
Leisler, Jacob, takes possession of Fort James, 175 ; executed for treason, 175
Lenni Lenapes, territory of, 35 ; signification of name, 44 ; tradition respecting origin, 44 ; traditionary war with the Allegewi, 45 ; form of government, 46 ; tribal divisions, 47, totemic divisions and emblems, 49 ; subjugation of, by Iroquois, 64 ; wars with the Senecas, 68 ; made tributary to the Senecas, 69 ; strengthened by emigrants from Shawanoes and Mahicans, 194; strength of, in 1750, 202 ; sale of lands of, 213 ; in alliance with the French, 212 ; action of, concerning lands, 216 ; declare war against the English, 219 ; devastations by, along the Kittatinny mountains, and on the Susquehanna, 220 ; hostilities in tht Minnisinks, 221, 238 ; declare themselves men, 225 ; Johnson sends peace embassy to, 224 ; Johnson appoints conference with, 228 ; Johnson removes petticoat from, 229 ; make peace with Pennsylvania, 236 ; take part in Pontiac's conspiracy, 243 ; massacre Connecticut settlers at Wyoming, 1763, 244 ; join the Western alliance, 244 ;

## INDEX. 409

Lenni Lenapes, continued —
country of, invaded by the English, 247; included in the peace of 1765, 249; condition of, in 1768, 251; declare war against Virginia, 256; more powerful than the Iroquois, 258; east of the Alleghanies unite with the Americans in the Revolution, 272; war cry of, at White Plains, 272; encouraged by the English to renew war, 290; renew hostilities in the west, 291; make treaty with Gen. Wayne, 292; on the banks of the Mississippi, 292

Lenapewihituk, name of Delaware river, 45

Lewis, Colonel, death of, 257

Logan, attack on encampment of, 255; commands war party of Senecas, etc., 257; biographical sketch of, 314

Long Island, Block builds ship on, 77; Dutch settlers on, 101; settlements ravaged, 136; territory of, divided between Dutch and English, 124; treaty with Indians of, 124; aboriginal name of, 365

Long Reach, Indians of, 177

Losses sustained by the Dutch in war of 1643, 108

Mahican confederacy, nine nations composing, 41, 85; original seat of, 41; subdue tribes on the sea-coast, 41

Mahicans, a nation of the Mahican confederacy, 41, 85; welcome Hudson at Castleton, 9; territory of, 34, 85; sub-tribal divisions, 85; national council fire, 41, 62, 88; villages and castles of, 85, 86; tradition respecting origin, 42; form of government, 42; relation of, to the Mohegans, 43; totemic divisions and emblems, 50; and Wappingers constitute one nation, 51; make treaty of friendship with the Dutch, 54; alleged subjugation of, 56; wars with the Mohawks, 57; ravage the east side of the Hudson, 60; officially recognized by Massachusetts, 62; relations with the government of New York, 62; sell lands to Van Rensselaer, 87; sell lands to Robert Livingston, 86, 87; obtain fire-arms from the Dutch, 66; attack the Manhattans, 105; defeat the Mohawks, 60, 61; murder Dutch soldiers, 131; solicit peace on behalf of Esopus Indians, 137; included in

Mahicans, continued —
peace of Esopus, 145; at war with the Mohawks, 149, 156; meet French Indians at Cohoes, 145; united in covenant with the Iroquois, 161; instigated to hostilities against the Dutch by the English, 160; assist the Mohawks, 175, 176; strength of, in Albany county, 184; equality of, with the Iroquois, 186; chiefs of, visits England, 188; in expedition against Canada, 189; removal of a portion to Pennsylvania, 194; hold conference with the Mohawks, 204; attend conference at Albany, 214; strength of, in 1750, 203; condition of, in 1768, 252; unite with Americans in Revolution, 262; take part in the battle of Lexington, 271; sent on mission to western tribes, 269, 272; take part in the battle of White Plains, 272; under Lafayette at Barren Hill, 286; operate against English in Westchester county, 286; Washington's testimony regarding, 287; removal of, to Oneida county, 292; removal of, to Wisconsin, 292

Mahak Niminaw, sachem of Katskills, 96

Mahican, Abraham, 88

Mahikanders, Mahicans, so called, 41

Mamekotings, location of, 95

Manhattans, the old, subjugated by Wappingers, 51; enemies of the Sanhickans, 71; language of, 51, 77; the Dutch settle among, 77; Adrien Block among the, 77; massacre of, by order of Kieft, 106

Manhattan, explanation of term, 77; wars, 99, 100

Manhassets, location of, 74

Manners and customs, 16; attention in sickness, 23; alliances, manner of forming, 32; chastity of females, 22; child-birth, 23; castles and mode of constructing, 25; dwellings and mode of constructing, 24; dress of an Indian belle, 21; disposition of prisoners, 32; declaration of war, 31; food and mode of preparation, 24; government and laws, 29; medicines, 27; occupation, 24; organization of armies, 31; plurality of wives, 22; punishment for murder, 33; religious belief and worship, 27; rank and titles, 30; title to lands, 30; wampum, 26; war, preparation for, 31

410 INDEX.

Manners and customs, continued —
war address, 31; war song of Lenapes, 32; weapons of war, 25; Van der Donck's description of appearance, 20; Verazzano's description of appearance, 19

Maquas, Mohawks so called, 35; castle of the Praying, 97

Maringoman, sachem of Waoranecks, 94; castle of, 94

Marsapequas, location of the, 73; take part in war of 1643, 73; aid the Dutch in Esopus wars, 73, 149, 153

Maramaking, sachem of Siwanoys, 82

Massachusetts, sends war belt to Mahicans, 269; reply of, to Mahican address, 271

Matinecocks, location of the, 74

Mattano, sachem of Raritans, 90

Mauwehu, sachem of Schaticooks of Kent, Connecticut, 195

Mayane, a Wappinger chief, 82, 113

Medicines, 27

Mechkentowoons, a Mahican chieftaincy, 71, 85, 96

Megriesken, sachem of Wappingers, 84

Merricks, location of the, 73

Mespath, village of, destroyed by Dutch, 114

Metzewakes, sachem of Kikhawongs, 79

Miantonomo, sachem of Narragansetts, 103

Miami Rapids, council of tribes at, 291

Mingoes, origin of, 257

Minichque, a Mahican sachem, mortally injured by negroes, 185; biographical notice of, 319

Minnisinks, a chieftaincy of Minsis, location and villages of, 96; one of, charged with murder at Esopus, 127; take part in war of 1689, 178; visited by Arent Schuyler, 181; invite Shawanoes to settle among, 181; Minsis defrauded of lands at, 217; settlers at, killed, 222; devastations in war of 1756, 238; Count Pulaski stationed at, 277; destruction of settlement at, 278; battle of, 278

Minsis, a tribal division of Lenapes, 50, 93; totem and chieftaincies of, 50, 93; at war with the Senecas, 68; obtain fire-arms from the Swedes, 69, 120; Senecas aided by Mohawks against, 68, 165; subjugated by Senecas, 68, 165; a portion settle among the Ottawas, 177; decimated by small pox, 181; Shawa-

Minsis, continued —
noes settle among, 181; devastate western Orange and Ulster, 221; murder settlers from Canastota to Esopus, 231; hostilities of, in Minnisink country, 238; paid for lands in New Jersey, 241

Mississagies, accepted as the seventh nation of the Iroquois confederacy, 199; alliance of, with Iroquois broken, 200

Mitchill, Dr. theory of, 16

Mohawks, a tribe of the Five Nations, 36; territory of, 96; villages and castles of, 97; totems of, 49; mode of declaring war, 31; conversion of, by Jesuits, 56; obtain fire-arms, 66, 100; at war with the Hurons, 53; first treaty with the Dutch, 54; wars with the Mahicans, 57, 61; drive the Soquatucks from their land, 59; weakened by the Mahicans, 60; solicit the gov. of Canada, for protection against the Mahicans, 59; attacked by the Mahicans at Caghnawaga, 61; defeated by the Mahicans at Kinaquariones, 61; obtain assistance from the Oneidas, Cayugas, and Senecas, 61; send embassadors to Fort Orange, 131; Dutch send embassadors to, 132; promise not to aid Esopus Indians, 133; send embassy to Esopus to negotiate peace, 136; regard Esopus war as having been caused by the Dutch, 141; included in peace of Esopus, 145; complain of bad treatment, 144; castles destroyed by the French, 175; Zinzendorp's statement concerning, 187; chiefs visit England, 188; in expedition against Canada, 189; in expedition against Crown Point, 223; aid the English in war of Revolution, 273; retirement of, to Ouise river, 289

Mohegan, meaning of, 50

Mohegans, a Pequot clan, 63

Monemius, castle, 85

Monakadook, Seneca half-king, mission of, 233

Montauks, location of, 75; chieftaincies of, 72; originally a part of Mahican confederation, 51; originally styled Manhattan, 51; at war with Narragansetts, 76; small-pox among, 76; accept protection of English, 76; divided between English and Dutch, 76; removal of portion of, to Oneida county, 293; reservation of, on Long Island, 294

# INDEX. 411

Montague, Rachel, taken prisoner, 150; pilots Dutch forces against Shawangunk, 150
Montour, Catharine, the Queen Esther of the Senecas, 276
Moody, Lady, house of, attacked, 123
Moravians, testimony of, 88
Morton, Thomas, theory of, 16
Mount Misery, traditionary battle at, 81
Muhhekaneew, original names of Mahicans, 41; orthography of, 41, 42
Murderer's kil, Indians of, 93
Murder, atonement for, 31
Murders committed by Indians, 120
Nanfan, Lieut. Gov., attends conference at Albany, 184
Nanticokes, a portion of settled at Katskil, 95; removal of, from Maryland to Pennsylvania, 199; accept Mahicanders as brothers, 231
National and tribal organizations, 34
Navisinks, location of the, 89; Hudson's intercourse with, 9, 89; kill John Coleman, 9, 89
Nawaas, location of the, 85
Necariages, application of, for acceptance as seventh nation of Iroquois, refused, 200
Nesaquakes, location of the, 74
Neversink, explanation of term, 376; river, 591
Nicholson, Gen., expedition against Canada, 188, 189
Nicolls, Richard, takes possession of Fort Amsterdam, 158; proclaimed deputy governor, 158; makes treaty with Iroquois, 158; renews treaty with Esopus Indians, 163
Niessen, Ensign, sent to Esopus, 149
Nimham, chief sachem of Wappingers, 51, 81, 84, 202; visits England, 253; killed in battle of Cortland's ridge, 287; biographical sketch of, 329
Nochpeems, location of, 80; treaty with, 117
Novisans at war with Iroquois, 68, 159
Nowedonah, sachem of Shinecocks, 75
Occum, Rev. Samson, mission of, 293; biographical sketch of, 325
Ochtayhquanawicroons, settlement of, on the Susquehanna, 200; subsequently called the Oghkawagas, 200; Mahican clans settle among, 200; Skaniadaradighroonas settle among, 200; Chugnuts settle among, 201; Esopus Indians settle among, 201; King, Thomas, chief of, 201; connection of, with war of Revolution, 201

Oghkawagas, elements composing, 200
Oghkawaga, head-quarters of Brant, 267
Ohio company, organization of, 208 valley, French endeavor to secure possession of the, 208, 209, 210
Onackatin, sachem of Warranawonkongs, 95; party to treaty of 1665, 165; lands of, 165, 387
Oneidas, a tribal division of Iroquois, 97; assign lands to Tuscaroras, 190; second castle of the, 201; accept war belt of colonists, 273; dispersion of, by Brant's forces, 275; retaliatory descent of, upon the Mohawks, 275; severed from Iroquois confederacy, 288; secured in possession of lands, 289; Mahicans settle among, 292
Onderis Hocque, a Minsi chief, address of, 141
Onondagas, a tribal division of Iroquois, 35; make treaty with the Dutch, 54; capital of the, 98; Spangenberg's account of confederacy of, 40; territory of, invaded by French, 176; Zinzendorf's opinion of, 187; declare themselves independent, 208; accept war-belts of the crown, 273; capital of, destroyed by Sullivan, 280; apply to Oneidas for relief, 281
Onondaga, capital of Iroquois confederacy, 98; Jesuit missionaries at, 170; war belts taken to, for consultation, 213; council at, repudiates sale of Wyoming lands, 219; conference with Lenapes at, 227; destroyed by Sullivan's expedition, 281
Organization of armies, 31
Origin of the North American Indians, 16
Oriskany, battle of, 274
Oritany, sachem of Hackinsacks, 91; treaty of, with the Dutch, 110; party to treaty of 1645, 118; solicits peace on behalf of Esopus Indians, 139
Ottawas, location of the, 177; a number of, die of small pox at Esopus, 177; Pontiac, king of, organizes alliance against the English, 243
Pacham, a chief of the Tankitekes, 80; advises massacre of the Dutch, 111; surrender of a condition of peace, 117
Papequanaehen, an Esopus chief, killed, 152
Parnau, sachem of Rockaways, 73

412  INDEX.

Passachquon, sachem of Navisinks, 90
Patchogues, location of the, 75
Patthunck, sachem of Siwanoys, 82
Pauw, Michael, settlement of, 106, 107
Pavonia, Jersey city so called, 106; Manhattan fugitives at, 106; massacre at, 107, 108
Paxinos, a sachem of Minnisinks, 178; attends conference at Mt. Johnson, 229; attends conference at Lancaster, 235; biographical sketch of, 305
Peekskill, aboriginal name of, 79
Pemerawghin, chief sachem of Warranawonkongs, 95
Penhawitz, sachem of Carnarsees, 73; sends delegates to negotiate peace, 109; conference with, at Rechquaakie, 110
Pennacooks, location of, 85; dispersion of, 62; a portion of, settle at Schaticook, 63; invited to remove to Canada, 184; remnant of, carried away to Canada, 216
Pennsylvania, proprietaries of, purchase lands, 216; Lenapes dispute title, 215, 218; declares war against Lenapes, 228; deeds surrendered, 241; makes peace with Lenapes, 241
Pequots, origin of the, 41; country of, 43; destruction of, 44; jurisdiction west of the Connecticut, 63
Petroleum, use of, as a cure for smallpox, 181
Pierron, a Jesuit missionary, labors of, 97
Plurality of wives, 22
Pocahontas, reference to, 144
Pontiac, king of Ottawas, conspiracy of, 243; tribes in alliance with, 248; failure of conspiracy, 246
Ponus, sachem of Toquams, 80, 82
Ponupahowhelbshelen, sachem of Weckquaesgeeks, 79
Pos, Captain, taken prisoner, 123; negotiates treaty of peace, 124
Potick, a Mahican village, 63, 395; fugitives from King Philip's war at, 63
Poughkeepsie, aboriginal name of, 371
Poygratasuck, sachem of Manhassets, 74
Praying Indians, Jesuit converts so called, 179
Presents, use of, in negotiations, 29, 31, 214
Preummaker, a chief of Warranawonkongs, 95; killed by the Dutch, 138; land of, 138
Prisoners, ransom of, 124
Proprietaries, (see Pennsylvania).

Punganis, lands of, 177, 387
Punishment for murder, 33
Quassaick creek, 382
Quaquasno, sacnem of Shinecocks, 75
Quebec, the Iroquois at, 172
Queen Anne's war, 183
Rank and titles, 30
Raritans, a chieftaincy of Lenapes, location of, 90; called Sanhikans or fireworkers, 90; remove to the Kittakeny mountains, 90; accused of plundering, 101; attacked by the Dutch, 101; destroy a family at Mespath, 131; remove to Oneida lake, 90, 293; remove to Lake Michigan, 90; New Jersey pays claim for lands, 293
Rauch, Christian Henry, missionary, 197
Rechtauck, Manhattan fugitives at, 106; location of, 362
Reckgawawancs, location of the, 77; attack Hudson's ship, 11, 77; included in treaty of 1643, 78
Red Hook, traditionary battle at, 57
Red Jacket, a Seneca chief pleads with his people for peace, 282; reference to, 317
Religious belief and worship, 27
Rochambeau, proclamation of, to French Indian allies, 258
Rockaways, location of the, 73
Rodolf, Sergeant, commands in massacre at Pavonia, 106
Ronduit, a small fort, erected at the mouth of the Walkill, 130, 146
Sachus, sachem of Kitchawongs, 79
Sackagkemeck, sachem of Haverstraws, 92
Sager's kil, Indian village on, destroyed, 138
Sanders, Robert, commandant at Schenectady, 174
Saraghtoga, settlement at, destroyed, 205; aboriginal name, 398
Schabash, a chief of Shekomeko, 89; biographical notice of, 328
Schaticooks, elements composing the, 166, 186; date of organization, 166; take part in war of 1689, 178; in expedition against Canada, 189; of Connecticut, 166; elements composing, 195
Schaticook, orthography and signification of, 195
Schenectady, destroyed by the French, 174; Albany, so called by Iroquois, 398
Schodac, capital of the Mahicans, 88, 374

## INDEX. 413

Schuyler, Col. Peter, secretary to commissioners of Indian affairs, 186; accompanies chiefs to England, 188 Col. Philip, 263 Hon. Yost, the story of, 274
Seatalcats, location of the, 74
Secatogues, location of the, 75
Senecas, a tribal division of Iroquois, 33; villages of, 98; at war with the Minsis, 68, 145; delegation visits Fort Orange, 144; included with Mohawks in peace of Esopus, 145; Stuyvesant urges them to make peace with Minsis, 146; subjugate Minsis, 69; attack French trading canoes, 169; French expedition against, 172; estranged from the English, 211; action of, concerning Wyoming lands, 216; encourage Lenapes to war, 216; remove petticoat from Lenapes, 219; make peace with the French, 242; invite an alliance against the English, 243; war against the English, 247; Johnson makes treaty with, 147; accept the war belts of the English, 273; country of, invaded by Sullivan, 279
Senecas of the Glaize in western alliance, 292
Sequins, location and cantons of, 82; sell lands to West India Company, 82; sell lands to the English, 83; chief of, imprisoned of Eelkins, 63, 83; compelled to pay tribute to Pequots, 83
Sergeant, Rev. John, missionary, 196
Sessekemick, sachem of Tappans, 91
Sewackenamo, sachem of Esopus, 95, 139; address of, 155
Shanasockwell, an independent nation of Siwanoys, 82
Shawangunk, castle at, 93, 149, 388; expedition for reduction of, 150; new fort at, 152; expedition for reduction of, 152; third expedition to, 153; Miss Mack killed at, 283; location and signification, 388
Shawanoes, removal of, from Maryland, 180: aided by Mahicans, 180; make peace with Iroquois, 180; settle among the Minsis, 180; number in expedition against Canada, 189; take part in Lenape wars (see Lenapes).
Shawuskukhkung, address by, 293
Shekomeko, a Mahican village, 86; missionaries at, 86, 197, 198

Sheyickbi country, 46
Shinecocks, location of the, 75
Shingas commands war party of Lenapes, 219; reply of, to Johnson's commissioners, 225
Shirley, Governor, expedition of, 252
Sickenames, Pequots so called, 83
Silver Heels, murder of, 256
Sing Sing, aboriginal name of, 79, 366
Sint-sinks, location of, 79; treaty with, 117
Sirham, sachem of Kitchawongs, 79
Siwanoys, location of the, 81
Sloughter, Col., appointed governor, 175
Small-pox, ravages of, 181
Smith, Ensign, in command at Esopus, 134
Smit, Claes, killed by a Weckquaesgeek, 102
Soquatucks, location of, 59, 85; removal of, from west side of country, 59; treaty of peace with Mohawks, 156
Soquans, a Mahican sachem, 184, 186
Souwenaro, sachem of Weckquaesgeeks, 79
Staats, Abraham, house of, burned, 60
Stamford, Dutch expedition at, 114, 115; massacre of Indians near, 116
Staten Island, DeVries's plantation on, 101; aboriginal name of, 362
Stockbridge, mission established at, 196
Stockbridges, Mahicans so called, 89
Stuyvesant, regards Manhattan wars as having been caused by Dutch, 124; holds conference with Esopus Indians, 126; demands Esopus lands as indemnity, 127; declares war against Esopus Indians, 137; makes treaty with Esopus Indians, 141, 155; holds conference with Senecas, 145; controversy with the English, 154
St. Clair, Gen., concludes treaties at Fort Harmar, 290; defeated by Lenapes, 291
St. Francis, Indians, descent of, upon Schaticook and Hoosic, 205, 216
St. Regis Indians, organization of, 179
Sullivan, Gen., commands expedition against Iroquois, 279
Susquehannas, subjugation of, 55
Susquehanna Company, organization of, 215
Swannekins, the Dutch, so called, 108
Tackapousha, sachem of Marsapequas, 74, 76; treaty of, with the Dutch, 124
Tackarew, sachem of Reckgawawancs, 78

# 414    INDEX.

Tadame, king of Lenapes, murder of, 227, 301
Taghkospemo, sachem of Tappans, 91
Tankitekes, location of, 80; treaty with, 117
Tanadiarisson, speech of, 209
Tappans, location of the, 91
Tarrytown, aboriginal name of, 79, 366
Teedyuscung, chief sachem of Lenapes, 69, 227; commands war-party of Eastern Lenapes, 219; holds conference with Shawanoe and Mahican allies, 220; attends conference at Mount Johnson, 228; attends conference at Onondaga, 228; makes treaty with Johnson, 231; holds conference with governor of Pennsylvania, 232; speech of, at Easton, 233; empowered to make peace, 234; final treaty with, at Easton, 241; murdered by Senecas, 244; biographical sketch of, 301
Teller's Point, aboriginal name of, 79, 366
Thayendanega, (see Brant, Joseph),
Thompson, Charles, clerk to Teedyuscung, 235
Throgmorton, settlement of, destroyed, 112
Ticonderoga, fortifications erected at, 224; aboriginal name of, 375
Title to lands, 30
Tobaccus, sachem of Patchogues, 75
Totems and totemic classifications, 49
Traditions, 361; Dans-Kammer, 383; Hiawatha, 36; Iroquois respecting origin, 35; Lenapes, respecting origin, 45; Lenapes, respecting subjugation, 64; Mahicans, respecting origin, 42; Mahicans, respecting Hudson's visit, 43; Mahopac lake, 368; Manetta hill, 364; Naoman, a tradition of Murderer's creek, 378; stepping stones, 362; Wanton Island, 395; Wawanaquassick, 373
Trade, mode of conducting, 120
Treaty with Iroquois, 1623, 54; with Mahicans, 1623, 54; with Weckquaesgeeks, etc., 1644, 117; with Mohawks and Mahicans, 1644, 117; with Weckquaesgeeks, etc., 1645, 118; with Esopus Indians, 1660, 142; with Esopus Indians, 1664, 156; with Esopus Indians, 1665, 163; with Iroquois and Mahicans, 1664, 158; with Tackapausha, 1656, 124; with Iroquois, 1768, 250
Tryon county, committee of safety of, 262

Tschoop, a Mahican chief, conversion of, 197
Tuscaroras, an original Iroquois tribe, 36; remove to North Carolina, 36; defeated by English in North Carolina, 190; return of, to Iroquois country, 190; constituted the Sixth Nation, 190; accept war-belts of colonists, 273
Tusten, Lieut. Col., commands in battle of Minnisink, 278
Umpachenee, commissioned lieutenant, 196
Unamis, a tribal division of Lenapes, 47, 50, 89; chieftancies of, 89; totem of, 50; the ruling tribe of the Lenapes, 47
Unalachtos, a tribal division of Lenapes, 47; totem of, 50
Uncas, a Pequot chief, 43
Underhill, Capt. John, enters the Dutch service, 113; commands expedition against Canarsees, 114; commands in expedition against Weckquaesgeeks, 115, 116
Unukat's castle, 85
Van der Donck, description of Indians of New York, 20; sub-tribal classifications of, 72
Van Dyck, Hendrik kills a squaw, 121; shot by the Indians, 122
Vaudreuil, invades neutral territory, 204
Van Voorst, Garret Jansen, killed, 104
Van Tienhoven, secretary, mother of, 108
Verazzano, description of Indians of New York, 19
Verdrietig Hook, 92, 93, 377
Vriesendael (see De Vries)
Vielle, Arnout, interpreter, 181
Virginia, operations of, in Ohio valley, 209, 210; war of, against the French, 210
Walking treaty, the, 216
Wampum, description of, 26
Wanton Island, traditionary battle on, 57, 395
Wantage, sachem of Merricks, 73
Waoranecks, location of, 93
Wappingers, a tribal division of Mahicans, 42; chieftaincies of, 77; sovereignty of, 63; no jurisdiction west of Hudson, 84; a portion remove to Pennsylvania, 85; attack boats on the Hudson, 111; war party of, visit New Amsterdam, 121; attacked by burgher guard, 122; destroy Hoboken and Pavonia, 122; retain prisoners as hostages, 124; treaty

# INDEX. 415

Wappingers, continued —
  with the, 136 : encouraged by English to revolt, 155; solicit peace for Esopus Indians, 155; take part in war of 1689, 178; removal of clans to Otseningo, 231 ; claim lands in Dutchess county, 252; aid Americans in war of Revolution, 286; signification of name, 370
Wappinger's creek, aboriginal name of, 84, 370
Warrawakin, sachem of Seatalcats, 74
Warranawonkongs, location of, 71, 94; wars with the Dutch (see Esopus Indians),
Warren Bush, settlement at, destroyed, 285
War song of Lenapes, 32
Wars, Cresap's, 285 ; Esopus, first, 120, 133; Esopus, second, 146; French, and Indian, 1787, 171 ; 1702, 187; 1744, 203; 1785, 208; Iroquois and the French, 172 ; King Philip's, 62; Lenapes for independence, 216; Lenapes, etc., 1793, 291 ; Mahicans and Manhattan, 105; Mahicans and Mohawks, 58, 158 ; Minsis and Senecas, 67, 145 ; Mohawks and the French, 131, 174; Montauks and Narragansetts, 76 ; Pontiac's conspiracy, 243, 246; Queen Anne's war, 187 ; Revolutionary war, 258 ; Raritans and the Dutch, 101 ; Senecas and Minsis, 67, 145 ; Senecas and the French, 145, 169 ; Tuscaroras and North Carolina, 190 ; Weckquaesgeeks and the Dutch, 102, 108, 111, 119, 121
Wassenaar and De Laet's account of sub-tribal organizations, 71
Wasenssne, sachem of Tankitekes, 80
Washington, Major George, commands expedition against the French, 210; holds conference with Lenape and Seneca chiefs, 210; attacks the French in ambush, 210; retreats to the great meadows, 211 ; withdraws from Ohio valley, 211

Warwarsinks, location of, 95
Wawayanda, signification of, 385
Wawiachech, sachem of Pennacooks, 193
Wawyachtonocks, location of, 85
Wayne, Gen., defeats Western tribes, 292; makes treaty of Greenville, 292
Weapons of war, 25
Weckquaesgeeks, location of, 78 ; a warrior of, killed, 101 ; attacked by the Dutch, 103; murder Ann Hutchinson, 112; castles of, destroyed, 114; treaty with, 117
Weckquaesgeek territory, 366
Welsh colonization of America, 17, 45
Werekepes, a Haverstraw chief, 92, 94
Weskheun, sachem of Kitchawongs, 79
Weskora, sachem of Weckquaesgeeks, 79
Wessickenaiuw, sachem of Weckquaesgeeks, 79
Westenhucks, location of, 85
Westenhuck, Mahican national council at, 89
Western controversy, parties to, 258
Western tribes, alliance of 1793, 292
Whitneymen, sachem of Matinecocks, 74; negotiates peace, 117
Wiekajocks, location of, 85
Willehoosa, cavern on Shawangunk mountains, 96
Wiltmeet, Indian castle of, 95 ; destroyed by the Dutch, 137
Wiltwyck, the old village of Esopus, 147 ; houses burned at, 147; council of war at, 149
Winnequaheagh, sachem of Secatogues, 75
Wyandance, sachem of Montauks, 75 ; death of, by poison, 76
Wycombone, sachem of Montauks, 76
Wyoming, lands at, purchased by Susquehanna Company, 215
Wyoming lands, 250, 25, 264, 265 ; massacre at, 276, 277
Yonkers, aboriginal name of, 77, 365

DATE